Biography of an Empire

The publisher gratefully acknowledges the generous support
of the Ahmanson Foundation Humanities Endowment Fund
of the University of California Press Foundation.

The publisher also gratefully acknowledges the
generous contribution to this book provided by
The Institute of Turkish Studies.

# Biography of an Empire

*Governing Ottomans in an Age of Revolution*

———

## Christine M. Philliou

UNIVERSITY OF CALIFORNIA PRESS

*Berkeley   Los Angeles   London*

University of California Press, one of the most distinguished university presses in the United States, enriches lives around the world by advancing scholarship in the humanities, social sciences, and natural sciences. Its activities are supported by the UC Press Foundation and by philanthropic contributions from individuals and institutions. For more information, visit www.ucpress.edu.

University of California Press
Berkeley and Los Angeles, California

University of California Press, Ltd.
London, England

Library of Congress Cataloging-in-Publication Data
Philliou, Christine May.
   Biography of an empire : governing Ottomans in an age of revolution /
Christine M. Philliou.
       p.   cm.
   Includes bibliographical references and index.
   ISBN 978-0-520-26633-9 (cloth : alk. paper)
   ISBN 978-0-520-26635-3 (pbk. : alk. paper)
   1. Turkey—History—Tanzimat, 1839–1876.   2. Phanariots—Turkey—
History—19th century.   3. Vogorides, Stephanos, 1780–1859.   I. Title.
   DR565.P456   2011
   956'.015—dc22                                      2010013361

20   19   18   17   16   15   14   13   12   11
10   9   8   7   6   5   4   3   2   1

*To Reza, Daphne, and Erfan*

CONTENTS

ILLUSTRATIONS

FIGURES

MAPS

TABLE

NOTE ON TRANSLITERATION

There are a number of transliteration systems for Ottoman Turkish and modern Greek, the two languages that predominate here, as well as for Bulgarian and Romanian, terms and names from which also appear from time to time in this book. I have tried to stick with a basic modern Turkish rendering of Ottoman Turkish words and a simplified modern Greek transliteration style whenever possible for terms and phrases. As far as proper names, phanariots are particularly hard to standardize, behaving as linguistic chameleons as much as political ones (e.g., the Soutso/Soutzo/Suçu/Drakozade/Souzzo family). For the better-known families, I have opted for the most commonly used variant of their name, and for the lesser-known clans, I have tended toward the modern Turkish phonetic rendition whenever possible. For Stephanos Vogorides, I have chosen the Greek variant (rather than Stoiko Stoikov, his original name, the Bulgarian variant of his adult name Stefan Bogoridi, or the Turkish Istefanaki Bey), and I have done so for Kostaki (Constantine) Musurus (rather than Kostaki Paşa, Musurus Paşa, or Constantine Mousouros) as well. For nonphanariots, I have opted for the modern Turkish variant of names (Mehmet Ali rather than the Arabic variant, Muhammad Ali, for instance). Finally, when I provide multiple variants for a term, *T.* signifies Turkish; *G.*, Greek; *B.*, Bulgarian; *R.*, Romanian; and *Sl.*, Slavic.

Christians with Greek names were often referred to in Turkish by their Greek diminutive form. Someone named Constantine (Konstantinos) in Greek, for instance, would be called Kostaki, the diminutive Greek form, adapted into Turkish. This book abounds with characters such as Manolaki (Emmanuel → Manolis → Manolaki) Efendi, Istefanaki (Stephanos → Stefanaki → Istefanaki) Bey, and Yanaki (Ioannis → Yanni → Yanaki). Not wanting to lose this pattern of linguistic/cultural transmission and adaptation and also not wanting to confuse the reader, I have included the diminutive nicknames when relevant but placed the fuller name in brackets after the first mention of that name.

For place names I have tried to stay with the Turkish variant, which is why I refer to the Ottoman capital as İstanbul rather than Constantinople, despite the fact that in the nineteenth century it was commonly known in English as Constantinople. For other places, which lie outside of Turkey today, I have tried to provide the standard national variant (Ioannina in Greece) but have provided the Turkish variant (Yanya) in brackets.

Since I have opted for the use of Turkish diacritics, I provide below a guide to Turkish pronunciation:

| | |
|---|---|
| *a* | like *o* in *oz* |
| *e* | like *a* in *hay* |
| *i* or *İ* | like *ee* in *meet* |
| *ı* or *I* | like *u* in *muddle* |
| *o* | like *ow* in *low* |
| *ö* or *Ö* | like the German *ö* |
| *u* | like *oo* in *tool* |
| *ü* or *Ü* | like the French *u* |
| *ç* or *Ç* | like *ch* in *chimney* |
| *ğ* | soft "*g*," hardly pronounced |
| *ş* or *Ş* | like *sh* in *shed* |

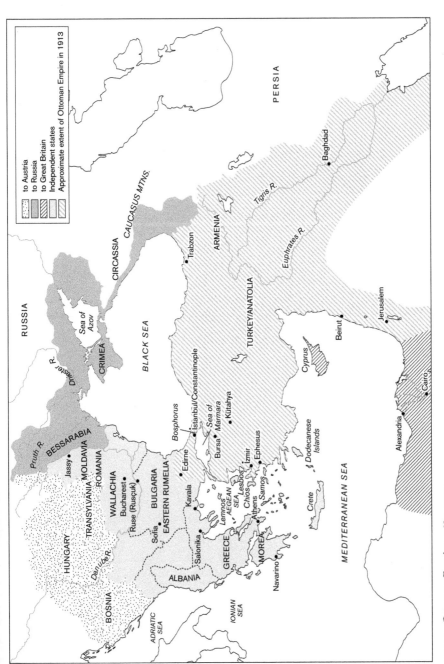

MAP 1. Ottoman Empire, 1683–1913.

Legend:
- to Austria
- to Russia
- to Great Britain
- Independent states
- Approximate extent of Ottoman Empire in 1913

RUSSIA

PERSIA

Baghdad

Tigris R.

Euphrates R.

CAUCASUS MTNS.

CIRCASSIA

ARMENIA

Trabzon

Sea of Azov

CRIMEA

BLACK SEA

TURKEY/ANATOLIA

Dniester R.

Prut R.

Jerusalem

Beirut

BESSARABIA

Jassy

MOLDAVIA

TRANSYLVANIA

ROMANIA

Cyprus

Cairo

Bosphorus

Istanbul/Constantinople

Sea of Marmara

Bursa

Kütahya

Alexandria

WALLACHIA

Bucharest

Ruse (Ruscuk)

BULGARIA

Sofia

EASTERN RUMELIA

Edirne

Izmir

Ephesus

HUNGARY

Danube R.

Kavala

Dodecanese Islands

Lemnos

Lesbos

AEGEAN SEA

Chios

Samos

BOSNIA

Salonika

GREECE

Athens

Crete

MEDITERRANEAN SEA

ALBANIA

MOREA

ADRIATIC SEA

IONIAN SEA

Navarino

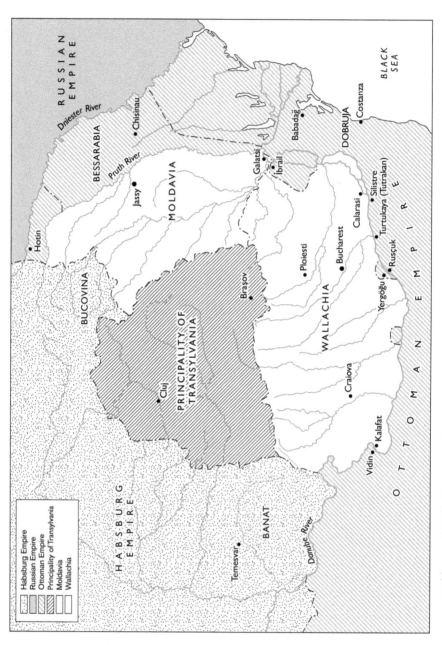

MAP 2. Moldavia and Wallachia, 1774–1812.

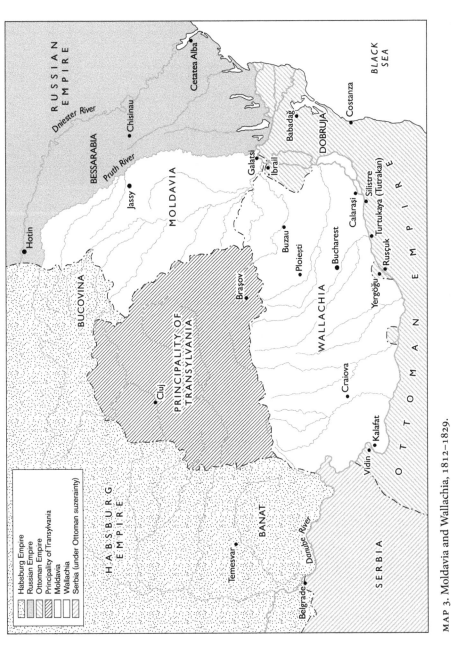

MAP 3. Moldavia and Wallachia, 1812–1829.

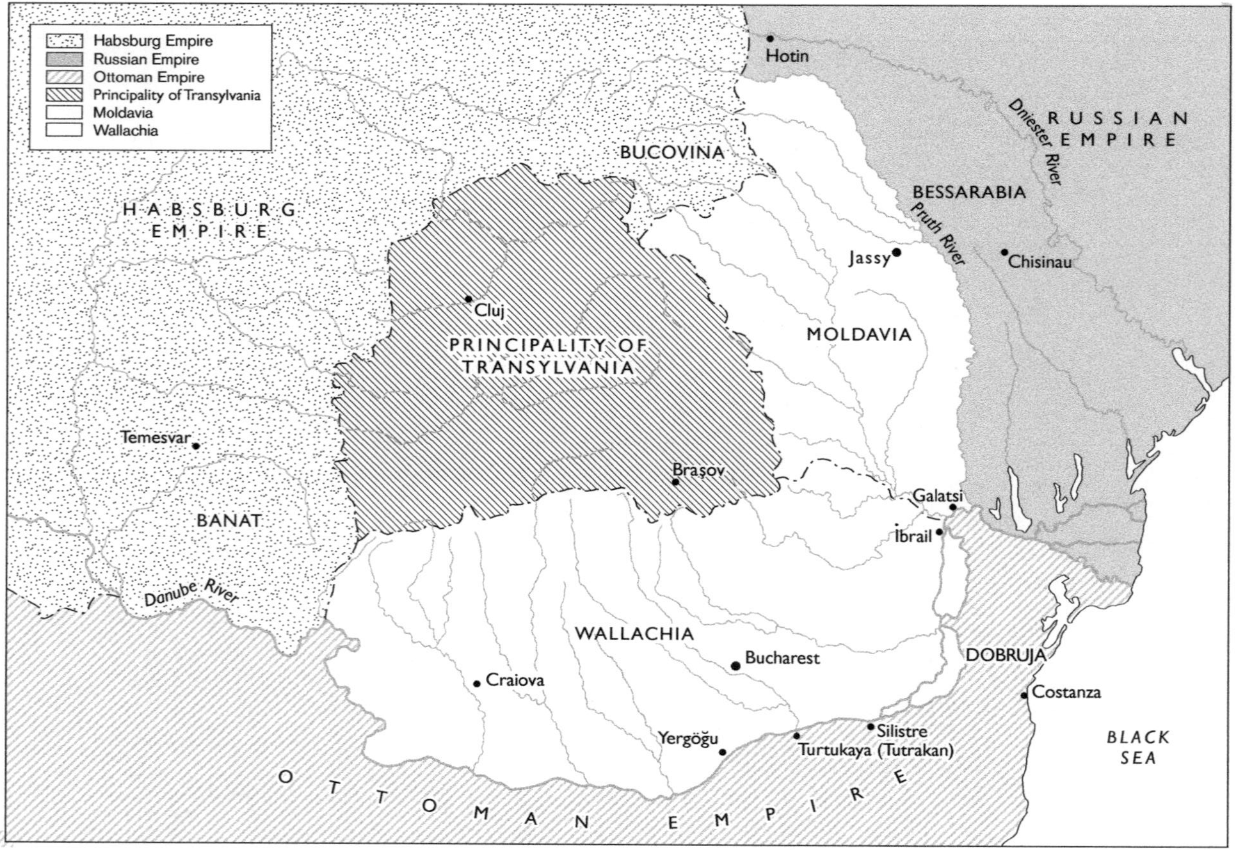

MAP 4. Moldavia and Wallachia, 1829.

# The View from the Edge of the Center

The origins of this book lie in a fundamental split in the way we remember the Ottoman Empire. For much of the twentieth century, the prevailing assumption was that the "Ottoman legacy" was one of authoritarianism, ethnic strife, and economic and cultural backwardness in the Middle East and Balkans. More recently, scholars have begun to hark back to a cosmopolitan multiconfessional Ottoman Empire, where Jews, Christians, and Muslims lived virtually free of communal strife under the umbrella of a flexible and accommodating Ottoman state. Were the Ottomans a force for stagnation and repression that kept the modern world at bay, or were they early modern pioneers of tolerance and cosmopolitanism?

The implicit question in this debate is whether the Ottoman Empire was behind or ahead of the (western European) norm. The one view, that the Ottomans were behind, is based on entrenched orientalist stereotypes that date back to the Ottoman period itself. The other view, which implies that they were ahead of their time, and thus ahead of Europe, with their tolerance for a multiconfessional subject population, springs from a strong revisionist impulse. Adherents of both views have a wealth of evidence from which to draw. It is the very acceptance of these terms—*ahead/behind, regressive/progressive*—however, and of the implicit norm against which to compare the Ottomans that necessarily limits us to two diametrically opposed visions.

A major aim of this study is to shift the terms of the debate about the Ottoman past. It achieves this aim by turning to what has been a black hole between tolerance and violence. Chronologically, this means the first half of the nineteenth century, when the supposed fluidity and tolerance of the early modern period shifted into an era of top-down attempts to reform, modernize, and Westernize and ultimately into mass and state-perpetrated violence. In retrospect we can also see that this period was the common starting point for three now-separate historical trajectories that would undo the empire over the course of the long nineteenth century (1789–1922): that of nation-state formation in the emergent Balkans, imperial modernization initiated from İstanbul, and European colonial projects that brought into being the modern Middle East. This period, in fact, is perhaps the central pivot in the statist master narrative that still haunts the modern field of Ottoman history: the narrative of rise (fourteenth to sixteenth century), decline (late sixteenth to late eighteenth century), and Westernization (the long nineteenth century). Indeed, the early nineteenth century is still implied to be the turning point between centuries of decline (even for those who have switched to its revisionist variants, such as decentralization, transformation, and change) and the new trajectory of top-down modernization (or Westernization) that would revive the empire for another century before its final demise in the wake of World War I.[1] And yet, as pivotal as it is, this period, and in particular the reign of Sultan Mahmud II (1808–39), has never been studied in depth.[2]

What has been seen as a prolonged transition period, however, roughly between the 1770s and the 1850s, contained an entire lifetime of crises and transformations. What follows is a close look at these crises and transformations in and for themselves, not merely as a starting or stopping point on the way to successful (or unsuccessful) modernization, nation-state formation, or the final demise of the empire and the establishment of the Turkish Republic in 1923. What follows is an attempt to grasp experiences of Ottoman governance during the fraught decades between the 1770s and the 1850s.

In order for us to appreciate the range of experiences that were possible in the Ottoman early nineteenth century, a broadened definition of the political is necessary. Oftentimes, who and what constituted "the state" is taken for granted as a unit of analysis in scholarship on the Ottoman Empire and is assumed to coincide with formal categories of status and power in the Ottoman period. In this period more than in many others of Ottoman history, it was glaringly clear that the state was not an autonomous actor, nor was it an "independent cause of events."[3] The state could hardly even be considered an "it," in fact, breaking down into constituent institutions and competing factions at several points in these decades.

Therefore, we must broaden the field of analysis in order to understand not only who and what constituted the Ottoman state but also how the institutions, networks, and individual personalities that functioned within the state were in flux and being shaped by forces and ideas outside the formal state apparatus. In an important sense, this study is a response to the calls of scholars such as Timothy Mitchell to historicize the distinction between state and society.[4] Using Rifa'at Ali Abou-El-Haj's plea for a comparative framework for analyzing crises and changes in the middle Ottoman centuries as a starting point, this study also takes inspiration from Abou-El-Haj's and Cemal Kafadar's calls to move beyond national(ist) versions of Ottoman history and to examine the syncretic and multiconfessional aspects of Ottoman governance through the centuries.[5]

Pushing beyond the binary division between "state" and "society" as much as that between "nation" and "empire," then, this book explores the practice of Ottoman governance in a time when the disjuncture between political realities and political discourse persisted for decades (ca. 1770–1860). On a microlevel I focus on an individual who operated both within and between institutions in order to practice governance in the absence of a formal share in the Ottoman ruling apparatus. In this individual life, as in the "life" of the empire, we begin to see the grave political crises of the 1820s in an arc of change with a kind of discursive crisis that took place in the early 1850s. Ottoman governance at the dawn of the nineteenth century was operated by individual actors using family and patronage relationships to forge projects across formal institutions and confessional divides. The series of revolutions that shook the Ottoman Empire in the first three decades of the nineteenth century—from the Greek-hetairist rebellions to the abolishment of the janissary (Ottoman infantry) corps and the rise of Mehmet Ali from Egypt—grew out of these realities of governance.[6] The restoration of the Ottoman sultanate was achieved in the 1830s only through a new ordering of governance. This new ordering synthesized Great Power, imperial, and often provincial and confessional politics and involved an inversion in the relative importance of diplomacy and domestic military power. The trumping of diplomacy over domestic military power would transform the calculus of Ottoman governance from within and lead, in stages, to the formation of the modern Middle East and Balkans throughout the subsequent century. Finally, the impasse of the 1850s occurred when the changed realities of international, imperial, and confessional politics could no longer be accommodated with the Ottoman discourse of empire. Out of this impasse emerged the 1856 discursive framework of the Tanzimat, which would dominate the subsequent twenty, if not the remaining sixty-five, years of the empire's history.

## SEEING LIKE A QUASI STATESMAN

In many ways the world I am trying to capture is unimaginable today—an impossibility within modern frameworks of political belonging.[7] The project arose from an encrypted memorandum I stumbled upon while conducting research for my doctoral dissertation. After spending the better part of three weeks deciphering and translating the document, I discovered it was in effect an apologia written by an Ottoman loyalist who had found himself at the center of the international crisis that led to the Crimean War and who happened to have been Orthodox Christian.

In justifying his unwavering loyalty to the Ottoman sultanate despite his having been Christian, the apologist-statesman reviewed his long career in defense of the well-protected domains of the sultan. Among many moments, he focused in particular on what was to him the climactic moment of 1821–22, when, in the heat of Greek secessionist rebellions, he found himself in a "supreme dilemma" as the governor of Ottoman Moldavia. The terms by which he described his dilemma—as one of whether to flee to Russia or to appease the janissaries clamoring at his doorstep to demand their grain rations—were nothing less than a radical departure from those of any modern historiography, Ottoman or national, with which I was familiar.

To begin with, I wondered, why did this dilemma have so little to do with the sentiments or even the military forces fighting in support of Greek statehood, despite taking place in the midst of what we now recognize as the first phase of the Greek War of Independence? Why was an Ottoman Christian in the 1850s attempting to justify his stance against not only the Greek national project but also the Russian Empire, so often portrayed as the coreligionist "protector" of Orthodox Christian Ottoman subjects since the eighteenth century? What could he have to gain with such a stance? And what could janissaries and grain rations have to do with a Christian's dilemma over loyalty to the Ottoman state?

This apologia supplied me with a series of trails to follow, drawing me into a quest to understand this world of Ottoman governance as experienced and imagined—in all its contradictions and immediacy—by its own practitioners and on its own terms, perhaps beyond those of modern historiography of the Ottoman Empire or the nation-states that emerged out of it. After I spent years of research in no fewer than eleven archives spread across six countries and containing documents written in five languages, the resulting book illuminates a political history in the broadest sense, told from a perspective at the imperial center of İstanbul but not the perspective of the sultan and his vezirs.

The life, career, and writings of one man have not only served as a map for my research, but have come to frame this book—none other than the Christian Ottoman apologist mentioned above. Stephanos Vogorides, also known as Istefanaki Bey in his Ottoman milieu, was born in the 1770s as Stoiko Stoikov in a town in Veliko Turnovo, a region in central Bulgaria today. As a young man he shifted away from his Bulgarian-speaking origins and assimilated into a Greek-speaking milieu, marrying into phanariot circles before 1821.

The term *phanariot* refers to the quarter in İstanbul—Phanar (T. Fener; G. Phanari)—where the Orthodox Patriarchate was and is located and the area where phanariots had their residences and therefore their base of power, because they dominated the lay and sometimes the clerical offices of that institution. While the term *phanariot* has a range of connotations in Ottoman, Balkan, and Arab historiographies, I use it loosely to mean Phanar-based elites and their retinues or affiliates. They differed from nonphanariot Orthodox Christian elites (such as local notables

[T. *kocabaşı; G. demogerontes*] and wealthy merchants) because they held offices associated with the Ottoman central state or the phanariot administration in Moldavia and Wallachia or both and were therefore servants of the Ottoman state in addition to being merchants or Church functionaries. They did not, however, enjoy the official *askeri,* or tax exempt, status of their Muslim functionary counterparts.

Originally a creation of the phanariot ascendancy in Ottoman governance before 1821, Vogorides bounced back from the crises of the 1820s that decimated many of the networks associated with phanariots in İstanbul and many Ottoman provinces. He remade himself to become indispensable not only to Sultans Mahmud II (r. 1808–39) and Abdülmecit (r. 1839–61) but also to an emerging generation of "neophanariot" statesmen and diplomats who were his protégés. Further, and perhaps most important, he made himself indispensable to Stratford Canning, the British ambassador in İstanbul. He did all of this from his base in İstanbul and under the deceptively trivial title of prince of the autonomous island polity of Samos. His life and career are nothing less than a tutorial on the nature and vicissitudes of Ottoman governance in the decades before the 1856 declaration of the Tanzimat reforms, themselves so often the starting point of scholarship on the Ottoman nineteenth century.

In an age of innovation and challenges to the imperial status quo across Europe, Vogorides was the leader of no movement—either popular or intellectual. He in fact resisted the calls of his contemporaries to join secessionist movements from Greek to Bulgarian and Romanian. On the surface he seems an aberration, even by the standards of his day—both as a Bulgarian-born phanariot and in a broader sense as a Christian Ottoman loyalist during and after the movement for Greek independence. And yet there were many like him who quietly remained in the arena of imperial politics, above the masses of non-Muslim Ottoman subjects and below the top-ranking Ottoman statesmen of their day.

It is revealing that Vogorides has largely been overlooked by modern scholarship of the Ottoman nineteenth century, receiving only rare and passing mention, and that only for his appointment as the first Orthodox Christian representative to the Meclis-i Vala-yı Ahkam-ı Adliye (Supreme Council of Judicial Ordinances) three years before his death, at the age of eighty-six, in 1856.[8] While perhaps an important watershed in the forward march toward representative institutions for a modern, secular, liberal (Turkish) state, this was in fact one of the least consequential of his achievements. The erasure of Vogorides from modern scholarship is not surprising, perhaps, given the traditional focus on institutions; writing Vogorides back into history thus sheds light on the ways in which the institutional focus has skewed our perceptions of Ottoman politics.

During his lifetime, Vogorides had a conflicted relationship to several ethnic-national projects for autonomy if not secession, including the Greek-hetairist, Serbian, Romanian, and Bulgarian movements between the 1830s and 1850s. The rare mentions he receives in Greek and Romanian historiography portray him as a villain, in the former case for his resistance to Greek national interests, and in the latter case for his and his son Nicholas's thinly veiled attempt to sabotage the 1856 plebiscite for the union of the two Romanian principalities, a defining moment in Romanian nation-state formation. He enjoys more, if conflicted, attention in Bulgarian national historiography, principally because he was the grandson of Sofroni Vracanski, the archbishop of Vratsa—the first self-proclaimed Bulgarian archbishop in a Greek-dominated Church hierarchy and the individual credited post facto with sparking a Bulgarian cultural revival that would eventually lead to independent statehood.[9] And yet the conflict lies in the fact that Vogorides was hardly a consistent champion of Bulgarian causes himself. This series of national movements has often served as the main plotline for scholarly treatments of Balkan and Ottoman Christians in the nineteenth century. From the perspective of Vogorides and phanariots such movements appear only obliquely, as challenges, crises, and even annoyances to a much larger and more entrenched imperial system of thought and governance.

Framing a structural and historical analysis around a biography animates the question of agency in a period that is often seen as merely neoabsolutist (as Mahmud II took back the reins of power) and as the starting point of "top-down, outside-in" reforms.[10] Vogorides' actions—indeed his political existence—cannot be explained within a purely structural or ideological matrix. He did not *have* to practice Ottoman governance, either before or after the 1820s. As he himself would explain in the apologia mentioned above, he had many opportunities to abandon his post as a loyal servant of the sultan, whether it be to escape to the Russian Empire, join forces with Greek revolutionaries (as his own brother Athanasios did), or simply pick up and move to any number of European states. From our perspective the question that persists is why he would continue to practice Ottoman governance when so many competing national ideologies were at play and dynastic loyalty was no longer sufficient to justify a Christian's adherence to Ottoman politics. What were the duties of servitude, as he refers to them? Most fascinating are the many moments his personality bursts through in his correspondence, forcing us to identify with him across the political and historical gulf that seems to separate the early nineteenth from the early twenty-first century.

To approach the phanariot ascendancy before 1821 and the reconstitution of phanariot power after the 1820s from Vogorides' vantage point allows a glimpse into his own grand ambitions and strategies as well as into the experiences of those with more humble projects—limited to one province, institution, or patron—that fit into or worked against Vogorides' phanariot scheme. While Vogorides' biography and writings frame the book, several other—Muslim as well as Christian—individuals' lives and careers are sketched out in the following pages. Vogorides' maverick predecessor Mavroyeni Bey, phanariot functionary-chronicler Dionysios Photeinos, Ottoman statesman-turned-villain Halet Efendi, Vogorides' nemesis Aristarchi Bey, and more prominent figures such as Husrev Paşa, Mehmet Ali Paşa of Egypt, and even Sultan Mahmud II are all featured so as to demonstrate the interconnectedness of Ottoman governance as well as the limits and possibilities of action in an age of institutional—and ideological—flux. These were all men who violated, changed, or established formal institutional boundaries in an age that is as fascinating for its indeterminacy as it is for its formative place in the creation of the modern Middle East and Balkans.

## GOVERNANCE: TOWARD
## A NEW POLITICAL LANDSCAPE

On the broadest level of the study, governance—rather than state, sovereignty, or government—is the operative concept. By governance I mean the project of keeping a political order in place, including the formal state apparatus but also the many relationships in society involving institutions, networks, individuals, customs, and beliefs that contribute to upholding that order. This concept sets up the broader canvas necessary to see the Ottoman state in its historical and cultural context and in a larger comparative framework of empires. By extension it allows for a discussion of lived governance, formal structures of power, and the multiple and changing discourses of politics that were available in the early nineteenth century, all in the same analytical field.

Michel Foucault has of course written the most illuminating studies of power and "governmentality" with reference to the French and a broader European context, noting that power is dispersed in myriad ways and not "localized in the State apparatus."[11] To apply the related term *governance* to an Ottoman context is to take inspiration from this work but to set a framework that captures the specificity as well as the universal dimension of power in the Ottoman Empire in the first half of the nineteenth century. We may be talking about processes that resemble those in European experiences of "modernity" and are certainly talking about a crucial period of transformation in the nature of power in the Ottoman context, and yet in trying to capture the levels of unarticulated change in the Ottoman Empire to project the term *modernization* or *modernity* is to accept its many implications about twentieth-century paths of development. Similarly, to assume that in this period the loci of changes were the prison, the hospital, and the asylum is to project a universal modernity onto the Ottoman Empire before it had necessarily entered the same discursive arena with western Europe. For an Ottoman context, I am exploring the possibility that the arenas through which we can track changes in the calculus of power were those of diplomacy and the military, and I track those through the lens of phanariots and related groups, such as janissaries and *ayans*.

Neither Vogorides' career nor the larger phanariot ascendancy that made his career possible took place strictly within the confines of Ottoman state institutions. Rather, both Vogorides and his phanariot associates operated with actors and institutions associated with the Ottoman state and yet did so without formal status as *"askeri,"* or official members of the ruling apparatus. The term *governance,* then, allows us to capture phanariots' political landscape in full and compels us to expand our understanding of the political, encompassing all of the common alternatives— state, society, and economy, as well the realms of locality, family, military force, diplomacy, and foreign relations and the gamut of roles played by religion, from doctrine to practice and ceremonial—as legitimating forces for the social and political order.

Within the broad concept of governance, I differentiate at several points in the book between formal, official politics—which includes formal positions and titles, state-sanctioned meetings and social events, official receptions of ambassadors, and official memos and documents sent between official representatives of state or individual agents—and unofficial, informal politics, by which I mean meetings that occurred in private residences, with or without the express consent and sanction of the central state, meetings that were ordered to be covert or informal, that involved individuals without official political positions, and that were arranged to convey information on behalf of official state actors.

My point in drawing this distinction between formal and informal politics is to pinpoint the space in which phanariots operated—the gap between political ideals and political realities. And this is what makes the early 1830s a pivotal moment in the book: while on the one hand a formal apparatus of Ottoman diplomacy was emerging (which superseded the informal matrix of diplomacy conducted through the members of the phanariot system), on the other hand, various actors used, manipulated, and circumvented those men in formal positions of power through informal negotiations and information gathering. While certainly all systems of governance feature such a gap between formal structures and informal practices of politics, what makes the Ottoman case stand out are the ramifications this had for the political and confessional order of the empire, for that empire's changing relationship to the "Great Power" states around it, and ultimately for the way the subsequent decades of the empire's history played out.

When we consider phanariots in the broad political landscape of governance rather than the state, we begin to see that they were not the only Ottoman elite that was proliferating at the interstices of formal state and religious institutions and local communal structures. But theirs is a case that brings to the fore the dilemmas and contradictions of Ottoman governance more dramatically than the cases of their more familiar janissary (Ottoman infantry) and *ayan* (provincial notable) contemporaries, cases that mirror the phanariot ascendancy in a number of important ways. These Muslim Ottoman groups, the former centered around formal military institutions and the latter around formal provincial administrative institutions, were also remarkable for their instrumentalization of existing institutions toward new ends, which were likewise threatening to the interests of the formal central state.[12] But, whatever the dramatic class and political shifts were that they signified, those of janissaries and *ayan*s were underway in an intra-Muslim (and ultimately intra-*askeri*) context. They certainly threatened the military and administrative capacity of the formal structures of state, but as Muslims (even when they disagreed about the meaning and obligations associated with this) they did not threaten the fundamental consensus of Ottoman governance as articulated since at least the sixteenth century—the formal predominance of institutions and adherents of (Sunni) Islam over non-Muslims (and non-Sunni Muslims) in and for the Ottoman state.[13]

While the Greek Revolution, or War of Independence, from a national perspective is outside the purview of this discussion, the post-1821 phanariot ascendancy within Ottoman governance is crucial; this second ascendancy was perhaps even more remarkable than the first one. The Greek War of Independence was a bloody, prolonged civil war between Greek-aligned rebels and Ottoman loyalist forces, which was perceived in national historiographies from Greece to Turkey, if not at the time by Ottoman statesmen, as a betrayal on the part of the Orthodox Christian community. It ended in the cession of territory under Great Power guarantee and the establishment of the kingdom of Greece. Better-known phanariots joined this new national enterprise, even as many other phanariots managed to recoup their strategic functions deep within the project of imperial governance. In doing so they reconstructed patronage networks in a shifting institutional landscape, even while continuing to employ an operational logic similar to that before the conflict. Neither the janissary corps, which was formally and violently abolished in 1826, nor *ayan*s, whose power was squelched in many regions by the second decade of the nineteenth century, could be said to have had the same resurgence.[14] After the 1820s, then, phanariots in their Ottoman context present a paradox for those focused on the forward march of centralizing and modernizing reforms, looking like a holdover from an earlier age of governance or an aberration in an age of Tanzimat institutional encroachment. As will be clear in the following pages, they demonstrated an ability to adapt to manifold changes and an ability to survive and prosper well into the supposedly new age of reforms.

## ARCHIVES, EMPIRE, AND
## THE HYBRID VANTAGE POINT

This project would not have been possible without the foundations of scholarship on the late eighteenth and early nineteenth centuries laid by Ottoman historians as well as Balkan/southeast European and Middle East history scholars.[15] While this project builds on a synthesis of their work, it occupies what is a fundamentally new perspective, situated at a historical crossroads : the period conventionally understood to be the chronological intersection between Ottoman "decline" and "Westernization," in the spaces between Greek, Bulgarian, Romanian, Turkish, and Egyptian national narratives and even between the larger categories of military, national, regional (Middle East and Balkan), international, and confessional trajectories of Ottoman history. The task of writing a postnational history of Ottoman governance has demanded the dissolution of longstanding divisions regarding archives and empire that have dominated Ottoman, Balkan, and Middle East studies over the past several decades.

George Steinmetz has noted the need for multiple theoretical strategies and perspectives to analyze properly any specific modern state in its full complexity.[16] Applying that to the specific context of Ottoman governance in the early nineteenth century, the new perspective put forward here amounts to a hybrid vantage point on Ottoman governance. Phanariots, and Vogorides himself, were operating not only between rulers and ruled but also between Ottoman and national. Fundamental to capturing their hybrid vantage point is a synthesis between Ottoman state archival sources and Greek-language phanariot sources.

Students of Ottoman history are often taught that official, state-generated documents in Ottoman Turkish constitute the most authoritative and definitive source for the history of that empire.[17] Sources in other languages—be they Greek, Armenian, Ladino, Kurdish, or even Arabic—are assumed to be of use only for particular religious-ethnic or local communities, not to revise the core narrative of the Ottoman state. This assumption may hold if we are tracking official policy outcomes, formal power arrangements between the central state and provincial or social-occupational groups, or even less formal patterns in crucial economic affairs such as tax farming. And yet, I argue that one reason we have missed the complex realities of politics at the turn of the nineteenth century is that scholars have neglected the role, both productive and destructive, of phanariots—and the significant volume of Greek-language as well as Ottoman-language sources they left behind—in the day-to-day work and the high politics of the empire.

By placing a dialogue between Ottoman- and Greek-language sources at the center of this study, a virtual first in the context of Ottoman imperial and Balkan national traditions, this book opens new vistas onto Ottoman governance in a period scholarship has long taken for granted. Ottoman Turkish sources from the Başbakanlık Devlet Arşivleri (Prime Ministry State Archive) and Topkapı Sarayı Arşivi (Topkapı Palace Archive), as well as the Archivele Statului (National Archives) in Romania, provide a window into the official operations and language of governance in the empire. They also supply much evidence for the direct involvement of phanariots in Ottoman governance and the changing political realities in which they were engaged. Greek-language sources from the ecumenical patriarchate in İstanbul (even though only a small portion of these are accessible to researchers), phanariot-authored chronicles, and correspondence among phanariot Christian diplomats and interpreters in the service of the Ottoman Empire bring to life the informal relationships and processes crucial for the practice of Ottoman governance at this time.

Research for this project involved not only integrating Ottoman Turkish- and Greek-language sources but also an intimate knowledge of the blended nature of phanariot Ottoman identity through the unique and hybrid language they employed in creating and maintaining their connections and power. While we have few if any examples of personal or candid correspondence among Muslim Ottoman officials in this period, phanariot correspondence reveals the more candid (and messier) side of political life that Muslim Ottomans must have also experienced.[18] Given that they were translators and interpreters, phanariots often tacked back and forth between their two major languages—Ottoman Turkish and Greek—in their writings to each other. At times they wrote in a secret code—wherein numerals represented Greek letters, which were used to spell Ottoman Turkish words—knowing that those outside their ranks would have no hope of understanding. At other times they improvised their own transliteration system of Ottoman Turkish words and phrases into a Greek alphabet (placing three dots over a Greek *sigma* to make the Arabic/Turkish letter *shin*, in imitation of the three dots that would represent that letter in the Arabic/Ottoman alphabet, for instance). These details are crucial for understanding the depth of integration that was possible in this world, which scholarship has falsely tried to imagine and understand as either distinctly Greek or as Ottoman and therefore Turkish.

The papers of Stephanos Vogorides and his son-in-law Constantine Musurus are a treasure trove for addressing questions of lived Ottoman governance in the nineteenth century. Vogorides' undoubtedly tremendous personal archive did not remain intact; one biographer noted, "Upon the death of Vogoridi, his archives were scattered. For more than a year, the cinnamon, salt, and pepper sold by boutiques in Arnavutköy and Bebek [Bosphorus villages] were wrapped in paper from it."[19] Constantine Musurus's personal papers, however, including his correspondence with Vogorides, were preserved and eventually sold to the Gennadeion Library, in Athens, by an İstanbul Greek collector in the early 1970s. The Greek- and French-language papers had already been well-known if rarely used by scholars. I also discovered that some eight hundred additional papers existed in Ottoman Turkish. These added another dimension to the study, together providing a magnifying glass into the daily work of Ottoman governance, from the island of Samos to Jassy, in Moldavia, and from İstanbul to London and Vienna.[20] As a whole they show, for one, that the larger Ottoman story does not begin and end in the Prime Ministry Archives of İstanbul (as important and abundant as those archives are) and cannot be fully appreciated without the experiences, activities, and vantage point of Ottoman Christian elites, some of whom, such as the dragomans and diplomats expounded on in the following pages, had key roles to play in the official (and sometimes more important, unofficial) operations of imperial governance in the eighteenth and nineteenth centuries.

British and French consular reports are also most useful for this study for their vantage point as outside observers of Ottoman governance and also precisely because of Vogorides' regular contact with such diplomats. They also demonstrate the changing role of diplomats in İstanbul from observers to participants in Ottoman governance in the early 1830s, a change that constitutes a crucial turning point in the argument that follows. The memoranda sent from İstanbul to the British and French foreign ministers indicate how consuls on the ground understood the changes and workings of Ottoman governance and reflect the new political calculus that was coming to determine Ottoman decision making by this decade. As a result of employing these sources, some of the analysis that follows may appear similar to a well-established literature on the Eastern Question, and yet this is only part of the story as told from the perspective of phanariots at the interstices between international, imperial, and provincial arenas of Ottoman governance.

A series of five interludes is interspersed throughout the book. These interludes sketch the life and career trajectory of Stephanos Vogorides and, in the post-1830 period, that of his archrival Nicholas Aristarchi. Vogorides' path through Ottoman governance (and struggle against Aristarchi) is a thread of continuity connecting the long-term changes underway before 1821, the breakdown in multiple arenas of the 1820s and their restoration of the 1830s, and the discursive impasse of the 1850s that led to the second round of the Tanzimat.

Six chapters open out from Vogorides' personal story and provide a kind of sociology of empire to complement and contextualize his biography of empire. Chapter 1, "The Houses of Phanar," focuses on the pre-1821 phanariot ascendancy, arguing that the phanariot project within Ottoman governance at the turn of the nineteenth century, like the houses of the Phanar quarter in İstanbul, had a deceptively simple exterior that hid intricate and lucrative relationships to the larger world of governance. It was in this phanariot "house" that Vogorides came of age and learned his operational logic, and chapter 1 demonstrates both the coherence of a phanariot project in Ottoman domains and the parallels and connections between that project and better-studied projects of Muslim Ottoman provincial notables and janissary members at the same time.

Shifting from the structures of the phanariot ascendancy, chapter 2, "Volatile Synthesis," moves to the contingencies of Ottoman governance in crisis—as seen from the phanariot house. This chapter follows a series of lives, Christian and Muslim, that were intertwined with one another and bound up in often surprising ways with

the project to launch a new Ottoman military between 1791 and 1808. Arguing that
the period following the "failure" of the New Order reforms was not so much a pause
as a volatile synthesis between factions that had been on opposing sides of the reform issue, I demonstrate this through the conjunction of interests that brought
phanariots and master courtier Halet Efendi into close cooperation between 1808
and the outbreak of rebellions in 1821. These were the years of Vogorides' education,
training, and induction into phanariot networks, and as such they left an indelible
imprint on his understanding of and approach to politics in the subsequent four
decades of his career.

Chapters 3 ("Demolitions"), 4 ("The Struggle for Continuity"), and 5 ("Diplomacy and the Restoration of a New Order") go on to use—and extrapolate—a phanariot perspective on the larger world of Ottoman governance. This phanariot perspective continues, even though the 1820s saw the demise of the phanariot house
and the transformation in relationships of governance that extended into the early
1830s. In one sense, this is meant to be a close-up look at a period that has not been
ignored so much as taken for granted in modern historiography, a period of momentous events, such as the first successor-state based on a national principle (the
Greek kingdom) was established, the nominal military force of the empire was abolished, and the sultanate was nearly usurped by Mehmet Ali (Muhammad Ali) from
Egypt. All three events constitute the starting points of divergent historical narratives—Balkan national movements, imperial (military) modernization, and the formation of the modern Middle East. But for those living at the time, all three conflicts
were experienced in the same historical moment and interpreted in the same framework of governance.

The 1820s and early 1830s were also the most decisive—and risky—period in
Vogorides' life and career, when his loyalty was tested and his skills in politics and
diplomacy were stretched to the limit. Each of the three chapters thus takes a different level of change: the day-to-day violence in İstanbul in the 1820s that led to the
demise of the phanariot (and janissary) house (chapter 3); the undoing of major
structures of governance and the solutions devised by the central state to remake
structures of diplomacy and military in new ways (chapter 4); and the formation
of a new politics of diplomacy in İstanbul that signified a new order of governance,
both imperial and international (chapter 5). Taken together, the changes detailed
in these three chapters help explain how the world had changed and what allowed
men such as Vogorides, his friends, and rivals from before 1821 to find renewed
relevance and step back into niches of power within Ottoman governance in the
1830s and beyond.

Returning to Vogorides at center stage, chapter 6 ("In the Eye of the Storm")
zeroes in on the political, and ultimately discursive, crisis that he—and the Ottoman
Empire—faced in the early 1850s, when international conflict loomed in Ottoman
domains. The disjunctures of international, imperial, and confessional politics cul-

minated not in an Ottoman military crisis, or in one of provincial administration, or even in Balkan nationalism, but in a kind of discursive and jurisdictional crisis revolving around custodianship of Christian Holy Sites in Ottoman Palestine. This crisis, which led soon after to the Crimean War and ultimately to the 1856 promulgation of the Tanzimat, prompted Vogorides, for the first time it seems, to try to claim a place for himself as an Orthodox Christian, Ottoman loyalist whose position would not be blurred with that of Russia, the premier Orthodox Christian power involved in the dispute. His emergent ideology would soon be buried by the administrative-political framework of the Tanzimat, a product of Great Power politics as much as Ottoman imperial necessity. But his very attempt to form a kind of ideology to weather the storm is a fascinating reflection of what must have seemed possible at that moment.

I seek to demonstrate in the following chapters that there is a history of governance before (and outside) the institutional and discursive framework of the Tanzimat. To do this is not to belittle the transformative potential of the Tanzimat or its tremendous consequences for the epistemic framework, institutional structures, and even day-to-day practices of governance post-1839 and more profoundly post-1856. Indeed it was the legal and ideological framework of the Tanzimat that brought the Ottoman Empire into a common political arena with the competing and allied states of Europe, for better and worse "bring[ing] the Ottoman Empire into the modern world for the first time."[21] The goings-on of the first half of the nineteenth century, through the eyes of a group—and an individual—that was institutionally excluded from power and yet as intimately bound up with Ottoman power as any Muslim group could be, are remarkable for taking place before the onset of a deliberate integrationist project (with a concomitant discourse of integration). The fact that so many changes could happen, with so little political language to articulate and accommodate such changes, can only make the subsequent Tanzimat experiment seem at once more significant—for the discourse that accompanied it—and less novel, given this "prehistory" of integration. Here is a story of Ottoman governance before the telos of the Tanzimat.

# Stephanos Vogorides' Apologia

## November 1852

Enlightened by the theory of the Evangelical Logos,[1] which commands us to render unto Caesar what is Caesar's (idol worshipers though they were then), to love one's neighbor as thyself, even the Samaritan who does not glorify the Resurrection as we Christians do, and to avoid anything that brings about scandal, abnormality, or disorder to human society, where divine Providence deigned to form us out of nonbeing, I have thus always been bound not to give occasion for discord, for responsibility and accusations of suspicion against Christians of the Ottomans (under whom God has subjected us for our sins). I am shamed to give my fellow Christians an example of submission and forbearance, so that our most holy Christian religion not be blasphemed by the exploitation of some other Christians. I never failed to take care in executing the political duties that were incumbent on me, nor to be bought out by or take advantage of the circumstances of the day that come with this awareness.

If I had had a tender and coddled upbringing like the phanariots and most of the Ottoman ministers in İstanbul, I surely would not have been able to tolerate so many dangers, and I would have fled or been killed, like so many of my phanariot compatriots. Having as I did this physical and moral upbringing, I was able to remain constant in the duties of my servitude when the revolution of the Greeks [Graikon] broke out in 1821, when I was already of a vigorous age, and during the wars against the French in Egypt, and then again later when I found myself in Rumelia with the imperial army against the Russian forces, emboldened by the booming of the cannons and rifles not to shy away from dangers and wars, and the times I was thought to be Rumeliot and a compatriot of the Bulgarians, and when the paşas were politically asleep, and when I was invited by Hypsilantis and the other commanders of the apostasy of the Greeks to join them, I remained steady in the duties of my servitude. Other-

1

*wise, neither Moldavia and Wallachia nor Turkish Europe [Tourkike Evrope] would be in their current state of submission and obedience. It was I who roused the* paşas *on the Danube and caused them to take the necessary military and defensive measures in time. Let me say something else that might seem paradoxical to those who have had a different upbringing and have different convictions from us local Christians:*

*It was the time when the janissaries came and flooded into Moldavia [in 1821–22], saying it was to fight the apostates,*[2] *but in reality to fight the impending invasion of the enemy Russians, and when the hetairist Greeks had been expelled by me to the other side of the river Pruth, that the Greeks propagated the rumor from across the river among the janissary sycophants at my side, that supposedly I as the* kaymakam *in collusion with the Russians was selling the Russians the grains of Moldavia in order to leave the janissaries to desert from hunger. It was at this time that, one night, the* ustas *[oustades], or the elders/notables [prouchontes] of the janissaries, were gathered together to demand money from me so as not to complain about the ringing of the [church] bells in the city. At that moment a Greek [Graikos] from among the archons and someone who was honestly well-disposed toward me, whom I had dispatched to be on guard and to gather information from Bessarabia [across the Pruth] and notify me so that I could arrange the* paşas *appointed to the Danubian region in a timely manner, and subsequently to notify the Sublime Porte of my actions, came and whispered into my ear (in the presence of the* ustas*). He said that General Insoff (Dutch by genos and military commander of the Russian troops in Bessarabia) sent him to come and tell me secretly that the then-Russian ambassador Baron Stroganoff had suddenly left Constantinople, and that Russian forces were awaiting orders from St. Petersburg at any moment to cross the Pruth and expel the janissaries and other Ottoman forces, and that I, the* kaymakam, *will be in great danger when that happens, and that the hetairist Greeks that I threw out, accompanied by the Cossacks on the road, will cut me up into pieces, and that if I leave with the janissaries they will murder even their own vezirs/commanders in the retreat, and that he had information that the all-powerful Christian-killer [Christianomachos] in Constantinople, Halet Efendi, was looking for an opportunity to slit my throat, and that if I were to leave immediately for Russia, they would honor me with the title* général en chef, *of equal status to my title of* kaymakam *bestowed by the sultan in Moldowallachia, and the imperial court [in Russia] will reward and compensate me with land and money. I, in a state of great agitation, sent the* ustas *away on a pretext and with great warmth* dans un moment si suprême *turned to the all-powerful and all-merciful God and said inside myself that, if divine Providence had deigned to make me born Russian, then I should have been born in Russia. Since I was created in Turkey [Tourkia], I will owe a great explanation to God if, because of my flight to Russia, I gave a blessed cause for Halet*

FIGURE 1. Portrait of Stephanos Vogorides. Photograph courtesy of Christos Landros.

*Efendi to murder many Christians, and would justify his anti-Christian and murderous policy, allowing him to allege that, since Stefanaki became a traitor [G. haines; T. hain], the Sublime Porte should not trust any Christian subject. . . . Weighing all of this I stayed and fought then and subsequently, swimming through so many dangers, but by the grace of God I have been saved until now. Great is the Lord, and miraculous are his works. I neglect to describe other great, faithful, and warm labors of mine over the past fifty years.*

*So what would the Duke of Wellington, that man rare in history for his moral and martial virtue, who has completed works of the utmost importance for England and is worthy of the honor bestowed on him by his ethnos in life and in death, do if he were in my place, if he were serving an anti-Christian ethnos, which looks askance at the loyalty [sadakat] of a Christian and can't bear to believe that the Christian can be most well-behaved and most loyal toward the Sublime Porte? Would he put up with it and try to save Moldavia and Rumelia, that is to say Turkey, from all of the misunderstandings and inroads of fanaticism or not? It is this problem I would like my old and good friend Mr. [Stratford] Canning to answer for me.*[3]

# 1

# The Houses of Phanar

It was with difficulty that I could collect my scattered senses when the time came to step into the nut-shell, all azure and gold, which waited to convey the [dragoman]'s suite to the [Phanar]. . . . Each stroke of the oar, after we had pushed off from the ship, made our light caick [T. *kayık*] glide by some new palace, more splendid than that which preceded it; and every fresh edifice I beheld, grander in its appearance than the former, was immediately set down in my mind as my master's habitation. I began to feel uneasy when I perceived that we had passed the handsomest district, and we were advancing toward a less showy quarter. My pangs increased as we were made to step ashore on a mean-looking quay, and to turn into a narrow, dirty lane; and I attained the acme of my dismay, when, arrived opposite a house of a dark and dingy hue, apparently crumbling to pieces with age and neglect, I was told that there lived the [phanariot] lord. . . . A new surprise awaited me within. That mean fir-wood case, of such forbidding exterior, contained rooms furnished in all the splendor of eastern magnificence. Persian carpets covered the floors, Genoa velvets clothed the walls, and gilt trellis work overcast the lofty ceilings. Clouds of rich perfumes rose on all sides from silver censers. . . . The persons of [phanariot] grandees were of a piece with their habitations. Within doors, sinking under the weight of rich furs, costly shawls, jewels, and trinkets, they went forth into the streets wrapped in coarse, and dingy, and often thread-bare clothing.[1]

Orientalist hyperbole aside, phanariots were engaged in a paradoxical imperial enterprise from the late seventeenth century until 1821. They were a composite Orthodox Christian elite that grew out of the social and political fabric of Ottoman governance. Their rise to power flew in the face of religious dogma and political ideology underpinning Ottoman governance, which forbade Christians a formal share in Ottoman sovereignty. Their political success transcended (and often effaced) their mercantile origins and connected them with Ottoman governance in several ways: as translators, purveyors, tax farmer–governors, and diplomats and through their association with the Ecumenical Patriarchate in İstanbul, itself deeply connected to Ottoman administration. Phanariots had built a house (and households) of their own within Ottoman domains. In a taxonomy of elites at the turn of the nineteenth century, theirs was a house that shared many features, not just with diasporic merchants and social groups of contemporary Eurasian empires, but also with the major Muslim Ottoman social groups operating all around them—and with them—in the provinces and the imperial center.

Phanariots in the Ottoman Empire have received much less scholarly attention than Greek mercantile elites in the larger Mediterranean world, with whom it is of course tempting to frame a comparison. Both enjoyed prominence in precisely the same period and were connected by ties of commerce, blood, and local origins.[2] The well-known story of the Greek merchant diaspora, operating from London to Marseille through Odessa, which amassed the capital, built the information networks, and imported the ideas necessary for a secessionist revolution and the establishment of an independent Greek state obscures the fact that there was also a Greek-identified elite who were products and agents of Ottoman governance.[3] This was an elite that can hardly be termed part of a diaspora, for its members were increasingly involved in the work of Ottoman governance and were concentrated at the Ottoman metropole, which had, of course, once been the chief city of Byzantium. Phanariots did not belong to the imperial ruling house, nor did they share the dominant religion of Sunni Islam. And yet, while other transregional networks of "middleman minorities" could be deeply involved in the political economy of the states that gave them shelter, phanariots went well beyond this arena to serve as functionaries—governors and diplomats—for the Ottoman state, and thus confound the national and diasporic frameworks. It should not be a surprise, then, although it has been all but ignored up to now, that phanariots deployed a number of strategies to gain status and legitimacy—and wealth—*within* the political culture and economy of the Ottoman Empire. Key to these strategies was not just the mobilization of family relationships but also the formalization of those relationships in a specifically Ottoman Turkish idiom.

In modern scholarship on the Ottoman Empire, phanariots have been accounted for within the framework of *millet*s. The system of *millet*s—confessional nations that were the basis for Ottoman administration—was once accepted as a mechanistic explanation for how the Ottoman system could sustain a multiconfessional subject population. In this vein scholars have long argued that non-Muslims inhabited their own autonomous communities and had little interaction with the Muslim state apparatus throughout the Ottoman centuries. The *millet* system has become a subject of debate over the past generation, however. Newer work has suggested a more fluid administrative apparatus, arguing that there was no fully institutionalized *mil-*

*let* framework until the Tanzimat reforms of the mid-nineteenth century.[4] The very terms of this debate reflect a preoccupation with formal institutional and legal definitions. Such definitions shed little light on the social realities of Ottoman governance, particularly at century's turn when formal institutions were by all accounts in profound crisis.

One would not want to deny that confessional identity had a tremendous impact on phanariots' activities and possibilities. Certainly in the legal arena there were basic divisions between Muslims, who were adherents of the ruling state religion, and Christians and Jews, who enjoyed the in-between status of *zimmi,* or People of the Book, both protected and shunned as second-class subjects. The Orthodox Church apparatus and doctrines no doubt overshadowed the lives of Orthodox Christians in the Ottoman Empire. Indeed, the identity of phanariots may have been first and foremost as Christians in a Muslim-dominated state. Recruitment into phanariot networks occurred through Church affiliations in addition to family relations and more formal schooling opportunities in the principalities and elsewhere.

And yet beyond the scope of any real or imagined *millet* system, a significant faction of phanariots was in the midst of consolidating transregional households—comparable to those of their Muslim peers in structure and function—by the turn of the nineteenth century. If we have an understanding of phanariots' rise, the internal composition of their households, the range of connections they sustained to the broader matrix of Ottoman governance, and the strategies for legitimization they employed within Ottoman political culture, a picture emerges of an imperial project that was, on the surface, fleeting but remarkably durable and adaptable to shifting realities within. Like the British Empire in India that dwarfed phanariots' project and that of their Ottoman superiors, phanariots even made the transition from mercantile to territorial control over their domains in the late eighteenth century. While in the British case this led to indirect and eventually direct imperial rule over an entire subcontinent, in the phanariot case, their house split by 1830 into a Greek nation-state kingdom and a new kind of enterprise within Ottoman lands.

A quantitative and comprehensive study of political involvement or even kinship patterns among phanariots, as among *ayan*s and janissaries, is hardly a possibility given the fragmentary evidence available. This is not merely because records have been lost but also because the very phenomenon of the phanariot ascendancy—like the *ayan* phenomenon and the range of de facto janissary roles in Ottoman governance—was not fully institutionalized.[5] While families formed webs of patronage ultimately replaced by institutions such as the Tercüme Odası, or Translation Office (est. 1833), they did so in what seems to have been an improvised way, and this is reflected even in the little we can glean about kinship patterns.[6] Thus, anecdotal evidence from contemporary chronicles, personal correspondence, secondary sources regarding phanariot genealogies, and Ottoman state archival sources that make reference to particular offices and functions performed for the Ottoman state is necessary in capturing both the ramshackle exterior and the plush interior of the phanariot house.

## THE OFFICIAL STORY

Situating the neighborhood that was the phanariots' power base in İstanbul encapsulates much about their rise: Phanar was conveniently located near the many docks of the Golden Horn, where crucial provisions arrived in the capital. It was a short boat ride from Topkapı Palace, the imperial palace and seat of the sultanate, and an even shorter one across the bay to Kasımpaşa, where the imperial shipyards and arsenal were located. Phanariots derived their power from the operations going on at all of these sites: from their commercial activities and emergence as local elites on Aegean islands (administered by the Ottoman admiral) and in İstanbul in the seventeenth century, their accumulated knowledge of medicine and European languages useful to the Ottoman imperial project, and their political relationships to and offices in the Orthodox Church, which had special authority over dispersed Christian populations in the empire.

This phanariot house was built thanks to the changes both in the regional political-economic landscape and in the structures of Ottoman imperial governance from the later seventeenth century. Historians of the Ottoman Empire have long noted the shift from a military to bureaucratic state emerging from the crises of the mid-seventeenth century.[7] This entailed changes on countless levels, such as revenue collection and expenditure, provincial administration, trade and food provisioning, and writing about politics and statecraft.[8] But perhaps most important for the emergence of phanariot elites in this transformation was the 1699 Treaty of Carlowitz, which signaled the closing of the Ottoman frontier with Europe, the end of an expansion-driven regime, and the first official cession of territory to Christendom.[9] This treaty prompted a realignment of Ottoman diplomacy and a reconfiguration of administration in the border areas and populations as well as in the diplomatic apparatus in İstanbul. It also coincided with the rise of Russia as a major power and threat to Ottoman ambitions for expansion and eventually political survival. Together, these changes offered a host of building materials for an aspiring Orthodox Christian elite, such as the phanariots, with linguistic and political knowledge useful for diplomatic intercourse with the states of Christendom.

A handful of individual phanariots and families had already attained positions of great influence in the decades before Carlowitz. Panagiotes Nikousios, a native of the formerly Genoese island of Chios, and Alexandros Mavrocordato, from an already prominent İstanbul family with roots in Chios, were the two major examples of this.[10] The Mavrocordato family, like several other emerging phanariot families in the seventeenth century, apparently accumulated capital from a monopoly

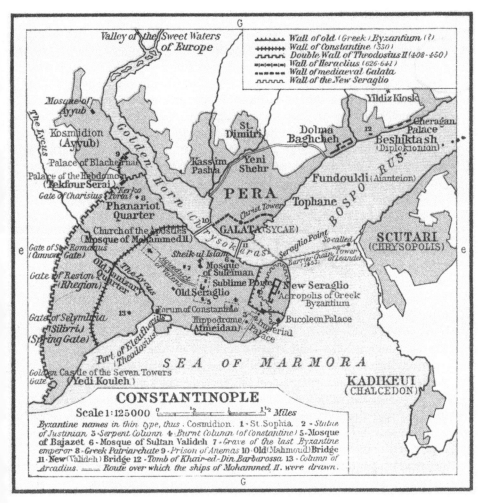

MAP 5. İstanbul/Constantinople, early nineteenth century. From William Shepherd, *Historical Atlas* (New York: Henry Holt, 1911), 93.

of particular commodities, such as salt, meat, and grain, which were crucial to provisioning the capital city of İstanbul. They then used this money to purchase titles in the Orthodox patriarchate Church of St. George in the Phanar district of İstanbul, "a practice which eventually gave them complete control of the Patriarchate and its various functions."[11] In contrast to Indian portfolio capitalists seizing on disconnected regional state formations in the Mughal Empire, phanariots seized on the sinews still holding the empire together—such as the Orthodox patriarchate—in which they were formally eligible to participate as Orthodox Christians.[12]

At the same time that particular families were accumulating wealth and influence within the Ottoman imperial domains, members of these families also seem to have been sent abroad, often to Italian cities, to study medicine. This was the case with Panagiotes Nikousios, who studied in Padua, as well as with Alexandros Mavrocordato, who studied first at the College of St. Athanasius, in Rome, and then went on to study medicine at the Universities of Padua and Bologna. Upon their return to İstanbul, both took up positions teaching at the Patriarchal Academy and entered the service of the Ottoman grand vezir as physicians. Once they began working as physicians, they enjoyed privileged access to the grand vezir, who eventually came to see the usefulness of their expertise in the Italian language for the burgeoning area of diplomacy. Despite their many similarities, here phanariots differ yet again from the "portfolio capitalists" of early modern India. The latter were brought down by European competition, whereas phanariots rose to power on the waves of change brought about by increasing European involvement in the commerce and politics in Ottoman domains.[13]

Both phanariot pioneers, Panagiotes Nikousios and Alexandros Mavrocordato were granted the office of grand dragoman during the grand vezirate of Fazıl Ahmed Köprülü (r. 1661–76), himself a member of the dynasty credited with restoring Ottoman imperial governance during the crises and rebellions earlier in the seventeenth century. This fact points to two key conjunctures. First, it was with the Köprülü Restoration that a model of politics based on the military-grandee household expanded beyond the sultan's palace throughout the Ottoman provinces.[14] We indeed find that many prominent Muslim Ottoman families of the eighteenth century—associated with *ulema* (religious learning and jurisprudence), bureaucratic office, regional commerce, and the military—traced their origins to the late seventeenth century.[15] As their dominance of the Orthodox patriarchate led to a monopoly of the office of grand dragoman and the top administrative offices of Moldavia and Wallachia (in 1711 and 1716, respectively), phanariots borrowed kinship practices—and terminology—from their vezir and *ayan* counterparts.[16]

In the aftermath of the Treaty of Carlowitz, particular phanariot families on the rise were strategically placed to capitalize on what was no doubt an unpleasant reality for members of the Ottoman central state—that negotiators could command the power to defend the empire, a power that military men once enjoyed. Not only did these families share Orthodox Christianity with the Russian Empire, which made them both valuable and threatening, but also some of those families from the formerly Genoese island of Chios had maintained ties with Italian states and possessed the ever more important knowledge of European languages such as Italian and French.[17]

With the accession of Nikousios and then of his protégé Alexander Mavrocordato to the office of grand dragoman, trade in information became central to phanariot political livelihood and the basis for their further expansion of power. By the second decade of the eighteenth century, Alexandros Mavrocordato's son Nicholas was appointed *voyvoda* (T. *bey, voyvoda*; G. *hegemonas, pringips*; Sl. *voivode, hospodar*) of Moldavia and then Wallachia, crucial provinces in the continuing territorial conflicts with the bordering Habsburg and Russian empires. These provinces were together known as the Danubian Principalities (T. Eflak and Boğdan; G. Moldo-vlachia), and bordered both the Austrian and Russian Empires, comprising much of present-day Romania.

These four supreme positions of dragoman and *voyvoda* served as the skeleton of what I am calling the phanariot house. The two *voyvoda*s of Moldavia and Wallachia managed tax collection, provincial administration (including church administration of the many lucrative monasteries), policing of the imperial boundaries with Russia and Austria, and foreign relations conducted at the border. From the mid-eighteenth century onward, the *voyvoda*s of these two provinces also had special agreements with the sultan to provide ever more grain and meat for the imperial capital and, in times of war, for the Ottoman military.[18] As tax farmer–governors in these principalities, they co-opted and married into the local Romanian-speaking class of boyar landowners and supplied the Ottoman military and its capital of İstanbul with crucial food provisions and maintaining dense patronage relationships to Orthodox Church institutions so prominent in these provinces.

Back in İstanbul, the dragoman of the court was the liaison between European envoys and the sultan and his inner circle, as well as between the Orthodox patriarch (and his lucrative empirewide ecclesiastical administration) and the court.[19] The dragoman of the fleet, the final office to be created and granted to phanariots, was second in command to the *kapudan paşa* (Ottoman admiral) and was de facto the administrator of many Aegean islands and Anatolian coastal localities. He was also responsible for naval operations, including shipbuilding and warfare. In order to be translators, they were required to be proficient in European languages (usually Italian and French) in addition to the *elsine-i selase,* or the Three Languages—Arabic, Persian, and Turkish—that constituted Ottoman Turkish.[20]

Finally, several other dragoman positions were of strategic importance but were not as formalized as that of the divan and the fleet. These included the dragoman of the imperial army *(tercüman-ı ordu-yu Hümayun)* and dragoman of the Morea (T. *mora tercümanı*).[21] Such positions allowed phanariots to broaden their patronage networks into Ottoman military circles on the one hand and a range of localities, each with its own contending elites, on the other. Given these interlinked patronage networks, few degrees of separation existed in practice between monks on Mt. Sinai, merchants in Anatolia, diplomats in İstanbul, soldiers on the Danube, sailors in the Aegean Islands, administrators at the imperial arsenal and mint, and scribes in Bucharest. This is not to imply that these figures were all phanariots per se (monks and sailors, for instance, were not) but rather to point out that a vast range of contacts—across what we now call the Balkans, the Aegean Islands, and

Anatolia, and even the trade entrepôts, churches, and monasteries of Egypt, Syria, and Palestine—was possible through these phanariot networks. For example, should a phanariot need information or goods from a monastery such as St. Catherine's of Sinai, contact was quite easily established given the many monasteries under phanariot control in the principalities that St. Catherine's held. Family and patronage connections among such groups could be mobilized for an exceptionally wide range of pursuits, whether for personal profit or state gain, the distinction between which grew increasingly fuzzy.

## PHANARIOT INTERIORS

Dionysios Photeinos, a midlevel phanariot functionary in the first two decades of the nineteenth century, provided us with a window into the social composition and internal workings of phanariot networks—a tour of the plush interior of the phanariot house. He did this through his three-volume history, *Historia tes palai Dakias ta nyn Transylvanias, Wallachias, kai Moldavias* (History of the Former Dacia, or the Current Transylvania, Wallachia, and Moldavia), published in 1818–19, just months before Greek-hetairist insurrections broke out against the Ottoman sultanate. It contains the fullest—and latest—elaboration by, for, and about the phanariot house.

Photeinos actually worked on two histories in his spare time. One, never completed, was a history of the Ottoman sultans from Mehmed II to Mahmud. The other was the three-volume *Historia tes palai Dakias* under discussion here.[22] At first glance, Photeinos's use of Dakia, or Dacia, in the title of his completed oeuvre for Moldavia, Wallachia, and Transylvania seems odd, since the name is neither the Ottoman demarcation of the area nor a national category, but rather a Roman administrative label. But it also evokes the Russian empress Catherine the Great's (and the Habsburg emperor Joseph II's) "Greek plan," of a few decades earlier, to create an independent kingdom out of Moldavia and Wallachia under that name.[23] The reference to Dacia in the title, together with much of the content of Photeinos's history, betrays not only a classicizing tendency typical of his well-educated contemporaries to the north and west but also an elaborate, if incipient, imagination emerging from phanariot involvement in Ottoman governance. This imagination was neither national, in the sense that would emerge in the course of the nineteenth century, nor simply an Orthodox Christian commonwealth vision of uniting with Russia and resuscitating Byzantium.

A key to understanding Photeinos's horizons lies in the multiple meanings of the term *Romaios* (T. Rum), meaning Roman (and by extension what we would call Byzantine) and Orthodox Christian subjects of the Ottoman sultan. The term has also been used as a geographic signifier in Arabic and Persian for what we now call Anatolia (Rum) and in Ottoman for what we now call the Balkans (Rumeli

[Rumelia]). It would seem, then, that Photeinos and presumably his fellow phanariots took the connection to the Roman Empire seriously and were implying that
their patrimony was not a Byzantine one (in the Greek national sense) but instead
a Roman, truly imperial one. Add to this a passage from *The History of the Ottoman
Empire,* penned early in the eighteenth century by proto-phanariot Dimitri Cantemir, under the heading of "Muhammad's magnanimity," and we begin to see the
conjunctions inherent in belonging to an imperium that had blended Roman, Greek,
and Ottoman Islamic elements: "For I call not them Greeks who are born in Greece,
but those who have transferred the Grecian learning and Institutions to themselves.
It is justly said by Isocrates in one of his Panegyricks, I had rather call them Grae-
cians, who are Partakers of our Discipline, than those who only share with us the
same common birth and nature."[24]

Given these "Rum" horizons, it makes sense that Photeinos would narrate the
history of Dacia as a geographic entity and administrative district, peopled and ruled
by a succession of groups over the ages, with the Ottomans neither the natural sov-
ereigns nor merely foreign interlopers in the region. He begins with the area's first
human habitation as narrated by historians in the fourth century B.C. By the third
volume, which begins with the founding of the principality of Moldavia in the fourteenth century and covers the entire Ottoman period (from the fourteenth to the
nineteenth century), particularly when he reaches the events and reigns he personally witnessed, the descriptions are, as one would expect, more detailed and complex in their presentations of Ottoman and phanariot politics. One is even reminded
of Kritovoulos's pragmatic notion of political power in his fifteenth-century *History of Mehmed the Conqueror.* There, the Byzantine-turned-Ottoman panegyrist
and historian portrays the Ottomans at once as successors to the Romans (Byzantines) and as analogues to the Romans in their triumph over the Jews, writing,

> Who does not know that since men have existed the kingly or ruling power has not
> always remained in the same people, nor has it been limited to one race or nation?
> Like the planets, rule has gone from nation to nation and from place to place in suc-
> cession, always changing and passing, now to the Assyrians, the Medes, the Persians,
> and then to the Greeks and Romans, according to the times and epochs establishing
> itself in a place and never returning to the same. . . . There is therefore nothing as-
> tonishing if the same things happen and are endured now also, and the Romans
> [Byzantines] lose their rule and prosperity, which pass on and are transferred to others,
> just as they came from others to them, so forever preserving the same nature and or-
> der or events. . . . This is what Josephus the Hebrew recognizes in his book about the
> capture of Jerusalem. He praises the skill and valor of the Romans, and exalts them
> truthfully in his discourse.[25]

In regard to the immediate horizons of phanariots in the early nineteenth century, one of the many illuminating features of Photeinos's work on Moldavia and
Wallachia was the list, or *katalogos,* of "*philokalon kai philomouson syndrometon,*"

or "subscribers who were lovers of beauty and letters," that precedes the history.[26] This list of subscribers not only documents the specific—phanariot—audience for Photeinos's work but also in doing so provides important clues as to the intricacies within the sphere of Orthodox Christianity of the Ottoman Empire. Stephanos Vogorides, then just at the peak of his pre-1821 career as a phanariot, appears as a subscriber to the work. Both Vogorides and Photeinos had attended the Princely Academy of Bucharest (founded by phanariot pioneers, the Mavrocordatos, in the early eighteenth century), and both studied with the same teacher, Lambros Photiades. And they served together in the Wallachian-Moldavian administration at the time; Vogorides is listed in the book as *archon megalos postelnik* (foreign minister) of Moldavia along with eight others.

In the list of subscribers, in addition to Vogorides we also see many who would go on to fight for Greek independence and, more strikingly, the traces of the processes of socialization and acculturation into a phanariot—and by extension Ottoman— political culture of which he and many others were part. The list includes approximately 350 individuals, divided into forty categories, which together form a sociopolitical portrait of the group I am calling phanariots in the 1810s. The resulting portrait reveals both identity and difference within the world of Orthodox Christian Ottoman subjects as well as between that world and the larger Ottoman world in which it was embedded.

The subscribers are organized into categories that are ordered at once according to administrative hierarchy, geography, and profession. Presiding at the top of the list are the "most high and pious princes" *(hegemones)*, which include the reigning phanariot prince of Moldavia, Skarlatos Voyvodas Alexandrou Kallimaki (Skarlato Kallimaki) (r. 1812–19), and the two phanariots who were vying for the vacant throne of Wallachia at that moment, "Alexandros Voyvoda Soutso" and "Alexandros Voyvoda Hantzeris Han" (Alexandros Hançerli). After this illustrious group comes the geographical designation "in Bucharest," made up first of a *beyzade* (prince; son of a prince) and two major generals, then twenty-one categories of officials of the Wallachian princely administration. Sixteen of these groups of officials are also called "archons," and their subdivisions include a combination of Romanian, Byzantine-ecclesiastical, and Turkish titles, from *banoi, vorniks,* and *kloutziarides,* through *logethetes* and *megaloi vestiaroi,* to *ağas* and *serdars*—reflecting the range of idioms being melded into this phanariot world. After these official functionaries come the professions: *oi exohotatoi giatroi* (his excellencies the doctors), the *timiotatoi pragmateutai* (the most honorable merchants), the *ellogimiotatoi didaskaloi* (the most learned teachers), and finally the members of the *hierou katalogou,* or clergy.

After this assemblage of social groups in Bucharest comes a mixed social group of fourteen, all in Craiova (a commercial city west of Bucharest), and then six distinguished Constantinopolitan archons, including the current grand dragoman of the "ruling Ottoman kingdom," Michael Soutso, the former grand dragoman

Iakovos Argyropoulo, and the grand *postelnik*s Iakovos Rizos-Neroulos (with his four sons) and Alexandros Mavrocordato.[27] The Istanbuliote subscribers are sandwiched between the categories of Bucharest and Jassy, the latter being Moldavia's capital. The categories of officials in Moldavia—territorially the smaller of the two principalities—mirror those in Wallachia, in that they are organized hierarchically, although they display some extra categories, such as the *archontes megaloi postelnikoi* (quasi-foreign ministers), and there are fewer officials (57 names) than for Wallachia (about 150 names). Finally, there are four geographic categories: in Galatsi (a port city on the Danube in Moldavia—containing six names), in "Peloponnese" (the Morea—four names), in "Patras" (Paliai Patrai—eighteen names), and in Vienna (three names, one of whom is noted as having subscribed through an acquaintance in Wallachia).

The subscriber categories reveal that there were both an explicit structure associated with phanariot rule, expressed in the hierarchy of offices under the two phanariot *voyvodas*, and an implicit social and geographical structure, which held the principalities to the Ottoman capital and to particular localities, such as the Morea (Peloponnese) and even—at least through a few individuals—Vienna (the only city mentioned from outside Ottoman domains). But how did individuals fit into and, presumably, move through this structure? To address this question, we can examine this same subscriber list as a snapshot of 350 individuals at particular locations on their way up the hierarchy.

The life of one Iosipos (Joseph) Moisiodax (ca. 1725–1800) has attracted the attention of intellectual and cultural historians of southeastern Europe. Moisiodax was, like many phanariots, an Orthodox Christian of Vlach-speaking origins, from today's northern Bulgaria. Again, like many of his fellow countrymen that engaged in trade in central Europe, he became hellenized, and he entered the Orthodox Christian clergy, in which knowledge of Greek, the language of the Church and letters, was a necessity. This process of hellenization was hardly unique to Moisiodax, whose case reinforces the earlier arguments of scholars such as Traian Stoianovich regarding the hellenization of Bulgarian-, Romanian-, Vlach-, Albanian-, and Serbian-speaking Christians as a vehicle for social mobility into the Balkan Christian mercantile classes in the eighteenth century.[28] However, rarely have attentions focused on the Ottoman context; rather, the focus has been on how the motivation to learn Greek and, for some, to identify oneself as culturally "Greek" related to entering Christian merchant networks or the Christian clergy or both, all as a kind of implicit preparation for national awakening.

Linking this world of Greek or hellenized merchants and clergy to the larger world of Ottoman governance, however, allows us to see an additional dimension—not only the daily social and political realities of these Balkan Christians as Ottoman subjects, but also the symbolic, cultural, and political connections that were forged between phanariot retinues and networks on the one hand and elements of what is considered specifically Ottoman governance on the other. That more complete picture, in turn, reveals that another career path was taking shape for Orthodox Christians in the late eighteenth century: the path into the retinues of phanariot princes and dragomans. This, like the paths to commerce and the clergy, necessitated hellenization, for the Greek language enjoyed primacy among the phanariot *nomenklatura*, as it did in the Greek Orthodox Church and in the networks of Greek merchants. Hellenization meant for these people, as it meant for Stephanos Vogorides, learning Greek letters, but also changing one's name to fit Greek linguistic and cultural conventions.

The most famous cases of this hellenization were the *voyvodas* themselves, such as "Skarlatos Voyvodas Alexandrou Kallimaki" (Skarlato Kallimaki). The Kallimaki family was originally Romanian-speaking and hellenized into the phanariot elite in the later seventeenth century. They were thus well placed to qualify for the office of prince when "indigenous" Romanian boyars were ousted from power and phanariots gained ascendancy in ruling the principalities in the second decade of the eighteenth century.[29] The Ghika family, also listed in the top category of Photeinos's roster, and therefore the top echelon of phanariot society, had migrated from "Albania" to the Ottoman capital in the seventeenth century. Their ancestor Georgios was said to have been a childhood friend of Mehmed Köprülü, founder of the Köprülü dynasty of grand vezirs that was credited with restoring Ottoman power in the second half of the seventeenth century.[30] In a striking parallel between processes of social mobility among those who remained Christian and those who converted to Islam from Christianity, the Albanian Ghika family remained Christian but hellenized, while the Albanian (T. Arnavut) Mehmed Köprülü was a Muslim convert from Christianity who then assimilated into the Ottoman ruling class through the slave *(devşirme-kul)* system—and likely suppressed his Albanian origins in some contexts.[31] A biographer of the Ghika family suggests Georgios joined Mehmed Köprülü's faction in İstanbul in 1653 and achieved commercial and political successes with the latter's support.[32]

Beyond these prominent phanariots who shifted "ethnic" identities within the bounds of Orthodox Christianity were lower-ranking officials with hellenized Romanian names, such as Nicholaos (Nicholas) Philippeskos (archon *ağa* of Bucharest and an important patron of Photeinos's) and Pavlo Patresko (archon *serdar*).[33] There were also hellenized names indicating more complicated social shifts, such as Konstantinos (Constantine) Tattareskos (containing the word *Tatar* with a hellenized Romanian -*escu* ending), Skarlato Tzerkezis (with a hellenized -*is* ending to the Turkish designation for a Circassian [Çerkez]), Skarlato Stoigianneskos ("Stoian," a common Serbian/Slavic name, hellenized into "Stoigiannes," with a Romanian -*escu* and a Greek -*os*), and Ioannitzas (Ioannis) Tsalikovitz (with a Greek rendering of the Serbian/Slavic -*ovich* ending to the Turkish *çelik,* meaning "steel").

Other names indicate origins geographically remote from the Danubian Principalities, demonstrating that geographic mobility often accompanied social and ethnic mobility. One example is of a man of possibly Turkish-speaking Christian origins, Radoukanos Karamanlis (denoting origins in central Anatolia, where Christian populations were overwhelmingly turcophone).[34] Another is Gregorios Mavrodoglous (with a hellenized Turkish *-oğlu* ending, common among the Karamanli of Anatolia). Even names of Armenian origins exist, such as Gregorios Balianos (with the title of archon *megalos vornik*) (also known as Krikor amira Balyan [1764–1831], the Armenian palace architect for the Ottoman state and the father of Garabed amira Balyan, architect of Dolmabahçe Palace in the mid-nineteenth century) and the archon Logothetes Gregorios Baltzianos, not to mention those of closer-to-home Vlach origins, such as Archon Grammatikos Manuel (Emmanuel) Vlachides.[35]

Finally, in addition to the one name with known Bulgarian-language origins, Stephanos Vogorides, there are several with indications of geographic origins, such as the archon Serdar Georgios Laskari Peloponnesios (from the Morea, or the Peloponnese), the "*eugenestatos kyrios* Andreas Soteriou Lontou ek Vostitsis" (from Vostitsa), the *ellogimiotatos didaskalos* Demetrios Ithakesios ("the most learned teacher Demetrios from the island of Ithaka," placed among those on the list living in the port town of Galatsi), and the archon *hatman* of Bucharest Konstantinos (Constantine) Karydes ho Kyprios (the Cypriot).

These examples show, first, that hellenization was going on beyond the spheres of commerce and the clergy, which have heretofore been the focus of scholarship. But they also illustrate the ways that the phanariot administration of Ottoman Moldavia and Wallachia was serving as a portal for Orthodox Christians—of both Greek- and non-Greek-speaking origins—to enter the world of the phanariot and, by extension, Ottoman governance. Their titles, though derived from Byzantine Church and Romanian contexts as well as Ottoman Turkish sources, were important to their names and identities, and in most cases a hellenized name was a prerequisite to belonging in the Ottoman imperial administration, through employment in a phanariot retinue. Also, in addition to performing their "day jobs" as *voyvodas*, *vestiars*, or *ağas*, at least 350 of them seemed to be subscribing to and reading works of history that reflected their social and political outlook as Christian Ottoman subjects and phanariot functionaries associated with Moldavia or Wallachia or both.

There were not only multiple strata but also multiple processes of social mobility underway among these strata, all within the Orthodox Christian sphere. So far, this only reinforces the *millet* paradigm that places Christians in separate, autonomous confessional communities, set apart from Muslims and from participation in Ottoman governance. In addition to the social and "ethnic" mobility practiced by humbler Orthodox Christians at work under phanariot princes, however, those princes and commoners alike were themselves hard at work striving for Ottoman

FIGURE 2. Inscription at St. Spiridon Hospital, Iași (formerly
Jassy), Romania. Author's photograph.

cultural and political status and linking up with the larger world of Ottoman governance. This begs the question of how the phanariot house looked to the outside—
Ottoman—world. Were phanariots convincing to others in their attempts to blend
into Ottoman political culture?

### The House of Phanar—as Seen from the House of Osman

No "phanariot dossier" sits in the Ottoman state archives. This indicates, for one,
the lack of systematic consideration that phanariots received from their Ottoman
superiors. It also implies that the phanariot house, like the houses of Phanar, had a

curious place in the official landscape of Ottoman governance. We know that early phanariot pioneers such as Alexandros Mavrocordato, appointed minister of the secrets *(ex aporiton)* in the wake of his successful performance at the Treaty of Carlowitz, were the confidantes of earlier sultans and therefore enjoyed their attention and trust. But by the reign of Selim III (r. 1789–1807/8), this sultan had developed a deeply conflicting stance toward what he called the "phanariot clique" *(fenarlı takımı)*.

In one undated memo written by Sultan Selim to his grand vezir sometime between 1800 and 1807, the sultan condemns the phanariot clique for "pursuing their own aims and spreading false rumors." He asks his grand vezir, "Why can't you and your servants take notice and try to put a stop to this?" and wonders, "Can't anything have an effect on these infidels?" (Bu kafirlere hiç bir şey tesir etmez mi?) He goes on to say that this is what can be expected of this Wallachia and Moldavia set (Böyle şeyler Eflak ve Boğdan takımından çıkar), ordering the vezir to kill those involved in the conspiracy in order to "open the eyes" of the others (gözlerini açsunlar sonra kenduleri bilur).[36]

Despite the sense of powerlessness and frustration evident in the sultan's memo, there is much evidence that phanariots were held in high esteem by sultans and their advisers. A draft of an *irade* (sultanic decree) from the same period (A.H. 1216; M. 1801–2) declares that appointments to Ottoman embassies in Europe should be made from among the "princes, sons of princes, boyars, and sons of boyars" *(beyzadeler ve beyzadeler oğulları ve boyarlar ve boyar evladlarına)*, all of whom were part of the existing Wallachia and Moldavia service.[37] While appointments to European embassies were never made from among phanariot princes and boyars exclusively, they did constitute an important contingent of the diplomatic service under Selim III.[38] The memo outlines specific rules to be put in place that would weave these phanariots into the existing bureaucracy, for instance, their terms of office, how their previous ranks and salaries as dragomans or *voyvoda*s would affect their status when their terms as ambassadors ended, and who they would be allowed to take with them for staff (including wives and other family members).[39] In an attached memo, originally written in code by a Muslim patron of phanariots, the author notes that Orthodox Christians, already "intermixed" *(ihtilata)* with the work of diplomacy, were "now our number one infidel *millet* in terms of loyalty" *(ancak al-küfr milla-i vahide[-i] ma sadıkınca rum ta'ifesi).*[40] He goes on to say that those from among the Orthodox Christian *ta'ife* who are of "gentility by birth" *(kişizadelerinde),* that is, the sons and grandsons of former *voyvoda*s of Moldavia and Wallachia *(evlad ve ehfad ve kişizadelerinden),* are well suited to do such work by dint of their demonstrated loyalty and "inquisitiveness."[41] He even goes on to say that it is not suited to Muslims to live for long periods in Christian kingdoms *(ehl-i İslamın memalik-i nasarada tul müddet ikametleri uyamayup),* whereas for Orthodox Christians in such employ this "comes with ease" *(suhulet).*

A third document comes from a slightly later period (A.H. 1225; M. 1810–11), just after Sultan Mahmud II took power in the wake of the executions of his predecessors Selim III and Mustafa IV at the hands of janissaries—and in the midst of Russo-Ottoman hostilities. It is not a formal document but rather the scrawl of a high state official trying to pin down which phanariot families were allied with which foreign powers, and indeed which family members were holding which high office at that moment. It reads, for instance, "They accuse the following of being Russian-aligned: Moruz Aleksandır Bey (Alexandros Muruzi)—four-time *voyvoda;* called French-aligned: Suçu Aleko Bey (Alexandros Soutso), currently *voyvoda* of Wallachia; they accuse the following of being Russian-aligned: Moruz Bey's (Muruzi's) second brother Dimitraşko (Demetrios), today the dragoman of the imperial army."[42]

Phanariots, whose allegiances were apparently unclear to their Ottoman superiors, nevertheless regularly submitted dispatches in Ottoman Turkish to the highest of state functionaries. In these they relayed the goings-on of the French Revolution and the Napoleonic Wars just over their borders or advised on matters of diplomacy and proper state etiquette toward foreign powers.[43] From the perspective of the official documents they generated that made it into the Ottoman archives, phanariots were suppliers of necessary, strategic intelligence to an Ottoman state that was itself becoming increasingly enmeshed in intraimperial continental politics. But the documents produced by officials of the central state portray a far more ambivalent phanariot role in the project of imperial governance. Their Ottoman superiors seemed unable to fully accommodate the contributions of phanariots as a group *(takım)* into their explicit ideology of statecraft, even as the points of engagement between phanariots and the matrix of day-to-day Ottoman governance proliferated.

Collecting information was crucial to the phanariot repertoire, and for this phanariots did receive acknowledgment from Ottoman authorities. By 1800, the task of phanariot *voyvoda*s-cum-ambassadors in Europe was repeatedly acknowledged in Ottoman documents as "procuring of news" *(celb-i havadis).*[44] In an early nineteenth-century investiture ceremony for Wallachian and Moldavian *voyvoda*s, the sultan explicitly charged the initiate with the following duties and concomitant privilege, which lay at the core of the entire phanariot enterprise: "The arrangement demanded of you from my imperial pantries [coffers] is this: you bring back news from the European parts; the office of *voyvoda* of Wallachia is granted to you with full freedom and plenipotentiary powers; in return, your loyalty is demanded."[45]

While, as we will see, their contemporary Muslim Ottoman elites in the Balkans, Anatolia, and Arab lands were necessary for revenue collection and domestic stability, phanariots supplied crucial information from abroad through posts in the border provinces, in their capacity as dragomans, and eventually in naval service alongside the *kapudan paşa.* The often exorbitant taxes they were allowed to collect in the Danubian Principalities were a perquisite they received in exchange for procuring information and supplying staple foodstuffs, such as grains and meat, to the Ottoman capital.

By the end of the eighteenth century, phanariots had set up far-reaching webs for the transport of information and goods. Such webs were staffed by relatives stationed in İstanbul, the Danubian Principalities, and beyond. Ottoman authorities described them in this way: "Members of the Rum *ta'ifesi* who are in the Wallachian and Moldavian service, *like a chain [zincir mesellu],* have continual contact with their families across long distances," and countless *yol tezkeresi,* or travel documents, confirm this.[46]

Family members served a variety of purposes in this chain. Male relatives (sons, brothers, and sons-in-law) of the reigning *voyvoda*s in Wallachia and Moldavia were kept in captivity in İstanbul as hostages *(esir)* to ensure loyalty, and since they were in communication with their families and important conduits of information, they might be interrogated whenever the Ottoman authorities found it useful.[47] The position of *kapıkahya* (or *kapıkethüdası*) was an important office, often filled by a male family member (with ties of blood or marriage) of the reigning *voyvoda*.[48] The *kapıkahya* was the representative of the *voyvoda* to the Sublime Porte and would remain in İstanbul (in his own residence) and regularly visit the Porte to convey information from his superior in the provinces and to keep abreast of goings-on at the palace that might affect the *voyvoda*.[49]

Women family members, too, were deemed important, even in official documents, for securing information. Arguing in favor of phanariot *voyvoda*s-cum-ambassadors bringing their wives with them to their posts, an anonymous official noted, "Given that it is obvious that in Europe the *ta'ife* of women have great insight, ambassadors should be permitted to have their wives and families accompany them, so that the latter can procure information (from the wives of European statesmen)."[50] Family relationships, then, were acknowledged even from the outside to be key to the task of information management between phanariot elites and the Ottoman central state.

### Performing Ottoman Governance

Despite their conflicting policies and feelings toward phanariots as they ascended to power, leaders of the Ottoman state continued to participate in ritualized performances that symbolized and even idealized phanariots' role in imperial governance. Phanariot historian Dionysios Photeinos has again provided us with a vivid entrée into the interconnections between phanariots and this matrix of governance with his description of their investiture ceremony—a ceremony that would have warmed the hearts of both the emperor Justinian and Eric Hobsbawm.[51] Held for phanariot *voyvoda*s leaving İstanbul for their provincial seats of power in Bucharest and Jassy, it was a vivid representation of the phanariot house, expressed in the idiom of Ottoman political ritual.[52]

The two *voyvoda* positions were the crowning glory of the phanariot network. Like the offices of grand dragoman and dragoman of the fleet, they were of near royal status. In one Ottoman document from around 1801–2, these *voyvoda*s were declared to have been considered equal in rank to the kings in Europe (saye-i Padişahide memleketeyn-i merkümeteyn voyvodalığı Avrupa'da kral payesinde itibar olunduğuna).[53] *Voyvoda*s enjoyed free rein in setting taxes and eventually in setting up a civil code in their respective provinces. They thus could deem themselves autonomous Christian rulers, even if under the authority of the sultan, and in many ways their ceremony was similar to visits of foreign envoys to the Ottoman court.

Ritualized acts symbolizing affiliation, submission, and sovereignty were performed at several places in İstanbul, on the road to the provincial capital, and at significant sites in and around Bucharest or Jassy, revealing the many sites and actors that melded phanariot networks with the larger matrix of Ottoman governance.[54] The İstanbul portion of the investiture ceremony began with a ritualized invitation ceremony to summon the initiate and transport him by water along the Golden Horn from his Phanar residence to the grand vezir's quarters near Topkapı Palace.[55] At this point the initiate would already have selected his cabinet, the retinue of twelve or more officials who would follow him to his post and man his upper administration. Together they would meet with the grand vezir and secure his official appointment in preparation for the investiture ceremony the following day. On the way back to his Phanar residence, the initiate and his now sizable procession, including Ottoman military figures, a military marching band, and his own retinue, would stop for a benediction ceremony at the patriarchate complex, also in the Phanar district, during which the patriarch and the members of his Holy Synod would approve the *voyvoda*'s appointment.[56] The Byzantine ceremonial was thus contained within a larger Ottoman ritual framework.

The investiture ceremony itself, continuing the next day at Topkapı Palace, took several hours and included a ritualized meal. Accepting the sultan's food had, since the *gazi* days, been an Ottoman sign of loyalty to the sultan, which is why, when the janissaries rebelled, they banged pots and why Topkapı Palace was designed so that the smoke from the chimneys could be seen from far away, giving visual form to the fact that so many people in the palace were accepting the sultan's food.

In the phanariot ceremony a special soup was shared with representatives of the Janissary *(yeniçeri)* Corps in the palace's outer courtyard. The symbolism of sharing this meal was manifold. Phanariots would be responsible not only for feeding the janissaries who went on campaign but also, it seems, for working with those who doubled as merchants in the peacetime state-administered grain trade from the principalities to İstanbul via the ports of the Danube and the Black Sea.[57] Cooperation was signified by the act of sharing a meal—janissaries formed *ocak*s, or units, that cooked and ate together—and in this way the phanariot initiate was inducted into that community as well. This portion of the ceremony even included the initiate being shown the *esame defteri,* or pay register of the janissaries, and "giving assent" to it.[58]

The core moment of the ceremony was the carefully staged encounter with the sultan. Its similarities to audiences that foreign ambassadors would have with the Ottoman sovereign demonstrate the dual nature of phanariot *voyvodas* as both autonomous rulers and administrator-subjects of the sultan. A document, known as a *telhis,* asking for an audience would be delivered to the sultan, and the sultan would sign off, allowing the initiate to be escorted in.[59] The sultan would vest the *voyvoda* with the *kaftan* and *kuka* hat that symbolized his office and recite the pact to which the initiate would agree: The initiate would "bring back news" from Europe, receiving the office of *voyvoda* and the power that went with it in exchange for loyalty to the sultan.[60]

The very apex of the phanariot network, then, was held in place by a contractual relationship with the person of the sultan: the seemingly simple tradeoff—information and loyalty for regional political autonomy—in practice meant that the *voyvoda* was to maintain a many-tiered relationship with the merchants, soldiers, and officials involved in the Ottoman administration.

The initiate would then travel once again back to his residence in the Phanar and assemble his Princely Council, making the preparations for a journey of several weeks or more, depending on the weather conditions, to Bucharest or Jassy. After completing these preparations, he would set off with a procession of hundreds and be cheered by hundreds more as he departed the capital and went on to make ritualized rest stops at particular villages and towns along the way. This was a peacetime mimicry of the many military campaigns (replete with military marching music for the duration) that had not long before traversed the same lands to fight *ayans,* Russians, or Austrians.

When the new Wallachian *voyvoda's* procession neared Bucharest it would stop at the Vacaresti Monastery (built early in the eighteenth century by phanariot predecessors, the Mavrocordatoi) on the city's outskirts, assemble, and prepare for the entrance into the city and the arrival at the *voyvoda's* court that adjoined the city's cathedral.[61] While the Church was a minor presence in the İstanbul portion of the ceremony, limited to the benediction ceremony in the Church of St. George, it took center stage in the provincial phase. The monastery and cathedral acted as pivotal sites in the principalities, tolling church bells replaced the Ottoman military music in İstanbul, and the archbishop maintained continuity in the province between old and new *voyvodas* and led the delegation to greet the new initiate upon his arrival in the city. Once arrived, the *voyvoda* would greet representatives of the various local social strata and his cabinet and hold a reception at his new palace, replete with coffee, sweets, and hookah. His wife, whose title was *domna*, held a reception in her salon for the ladies of the retinue. Thus, a ceremony that had begun in the sultan's chamber in İstanbul was ended in the *voyvoda*'s personal court in Bucharest. In the final act, the new *voyvoda* vested his new officials with *kaftan*s, mimicking his own investiture with the *kaftan* and *kuka* hat by the sultan.[62] The phanariot house, in its ceremonial expression and ideal form, was nested into the mansion of Ottoman sovereignty while in İstanbul and allowed a more expansive presence in the provincial capitals, which in their geographic remoteness constituted another kind of interior.

## PHANARIOTS—AND OTHER OTTOMANS?

The phanariot specialization in procuring information made them functionally unique among eighteenth-century Ottoman elites and invites comparisons with members of trading diasporas who transcended Ottoman realms and rose to power at the same time. But their house was built in Ottoman domains, from Ottoman materials, and as such they also found it useful to adopt strategies and symbols of legitimacy to blend into the Ottoman political environment in which they thrived. Two questions remain: How did the phanariot house connect to and compare with contemporary Ottoman houses—not just the imperial house, but those of *ayan*s and even janissaries; and, in what ways were phanariots consciously fashioning themselves as Ottoman households?

The two major sociopolitical groups that were relevant to phanariots were, like them, composite groups whose political and economic activities in Ottoman governance extended far beyond their official titles and functions. Phanariots shared analogous features with provincial *ayan*s and the *hanedan*s, or dynasties, they formed. But they also were connected through a range of activities—from the ceremonial to the economic—with the Janissary Corps, which had by the late eighteenth century penetrated nearly every institution of Ottoman state and society. Examining phanariots alongside *ayan*s/*hanedan*s and janissaries in turn clearly shows that phanariots borrowed strategies from new elites while enmeshing themselves in domestic trade and politics long dominated by janissaries.

The *ayan* phenomenon is the central lens through which historians have viewed eighteenth-century Ottoman governance.[63] *Ayan* families began to dominate several sectors of governance in their respective provinces in the late seventeenth century onward.[64] Military power, tax farming, bureaucracy, and commerce were all combined in a patchwork of family dynasties across Ottoman lands. This has generally been seen as the period of decentralization for the Ottoman Empire before efforts to recentralize state power, first by Selim III, then by Mahmud II (r. 1808–39) and his successors. But what looks from the *ayan* or the central state standpoint to be decentralization (or privatization) appears from the phanariot perspective, which entails a consideration of both the imperial center and provincial administration, to be an intricate kind of integration.[65] A profile of these two groups—phanariots and *ayan*—in the course of the eighteenth century points to several parallels.

The precise recipe for each *ayan* family was different, but it always included military force and most often the purchase of life-term tax-farming rights.[66] Beyond that, commercial connections, bureaucratic posts, and connections to the Muslim hierarchy (or Christian, depending on the demography of the province) were handy. As the official Ottoman infantry and cavalry eroded by the eighteenth century, *ayan* became crucial providers of military manpower for the central state in domestic and cross-border conflicts. As one *ayan* or their variant, a *derebey*, rebelled against the Ottoman center, an alliance of other *ayan* would battle the rebels with troops raised from their localities. This prompted frequent migration of both military and civilian populations, and it became increasingly difficult to distinguish between the two.

Phanariots were related to but distinct from the cast of *ayan* characters that rose to power during roughly the same period. The origin myth for both groups is intriguingly similar. In the phanariot case, Panagiotes Nikousios was said to have been rewarded with the office of grand dragoman for his assistance to Grand Vezir Fazıl Ahmed Köprülü during the Ottoman siege of Crete in 1669, thereby making the first foray into the Ottoman court. One generation later Alexandros Mavrocordato, as a reward for his service as the Ottoman delegate (with Reisülküttab Rami Mehmed Efendi) at the Treaty of Carlowitz in 1699, succeeded Nikousios as grand dragoman and was made minister of the secrets *(ex aporiton)*. His son Nicholas Mavrocordato was appointed the first phanariot prince of Moldavia (1711) and then Wallachia (1716). With the removal of indigenous Moldavian and Wallachian notables (boyars) from the candidate pool for princely positions, İstanbul-based phanariots enjoyed eligibility to be invested with this office from İstanbul and to travel to their province to rule almost as they pleased. The period of phanariot ascendancy had begun.

As for the *ayan*s, some, such as the Pasvanoğlu family, were originally the agents of İstanbul-based tax farmers who were called in to fight off the banditry in the countryside, which had been caused by *sekban* troops demobilized in the wake of hostilities with Austria between 1683 and 1699.[67] This "began the process of official recognition and an increase in importance of the *ayan* in the eighteenth-century Ottoman Empire."[68] While the *ayan*s started at the territorial margins and phanariots at the imperial center, both were invited by actors within the struggling Ottoman state to take on roles in Ottoman governance in the late seventeenth and early eighteenth centuries. Both began with individualized personal connections to powerful officials and eventually earned their own formal power by performing military or diplomatic-political feats highly valued by the central state elite.

Many structural barriers set phanariots apart from *ayan*s. First among these was the absence of direct and formally sanctioned access to military force from the phanariot repertoire. They did maintain private militias in Wallachia and Moldavia and assisted as front-line interpreters in the many Ottoman military campaigns against the Austrians and Russians at the turn of the century. They even raised their own armies at a few key points in the later eighteenth century. But their power did not rest on their military capacity, and therefore they did not become provincial strong-men—or threats to the power of the central state—in the same way that *ayan*s did.

Unlike Muslim *ayan*s, phanariots were not eligible to acquire *iltizam,* life-term tax-farming systems that developed during the eighteenth century.[69] And yet this did not prove to be an insurmountable obstacle to their rise. Phanariot *voyvoda*s and other high officials not only circumvented such prohibitions by securing appointments as *mutasarrif*s and *mütevelli*s, or administrators, of such tax farms.[70] They also managed to accumulate land in the form of *möşye*s, and the privilege of collecting taxes and levying peasant labor associated with it, in Wallachia and Moldavia, as well as a monopoly on the *okna,* or salt mines, in these principalities.[71] This meant taking advantage of the liminal administrative and legal status of the Danubian Principalities with respect to Ottoman administration proper: autonomy gave them, as Christians, license not only to administer the principalities but also to imitate the means of accumulating power and revenue that their Muslim counterparts enjoyed in Ottoman lands.

Despite their formal exclusion from the *iltizam* system, phanariots who served as dragomans were generally well enmeshed in another way in the intricate webs of credit and patronage surrounding Ottoman governance in this period: their salaries were raised from the proceeds of several *mukata'a*s, or tax farms. The grand dragoman was paid his annual salary not from imperial funds *(mal-ı miri)* but from the personal tax yields of the Moldavian and Wallachian *voyvoda*s.[72] Ambassadors, whether Muslim or Christian, also received payments (*hediye pohçaları ve atları*— gift pouches and horses) through an arrangement that involved the Darphane, or the imperial mint, and individuals such as the "merchants *[bazirgan]* İskerlet and Düzoğlu" at the turn of the nineteenth century.[73]

In addition to collecting taxes and sending them to the capital, *voyvoda*s were under many other obligations that tied them to the imperial system, such as giving annual holiday cash gifts *('aidiye)* to no fewer than sixty-nine high Ottoman officials, according to the A.H. 1212 (M. ca. 1797–98) register. Totaling thirty thousand *kuruş,* these gifts ranged from eighty-five hundred *kuruş* to the grand vezir down to thirty *kuruş* to the *kaftan*-keeper and his assistant.[74] Each time an appointment or promotion occurred, specific payments were to be made. For instance, when one Todoraki (Theodore), the older son of one Tuğsuz Kamaraşoğlu, was recommended for appointment as an apprentice *(çirak)* dragoman, twenty thousand *kuruş* were offered to the grand vezir, ten thousand to the *kapudan paşa,* and a little present *(hediyecik)* to his servants, with Todoraki's future service being his gift to the *kethüda bey* (interior minister) and *reis efendi* (foreign minister).[75]

These gift-giving practices hint at another important feature of the house of Phanar: that in order to sustain transregional influence, phanariots cultivated more connections in and through İstanbul than their monoregional *ayan* counterparts seem to have done. Individual *ayan*s would often employ a representative at the capital to pursue their interests, or they were dependent on the titles and tax-farming licenses they garnered from the imperial center, but phanariots were interpreters for the sultan, grand vezir, and other high officials and were therefore integrated into the practice of foreign relations between the Ottoman court and European states. While *ayan*s such as Ali Paşa of Ioannina, the Karaosmanoğulları of İzmir, and Osman Pasvanoğlu of Vidin struck out on their own by conducting their own diplomacy directly with European envoys, phanariots conducted the sultan's diplomacy for the sultan.

We see these transregional and even international connections in the ways phanariots used the patronage of Muslim Ottoman officials in İstanbul to climb the social and professional ladder. For example, in A.H. 1215 (M. ca. 1800–1801), one Manolaki (Emmanuel), who had served in the retinue of İsmael Ferruh Efendi since his time as Ottoman envoy in England and was now among the *kapıkethüdas*, or representatives to the Ottoman court of Wallachia, wrote a petition on behalf of his son Yanko (Ioannis). Yanko was a dragoman of unspecified rank, and his father Manolaki petitioned to arrange his pay schedule with the chief accountant.[76] Another case shows Sultan Selim III pondering in another note to his grand vezir in A.H. 1220 (M. ca. 1805–6), whether to admit Kallimaki Bey, then *voyvoda* of Moldavia, into the retinue of (Alemdar) Mustafa Paşa, a pivotal figure in the upheaval of 1807–8.[77]

### *Phanariot* Hanedans

We have seen how phanariots were both distinct from provincial *ayan*s and analogous to them as aspiring Ottoman elites, and how phanariots were connected on several levels to imperial networks of credit and patronage. In addition, phanariots also seem to have self-consciously fashioned themselves as Ottoman households by the later eighteenth century. Although barred from access to titles and status with a particularly Muslim valence, they were able to attach themselves to Ottoman political culture through confessionally neutral terms, first among which was *hanedan*.

The term *hanedan* is of Persian derivation, meaning literally "a great tribe [or] family."[78] Once it passed into Ottoman Turkish usage, it was used as a conventional label to refer to those ruling families going back to the Abbasid dynasty and to the Ottoman dynasty itself *(hanedan-ı Al-i Osmani)*. It does not seem to have been used as a legal-administrative term within the classical Islamic Ottoman order of *askeri* (rulers) and *re'aya* (ruled), within the world of officeholders and scribes *(kalem)*, among *ulema* (religious-juridical experts), or among the elite *askeri* (men of the sword). Furthermore, it did not confer or confirm such status as could, for example, entitle a provincial family to a de jure privileged position within the central state. And yet, the term *hanedan* gained currency for phanariots in the eighteenth century at the same time that its use spread throughout the Ottoman political system. And I argue that its adoption is one of many signifiers of their integration into the imperial regime.

Phanariot *hanedan*s featured important structural differences from Muslim *hanedan*s. Since as Christians they could not own slaves, their households comprised family members and servants whose obligations arose from social patronage. As a result, their households and those of other elites, such as those in Egypt during Mamluk and post-Mamluk Ottoman rule containing legally imported slaves from the Caucasus, cannot simply be equated. And yet it is clear that they were striving for legitimacy and status by fashioning themselves as *hanedan*s.

The writer of an Ottoman *irade* around 1800 claimed that the "beys, sons of beys, boyars, and sons of boyars . . . are not descended from merchants and shopkeepers but are counted among the greatest dynasties [*hanedan*s]."[79] It seems likely that, at least in the case of beys and their sons, if not in the case of boyars (who were indeed indigenous to Wallachia and Moldavia and whose power had long rested on their landholding), their commercial origins were obscured to elevate them to the higher status of state officialdom.[80] The *irade* went on to say that *voyvoda*s of Moldavia and Wallachia were "acknowledged in Europe to have a rank equivalent to that of kings" and used the term *hanedan* to render a European concept of landed nobility into an Ottoman idiom.[81]

The social composition of phanariot *hanedan*s points to a number of convergences with contemporary Muslim Ottoman *hanedan*s. These dynasties, based in Wallachia, Moldavia, and İstanbul, like members of the Ottoman imperial and vezir households and those of eighteenth-century Egypt, were drawn from different areas of the empire and were of diverse ethnic-linguistic origins.[82] Even the most prominent phanariot families established already since the late seventeenth century had gone "transethnic" as well as transregional as a prerequisite to achieving power. In addition to the Ghika and Kallimaki families mentioned above, the Aristarchi family, originally Armenian, had come to İstanbul in the late seventeenth century from the Black Sea coast as *sarraf*s, or accountants, and had hellenized by the later eighteenth century.

Despite the many structural differences that divided them, transregional phanariot households and their more monoregional Muslim Ottoman counterparts exhibited some of the same strategies to augment their power and status. In eighteenth-century Aleppo, "the upper stratum of [Muslim] Ottoman provincial society was drawn from families associated with . . . respected careers: religious learning, mercantile activities, and service to the Ottoman state."[83] Career paths of members of phanariot families reflected a similar strategy, not of specialization, but of diversification, as one brother entered the clergy, and another the service of an Ottoman

THE HOUSES OF PHANAR 29

military or scribal official or an already prominent phanariot grandee, and a third
went into commerce or became, for instance, a physician. Accumulation of a range
of offices and titles, then, allowed for the building of influence by providing ever
wider access to information, expertise, and valuable goods. For these monoregional
Aleppan elite families, "economic power . . . was not grounded in a single form of
wealth, such as land or merchant capital, that would link them together through
shared economic interests. . . . Instead what they had in common was the diversity
of economic resources they controlled. They had acquired their wealth in different
ways: by engaging in commerce and money-lending, by appropriating rural sur-
pluses as tax farmers and owners of rural property, and by controlling *waqfs*."[84] Indeed we can say all of these things for phanariots as well, replacing only the term
*waqfs* (Muslim pious foundations) with Church properties throughout the empire
and in particular in the Danubian Principalities and the term *tax farmers* with *voyvodas*, who were essentially tax farmers on a grand scale. While Muslim Aleppan
families diversified within the local economy and provincial government of Aleppo,
phanariots diversified across professions but also across regions and ethnicities.

The common strategies phanariots and their Muslim Ottoman contemporaries
employed do not stop there. Throughout the empire in the eighteenth century, the
two groups also held in common the trend of acquiring family names "with the -
zade and -oghlu [-oğlu] suffix attached to a name or nisba being the usual form."[85]
If we recall Photeinos's list of subscribers to his history, it is clear that many phanariot families also came to add the Turkish -*oğlu* or even the Persian -*zade* suffixes
to their names just at the time they began to be termed *hanedan*. The Hançerlizade
(alternately known as Hançerli[s], Hantzeris, and Hançerlioğlu) family, İskerletzade
Aleksandır (whom we would recognize as Alexandros Mavrocordato, but who by
the late eighteenth century chose to be called İskerletzade, or the Turco-Persian rendering of "son of Scarlatos"), and the phanariot-affiliated Armenian Düzoğlu (also
known as Duzian) family are all evidence of this trend.[86] Ottoman documents at
times referred in passing to *hanedanzadelik,* or the quality of being descended from
a *hanedan*—better translated as "nobility," confirming that the choice to add -*zade*
and -*oğlu* to one's family name signified such pretensions for Christians and Muslims alike.

Maintenance and expansion of *hanedans* through marriage and fictive kinship
alliances also reflect parallels between phanariots and Muslim Ottoman elites. Men
who were already prominent in phanariot networks would marry their daughters
or nieces to aspiring men, bringing them into the household and larger network.
The father-in-law or uncle would then be responsible for providing opportunities
for the son-in-law or nephew *(damat)* and in turn would receive a client. Jane Hathaway notes the same pattern in eighteenth-century Egypt and points out that it is
similar not only to European dynastic practices but also to the sultans' practice of
marrying a princess to a prominent vezir, thereby admitting him to the House of

Osman.[87] In the case of godparentage, the specific custom of baptizing a child is a Christian practice, but the logic of expanding and reinforcing the patronage network through fictive kinship seems to have parallels in both the Ottoman imperial and Egyptian cases.[88] One need only consider the prevalent *ghulam/köle* system of elite slavery in the eighteenth-century Ottoman Empire, whereby a Muslim grandee would accumulate slaves, often from the Caucasus or the Balkans and, much like a godfather would his godchildren, train them as client-protégés in his household, eventually placing his slave progeny in key positions of power.

Phanariots even emulated their Muslim Ottoman counterparts in the realm of cultural and artistic patronage, demonstrating their aristocratic ambitions. In 1808, İskerletzade Aleko (Alexandros Mavrocordato) commissioned a *nasihatname,* meaning a work of "advice literature," belonging to the Persian Ottoman genre akin to *Mirrors for Princes.* His name is the Ottoman Turkish rendition of Alexandros Skarlatou Kallimaki, and he was likely the father of Skarlatos Voyvodas Alexandrou Kallimaki, the reigning prince of Moldavia in Photeinos's 1818 list of subscribers. This *nasihatname* was written in Ottoman Turkish and followed precisely the formula of works composed for and commissioned by Muslim Ottoman dignitary-patrons at the time. That Kallimaki chose at all to commission a *nasihatname* begs the question of whether he saw himself as a sovereign in need of advice or accepted that the sultan was the only sovereign. This question is complicated further by the fact that the work was commissioned in 1808, just as Sultan Selim III was executed by the janissaries and Sultan Mahmud II took the throne as a young boy. It is intriguing to consider whether Kallimaki was hoping to usurp an even greater share of sovereign power in an Ottoman idiom.

Furthermore, one need only look at the churches that phanariot princes had built in Moldavia and Wallachia throughout the eighteenth century to see their striking resemblance to contemporary Ottoman pavilions and other structures in İstanbul.[89] The same was true of the villas phanariots were building along the Bosphorus in the eighteenth century alongside those of Muslim Ottoman grandees—a stark contrast to the meager-looking houses they had inhabited in the Phanar district.[90]

By the turn of the nineteenth century, phanariot affiliates were being appointed ambassadors to the first permanent embassies established by the Ottoman sultanate in London, Paris, and Berlin.[91] As part of the Nizam-ı Cedid reforms, which are often heralded as primarily military in character, Sultan Selim III and his advisers also sought to institutionalize Ottoman diplomacy abroad, explicitly discussing how best to do it and whether to appoint members of phanariot *hanedan*s.

Phanariots were in a precarious position throughout the period of their ascendancy, charged with conveying sensitive information between the sultan and European states and thus always vulnerable to accusations of treachery. When such accusations were leveled and the accused fled to Russia or Austria, as was often the case, Ottoman authorities at times punished family members by confiscating prop-

FIGURE 3. Tombstone at Stavropoleos Monastery, Bucharest, Romania, reminiscent of Muslim Ottoman tombstones in style. Author's photograph.

erty but rarely disqualified the entire family from other offices or physically harmed them. Famous cases of early nineteenth-century *ayan*s, such as Tepedelenli Ali Paşa of Yanya, Osman Pasvanoğlu of Vidin, and Kavalalı Mehmet Ali Paşa of Egypt, point to a pattern of negotiation—and success or failure—for the entire family or dynasty. When Tepedelenli Ali Paşa and Osman Pasvanoğlu fell from power, their sons were prevented from succeeding them; when Mehmet Ali negotiated with the Ottoman Porte in the 1830s and '40s, his success resulted in the establishment of a hereditary dynasty in Egypt that lasted until the 1950s. Phanariot *hanedan*s could and did remain intact even when an individual member suffered exile or death, and yet they never managed to set up a stable, stationary, landed dynasty in their realms.

Phanariots, then, borrowed a number of features and strategies from their Muslim Ottoman counterparts, not least of which were specific practices of instrumentalizing family relationships for political and economic purposes. They built and consolidated *hanedans* outside the juridical mainstream of Ottoman landholding and tax-collecting regimes as part of a larger project to gain a kind of de facto legitimacy and importance in the realm of Ottoman rule. A major difference between phanariot and Muslim Ottoman elites, however, was that the phanariot enterprise was carried out on a geographically larger scale. While leaders of households in Egypt, Syria, and other Ottoman provinces diversified *within* the province (from military to tax collecting and commerce, for instance), phanariots, barred from direct access to military power, built ever denser relationships to Ottoman governance within the imperial capital while they were also cultivating ties beyond the empire, in the border zone of Moldavia and Wallachia as well as in European states and empires.

## Muslim "Riffraff" and Christian "Nobility"

Stephanos Vogorides' apologia, which inspired the structure of the present study, does not mention *ayan*s by name, either as threats or as allies.[92] Instead, by his own accounts janissaries played a much more pivotal role in threatening Vogorides' life and career, and this, I argue, has to do with phanariots' and janissaries' participation in many of the same operations of governance, from radically different starting points in society. The fact that both groups met their demise in the 1820s only makes juxtaposing them more intriguing. If phanariots and *ayan*s/*hanedan*s exhibited the common origins and legitimating strategies that were possible between monoregional Muslim elites and a transregional Christian one, a comparison between phanariots and janissaries brings out two very different groups that were transforming Ottoman governance from İstanbul.

Admittedly, even a cursory comparison between janissaries and phanariots seems bizarre—even more so than a comparison of either with *ayan*s perhaps. With a history dating back to the fourteenth century, the Janissary Corps was the elite infantry force, whose special, even sacred, duty was to protect the sultanate and, from the sixteenth century, the caliphate. The corps was designed, it seems, to be the bedrock of Ottoman governance, as close to the core of the state and dynasty as any group could be. Phanariots, in contrast, were institutionally marginal to Ottoman governance, were officially excluded from military activities, and had developed as a group only since the Treaty of Carlowitz in the late seventeenth century. And yet, there were several connections between the two, including structural isomorphisms, functional overlap, and lateral relationships of patronage.

The most striking parallel is the process of proliferation in the ranks of both janissaries and phanariot retinues, a process that became more pronounced as the eighteenth century wore on. The accuracy of estimates remains a subject of debate, but the number of janissaries on active military duty did seem to have been ever on the increase in response to expanding military campaigns, even in the sixteenth and seventeenth centuries—according to one estimate increasing from five thousand in the fifteenth century to thirteen thousand in the mid-sixteenth century, to twenty-five thousand in 1595, and to forty thousand in the late seventeenth century.[93] By this last period, the janissaries had "evolved beyond their role as an elite troop with principal responsibility for escorting and guarding the imperial presence to a position as the indispensable operational corps of the Ottoman army."[94] Still, frequent campaigns on several of the empire's frontiers maintained janissaries' connection to military activity.[95]

The janissary network continued to expand exponentially in the early nineteenth century, thanks to the now legalized habit of selling their pay tickets and thereby expanding the number of official titleholders.[96] Thus, by 1826, the year of their dissolution, about 135,000 names were on the books as janissaries. This had been an increase of 23,000 even since 1805.[97] Add to the number of titular janissaries those merchants, Christian and Muslim, who were paying for janissary protection in İstanbul and in the provinces, and the number who were involved in some dimension of the janissary complex grows to the hundreds of thousands.

Janissaries were originally drawn from the ranks of civilian subjects in the Ottoman Empire, but recent scholarship confirms that even in the earlier centuries they continued to participate in civilian and religious life when holding the janissary title.[98] Two interrelated activities exemplify this: janissaries' involvement in commerce and craft guilds, and janissaries' adherence to Bektaşi Sufism.[99] There are still more questions than answers regarding the evolution and details of the relationship among janissaries, commerce, and craft guilds, but several scholars have asserted that connections among the three were a widespread phenomenon in several provinces (Egypt, Bosnia, and Crete, for example) and in the capital since at least the seventeenth century.[100]

The details of janissary adherence to Bektaşi Sufism are also a vast topic in need of further exploration in Ottoman historiography, but it seems that there were associations between each janissary unit and a particular Bektaşi lodge and saint.[101] Important for this discussion is that the horizontal connections extending from the formal Janissary Corps into guilds, commerce, and Bektaşi networks expanded the political power at the disposal of the janissary networks by joining military power (both popular and elite) to religious, commercial, and artisanal networks. Thus, like the inhabitants of the phanariot house, who had begun as elites and structural outsiders to Ottoman governance and branched out into the lower social orders of the Balkans, the Orthodox religious establishment, Ottoman court networks, and foreign states and economies, the janissary networks evolved at the interstices of formal military and civil institutions.

In the eighteenth century, the multiple functions and associations of janissaries in society and politics continued while their participation in active military campaigns dropped off considerably. By the 1809 war with Russia, the leader of the janissaries was hard pressed to gather five thousand of his men for the march to battle from İstanbul to far-off Bender, even though more than fifty times as many names were in the formal janissary register. He managed to raise these five thousand men only by paying them extra compensation for leaving their shops.

While janissaries bought titles and failed to show up for military campaigns, phanariot *voyvoda*s handed out new titles with each new investiture. Entire retinues were removed and replaced with others when a new *voyvoda* was appointed, and yet members of former retinues retained their titles and often found other niches for themselves within the complex. Finally, with the creation of each new office in the provincial administration or in the *voyvoda*'s personal retinue, the recipient would bring in an officially prescribed number of servants or secretaries or both, as well as his family members.[102] Presumably, his previous business associates and patrons would also benefit from his new formal involvement in the phanariot networks.

Both groups—phanariots and janissaries—made concerted efforts to expand their base of associations by pulling in members of lower social orders and new arrivals to the capital. Phanariots accomplished this recruitment through personal, family, and locality connections, which could bring Balkan, Aegean, and Anatolian Christians of diverse ethnic origins into the Ottoman capital and hellenize them. Janissaries achieved the same goal by association with three groups: trainees (*yamaklar*), janissary guards at foreign embassies in the capital (*yasakçılar*), and the "riffraff" such as porters, coffee house assistants, and boatmen in the capital.[103]

Aside from their military duties, which seem to have been increasingly marginal to life as a titular janissary, members of regiments in İstanbul were officially responsible for many aspects of policing, urban security, and the policies and activities of the marketplace and the broader economy in the capital city of the early nineteenth century, as they had been in earlier centuries.[104] The janissary commander (*yeniçeri ağası*) was a member of the imperial council—and thus part of the central state—and was himself responsible for urban security in most areas of the capital city.[105] The janissary commander and *bostancıbaşı*'s troops were responsible for fighting the frequent and highly destructive fires in the capital city.[106] The chief butcher (*kasapbaşı*) was head of an important guild both for the janissaries and for the meat provisioning of the city. The newly established (1792) "grain minister" (*zahire nazırı*) was the intermediary among countless groups that participated in the grain provisioning of the capital—from local elites of grain-producing areas, through merchants involved in the transport of grains to the city, the Ottoman central administration, and the apparatus for military provisioning, to local distribution networks and the bakers of İstanbul.[107]

Like provincial *ayan*s, janissaries and phanariots were instrumentalizing their formal titles to expand the scope of their activities and patronage associations by the late eighteenth century. Some local *(yerli)* janissaries remained in provincial cities like Baghdad, Belgrade, Candia, and Salonica and in fortress garrisons throughout the empire.[108] Others were based in İstanbul and, although merchants or craftsmen, had memories of active duty in the 1770s. Still others, who could be engaged in a wide range of professions, had never performed a military drill and only collected their pay and enjoyed the privileges of having a janissary title and paybook. The upper echelons of the formal janissary structure were involved in the decisions and factions of the imperial palace, and the masses of janissaries had distinct customs and associations according to their particular regiment *(orta).* But for the purposes of this discussion, the focus is on their commonalities: they were each part of a heterogeneous janissary house, because they all held that formal title, collected their salaries, however measly by the eighteenth century, from the Ottoman state, and enjoyed a range of privileges in İstanbul and provincial society.

The phanariots and janissaries were forging connections with each other through ceremonies, patronage relationships in both the elite and the popular strata, and economic-institutional activities by the turn of the nineteenth century. The most obvious point of overlap between the two systems was in the performance of the investiture ceremony for *voyvoda*s of Moldavia and Wallachia. In that ceremony, janissaries played a role in legitimizing the new power of *voyvoda*s and in accepting them into state service. In return the *voyvoda*-elect would accept the validity of the janissary register, which by the early nineteenth century was no doubt bursting with new names. Leading representatives of the two systems would sit down and eat a meal together during the ceremony, symbolizing their joint participation in and loyalty to the imperial "kitchens" or coffers. Janissaries would also, as part of the ceremonial procession, escort the *voyvoda* to his court in Bucharest or Jassy and provide protection to him, however symbolic, during his tenure in the provinces.

Merchants and administrators associated with both groups of networks took part in important economic enterprises, such as the elaborate system of grain provisioning to İstanbul at the turn of the nineteenth century. As with the phanariot and janissary cases, the term *system* for grain provisioning must be used loosely, as it was far from monolithic. In fact, several systems were in place, depending on the geographical source of grains, the period, and whether provisioning was for the palace, for the military, or for the civilian population of İstanbul. In the second half of the eighteenth century, the Kapan merchants, who had "the commercial status of both semi-official and semi-private businessmen" in charge of procuring grains from the provinces and bringing them to the capital, were no longer able to purchase enough grain for the population of İstanbul. At this point the government "assumed direct responsibility for ensuring sufficient grain for Istanbul," ultimately, in 1793, establishing the Grain Administration (Zahire Nezareti) for this purpose.[109] With the creation of the Grain Administration, the methods of procurement and pricing also became more elaborate; the *miri* system, which had been used exclusively for military provisioning until the mid-eighteenth century, came into use for the provisioning of İstanbul, and the new *rayiç* system was also established.[110]

Moldavia and Wallachia were among the most important sources of grain for İstanbul after the Ottoman loss of Crimea to the Russian Empire in the 1780s. At the turn of the nineteenth century, in fact, the twin principalities were supplying one-third of the grain for İstanbul.[111] Given the administration of these provinces by phanariots, great and small, and the close relationships between janissaries and merchants of all kinds, several points along the grain supply chain likely depended on members of the phanariot and janissary networks in the late eighteenth and early nineteenth century.

At the sites of grain production, phanariot administrators and Moldavian-Wallachian notables collected (read requisitioned) the grains, either on the land they owned or in the territory they had been assigned.[112] At Black Sea ports such as Ismail, Kalas, and Galatsi, phanariot administrators and associated local merchants met Muslim Kapan merchants (who could also be titular janissaries) and boat captains who had come, with state permission, from İstanbul to pick up grains.[113] There, they presumably came into contact with representatives of a customs regime, phanariot or janissary or both, before setting off with their goods.[114] When they arrived in İstanbul, they docked at points on the banks of the Bay of the Golden Horn, such as Galata or Unkapanı, and unloaded their grain, either to wholesalers at the Kapan markets or to the state granaries such as that at Bahçe kapısı, the port of entry for Topkapı Palace, and the imperial naval arsenal at Kasımpaşa.[115] Recent studies suggest that transport workers at many of these quays were also titular janissaries. The final destinations of the grain meant for the civilian population were the bakeries of the capital, many owners of which were, likewise, titular janissaries.[116]

Phanariots at the turn of the nineteenth century were, like their *ayan* and janissary counterparts, fusing several institutions and coming up with novel combinations of operations to further their own ambitions but also to maintain the work of Ottoman governance—in effect, building a new kind of house. *Ayan*s, thanks in part to their military might and regional political legitimacy, could stand tall in their provincial strongholds, building palaces and fortresses that both emulated and threatened the Ottoman center. The house of Phanar, in contrast, was a more disjointed phenomenon: the power being accumulated on the inside, much as it matched the realities of Ottoman governance, could not be advertised to the outside world of Ottoman society. The connections forged by phanariots and the members of their entourages proliferated without much commentary and without a concomitant discourse to justify or augment the power that went with their knowledge. Their presence remained a vernacular one, as they fashioned themselves as *hanedans* or beys, with only a handful of official high-ranking positions around which to build their house.[117]

The traces Vogorides himself left behind of his involvement and personal ascent through the house of Phanar amount to a collection of silent appearances, exemplified by the presence of his name on the roster of students at the Bucharest Princely Academy, on a list of subscribers to Photeinos's history, and his signature as member of the house *(hanedan)* of Kallimaki on an official Ottoman document. In all likelihood he was a face in the crowd, at most a member of a princely retinue in the investiture ceremony of 1812 described by Photeinos. His silent presence combined with the range of expertise he must have garnered in these years is only further testament to the gap between political realities and representations, between vernacular and high politics, and between the outward structure and the internal activities of the house of Phanar.

# Becoming

*If I had had a tender and coddled upbringing like the phanariots and most of the Ottoman ministers in İstanbul, I surely would not have been able to tolerate so many dangers, and I would have fled or been killed, like so many of my phanariot compatriots.*

Stephanos Vogorides' personal journey through Ottoman and phanariot politics before the 1820s provided him with the skills, personal connections, and, according to him, the fortitude to survive wave after wave of major political upheaval and remain loyal to the Ottoman sultanate for another four decades.[1] His remains an excellent example of how people navigated and accumulated power in the phanariot moment—from the turn of the nineteenth century until 1821—and of how that power could be recouped in subsequent decades.

He was born—as Stoiko Stoikov—in the 1770s in Kotel (T. Kazan), a village in today's central Bulgaria, to Bulgarian-speaking Orthodox Christian parents. His father, Stoian, was a livestock merchant who traded in the nearby Wallachian and Moldavian principalities, and his grandfather Sofroni Vracanski was a cleric at Kotel who was ascending the Orthodox ecclesiastical hierarchy while Stoiko/Stephanos was growing up, ultimately to become archbishop of Vratsa in the midst of multiple crises in 1794.[2] Already on the fringes of the phanariot system in the 1770s and 1780s, the family reportedly fled their home village because of a combination of debts owed by Stephanos's father and a scandal involving local Muslim notables that had turned the Christian villagers against them.[3] The scandal was likely related to the *kırcali* (B. Kardzhali) movement, which involved local notables receiving payments to forcibly draft Christian and Muslim villagers of their districts into militias that were to put down brigandage and rebellions of Christian and Muslim Albanians moving through Rumeli. The family moved north to Arbanasi, a regional trading center near the border between Rumelia and Wallachia that was also the summer residence for prominent phanariot families such as the Mavroyeni and Muruzi families.[4]

There, Stephanos's family took two significant strides toward membership in phanariot circles. First, they became associated with "Muruz Bey," likely Constantine
Muruzi, who had in the 1770s served as grand dragoman (1774–77) and immediately after as *voyvoda* of Moldavia (1777–82).[5] Muruz Bey was well connected, not
only in the Moldavian and Wallachian administrations, but also with phanariot families in İstanbul and with high officials in the Ottoman navy.[6]

The second decisive step toward inclusion in the phanariot system occurred when
Stephanos's family hellenized their names while residing in Arbanasi; Stoiko became Stephanos, his father, Stoian, became Ioannis, and his mother, Guna, changed
her name to Anna, for instance.[7] While as Orthodox Christians they had been officially part of the Rum community in Ottoman administration, this meant that they
could transcend the subcategory of "Bulgar" and enter the Greek-speaking world
of *homogeneis*. The word *homogeneis* (homogeneous, of the same descent) was and
is a common way to refer to what we might now call a "fellow Greek." Interestingly,
this word does not specify Greek, Rum, Hellene, or any specific ethnic category and
does not connote belonging to any particular state.

Once they hellenized and became part of the *homogeneia*, it was possible to move
into the Greek-identified circles of phanariot elites. While grandfather Sofroni and
father Ioannis had their places—one as a cleric and one as a merchant—as Bulgarian speakers on the fringes of phanariot power, they sent Stephanos and his brothers to Bucharest for a phanariot, Greek-oriented education.[8] According to one source,
Stephanos's father was given the title of customs collector at the northern border of
Wallachia, leaving his father, wife, and children in Bucharest.[9] Whatever the circumstances, Stephanos and his family were among the many families entering the
service and culture of phanariots in the 1780s and 1790s. The best point of entry for
young men such as Stephanos and his brothers was the Princely Academies.[10]

At the Princely Academy of Bucharest,[11] Stephanos was a student of Lambros
Photiades, himself a philosopher and the director of the academy in the 1790s. We
do not know the exact dates of Stephanos's attendance but presume it was after
1791,[12] when the school reopened after the end of Austrian-Ottoman hostilities
and the Treaty of Sistovo, and likely before 1794, when plague and famine again
closed the school. The school had elements of "Enlightenment" education, but the
curriculum was ultimately under the control of clerics, such as the bishop of
Rimnik, who were appointed by the reigning *voyvoda*. Stephanos and his brothers learned Greek, Latin, and other subjects that would prepare some to continue
their education in medical and law schools of Europe, and others to enter the service of phanariots and other Ottoman officials. Perhaps more important, they entered the fray of phanariot power through their acquaintances with teachers and
fellow students, some of whom would also go on to officialdom in Moldavia, Wallachia, and İstanbul.

By his teenage years, Vogorides had become an inhabitant, even if a minor one, of the house of Phanar. He had not yet traveled to İstanbul or to its Phanar quarter, but he had embarked on an education and a career path that was tailored to the needs of the Ottoman imperial system, facilitated by phanariot elites that tacked back and forth between the imperial capital and their provincial power centers of Bucharest and Jassy.

2

---

# Volatile Synthesis

*The Grand Vezir Koca Yusuf Paşa, still in the field against the Russians, as-*
*sembled in his camp a small number of renegades captured in the course of*
*the campaign, including at least one Turk [sic] who had been captured by the*
*Russians years before and had served for some time in the Russian army. These*
*renegades, in cooperation with a few members of the grand vezir's personal*
*guard, began to train with captured Russian weapons, using European-style*
*exercises and maneuvers, and they performed periodically in front of their*
*master's tent as a kind of entertainment in order to divert the army's leaders*
*from their increasingly difficult military problems.*

STANFORD SHAW, "THE ORIGINS OF OTTOMAN MILITARY REFORM"

It is unlikely that Stephanos Vogorides or any of his contemporaries were aware of
this episode in Ottoman military history. And yet, this "toy" performance in the
grand vezir's tent in 1791 has become the starting point of a plotline that has overwhelmingly dominated modern accounts of the final, "long nineteenth century" of
Ottoman history. This is the plotline of Westernization and modernization of the
Ottoman military.[1] It has become so dominant, in fact, that this initial episode, which
could not have been witnessed by more than a few men, has come to obscure the
larger context of Ottoman governance during what was by all accounts—and for a
range of reasons—a crucial turning point.

Indeed, if the task is to trace the evolution of military reform or the Ottoman
central state's ongoing ambition to recentralize power, this performance in the grand
vezir's tent in 1791 is the logical starting point. It apparently encapsulates, even to
the point of caricaturing, an Ottoman pattern of reacting to defeat by mimicking
the strategies and even using the military equipment and uniforms of rivals such
as Russia, France, Britain, and eventually Germany. It also sets up an inevitable conflict among forces of modernization, secularization, and progress trying to impose
reforms on social groups entrenched in tradition, religion, and stasis. Modern historians of the Ottoman Empire still struggle with these polarities, even as they try

41

to eschew them for their profound implications for Western understandings—and misunderstandings—of Islam in the present.[2]

The term *Nizam-ı Cedid* means "New Order" and was used at the time to refer specifically to the new corps that was organized under Sultan Selim III between 1792 and 1807. It has since come to connote the broader spectrum of reforms under Sultan Selim III and the end of those reforms (the Nizam-ı Cedid events of 1807–8) and has been used as a catch-all term to characterize the period between 1792 and 1808 as a whole.[3] It would be nearly impossible, then, to examine this period without reference to the Nizam-ı Cedid in at least one of these senses. The phanariots' connections to the causes, application, and effects of the Nizam-ı Cedid project, however, also makes this chapter of Ottoman governance a perfect one to view anew through a phanariot lens.

The conventional narrative of the Nizam-ı Cedid era runs as follows. After a humiliating defeat by Russia and Austria (1787–91) and a massive mutiny on the battlefield, newly enthroned Sultan Selim III (r. 1789–1807/8) undertook military reforms to build a new, "European-style" army from among a group of janissaries and the militias of regional *ayans*. When he embarked on this military enterprise, his advisers realized that a new treasury (İrad-ı Cedid) would also need to be created in order to fund the basic needs and training of these troops. Such reforms threatened the interests of a panoply of existing power groups, such as janissaries and *ulema,* all of whom apparently benefited from the old system and were not convinced, whether for ideological or pragmatic reasons, that the reforms were desirable. By 1805 military reforms were suspended, and in 1807 civil conflict hit İstanbul, which saw the dethronement and eventual execution of Selim III as well as his cousin Mustafa IV and the reformist grand vezir Alemdar Mustafa Paşa. This ended in the enthronement of Mahmud II for the next thirty years and a pause in military and many other reforms until the 1826 so-called Vaka'yi Hayriye, or Blessed Event, in which the Janissary Corps was finally done away with, clearing the path for more comprehensive reforms.[4]

It would be difficult, and not particularly useful, to take issue with any particular step in this progression of events. But all of these events appear quite differently when viewed through a phanariot lens. Through that lens, the conflicts and activities of phanariots, janissaries, and *ayans* were intertwined at the political and geographical margins of military reforms, as were the realms of the military itself, foreign policy, and provincial governance. The actions of even a few prominent individuals, both Muslim and Christian, force us to discern some of the contingencies— and indeterminacies—in and around the houses of Phanar. A close-up look at a few individuals also sheds light on the connections between the phanariot Christian bid for power within Ottoman governance and the larger struggles underway for a dominant vision of Ottoman Muslim governance.

Three figures serve here as guides into the interrelationships of governance, first from 1791 through 1808, and then from that end point until the outbreak of Greek insurrections in Moldavia in 1821. The first figure is Nicholas Mavroyeni (1735–91), a self-made phanariot and Christian military leader who fought in defense of the sultanate in the course of the ill-fated war with Russia and Austria. The second is Osman Pasvanoğlu (1758–1807), a self-made *ayan* of janissary origins who presented the greatest challenge yet to Ottoman central power. And the third is Halet Efendi (1765?–1822), a bureaucrat and courtier who held together what I am calling the volatile synthesis of Ottoman governance—and the phanariot and janissary patronage networks—between 1808 and 1821. All three individuals were important to the causes, process, and outcome of the Nizam-ı Cedid reforms, but they were operating in the space between the house of Phanar and the larger house of Ottoman governance. And none of them was an ideologue, either for or against the "modernizing" reforms that have received so much attention in scholarship.

For the first two episodes, the history written by phanariot chronicler Dionysios Photeinos serves as a crucial narrative source to be read against and alongside Ottoman and foreign documents. Phanariot sources such as Photeinos's history are remarkable, highly valuable, and all but ignored. They represent the vantage of actors who were involved enough to understand the complexities of the conflict (unlike many European observers) but detached enough to present facts that would be suppressed by one or the other side in the reform–anti-reform conflict.

Photeinos was not only an eyewitness to many of the events he describes in his history but also was himself embroiled in political and factional tussles in the principalities. He had arrived in Bucharest in 1799, but by 1802 he and his patron Dimitraki (Demetrios) Ghika fled the rebel *ayan* Pasvanoğlu during the reign of Michael Soutso, and he later returned, still at the side of Ghika, the boyar, with whose support he rose in the hierarchy of the princely retinue. In 1808, while Wallachia was under Russian administration (1806–12), the Ottoman central state in İstanbul was in profound disarray, and Constantine Hypsilanti had been expelled as *voyvoda*.[5] The administration had been reorganized, and many of the "special" offices of the prince had been abolished. The significant income extracted from the provinces was no longer distributed among these special offices but was now concentrated in the hands of one archon, who each year reported and passed the income on to one official, the grand *vestiar*. Photeinos was apparently designated as this archon for one year of the Russian occupation, the first of several indications that he operated in the fields of both Russian and Ottoman governance.

In 1812, on the eve of the reinstitution of Ottoman phanariot administration in the principalities, Photeinos was appointed *ispravnik* in the district of Gialomitza,[6] likely by the grand *bano* and general-major Kostaki (Constantine) Ghika, who had himself been appointed "president of the Divan," or the imperial council, by the Russian Çiçakov. Photeinos remained in this office until the arrival of the Ottoman phanariot *voyvoda* Karaca. We know that he must have served in some official capacity from 1812 until the publication of his history in 1818–19, and therefore politically survived the transition from Russian to Ottoman rule in the principalities, but we do not know precisely how he survived. In 1818 he revealed in correspondence to his editor-publisher that he was waiting for a promotion to come through and thus could not yet refer to his title in his book. During this time he was on the outs with Voyvoda Karaca because of a satire he had composed targeting him, but the prince apparently forgave Photeinos when he saw the published first volume of the history in 1818, at which time he awarded him the title of grand *serdar.*

For the third episode in the present chapter, involving Halet Efendi, Photeinos's narrative silences reveal his own probable connections to the efendi. Such silences, while telling in themselves, force a reliance on fragmentary evidence from Ottoman sources and encrypted phanariot correspondence.

## CHRISTIANS IN ARMS—FOR THE SULTANATE

Despite his status as an outlier of established phanariot networks, Nicholas Mavroyeni's trajectory in many ways encapsulated the larger phanariot path—his triumphs, like the rise of phanariots more generally, were bound up with crippling military crises in the larger sphere of Ottoman governance and particularly with the defeat that prompted the Nizam-ı Cedid reforms. He was born in 1735, into a family who enjoyed regional importance on the Aegean island of Paros, and thus did not hail from the conventional phanariot areas such as Chios, İstanbul, or Rumelia. Like his uncle Stephanos Mavroyeni, he joined the İstanbul-based networks of the Ottoman naval administration under the *kapudan paşa,* which until the second half of the eighteenth century seemed to remain a wing of phanariot power apart from that which operated in the Danubian Principalities.[7]

Mavroyeni learned Greek, Turkish, and Italian, the last of which was undoubtedly of particular importance for naval administration (given the continued presence of Venetian commerce and Italian-speaking populations in the Aegean Islands). His tutor for these languages in İstanbul was reportedly one Hacı Nikolaki (Nicholas), the treasurer for the *kaptan-ı derya* Cezayirli (= Palabıyık/Gazi) Hasan Paşa.[8] This led, presumably through channels of patronage, to Mavroyeni's appointment as secretary to Cezayirli Hasan Paşa and ultimately to a very close patronage relationship, which lasted to the deaths of both men in the midst of war and mutiny on the Danube in the early 1790s.

Nicholas Mavroyeni was appointed dragoman of the fleet himself in 1770, by dint of his familial connection to Dragoman Stephanos Mavroyeni and his patronage connection to Cezayirli Hasan Paşa and before he could fairly be called a phanariot.[9]

In his sixteen-year tenure he dramatically raised the reputation and influence associated with that office and burst onto the phanariot scene in İstanbul and soon after in Wallachia and Moldavia. His investiture with the office took place in the midst of a grave naval conflict with Russia that would become perhaps the major turning point of the eighteenth century, ending with the historic Treaty of Küçük Kaynarca. The naval and administrative power he enjoyed was on par with that of Cezayirli Hasan Paşa himself as the admiral of the fleet and hero of the naval war against Russia.[10] Mavroyeni used this power not only to battle Russian forces but also to quell upheaval that occurred in the wake of the conflict, in 1774 and after, throughout the islands and the southern Balkans.

Having already proved his loyalty and competence in naval battles with Russia, Mavroyeni was promoted to the office of *voyvoda* of Wallachia in 1786, when hostilities with Russia and Austria were looming on the northern front after only twelve years of peace.[11] He was received with not a little trepidation by phanariot and boyar families already entrenched there. Chronicler Photeinos describes how the *kapudan paşa* Cezayirli Hasan, together with Grand Vezir Koca Yusuf Paşa, lobbied to have Mavroyeni installed as *voyvoda* of Wallachia—against the wishes of one Çelebi Petraki (Petro), the (Christian) *darphaneci,* or director of the imperial mint, described as the "strongest of all in the kingdom, not only of the Christians, but also of the Turkish grandees of the kingdom."[12] The *kapudan paşa's* faction won out, and, "snubbing the brilliant sons of princes *(beyzade)* who were starving," the appointment of the "crude islander" Mavroyeni as *voyvoda* of Wallachia was secured, as was the simultaneous execution (via *katle fermanı,* according to Cevdet and Photeinos) of Çelebi Petraki.[13]

Mavroyeni thus came to power through a patronage network that had already integrated Muslims and Christians, and he proved to be, for already-established phanariots, a "very strict and strange prince, with a different kind of character and strange and unusual behavior." Whereas "to the common people he was protective and sensitive, to the system of the nobles he behaved with derision and disdain— they even called him tyrant of the archons." He was accused of "believing in the religion of the Turks and of glorifying Muhammad, of respecting them and their law." In brief, sums up Photeinos, the essence of his spirit seemed a "concoction of fantasies and ideas that contradicted one another, his mind a monstrous synthesis of demons and superstitions." He apparently invested his horse with a high office of state and went into ecstatic states in front of the clergy and archons at his court, as well as in front of the many *paşa*s who gathered in Bucharest in times of war.[14]

But when military conflict began shortly after Mavroyeni took office (he reigned from 1786 to 1791, most of which time Wallachia and Moldavia were a war zone among Ottoman, Russian, and Austrian armies), he distinguished himself and took decisive action on a number of fronts.[15] He first expelled many Wallachian archons and their families for being *hains,* or disobedient to the Ottoman kingdom, according to Photeinos's definition. Once the allied Austrian-Russian invasion began, Mavroyeni gathered thirty thousand troops in Bucharest, made up of "Turks and various *ayan*s and *paşa*s," with about a hundred thousand troops gathering in all of Wallachia.[16]

Not only did he command Muslim troops in conjunction with *ayan*s and *paşa*s, but Mavroyeni also gathered an army of Christians, "made up of Albanians, Serbians, Bulgarians, and others, and he was the commander *(serasker)* of all these troops." Photeinos adds that, "he was Christian, and even so the *paşa*s, *ayan*s, and other Turks *[sic]* feared him and trembled when he appeared before them, as he abused and threatened them in various ways to keep them in line."[17] When enemy troops neared the principality, Mavroyeni even sent a group of Wallachian archons with an army made up of local (Christian) volunteers and Turks to a town in Moldavia so as to prevent them from entering Wallachia.

As Austrians entered Wallachia and set up a wartime administration there, Mavroyeni retreated to join the grand vezir (his patron Cezayirli Hasan Paşa) in Rusçuk (known as Ruse in English and Bulgarian), only to raise once again an army of "Bulgarians, Serbs, and others" to take back Wallachia, joining the grand vezir's troops when they arrived at the front.[18] In the course of these events, mutinies broke out among men under Mavroyeni's command but also among those under Cezayirli Hasan Paşa's.[19]

It seems to have been in the midst of these mutinies that Mavroyeni was executed by his long-time enemy, the newly appointed grand vezir, Çelebi Hasan Paşa Rusçuklu (= Çelebizade Şerif Hasan Paşa), upon his arrival in Soumla (= Şumnu), the military base of the region.[20] Photeinos asserts that Mavroyeni's execution was the result of machinations in İstanbul that began with the *valide kethüdası* Iosef "the Cretan" (G. *ho Kres*) who was at the time *darphane emini*.[21] Iosef "enacted" his death through Lala Mahmud, Sultan Selim III's tutor, and the two colluded to forge an imperial order for Mavroyeni's death, unbeknownst to the sultan—an order that the new grand vezir was apparently happy to carry out. Decapitation, Photeinos notes with sarcasm, "was his [Mavroyeni's] compensation for all of the works he had done for the Ottoman Porte, with so much loyalty and warmth."[22] Mavroyeni's patron, Cezayirli Hasan Paşa, meanwhile, had reportedly poisoned himself when he saw that it was impossible to conclude peace with Austria and Russia "without damage and dishonor to the Porte," as he had been charged to accomplish.[23]

We are unlikely to find a paper trail in the Ottoman archives to confirm the specific accusations of intrigue surrounding Mavroyeni's execution.[24] We can, however, surmise from the evidence that Sultan Selim III, who had taken power two years before Mavroyeni was executed, and his inner circle regretted the *voyvoda*'s execution. Evidence includes the flood of Ottoman documents that inventoried his assets in the few years following his death. Many of these assets were enumerated and explicitly granted to his wife and children rather than, as was standard practice, confiscated for the imperial treasury, and this corresponds to Photeinos's claim as well as to the claims of subsequent Ottoman biographers.[25]

Mavroyeni the individual was linked to Ottoman subjects in a wide range of social strata and across several regions of the empire. He was also intimately linked to Cezayirli Hasan Paşa and his patronage network, which went to the uppermost echelons of Ottoman governance, and pitted against the likes of Çelebi Hasan Paşa Rusçuklu and fellow Christian Çelebi Petraki. But most significantly, he not only commanded janissary and other Muslim troops but also spearheaded the direct participation of Christians in Ottoman military forces against foreign, Christian enemies (even if in Wallachia, territory that was technically autonomous from the Ottoman sultanate).

This episode was in turn bound up with one of the lowest points in Ottoman military history—the larger Ottoman military defeat by Austria (ending with the Treaty of Sistovo in August 1791) and Russia, ending with the Treaty of Jassy in January 1792. And it was this defeat that prompted the launch of the most ambitious experiment yet to reform the Ottoman military. As such, the Mavroyeni episode has been obscured by the arguably much less significant episode (for the time) involving military performances with stolen Russian arms and renegades in Koca Yusuf Paşa's tent that same year.

Modern historians have pointed out that it was during the conflict between janissaries and Ottoman state loyalists in the *paşalık* of Belgrade just after 1800 that Christians were first armed by the Ottoman state, to fight off the janissaries.[26] And from the mid-nineteenth century onward, with the inauguration of the Tanzimat project, aimed at political integration of Muslims and non-Muslims, service of non-Muslims in the Ottoman military would prove to be a persistent controversy, even through the Young Turk era and until World War I. Here was a case that predated the Belgrade one by almost fifteen years and the Tanzimat controversies by sixty years and would be forgotten almost immediately after it took place. Neither at the time nor in the course of later reforms did a language develop in which to accommodate such a de facto integration of Christians into the Ottoman military.

## FROM JANISSARY TO *AYAN*

The Nizam-ı Cedid reforms, which were initiated shortly after the death of Nicholas Mavroyeni, were of course not aimed at the integration of Christians into the Ottoman state apparatus. These reforms, however, were a reaction to the inroads Christians had made, which signified a collapse of the social order, exemplified by the Mavroyeni episode. They were conceived as a project to renew the Ottoman military, focused very much on the Janissary Corps and with a more ambiguous relationship to the *ayan*s who had been supplying the army with troops for decades.[27]

To phanariot chronicler Photeinos, the Nizam-ı Cedid was in fact merely a side show going on next to the real drama—the rise to power of Osman Pasvanoğlu of Vidin. In a seven-page footnote regarding Pasvanoğlu's life, Photeinos pauses to write, "In the meantime, Sultan Selim wanting to set up the Cedid Nizami [sic], that is to say the new military system in accordance with the order of the Europeans, and to wipe out the janissaries entirely, stopped giving the *garnizonous* [sic—garrisons? i.e., the janissary fortress guards] their *esame*, or their monthly royal wages, which they had always enjoyed for the duration of their lives."[28]

The Mavroyeni episode had represented the possibility of military integration of Christians into the Ottoman army, in the absence of a political language in which to formalize that integration. The larger defeat with which the episode was bound up provided the impetus for the Nizam-ı Cedid project. A focus on the process of reforms rather than their impetus reveals that the Pasvanoğlu phenomenon, which took place through almost the entire duration of the Nizam-ı Cedid experiment (1791 until Pasvanoğlu's death in 1807), included among other things a second example of Christian Ottoman subjects taking up arms in defense of the sultanate (when a phanariot *voyvoda* joined forces with Ottoman *paşas* against Pasvanoğlu). But in a larger sense and when viewed through a phanariot lens, it also lays bare the entangled loyalties on the ground as Sultan Selim III and his advisers attempted to launch the experiment for military renewal from above.

The personal trajectory of Osman Pasvanoğlu of Vidin both resembled and was bound up with that of Nicholas Mavroyeni.[29] Pasvanoğlu even served as a rear-guard officer under Koca Yusuf Paşa near Mavroyeni, in Wallachia, in the course of the Russo-Austrian-Ottoman war. Both Pasvanoğlu and Mavroyeni were catapulted onto the imperial stage in this watershed war between 1787 and 1791, but while Mavroyeni met his death in the wake of that conflict (and Pasvanoğlu's own father, Ömer, met his death early in the conflict), Osman seems to have used the conflict as a springboard, soon after establishing himself as *nazır* of Vidin, on the south bank of the Danube, and soldiered on to have forged the biggest military power—and posed threat to the Ottoman central state—throughout the 1790s and until his death (from illness) in 1807.

Chronicler Dionysios Photeinos looked back to the seven-year period from 1774 until the early 1780s as the "golden age" *(chryse epoche)* of Wallachia, when a just *voyvoda* (Alexandros Hypsilanti) ruled, archons were happy, and the people's tax burden was not too heavy. This golden age was broken first by Mavroyeni and the Russo-Austrian-Ottoman war, which ravaged the principalities, then by the upheaval caused by Pasvanoğlu, based just south of the Danube and the Wallachia border, in the Rumelian fortress town of Vidin.[30] Pasvanoğlu's bid for power was inextricable from the ongoing raids of *kırcali* brigands (thought to have been troops demobilized from the recent war) in the Rhodope Mountains throughout the 1790s. These raids, in addition to Pasvanoğlu's frequent incursions into Wallachia in search of grains, interrupted trade and cut off provisioning routes between the principalities and İstanbul. The first and second Serbian uprisings (1804–13 and 1815) were a crucial, if regional, by-product of these multilayered conflicts.

Pasvanoğlu was himself the son of a janissary from Bosnia who had come to Sofia as a guard (T. *pasvant*) of the bazaar there.[31] According to Photeinos, "The grand vezir happened to be there for the [1768–74] war between Catherine the empress of the Russians and Sultan Mustafa [III (r. 1757–74)]," when father Pasvanoğlu put out a dangerous fire in the bazaar and so "honored Pasvant for his bravery with the title *serdengeç ağası*, which means noble, and from there he advanced to various offices, moving to Vidin and acquiring estates *[çiftliks]* and status."[32] So Osman, the son, built on his father's achievements, rising to fame in Belgrade before returning to Vidin upon his father's death and taking over ever larger amounts of territory.[33]

By 1795 he had declared independence from the sultan, provoking the first of several attempts by state loyalist forces to break his power. He had joined up with *kırcali* insurgents and gave shelter to janissaries expelled from the *paşalık* of Belgrade, establishing an independent military and political center in Vidin. Furthermore, following Mavroyeni's precedent, Pasvanoğlu armed local Christians, but rather than deploying them in the defense of the sultanate, he "forced them to take part" in hostilities on the side of *kırcali* and janissary rebels.[34] While he built up his military power, he also assembled a coalition in opposition to the Nizam-ı Cedid military project, adding a dimension of social protest to the conflict.

After the Rumeli *valisi*, other *paşas*, and *kapudan paşa* Küçük Hüseyin were sent to put Pasvanoğlu down, these forces of the sultan were defeated, and Selim offered Pasvanoğlu a pardon, which was "brokered by the *voyvoda* of Wallachia, Alexander Mourouzis [Muruzi]." This was only a brief pause in hostilities, because soon after, in June 1798, an army of purportedly two hundred thousand was sent to oppose Pasvanoğlu.[35] In a move that echoed Mavroyeni's abrupt rise to the *voyvoda*-ship of Wallachia, Küçük Hüseyin, the Ottoman *kapudan paşa,* commanded the campaign and thus ordered that his phanariot dragoman of the fleet, Georgios Hançerli, be transferred directly from that office and appointed *voyvoda* of Wallachia so as to supply the troops properly with food. Hançerli went on to serve in that capacity from November 1797 until his execution in February 1799.

This campaign of Pasvanoğlu's was different from his earlier ones in that it involved seventeen *paşa*s surrounding Vidin with their royal troops and a naval force coming up the Danube, made up of "Saloups and Pergands, which are men trained in the art of naval warfare, such as Hydriotes and others, who had with them bombardiers and 'Intzinerides,' [engineers] or European geometrists, all under the command of the vice-Admiral İnci Bey."[36] Again, although we know that Christians were also fighting with Pasvanoğlu's forces, in Photeinos's rendering we have an example of Christians from the island of Hydra fighting with royal troops, this time not against Habsburg or Russian armies but against the internal threat of a Muslim rebel.[37]

Shortly after this round of fighting, the military calculus changed significantly for the Ottoman central authority because of Napoleon's invasion of Egypt. Thousands of irregulars from Rumelia (including a young Mehmet Ali, the future leader of Egypt) as well as phanariot secretaries and dragomans (including a young Stephanos Vogorides) left for Egypt, but Pasvanoğlu remained in his power base and fought on. After a few successive rounds of failed campaigns against and pardons of Pasvanoğlu, Christians of the area submitted two petitions recommending his pardon once again.[38] In one, Alexander Voyvoda Mourouzis (Muruzi) in Wallachia (reinstalled in that position in 1799 after the execution of Hançerli) presented him as "just and useful and beneficial for the area." The other petition was sent from Vidin by the ranking cleric there, Gregorios the Peloponnesian, in which he and the *protistoi* (notables) of the *re'aya* mediated for his pardon, claiming he was "most just and the warm defender of all the *re'aya* of the [Ottoman] kingdom."[39]

Pasvanoğlu was then forgiven and promoted, despite his open military challenge to the central state. "Selim, seeing the need for honor *[philotimia]* [no doubt the conflict in Egypt also played a major role], pardoned him, awarded him the royal title of *ibrohor,* and asked that he continue to pay his tribute." And that, according to Photeinos, was "when the general disorder began, the havoc in European Turkey, the rebellions of many *ayans* and *paşas* who no longer obeyed the Porte, because, seeing Pasvanoğlu, who, rather than be eliminated by the royal forces, destroyed them himself and not only failed to suffer any damage but was pardoned and honored with a royal title, amassing more than he had before, many started to follow his example, dissatisfied with the Cedid Nizami."[40]

Photeinos and presumably many other phanariots were conflicted with regard to Pasvanoğlu's efforts. He shared the admiration for Pasvanoğlu held by Christian and janissary groups in the Balkans and, at the same time, the condemnatory stance that the central state took toward Pasvanoğlu. When he first mentions Pasvanoğlu in his account, it is to comment on the "absurd and constant demands" he made on the Ottoman kingdom and the "unbearable sufferings" he was causing in Wallachia, which were increasing by the day and became the impetus for Sultan Selim's first bout with him.[41]

By the end of Photeinos's description he reiterates his condemnation of Pasvanoğlu: "So this Pasvanoğlu was, in his time, the first leader of the apostasy, the impaler of the Ottoman kingdom, and the calamity of Wallachia, where he perpetrated infinite misery and hardship." And yet, when Photeinos discusses Pasvanoğlu's personal qualities, he praises Pasvanoğlu for his bravery, cleverness, generosity, magnanimity, and greatness of spirit, "so rare among the Ottoman *genos.*"[42]

The Pasvanoğlu episode hints at the complexity not only of the disorder throughout Rumelia and the Danubian Principalities but also of phanariot positions with respect to the Pasvanoğlu challenge. On the one hand, Pasvanoğlu damaged the economy and power of phanariot *voyvodas* (and merchants in their realms) and challenged the authority of the sultan. On the other hand, he was a self-proclaimed defender of the janissary system and traditional order (from which phanariots had benefited greatly) and was thus defended by those same phanariot *voyvodas*. While Pasvanoğlu was a hero of many who were inspired by the French Revolution and went on to work for Greek independence,[43] he was also bound up with a process of further integration of phanariots—and the many humbler Christians who were connected to them—into the Ottoman imperial project.

Phanariots benefited—and suffered from—integration into the structures and practices of Ottoman governance on at least two levels as the Nizam-ı Cedid project unfolded in the 1790s and 1800s. In one sense, they were of a piece with the kaleidoscope of alliances and rivalries to the south of Wallachia and Moldavia, in Vidin and Rusçuk and to the west in Belgrade. This is made clear through the examples of Mavroyeni and Pasvanoğlu. While the resulting conflicts among Pasvanoğlu, several other regional *ayan*s, *kırcali* rebels,[44] and loyalist troops made for an interruption in many points of contact between phanariots and the central state, they also further integrated those factions into local factions of janissaries and *ayan*s who were opposed to reforms emanating from the center.

In another sense, however, phanariots were part of a *nearly* formalized inclusion in that very same reform program initiated by the central state "from above." They were directly implicated, not in the military reforms, but in the reforms in Ottoman foreign policy, namely, the establishment of the first standing Ottoman diplomatic corps and the concomitant regularization of ties with states of Christendom. As discussed in chapter 1, they were appointed alongside the first Ottoman ambassadors to London, Paris, and Berlin. Yanko (Ioannis) Mavroyeni, himself the nephew of Nicholas Mavroyeni, was even made the Ottoman ambassador to Vienna in 1811 and was the only ambassador to be reinstated in the 1820s, when Greek insurrections raged and the Ottoman diplomatic corps was paralyzed.[45]

Phanariots' integration into the foreign policy structures of Ottoman governance was a logical extension of the roles they already played as negotiators and intermediaries with European envoys at the Ottoman court and in the principalities. Such informal diplomatic activities took on unprecedented importance as the Napoleonic Wars and the European alliance system took shape, precisely alongside the Nizam-ı Cedid reforms.

Such inclusion into the emergent diplomatic corps was also facilitated by phanariots' reform-minded patrons in İstanbul. These included Galip Efendi, İsmael Ferruh Efendi, and Yusuf Agah Efendi, as well as the infamous Halet Efendi. It was Halet Efendi—Ottoman ambassador in Paris between 1802 and 1806—who authored the coded memo that proposed phanariots as candidates for ambassadorial posts, mentioned in chapter 1. And once the Nizam-ı Cedid program was formally suspended in 1808 and the Russo-Ottoman war drew to a close in 1811–12, it was also Halet Efendi who seems to have maintained the volatile synthesis of Ottoman governance from that moment until the outbreak of domestic violence again in 1821.

Before discussing the politics involved in this volatile synthesis between 1808 and 1821, we must briefly examine the violent conflict that put an end to "top-down" reform efforts for the next decade and brought about such a synthesis. In this case phanariots were not the protagonists but were astute and clearly well-informed observers. Photeinos's depiction of this watershed moment is invaluable, both for the familiarity and for the ideological detachment from the conflict it demonstrates.

## THE END OF AN ERA?
## THE NIZAM-I CEDID EVENTS OF 1807-8

Sultan Selim, in an effort to set up his new military administration (Cedid Nizami), tried to convince his people *[omogeneis tou]* to agree to it, resorting to flattery, threats, and promises of money, but realized he was powerless. So he realized he had to quit altogether or to carry it off in this crucial moment, a time when the sympathy of the nation *[ethnos]*, so necessary for the maintenance of the kingdom, would be on his side. But he judged wrong, that the present time would be right to set this up. Instead, when people saw all the new uniforms, they got the idea that the current declaration of war [with Russia in 1806] was fake and the real aim was to obliterate the janissaries, and they started thinking up ways to resist the whole enterprise.[46]

The civil war that put an end to the New Order experiment of Selim III was indeed one that took place within the Muslim *askeri* class, with janissaries and *ulema* forming a coalition against pro-reform central state loyalists, who included *ayans* from the Balkans and Anatolia. And indeed, on the surface this conflict seems not to have involved phanariots. Phanariots, after all, were not direct or formal participants in the Ottoman military forces and therefore were not ideologically or materially invested in whether a new or an old military force would fight wars for the sultanate. And yet they were enmeshed not only in the ongoing struggle with Pasvanoğlu but also in another immediate conflict between the Ottoman sultanate and the Russian Empire, which lasted from 1806 to 1812 and involved Russian occupation of both Moldavia and Wallachia.[47]

As complicated as the alliances and rivalries around the Pasvanoğlu episode were, they were quite simple compared with those that would bring down the Nizam-ı Cedid project in İstanbul in 1807-8. And it is difficult to tell the story from a static phanariot perspective, because their regime in the principalities was in such upheaval—and many of them were in flight—at that moment. Bucharest had been abandoned numerous times as a result of the constant fighting among combinations of royal troops, Christian Albanian troops fighting with the royal troops, and Pasvanoğlu partisans. Pasvanoğlu died in 1807, but by that time the Ottomans had entered a war with Russia, whose armies were themselves at war with Napoleonic forces. Wallachia came under Russian occupation and wartime administration from 1806 to 1812, and it was during this time that the Nizam-ı Cedid conflict occurred in

İstanbul. Luckily for us, those phanariots who did not stay on for the Russian administration of the principality had fled Wallachia for Transylvania or İstanbul. Those that made İstanbul their destination arrived in time to have a front-row seat for what one French observer called the "revolution in Constantinople" in 1807–8.[48]

After suspicions in İstanbul had apparently been raised as to the veracity of the Ottoman declaration of war with Russia, revolution ensued when janissaries and their defenders faced off against the partisans of the sultan and his Nizam-ı Cedid. Much of the rebellion took place at janissary barracks *(kışlas)*, with Selim III reportedly "watching through a telescope from Dolmabahçe Palace." Photeinos gives a dramatic sense of the upheaval that took place, writing, "How things take on such a strange shape in human affairs! The prominent, the wealthy, the serious, the brightly and luxuriously decorated, in one fell swoop became inconspicuous, paupers, humiliated, wandering unknown through the narrow streets! The established ones throughout the Ottoman domains suddenly proved themselves to be gutless!"[49]

Indeed the world turned upside down and people scattered, hiding in sewers, shacks, anywhere to seek safety.[50] All of this subsided by May 17, 1807, and, as Photeinos comments with relief, all "without the slightest injury to a Christian."[51] Phanariots—and Christians more generally—were indeed merely observers of this particular conflict.

The next round of revolution broke out in September 1807, when Bayraktar Mustafa Alemdar Paşa, leader of the pro-Selim III camp known as Rusçuk Yaranı (Rusçuk Committee), marched in from self-imposed exile in Rusçuk to reinstall Selim on the throne. (Mustafa had been made sultan in the meantime.) A confrontation then resumed between the pro- and anti-Nizam-ı Cedid forces. This ended with the corpse of Sultan Selim being dumped from the palace walls and the replacement of Mustafa IV with Mahmud II, who would be sultan from 1808 until 1839. Together, Mahmud II and Bayraktar Mustafa negotiated a (short-lived) peace treaty with Russia. All the while the janissaries were planning for a third round of rebellion for November 1807, during which time they burned and looted the city, taking revenge on all the supporters of Bayraktar they could find. Bayraktar Paşa's corpse was found under a slab of marble, at which time his pro-reform supporters fled the city to Rusçuk. These included several *paşas* and Dragoman Manouk, who was the Armenian treasurer of Mustafa Paşa, as well as two unnamed Armenian brothers.[52] Manouk with his household and "other Armenians" (such as his confidant Migirdiç, according to Ottoman sources) ended up in Russian-ruled Wallachia, where the emperor Alexander gave them honorary titles, and the others accompanied Ramiz Paşa to Bessarabia, with the *paşa* proceeding alone to St. Petersburg.[53]

Photeinos then turns away from the İstanbul events, cutting back to Wallachia to describe the Russian administration there (in which he served for a year during this time) and the conflict with Napoleonic and Russian armies between late 1807 and 1812. Peace negotiations, which soon broke down, were started in 1808, brokered in Jassy, of Moldavia, among Kahya Bey Galip Efendi, Bekirbey, the *ordu kadısı* (*kadı* of the army), and Beyzade Dimitrios Muruzi as agent of the grand dragoman.[54] Plans were finally made with General Kutuzov in 1812 for Russian withdrawal from the principalities and for the establishment of seven-year terms for *voyvoda*s there and for the Hatt-ı Hümayun, issued earlier by Sultan Selim, to be reinstated.

Photeinos ends his narrative of the Russian occupation (1806–12), an inextricable part of the Nizam-ı Cedid story, with a description of the disrespect and abuse suffered by Moldavians and Wallachians at the hands of Russians. The "rich and poor alike" apparently had welcomed the Russians as "coreligionist Christians," took care of them to the best of their ability, as "almost brothers by nature." The Russians, rather than reciprocate, "stripped them bare in unconscionable ways, levying heavy taxes without royal approval." They "abused them barbarically, rich and poor, like faithless ones, calling them Moldovan, which means barbarian and crude, and if a Russian encountered a Christian, he would scoff at him and call him *Tureski duh*, or Turkish soul, which," Photeinos adds, "other religions would never call their coreligionists, not even the Jews to those of other religions."[55] Such disillusionment with Russia no doubt drove some phanariots into closer allegiance with the Ottoman state.

## A VOLATILE SYNTHESIS

Phanariots, as resident outsiders of Ottoman military life, not unsurprisingly found themselves on both sides of the reform–anti-reform controversy. They could be found alongside janissaries or insurgent Serbs, consorting with Pasvanoğlu, and among the ranks of the elite reformers of the Ottoman diplomatic corps. As violent conflict subsided in 1808 and more so as hostilities with Russia drew to a close in 1811–12, phanariots had more opportunities than ever to practice Ottoman governance from these varied positions. While the period between 1808 and the 1820s is normally presented as a pause between central state assaults on the old system of the janissaries, for many groups it looked more like a volatile synthesis. For phanariots in particular it amounted to a golden age of opportunities.[56]

Halet Efendi facilitated many of these opportunities for phanariots, janissaries, and many local *ayan*s, and by doing so he held in place the volatile—and lucrative— synthesis of Ottoman governance for over a decade.[57] He had made his way to power in İstanbul through service as a secretary to various provincial officials in the late eighteenth century.[58] He is often depicted as a master puppeteer, pulling the strings of power behind the scenes at the Ottoman court. Such a simplistic image fits well into a modernization perspective, where corruption and patronage are undifferentiated and stand in contrast to modern meritocracy and rule of law. Upon closer inspection, Halet Efendi indeed seems to have amassed enormous power, all at a time when the central state was forced to synthesize reform and anti-reform groups and ideas.

His first connection *(intisab)* in İstanbul was the Bektaşi poet and spiritual leader Galip Dede, who likely played a role in Halet's appointments as secretary to the *zahire nazırı* (grain minister) Rasih Mustafa Efendi, the *kasapbaşi* (chief of the butchers' guild) Hacı Mehmed Ağa, and the Galata *kadı* Keçecizade İzzet Molla.[59] The former office was a Nizam-ı Cedid–era creation, and all three offices were tied to janissary networks as well as phanariot-run provisioning networks for the grain and meat supply for İstanbul.

In the 1790s Halet worked as a secretary to phanariot officials, such as Dragoman of the Fleet Alexander Ioannis Kallimaki and Yanco (Ioannis) Karaca. (Karaca would go on to be dragoman of the fleet and *voyvoda* of Wallachia.)[60] He was subsequently appointed *beylikçi kesedarı* under the protection of Rikab-ı hümayun reisi Mehmet Raşid. From 1802 until 1806 Halet was Ottoman ambassador to Paris, making him a member of the first generation of the Ottoman diplomatic corps under Sultan Selim III.[61] Fellow attachés included (phanariot) Yakovaki (Iakovos) Argyropoulo in Berlin.[62]

Upon his return to İstanbul from Paris, Halet went through several changes of appointment and internal exile before settling back at the court in İstanbul. He is referred to as "Reisülküttab Vekili Halet Efendi" in A.H. 1220 (ca. 1806) and was promoted to *reis efendi* during Mustafa IV's short tenure as sultan in 1807.[63] He was exiled to Kütahya for pro-British loyalties amid the events of 1808. In 1810 he returned to the court to join "Mahmud II's inner circle" and was quickly sent to Baghdad to battle Küçük Süleyman Paşa, the rebel *vali* (governor) of the region. In March 1810 he marched on Baghdad with ten thousand men and overthrew Süleyman.[64] He was then appointed minister of domestic affairs *(rikab-ı hümayun kethüdası*—literally meaning steward of the imperial court) in İstanbul in 1811.[65] From this point, Halet Efendi began to use his influence at court to promote particular phanariot families,[66] such as İskerlet [Skarlatos] Kallimaki—the son of his former employer and a classmate in the household of the elder Kallimaki—and to use the funds he received from Kallimaki to pay off janissary commanders and *ulema* to gain their support.

In addition, he engaged in less sentimental patronage relationships, receiving bribes and gifts from Mehmet Ali, who was himself gaining influence as a military leader and provincial governor in Egypt in these years. He was connected to other powerful provincial figures such as Ali Paşa of Ioannina (Yanya) and established his own network of patronage at the interstices of those networks and the Ottoman court in the decade before 1821. He worked to keep the system of *ayan*s and privileges of janissaries in place when Sultan Mahmud and others began to suggest supplanting the latter with a new military force. His network included, in addition to phanariots and janissaries, members of the imperial bureaucracy and in particular members of the Bektaşi Sufi orders, to which janissaries and members of many guilds belonged, as well as members of the Mevlevi dervish order, which was more popular among elite *ulema*.

During this time Halet installed many men in official positions through his influence as court favorite in the 1810s. These included Hacı Salih Paşa, who would become grand vezir in May 1821 with the help of his patron, Halet; Mufti/Şeyh-ül-İslam Yasıncızade Abdulwahhab; and Keçecizade İzzet Molla, the *kadı* of İstanbul's Galata quarter.[67] Halet himself, despite his connections with janissaries and *ayan* military leaders, was not a military leader and instead had risen to power through bureaucratic and diplomatic posts. Furthermore, Halet came to power in a rare decade—one that did not see significant foreign military conflict for the Ottoman Empire.[68]

In August 1812, shortly after his own appointment as *kethüda* at the court, Halet saw to the appointment of Yanko Karaca to the *voyvoda*ship of Wallachia and Skarlatos Kallimaki to the *voyvoda*ship of Moldavia. It was this investiture ceremony, in all its splendor and detail, that Dionysios Photeinos described in his *Historia tes palai Dakias*. It was not a coincidence, in fact, that Photeinos composed his history during this seven-year reign of Karaca and Kallimaki, as it was a period of remarkable stability, marked by an institutionalization of phanariot networks on a number of levels. Civil law codes (Code Callimache [Kallimaki] and Code Caradja [Karaca]) were drawn up and published in both principalities likely in imitation of the Napoleonic and Austrian codes of the time, for instance. Academies in Bucharest and Jassy were operating in full force, training the next generation of personnel for phanariot retinues.[69]

The internal institutionalization of phanariot power in the Danubian Principalities and the larger volatile synthesis of which it was part post-1812 also led to a rapid expansion of personnel serving phanariot *voyvoda*s and dragomans. This expansion has been noted by modern historians studying the larger arena of Ottoman bureaucracy. In describing the phanariot administration of the 1810s, Photeinos condemns the expansion in official personnel:

> Promotions of the archons and the hierarchy of offices always depends on the will of the *voyvoda*, and whereas in old times sudden promotions and the skipping of ranks were rare, in recent times the need of the *voyvoda* to please the Ottomans, the Orthodox Christians [Romaious], and the Wallachians and the selling of offices have caused a proliferation of titles; that is, too many people are given *paye*—only the titles of offices—and these people are made happy with high appellations, because with those they enjoy the designated number of serfs for life, the preeminence granted by the rank of their title, and the honor and other privileges accompanying such offices.[70]

Even though Photeinos claims that the *voyvoda*s created new offices to please the Ottomans, the Ottoman central state had noted the expansion of offices as wrongful even while Photeinos's history was under publication.

Just as Photeinos's *Historia tes palai Dakias* was hitting the shelves, a solution was devised to stem the expansion of phanariot retinues. This was the 1819 Kanunname, or Regulation.[71] With the support of phanariot patron and court favorite Halet Efendi, the Kanunname was drawn up to "take back the reins" of phanariot power and limit access to the highest four offices to four specific phanariot families, who were to be known as the Hanedan-ı Erbaʾa, or the Dynasty of Four. The need for such a regulation is described by an Ottoman source:

> Those descending from the phanariot faction have been preferred for employment and have been close to the esteem of the strong state for some time now. The people who have reached the offices of imperial dragoman, dragoman of the fleet, and *voyvodas* of the twin principalities, who are at times appropriate and at other times coming from the outside and deserving as well as undeserving of these offices, has multiplied. Their love of advancement has become a breeding ground for them to intrigue against each other.[72]

While this observation was certainly true overall, the writer of the document (an anonymous informant) may also have been referring to the recent (1818) flight of Yanco Karaca, *voyvoda* of Wallachia since 1812, to Geneva.[73] This had apparently been in connection with a *fesad* (sedition or intrigue) that had soured Halet on phanariots. (Long a protégé and patron of phanariots, by the time the Greek rebellions erupted in 1821, Halet had become known in phanariot circles—and in Stephanos Vogorides' apologia—as the *"Christianomachos,"* or Christian-slayer.) In an encrypted report to Alexander Soutso, still the reigning *voyvoda* in Wallachia, Halet's banker Haskel had reported the following statement of Halet's to the informant: "Your entire *millet* became my enemy. After that Karaca also became my enemy and fled" (Bütün milletiniz bana hasm oldi. Sonra Karaca da hasmim oldi kaçtı).[74] Halet's code name in the document, incidentally, was the French *"dans,"* undoubtedly a reference to him as the insider at the court.[75]

According to the Kanunname, the problem of phanariot ambitions and intrigues would be resolved by giving four families a monopoly of the four high offices—those of the reigning Moldavian *voyvoda* (and friend of Halet) Kallimaki; the current Wallachian *voyvoda* Drakozade Aleko Soutso (who had taken office after Karaca's flight); Mihal (Michael) Bey's line descending from the current imperial *dragoman* Drakozade Mihalaki (Michael) Soutso; and the "houses of the three brothers of the deceased Alexander Muruzi." The other families who would be excluded from eligibility—such as the Yakovaki (Argyropoulo) and the Hançerli (Hantzeris) families—would be paid a pension of sixty thousand and forty thousand *kuruş*, respectively, by the four reigning families.[76]

If Halet Efendi's original move to install Karaca and Kallimaki in 1812 had been the result of patronage ties, the decision to appoint these four families to the Dynasty of Four in 1819 seemed to be a result of bribery as well. In A.H. 1234–35 (sometime between 1818 and 1820), Halet acknowledged in writing his receipt of two hundred *"rumi altını,"* equal to six hundred purses of *akçe*, from Alexander Soutso.[77]

This transaction could have been aimed at securing Soutso's appointment to the throne vacated by Karaca and his family a place in the Dynasty of Four. Both signified a triumph over the Hançerli family, who were also vying for the throne of Wallachia but who were, in the end, formally excluded from the Dynasty of Four.

## THE SENED-İ İTTİFAK AND THE HANEDAN-I ERBA'A KANUNNAMESİ

Many of the particular motives, machinations, and alliances, both foreign and domestic, that led to the issuance of this regulation revolved around Halet Efendi. But in the end this regulation also represented a desire to integrate specific phanariots formally into the matrix of Ottoman governance, to transform them from an amorphous (and uncontrollable) group into a collection of four organized dynasties, and to winnow down their numbers at the top, and to regularize membership in their retinues, rules for their election, and terms of office. And all of this just months before the outbreak of the Greek rebellions, which would, we know now, lead to the establishment of an independent Greek kingdom under great-power protection, the first independent successor-state of the Ottoman Empire.

The Hanedan-ı Erba'a Kanunnamesi was quickly buried and forgotten when Greek-hetairist insurgencies erupted less than two years later. We do, however, know that the Kanunname must have been hotly debated in phanariot circles at the time of its promulgation. Phanariot Stephanos Vogorides, who was a signatory of the Kanunname as a member of Scarlatos Kallimaki's *hanedan*, refers decades later to a pamphlet he had written, called *He Tetrarchia stes Paradounavies Hegemonies* (The Hanedan-ı Erba'a in the Danubian Principalities). He had lost the pamphlet when his home burned down in the 1840s, but he comments that Mavrocordato, his former cophanariot who had since become a leading figure in the new kingdom of Greece, must have kept a copy.[78]

The all-but-forgotten 1819 Kanunname is evocative of a better-known document issued a decade earlier—the Sened-i İttifak.[79] Meaning "Deed of Alliance," this document was the result of negotiations between Bayraktar Mustafa Alemdar Paşa and the young sultan Mahmud II in consultation with several loyalist *ayan*s and was intended to quell regional unrest among the notables and bring them into the fold of the centralizing state. The agreement was that *ayan*s would receive protection from the sultan in return for their loyalty and for supplying the sultanate with troops. This was a formalization of a de facto relationship between *ayan*s and the central state, and it was framed not as a mutual agreement or contract but as a beneficent gesture from the sultan.

Shortly after reaching and signing the agreement, Bayraktar Mustafa Paşa was killed and Sultan Mahmud went on to ignore the agreement and suppress the Sened-i İttifak, eliminating almost all *ayan* threats to his power one by one in the decade that followed. This document has nevertheless been touted in retrospect (since Tanzimat times) as the symbol of the federalist road not taken in Ottoman governance and as signifying the birth of constitutionalism.[80]

The Hanedan-ı Erba'a Kanunnamesi represents a fascinating counterpoint to the Sened-i İttifak in several ways. Issued under the reign of Mahmud II, both documents expressed that sultan's desire to regularize and formalize existing power relationships. Both were also doomed to obscurity—the Sened-i İttifak because of Mahmud's campaign to eliminate regional power centers and the 1819 Kanunname because of the outbreak of Greek insurrections. (Three of the four families included in the Dynasty of Four were already members of the Philike Hetaireia, or the Society of Friends, a secret society that would launch the insurrections in Moldavia in 1821.) Both could have been compacts between emergent political groups and the Ottoman central state had they been couched as such and not as dispensations from the beneficent sultan.

And yet, while the Sened-i İttifak has come to enjoy an afterlife as a sign of what could have been, the 1819 Kanunname has fallen into obscurity, overshadowed by the Greek national drama that would take off in 1821. It is tantalizing to imagine what could have been, however, if the institutionalization granted in the Kanunname had been realized. It would not have been an institutionalization based on a discourse of equality or separation of religion and state. Instead, it would have grown out of the existing framework of sultanic authority and sustained the inclusion of Orthodox Christians within a polity that claimed to give predominance to the political traditions of Islam. The Kanunname was also the result of the very real and not so savory politics of patronage that, thanks to Halet Efendi, was holding the synthesis of Ottoman governance together at this moment. While janissaries were enjoying a new lease on life and ayans were given nominal protection but in actuality came under continued assault by Mahmud in his project to centralize provincial governance, phanariots fared best of all. They had emerged unscathed from the violent conflicts of 1807–8, retained and even augmented their role in Moldavia and Wallachia when an Ottoman administration replaced a Russian one in 1812, and proliferated in numbers and in the range of tasks they performed in Ottoman governance.

The career trajectories, alliances, and downfalls of three individuals—Nicholas Mavroyeni, Osman Pasvanoğlu, and Halet Efendi—as seen through a phanariot lens force us to see the levels of integration that were and were not reached with the initiation of reforms in 1791; the layers of interests and factions under the surface of the binary opposition between pro-reform and anti-reform groups; and the volatile synthesis that was forged under the appearance of a pause in top-down reform efforts after 1808. Exploring the practice of governance before, during, and after the Nizam-ı Cedid thus highlights that the process of inadvertent integration of phanariot networks into the larger matrix of Ottoman governance, underway at the nineteenth century's turn, was advanced in the course of each new conflict, both within and outside the empire. Phanariots became ever more relevant and useful to the project of Ottoman imperial governance. This integration was often an unintended consequence of state policies, until finally, just before the outbreak of the Greek Revolution, it was sanctioned by the sultan himself in the form of the Hanedan-ı Erba'a Kanunnamesi.

Simultaneous with the phanariot ascendancy, ideologies emerged that would articulate anew both the Islamic character of the Ottoman state (so as to justify reforms) and the ethnonational ambitions of some phanariots for an independent Orthodox Christian polity. The 1819 Kanunname under Mahmud II amounted to a very different solution to the same problem Selim III had encountered two decades earlier: whether to integrate phanariots into or expunge them from Ottoman governance. At the turn of the nineteenth century, phanariots had ascended to become an Ottoman community on the verge not just of national secession but of imperial integration.

# New Orders

*Having as I did this physical and moral upbringing, I was able to remain constant in the duties of my servitude when the revolution of the Greeks broke out in 1821, when I was already of a vigorous age, and during the wars against the French in Egypt, and then again later when I found myself in Rumelia with the imperial army against the Russian forces ... and the times I was thought to be Rumeliot and a compatriot of the Bulgarians, and when the* paşas *were politically asleep.*

STEPHANOS VOGORIDES' APOLOGIA

When Stephanos traveled to İstanbul in the mid-1790s, he had already laid the groundwork for entrance into politics and imperial service through the connections of his family in Wallachia. He arrived in İstanbul with a letter from his grandfather to a combination of officials that varies according to one's source. Some say he first arrived with a letter to Helarion, bishop of Turnovo, who in turn recommended Stephanos to the Karaca phanariot family. They in turn introduced him into the service of Husrev Paşa, who was ascending the Ottoman military-administrative hierarchy in the 1790s.[1] This route seems plausible in that Stephanos's grandfather Sofroni, as a cleric from the district of Turnovo, could easily have been well-acquainted with Helarion, as bishop of Turnovo. An alternative story places Stephanos, immediately upon first entering İstanbul in the 1790s, in the joint protection of an Ottoman high official—Kahya İbrahim (the interior minister)—and the Psychares merchant family from Chios, who introduced him directly into the service of Husrev Paşa.[2] This was more certainly the case when Stephanos returned to İstanbul from Egypt in the opening years of the nineteenth century and could have been the case when he first arrived in the 1790s as well. Whichever the actual chain of connections that brought Stephanos into the service of Husrev Paşa, both versions demonstrate the symbiosis among clerical connections, phanariot families, and Ottoman military-administrative officials that made up the phanariot enterprise at the turn of the nineteenth century. These connections allowed Stephanos to advance from a Bulgarian-speaking background through a provincial Greek-phanariot education and enter the imperial service, not immediately as part of a phanariot retinue, but as a secretary-translator for an Ottoman military-administrative official.

Stephanos's first years in İstanbul were probably the most formative years of his career. He must have learned the language and social and political skills through informal apprenticeships, possibly to merchants, clerics, and clerks or scribes and acquired a base of personal connections to advance in Ottoman imperial and phanariot politics. Unfortunately it is the period for which we have the least information and know only that he somehow ended up in the retinue of Husrev Paşa by 1799, when he traveled with Husrev to Egypt to fight against the Napoleonic invasion there. By that time he had the language and technical skills to serve as a military translator and would continue to work as such until his 1812 appointment to the phanariot retinue of Voyvoda Kallimaki in Moldavia.

Vogorides' work as military translator to Arif Ağa, a member of Husrev Paşa's retinue to Egypt, made him a witness (and sideline participant, as translator) to the Battle of Aboukir, when allied British and Ottoman fleets defeated Napoleon's naval forces during 1799–1801. This was an experience Vogorides would often look back on in the 1830s and after, claiming it as part of his pedigree of service. In Egypt, he came into contact, if indirect, not only with British figures such as Admiral Nelson but also with a young Mehmet Ali, freshly arrived from his native Kavala with a contingent of Albanian irregulars to support the war effort. The reoccurrence of this conjunction of foreign and domestic actors would not go unnoticed by Vogorides in the course of the Mehmet Ali crises in the 1830s, and Vogorides would remind French and British diplomats of his presence and role, even if minor, in those world-historical events.[3]

When Vogorides, along with his patron–employer Husrev Paşa, was expelled from Egypt by Mehmet Ali and Tahir Paşa shortly after the end of hostilities with Napoleonic forces, he began anew to search for positions in İstanbul.[4] It was apparently at this time that he was under the protection of the Psychares merchant family and recommended to Kahya İbrahim, an important figure at the Ottoman court. In 1806, Moldavia and Wallachia were occupied by Russia, which, along with the Russo-Ottoman military hostilities, contributed to a rupture in the Ottoman-phanariot administration in the principalities. With phanariot positions in Moldavia and Wallachia temporarily out of his reach, Vogorides focused on work as a dragoman and secretary in the Ottoman military and Ottoman administration proper between 1806 and 1812. By the end of Sultan Selim's reign (ca. 1807), for instance, Stephanos was working again as a military dragoman, this time for the *kethüda* Mustafa Refik Efendi, during hostilities with Russia.[5] Around the same time, in 1807, he was reportedly working as a dragoman in Vahid Efendi's retinue and is said to have played an important role in the Treaty of the Dardanelles (1809), which served as a basis for the future Anglo-Ottoman alliance.[6] He was rewarded for his service with appointment as grand dragoman for a brief period, before moving on later in 1809 to represent the Porte in Moldavia.[7] It was perhaps at this time that Vogorides came under the patronage of Scarlatos Kallimaki, the *voyvoda* of Moldavia, not only from 1807 to 1810, during Russo-Ottoman hostilities in the area, but also from 1812 to 1819 as well, when the province had been returned to Ottoman control after a two-year Russian occupation.

In 1812 the Wallachian *voyvoda* Ioannis Voyvoda Karaca was invested with his office in an elaborate ceremony in İstanbul—likely the model for Photeinos's description of the investiture ceremony. This particularly grand investiture was a result of the Russian-Ottoman agreement to regularize the phanariot regime by establishing seven-year terms for *voyvodas*. And Karaca, it turns out, would be the last to serve a seven-year term before the system collapsed into rebellion.[8] Stephanos at this time was poised to enter the formal service of phanariot Scarlatos Kallimaki, newly reappointed as *voyvoda* of Ottoman Moldavia, having already served as the representative of the Porte to Kallimaki's administration, and would take advantage of this regularization and work for further consolidation of phanariot power vis-à-vis the Ottoman imperial state.

Stephanos took two important strides into the formal ranks of phanariot politics at this time. In 1812 he was appointed *kaymakam* (governor) of Craiova and Galatsi,[9] his first official position in the phanariot administration of Moldavia. From this position he would, living mainly in Jassy, rise through the official ranks of the Moldavian administration over the next nine years of relative peace in the area. He was granted the title of *ağa* in 1813,[10] then the following year made *postelnik,* or minister of foreign affairs, for Moldavia.

Aside from climbing the ladder of official positions in Kallimaki's Moldavian administration, Stephanos allied with Kallimaki in 1813 by marrying Ralou Skylitzi-Skanavi, who was related not only to Voyvoda Skarlatos Kallimaki but also to two prominent Chiote merchant-phanariot families, the Skylitzis and the Skanavis.[11] This marriage alliance made Vogorides an undeniable member of the innermost circles of phanariot power, and, although he was likely not a candidate for *voyvoda* because of his humble (and perhaps his recent Bulgarian-speaking) origins, he could reach the second-highest position of *kaymakam,* which he did in 1820–21. The marriage also meant that he would inherit land in the Phanar quarter of İstanbul, the epicenter of the phanariot system, thus further solidifying his membership in that elite.[12]

Stephanos's decade of acceptance into and advancement through the Moldavian phanariot administration coincided not only with years of relative peace but also with the period of Halet Efendi's ascendancy and the consolidation of phanariot power in Ottoman politics and in the twin principalities. Two projects point to this consolidation and institutionalization underway: one, the establishment of the Callimache Law Code (1818) in Moldavia; and two, the Hanedan-ı Erba'a Kanunnamesi in 1819. The former, often referred to in French as the "Code Callimache" (Kallimaki Civil Code), was, in imitation of Napoleonic Law Codes, an attempt to regularize power through the creation of a civil code for the province. In the latter, four families with close connections to Halet Efendi attempted to consolidate their hold on the four top offices open to phanariots. Vogorides participated in both of these projects; not only did he help draft the law codes, but he also contributed to what must have been a controversial debate about the Dynasty of Four by writing a pamphlet in favor of the rule.[13] Vogorides appeared as a signatory of the letter of gratitude submitted by the patriarch Gregorios and the Dynasty of Four to the central state for its promulgation of the 1819 Kanunname. Vogorides appears as "Hatman Istefanaki Vogori" in the roster of personnel at the end of the document.[14] Finally, in 1820–21 Vogorides as *postelnik* would travel to Wallachia with fellow *postelniks* Ioannis Samurkassis and Theodore Negri to negotiate a settlement with Wallachian rebel leader Tudor Vladimirescu, whose efforts to overthrow phanariot power came into direct conflict with Greek hetairist rebellions the following year.[15]

By 1821, after two decades of involvement in Ottoman politics and nine years of formal membership in a phanariot entourage, he was deeply involved in the internal politics of the principalities, in the "foreign affairs" of Moldavia, both with Wallachia and with the Ottoman central state, and in familial relationships at the highest echelons of phanariot power.[16] In fact, if the institutionalization of his patron Kallimaki's power, which was sanctioned in the 1819 regulation, had continued, Vogorides could have looked forward to a stable career in the highest reaches of phanariot power. His hatred for hetairists such as Hypsilantis—who apparently approached him as they were planning their insurgency—is understandable in light of the successes Vogorides had enjoyed within the Ottoman-phanariot world. For Vogorides, as for many of his fellow phanariots, the second decade of the nineteenth century was anything but a pause in the action, as it is often portrayed in scholarship. Instead, it was a decade full of opportunities and possibilities, only one of which turned out to be the Greek national insurgency.

# 3

## Demolitions

In September 1821, six months into civil wars sparked by Greek-hetairist insurgencies in the Danubian Principalities and the Morea, a British envoy in İstanbul noted a dilemma of the Ottoman government:

> As to the immediate re-establishment of the [Danubian] Princes, a . . . difficulty stands in the way. Are you aware of the public ceremony and pomp attending their investiture? Are you aware that these ceremonies are indispensable? That a procession, scarcely inferior in splendor to that of the Sultan himself, must be made through Constantinople? That the whole of the Greeks established here, attend the ceremony? Be assured that if under the present circumstances it were to take place (and without it the assumption of offices by the Princes [voyvodas] would be imperfect and their authority not acknowledged) it would be the signal for every sort of disorder, for massacre, and perhaps for Revolution.[1]

Almost a year later, despite the risk of revolution in İstanbul, the investiture ceremony for the Moldavian and Wallachian voyvodas was reinstituted—for non-phanariot, "native" voyvodas. In fact, the investiture ceremony was permanently terminated only with the abolition not of the Greek-identified phanariots, but of the janissaries in 1826. The customary investiture ceremony was, temporarily at least, detachable from the Greek-identified phanariot networks, performed as it was in 1822 with Moldavian and Wallachian figures instead of İstanbul Rum voyvodas. It was not, in the end, detachable from janissary networks.[2] This is one of the many connections between phanariot networks and the larger matrix of Ottoman governance before 1821 and one reflection of how the demise of one house—the phanariot—in 1821 was related the demise of the other—the janissary—in 1826.

The breakdown of the phanariot system in 1821–22, in İstanbul, was a reper-
cussion of Greek-hetairist insurgencies in the provinces. Those events can be understood in their larger imperial context by using the evolution and demise of the
janissary house for comparison. The demise of the phanariot house in the wake of
the Greek Revolution is conventionally examined in the context of Balkan nationalist movements, which would accelerate in the course of the nineteenth century.
The demise of the Janissary Corps in 1826, in contrast, is seen as the delayed reaction to the violent upheaval around the Nizam-ı Cedid in 1807–8 and a prerequisite for more sweeping military and administrative reforms that would follow in
1839 and 1856; as such the 1826 abolishment of the janissaries was a turning point
in the larger trajectory of modernization that led directly to the 1923 establishment
of the Turkish Republic. But what would happen were we to uncouple the demise
of phanariots from the Balkan national narrative and that of janissaries from the
tale of imperial modernization? To examine the phanariot demise in light of and
in relation to the destruction of the Janissary Corps would, I contend, illuminate
the common patterns and dilemmas of governance in the 1820s.

From the Ottoman imperial perspective, those who took part in Greek-hetairist
insurgencies—whether phanariot or not—were understood as traitors (in collaboration with Russia) to an already beleaguered Ottoman state.[3] Consequently, the goals
of the central state were to put down the rebellion in the provinces and to seek out
and purge the guilty "co-conspirators" lurking in İstanbul. Rebellions began far from
İstanbul, in Moldavia, in early 1821 and were first led by Tudor (Theodore) Vladimirescu against phanariot rule and immediately after by Alexander Hypsilanti, who
had arrived from Bessarabia (held by Russia at the time) with troops associated with
the Society of Friends.[4] Through reprisals by the central state and further insurgencies in Rumelia, the Morea, and the Aegean Islands, these rebellions precipitated a
breakdown in many of the relationships that had constituted the phanariot house.
Some of those relationships were of course reconstituted in the Greek kingdom that
was established in 1832, which is outside the scope of the present discussion.[5] In
order to understand the ways the phanariot house broke down, the breakdown's
effects on the Ottoman state, and the possibilities of reconstituting that system, one
must highlight the locations and ways the phanariot house first came undone in
1821–22.

It is important to note that no uprising occurred among Rum subjects in İstan-
bul itself. Thus, the central state's reactions in İstanbul to Greek-hetairist rebellions
were geographically remote from the actual theaters of insurrection, which included
Moldavia, the Morea, Epirus, and several Aegean islands. The story of whom the
central state chose to question, accuse, and execute and who escaped blame and
survived in İstanbul, then, reflects the way Sultan Mahmud and other policy makers may have understood the causes and development of the far-off Greek revolts.
In particular, the violence initiated by central state actors in İstanbul unfolded to

destroy many fundaments of the phanariot house. If we trace the path of this violence, the structure of that house and the repercussions for the state when it was
broken down emerge.

Several overlapping accounts of the İstanbul events of 1821–22 exist. Ottoman
chroniclers such as Şanizade, Cevdet, and Lütfi provide general mention of some
events, and the works of Spyridon Tricoupes, a Greek national(ist) historian of the
Greek Revolution, contain brief descriptions of the İstanbul episodes. The modern
Romanian historian Nicolae Iorga also provides a description of some of the main
events involved in the Ottoman reaction to Greek rebellions. But among the most
useful for the present discussion are two Greek-language eyewitness accounts. These
accounts are rare in that they describe events in İstanbul rather than the Morea or
the Aegean Islands. Furthermore, while they are written in the Greek language, they
are not framed within the context of a Greek *national* ideology. One is an account
of a Greek-speaking visitor to the city who likely originated from Heptanesus, or
the Ionian Islands. The anonymous writer seems to have witnessed much of the violence and also to have had access to phanariot circles, judging from the details he
provides. The second account is titled simply (as translated) "Unpublished Account
of an Official and Eyewitness Fellow Greek [*homogenes*]."[6] The author of this second account had "an official position," but specific information about his background and position are not disclosed in the publication of the account.

THE UNRAVELING

On February 28, 1821, news from the Danubian port town of Galatsi reached İs-
tanbul through the port of İbrail that "the Greeks had risen up against the Turks
and killed many of them."[7] The first reaction of the central state was to summon
the *kapıkahya*s, who were the resident representatives of the Moldavian *voyvoda* in
İstanbul. The oldest of the representatives (for they had proliferated from one official representative to several in the preceding years) was Nicholas, the brother of
the recently deceased Wallachian *voyvoda* Michael Soutso. The exchange that went
on between the *reis efendi* and the *kapıkahya* conveys the confusion of the moment:
the *reis efendi* asked the *kapıkahya*, "Hasn't your master written to you about the
events in Galatsi?" to which the *kapıkahya* replied, "No, he hasn't written us at all."
When told the news by the *reis efendi* that the *"giavur"* (infidels) of Galatsi had murdered the "Turks" there, the *kapıkahya* again replied innocently that it must have
been the outcome of "the fights that break out between them [Rum and Turks] over
women." His assistant *kapıkahya*s likewise evaded the question, whether out of ignorance or fear, saying, "Galatsi is the port of Moldavia—aren't the Turks there Stam-
buliotes anyway, who only travel there with their boats and load up with grain?"[8]
With that, they left the meeting with the *reis efendi* and went to their homes on the
Bosphorus.

The next day the ignorance of the *kapıkahya*s was dispelled when a messenger arrived from the *voyvoda* telling them to leave the capital immediately, "because Alexander Hypsilanti has arrived, and we, meaning also Russia, have a war against the Turks."[9] They left their homes and belongings and immediately boarded boats bound for Odessa, which had become a safe haven for Orthodox Christian Ottoman subjects. The day after that, government authorities learned of the uprisings in Jassy and the arrival of Hypsilanti, then came to arrest the *kapıkahya*s. Realizing the men had left for Russia, the authorities confiscated their homes and belongings.[10]

At this point, the state authorities, "in great fear that they were entering a war," looked to Russia and called in Minister Stroganoff, the Russian representative in İstanbul. They asked him, "Why did Russia enter our lands?" to which he replied that he had no news of any war or incursion. "Why did Russia let Hypsilanti enter our lands then?" they asked. Stroganoff answered, "He is an apostate, not someone sent by Russia, and besides, Russia has no need of such means, for we have a million bayonets to fight any enemy."[11] The leaders of the central state were coming to realize that this was an internal conflict, not one that could be fought with a foreign state.

There was no declared enemy or at least no representative of such an enemy within easy reach in the capital. After failing to pinpoint the cause or agent of the distant conflict, the central state, lacking access to swift and coordinated military force, turned to mobilizing the Muslim population with a *ferman,* or imperial decree, by the sultan to the "populace" that said,[12]

> Muslims: in the month of April, when the *giavur* [infidels] have their Easter, they have conspired on that day to set fire to Asia, across from Byzantium [the Old City quarter of İstanbul], the site known as Chryssopolis,[13] planning that we will cross the straits to put out the fire. At that moment they will enter Byzantium and take the throne from us by sword. Cursed and excommunicated is he who violates my order! Children, adults, young and old, arm yourselves immediately and be vigilant, day and night.[14]

The *ferman,* according to this eyewitness account, did not make reference to the uprisings already underway in the remote provinces of Moldavia or in the Morea.[15] Instead, the focus was on a betrayal that was yet to happen but that was much more immediate because it was to take place in the capital and it was a plan to subvert the sultanate altogether. Ottoman sources include news from Moldavia and Wallachia as well as a report signed by the "former *kethüda* Mustafa" that Rum in the Beyoğlu District and other quarters were collecting "cannonballs, rifles, and Muslim clothing" and had planned, with the help of the bishops of Kuşadası and İzmit and the grand dragoman, to rise up and take over İstanbul ("İstanbul'u zapt etmek üzere kıyam edecekleri").[16]

According to our eyewitness source, the "Turks" went en masse to the bazaar, bought guns and ammunition, and started shooting everywhere, "from in front of the sultan to the houses of the Rum." They provoked panic and fear, "impregnated women," and shot into the air, spending their money on ammunition until they started to yell, "We've made ourselves poor by shooting bullets!" Then they forced the government to give them gunpowder and bullets and started assaulting and robbing Rum in the streets and breaking into their workshops to take their money. Rum started to secure their shops by keeping them closed, but the state declared anyone who did not open his shop a criminal.[17] The same atmosphere, with different details, is described by another eyewitness, Rev. R. Walsh, who noted that "many thousand fellows of all descriptions completely armed, in addition to the populace of the town, [were] going about with loaded pistols, which they discharged in mere wantonness at every object that presented itself, so that day and night we were disturbed by a succession of reports, like the hedge-firing of an irregular engagement."[18]

The following week, on March 11 (a Friday), the imperial Divan was called "so that the decision of the sultan could be announced, that is, so that the müfti of İstanbul [şeyh-ül-İslam] could issue, according to his religion, a fetva document ordering the beheading of the reaya [Orthodox Christians]."[19] The şeyh-ül-İslam (who was Dürrizade at the time) and the kahya bey (steward of the grand vezir, whose post was evolving into one of a minister of home affairs) would not give their opinion, however, and the sultan exiled them. It seems that there was no consensus within the imperial council about the nature of or proper response to the outbreak of rebellion. The first to be punished in İstanbul, then, in the course of the "Greek Revolution" were not Greeks but the highest-ranking Islamic legal scholar and the Ottoman chief steward of the grand vezir.

At this point, the waves of public executions of suspected Christian co-conspirators began. Judging from the pattern of the executions, several criteria, not one, prompted the decision of whom to kill. One such criterion was physical proximity to the capital; the decision to execute the messengers who had arrived from Jassy and the postelniks who were in İstanbul reflected this.[20] Another criterion was family associations; one guilty individual would be executed along with any of his family members who were perceived as co-conspirators. A third criterion, whether expressly articulated or not, seemed to be to break the vertical connections of the phanariot house; in each group of executions were high-ranking phanariots, Church figures, merchants, messengers, and "unknown" or common people—barbers, butchers, or green grocers—and locals from the Morea and other areas of insurrection who happened to be in the capital.

The first day (in mid-March) saw ten executions: Postelnik Nicholas Skanavi; his son-in-law Hatman Michael (who had been dragoman of the fleet in 1815); the grand logothete of the Church Theodoraki (Rizos) Neroulos, brother-in-law of Skanavi, who had been dragoman of the fleet in 1807; the son of Alekos (Alexandros) Photeinos, who had arrived from Jassy to find Prince Skarlatos Kallimaki; the merchant Dimitraki (Demetrios) Tselikis, who was rumored to have been on the way to reaching the rank of Ottoman admiral; the unnamed messenger of Prince Soutso; and four "unknown Christians."[21] Together, they were a cross-section of inhabitants of the phanariot house, linked to one another by blood, marriage, and possibly patronage ties and holding an array of official positions.

At the same time as the state-sanctioned public executions, "masses of Turks" also began to kill people in the streets, according to an eyewitness report. An Ottoman document ordered that all Muslims stop their foolish squandering and arm themselves (bilumum Müslümanların sefaheti terk ile müsellah olamaları) in response to the alliance of Rum infidels against them (Rum gavurlarının ehl-i İslam aleyhine ittifaklarından dolayı).[22] At this point it seems that Rum could be killed for involvement in the Moldavian uprisings, for involvement in the perceived conspiracy to set fire to the Asian side of the Bosphorus and take over the throne from the Ottomans, or simply for being Rum Christians. Whichever the case, Rum as well as resident Franks (Europeans) tried to protect themselves, and "the Dragomans of the [European] Ministers could no longer visit the Porte."[23] The dragoman Kallimaki was exiled to Anatolia (the town of Bolu), and the family of the *voyvoda* Kallimaki was put under guard, for he was made *voyvoda* of Wallachia and was expected to conclude the Congress with Russia as the designated envoy of the sultan. The central state was still in search of loyal phanariots to play the roles of provincial administrator and diplomatic envoy, even as they sought out the guilty in the conspiracy to take over the empire.

The sultan again, according to this eyewitness source, gave an order to kill Rum, and shots were heard day and night until the women of the harem started to complain that they could not sleep at night and were afraid of the booming sounds of guns. British pressure to ease up on reprisals and offer clemency to rebels also contributed to a reconsideration of the policy. This reportedly caused the sultan to exile Musa Paşa, the grand vezir, and replace him with "Sahi" Paşa (Hacı Salih), who decided that the disorder of the populace "is not good in the capital," and moved the Sultan to disarm the masses and threaten to hang anyone found with arms.[24] This brought about peace and quiet, and the Rum were ordered to open their shops and sit in them. The peace lasted for only a few days, however, at which time the sultan brought back Musa Paşa, who rearmed the populace, and chaos resumed.[25] The sultan ordered the banishment of any Turks who, having Rum friends, whether merchants or anything else, defended or even greeted them.

The next move was to order a census to be taken of all "Graikoi" ("Greek," as opposed to Rum) merchants and phanariots, counting how many families, how many young people, and what their professions were and obtaining "guarantees of one another's character *[kefalet]*." The list was to contain "the names, places of origins, and places of business of many merchants, phanariot archons, and high clerics and bishops, as well as anyone who had relations with the Greeks [Graikoi], which of those had traveled to Europe, had interactions with Europeans, and which 'well-behaved'

Greeks were resident in the capital."[26] The *dragoman beyzade* (prince) Kostaki (Constantine) Muruzi, a member of one of the Hanedan-ı Erba'a (Dynasty of Four), established two years earlier, was ordered to compile an exhaustive list of all merchants, including their names, their land of origin, and the places they traded, and a list of all phanariots, including which were high clergy and bishops, which were associated with Rum, which had traveled to Europe and had European friends, and which of the Rum in the capital were reputable.[27] This census would serve as a map for the central authorities to designate executions in subsequent days and weeks.[28]

The order to compile a register of phanariots and their associates indicates the nature of the phanariot house up to that point. On the one hand, this house was an informal enterprise whose members were known predominantly to one another. As such, one of its members had to be called upon to provide the list of names. On the other hand, nonphanariots in the central state were aware of the existence and pervasiveness of the phanariot house. Only when betrayal was imminent did leaders of the state feel it necessary to obtain systematic and specific information about the house's members.

While the phanariot house was pursued through lay figures like the *voyvoda* and dragoman, Church officials who were associated with secular members of the house also came under attack. Among those executed early on were the archbishops of Ephesus (Efes) (Dionysios Kalliarches), Nicomedeia (İznikmit) (Athanasios ho Kyprios), Derkon (Gregorios ho Peloponnesios), Thessaloniki (Selanik) (Iosef ho Peloponnesios), Turnovo (Ioannikios ho Phokaeus), and Adrianople (Edirne) (Dorotheos Chios ho Proios). They had been called to the *bostancıbaşı* (the chief of the prison at the imperial arsenal, among other duties) and arrested. This in turn prompted the escape of several prominent phanariot families who were presumably associated with these clerics: former Wallachian *voyvoda* Alexander Hançerli; Beyzade (Prince) Georgios Karaca, Nicholas Soutso, brother of Michael and the *kapıkahya* who had been first questioned by the grand vezir; and Dimitrios and Ioannis Skina with their families.

Meanwhile, when Dragoman Beyzade Kostaki Muruzi had finished his task of compiling a register of the phanariots and clerics in İstanbul, he was the first to be executed on April 5, "since they [the authorities] had him in front of them every day."[29] The batch of executions during Orthodox Holy Week (the week preceding Easter) included at least twenty-eight men, many of them exceptionally wealthy. The second batch of executions seemed to have been designated on the basis of financial criteria in addition to the criteria of the first set of killings. Those who were owed money by the government, as well as those who held wealth and possessions needed by the central state for arms, were the focus. The institution and properties of the Church (if not its clergy) were still passed over as the main focus of hostilities and punishment in favor of prominent phanariot figures (Muruzi), wealthy merchants, "terrorist" conspirators, and even paupers. The sultan had decided to act with greater precision, ordering the populace not to kill people on their own but to let the sultan "sacrifice people a few at a time." The sultan reportedly "each day opened the register [that had been compiled by Muruzi] and chose from those names whom he would order to be killed."[30]

After the dragoman and census taker Muruzi was executed, the sultan ordered the executions of the merchant Antonaki (Antonios) Tsira, who, as a purveyor of silk to the palace, was owed 200,000 kuruş by the government; his son Stefanaki, who was also waiting to receive 150,000 kuruş; the "multimillionaire" merchant Paparrigopoulos from the Morea; Panos Panagiotakis, a kapıkahya of Prince Soutso; one Tsorpatoğlu from Üsküdar (on the Asian side of the Bosphorus), "from whom the state wanted to take his many possessions and wealth"; four Hydriotes; six green grocers; four "suslitzides," architects whose job was to bring water to the city and who were accused of a plot to poison the drinking water; Prince Michael Hançerli, who had been dragoman of the fleet in 1808; Ağa Alexander Ralli, who had been chargé d'affaires in Paris in 1800; Paharnik Theodoraki (Theodore) from Therapeia (on the Bosphorus); Paharnik Torakçi (kilnmaker) from the imperial shipyards; and four paupers.[31]

For the first six weeks of executions in İstanbul the state focused on those with financial power, political positions, and suspect family and patronage associations. It was unclear which members of the phanariot house were being punished for involvement in the conspiracy for uprisings in Moldavia and which for the conspiracy in İstanbul, which had not yet happened. The informal power of the phanariot house was being demolished in a way that seemed hasty and indiscriminate,[32] cutting across social lines; however, reprisal against the patriarch himself would prove to be much more carefully organized and staged.

Holy Week ended with the hanging of Patriarch Gregorios V from the door of the patriarchate in Phanar on Easter Sunday (April 22, 1821), an event that became a central symbol of Orthodox Christian martyrdom in the national narrative of the Greek Revolution. Within the sequence of events told here, however, the hanging of the patriarch appears as part of the breakdown in the phanariot house, and the story begins with the imperial dragoman. Dragoman Kostaki Muruzi had been executed earlier that week, and on Saturday night (Easter eve), Stavraki (Stavros) Aristarchi had been appointed to replace him as dragoman.[33] Patriarch Gregorios reportedly saw this news as encouraging, for Stavraki was a "good friend" of the patriarch.

After the patriarch had conducted the Easter service on Saturday at midnight, a new procession arrived from the palace, including the kesedar efendi (treasurer) of the reis efendi, escorted by a large number of çuhadars (footmen) and the imperial dragoman, Stavraki Aristarchi. The procession entered the patriarchate compound and went straight into the synodicon of the Church, where the patriarch was just sitting down to eat his customary Easter soup. The dragoman approached him, asking him to remain calm and to receive the dragoman alone in his quarters for a visit.[34] After this meeting, the *çavuşlar-emini* (chief of police) came and informed the patriarch of his removal, as was his customary role, and led him out of the patriarchate along with the archdeacon Nikiforos and the deacon Agapios. The patriarch believed he was to be led to Chalcedon (Kadıköy), as was the custom with deposed patriarchs. Instead, the patriarch was led to the prisons of the *bostancıbaşı* at the imperial arsenal in Kasımpaşa.

The imperial dragoman, Stavraki, then called a meeting at the patriarchate of upper clergy, the community representatives, and representatives of the boyars and notables to tell them of the removal and punishment of Patriarch Gregorios, which had been ordered in writing, along with the appointment of the archbishop of Pisidias, Eugenios, "whose homeland was Philippoupolis [B. Plovdiv; T. Filibe] and whose descent was Bulgarian," as the new patriarch.[35] Together with the dragoman, Eugenios traveled in procession to the Porte and was there invested with the civil authority of patriarch. When he left the Porte, "he was accompanied, as was the old custom, by the servants of the Porte and a portion of the janissaries, and, when they reached the patriarchate, the ceremony of patriarchal election and appointment occurred in the holy cathedral, and he ascended the *synodicon* with the high clerics."[36]

Only then, after observing the custom for the removal of the old patriarch and the appointment of the new, was Patriarch Gregorios brought from the prisons to the gate of the patriarchate and hanged there, with a sign suspended from his neck stating the cause of his execution.[37] Most striking about this account of the execution of the patriarch is the concern for process on the part of the Ottoman state—something that is left out of the martyrdom narrative of Greek national history. In this version, the patriarch was hanged only after a replacement had been located, brought to the palace, and invested with his new office. The office of patriarch, then, was not left empty, and perhaps Ottoman leaders could argue (to the Russians, who were likely to object) that they executed not the patriarch but the man who had served as patriarch and betrayed the Ottoman sultan. This procedural point was reportedly made by the Ottoman court to Russia on the occasion of the severing of Russian-Ottoman relations in 1821 because of the trampling of Orthodox Christian buildings and figures: "It was further stated [in the Ottoman response to Russia] that the Patriarch had not, in fact, been executed, for that he had been on the very morning deposed from his dignity, and so was no longer head of the Greek church when he was put to death."[38]

At this point religious institutions and buildings and religious differences in society became a focal point in the conflict. Several other clerics were executed shortly after Patriarch Gregorios, and, in reaction to a report that Christians were hiding armed men and arms for use against the government in the basements and courtyards of their churches, Muslim religious students entered the conflict. The "*softas* [*suhtas*] and *hocas*" (students and teachers) reportedly came and destroyed the church and holy spring at Balıklı.[39] They proceeded to the Church of St. George at the Edirne Gate of the city and to churches in several other neighborhoods, including the İstanbul *metochion* (dependency) of the Monastery of St. Catherine's of Mt. Sinai, destroying the buildings and contents of the churches. Some churches were protected—by janissaries, whom one might expect to be carrying out acts of revenge for the central state, but some of whom were instead paid by Christians to defend the churches.[40]

The aggression among popular strata of religious students and graduates against Orthodox Christian religious sites stands in contrast to the cautious approach of some elite members of the *ulema* establishment in the 1820s (recall the reluctance of Şeyh-ül-İslam Dürrizade to issue a *fetva* ordering reprisals against Christians at the start of hostilities). The *suhtas,* or religious students, numbered in the few thousands in İstanbul at this time and were predominantly of very humble means, receiving one free meal a day and living in squalid dormitory conditions.[41] They apparently harbored resentment toward the aristocratic caste of elite *ulema,* who passed their privileges on to their sons from a young age while humble students had to wait years for paid appointment, as well as resentment against janissaries and other groups.[42] While *suhtas* were perceived as a potential threat to the central state for their past support of janissary rebellions, when Rum Orthodox Christians were those in rebellion, the decision for the *suhtas* to attack the symbols and buildings of Orthodox Christianity was, apparently, clear.

While the Moldavian uprisings are ordinarily glossed over as a preamble to the main event of Greek Revolution in the Morea, from the imperial viewpoint the Moldavian events were crucial. Those events and the Ottoman central state's reaction to them tore apart the phanariot house at its geographic center—İstanbul—and along the points that served as its foundations, starting from the *kapıkahyas* and moving between İstanbul and the principalities and between the Ottoman court and the Orthodox patriarchate. The violence in İstanbul and the failure of the janissaries to defend the state from Greek insurgents in the provinces then precipitated an escalation of tensions within the central government and between the government and the Janissary Corps, tensions that came to an end only with the abolition of the latter four years later.

## FROM PHANARIOT DEMOLITION TO JANISSARY ABOLITION

The Greek insurgencies that started in 1821 and caused the breakdown of the phanariot house were also a precipitating factor in the collapse and ultimate destruction of the janissary house. The ineffectiveness of janissaries as a fighting force for the imperial state was made clear with their performance against Greek rebels. In this way, the Greek insurgencies heightened the existing tensions between members of the Janissary Corps and the central state and catalyzed the final breakdown of that corps. The connection of the two groups by key individuals and activities made their potential power as well as destruction all the more disturbing for a threatened Ottoman central state. Halet Efendi had successfully lobbied for the interests of both phanariots and janissaries for the fifteen years since his return from the Paris Embassy. The rebellions and reprisals against the phanariots that began in 1821 set off a profound crisis in Halet Efendi's networks at the epicenter of Ottoman governance. Phanariots, now executed, in hiding, or in internal exile, were no longer able or present to supply Halet with funds. Consequently Halet could not use such funds to continue paying off janissaries, who were now under increasing pressure to serve as a defensive force for the state against the Greek rebels. Furthermore, "the Janissaries, without the payments from Halet to which they had become accustomed, quickly began to shift their allegiance [and] Halet also lost the income which he had been receiving in gifts and bribes from [Mehmet Ali], Viceroy of Egypt."[43] The centrifugal forces in Halet's personal network were gaining momentum and, with them, the centrifugal forces exerted on Ottoman governance at large.

In the year and a half between the outbreak of the Greek rebellion and Halet's exile, Halet tried to reestablish an equilibrium of power for himself by attempting to influence military policies yet again. Still trying to deflect attention from and discourage changes to the Janissary Corps, Halet convinced Sultan Mahmud to move against Ali Paşa of Ioannina (Yanya).[44] Halet claimed this would be an easy victory, but it became yet another protracted conflict to deal with in addition to the Greek rebellions. Halet, it appears, persuaded Mahmud to sink his limited resources into a draining military conflict and, by doing this, only accelerated his own downfall, becoming the scapegoat for the empire's many ills.

While Halet's phanariot funding sources were drying up, the janissary recipients of his bribes were digressing further and further from their official role as defenders of the sultanate. At the start of conflicts in Moldavia, five companies of janissaries had been specially trained, but when the janissary commander was ordered to supply five thousand janissaries to march to the Danube, he, like other janissary commanders before him, found that these elite troops were also guild members and had no desire to leave their businesses. The janissary commander "had to call upon the treasury to supply funds to pay these recalcitrant warriors a bonus of 50 piastres per man for regular Janissaries and 100 piastres per man to each Janissary who was also a member of a guild."[45] Janissaries had gone on to fight against Greek rebels in the Morea in some numbers, in addition to tribal troops and Albanian irregulars, and had sustained serious losses there. This sparked janissary protests and agitation for change in the capital, and although "some of the leading trouble makers were secretly executed," dissatisfaction for Halet's role as courtier and janissary patron was building in the spring of 1822.[46]

As Halet's networks of payments and patronage were dissolving, an incident occurred that, although possibly apocryphal, is often pointed to as at least the immediate impetus for his removal. Sultan Mahmud went to the Bayezid Mosque to pray one Friday and reportedly overheard a group of janissaries airing their dissatisfaction with Halet Efendi to their commanders. This Mahmud saw as his opportunity to earn the trust and favor of the janissaries—by eliminating their former patron, whom they now saw as their adversary—and thus gain time to formulate a plan to do away with the janissaries themselves.

Sultan Mahmud then exiled Halet Efendi to the Sufi lodge of his choice, in Konya.[47] Although he had promised Halet that his life would be protected, when criticism of Halet Efendi continued unabated in İstanbul, the sultan sent a messenger to Konya, ordering his execution.[48] He was beheaded, and a note, attached to his nose and displayed in December 1822 at the court, expressed the favors he had received in serving the sultan and the zeal with which he had served the religion of Islam.[49] The note continued with the reasons for his execution:

> Because of the guile and machinations in which Halet took part, he necessarily carried this wickedness and this malice innately in him, and many people have been ruined by him up to now.
>
> He always sowed division and favored the bearing of dissension among Muslims. Furthermore, a hypocrite in his words and actions, he behaved, on the surface, like a faithful man; but, deep down, he sought nothing but to advance his personal interests, and without abandoning extravagance, without dissolving this perversity which had become familiar to him, he dared to commit, against the supreme will, many actions analogous to his character; and shortly this became constant.[50]

Halet Efendi had served a necessary purpose in holding the potentially conflicting groups of Ottoman governance together between 1811 and 1821. Nevertheless, when the system came unraveled with the Greek Revolution and the diverse crises the revolution set off in the Ottoman court politics and military, it was Halet's innate malice, hypocrisy, and personal interests that were portrayed as the causes of discord among Muslims and of the ruin of many individuals. The decision to kill Halet, then, was not only a decision to punish a wrongdoer. It was also a tactical decision made by Sultan Mahmud—to supplant Halet's networks and gain support of disaffected janissaries, who were already turning to Halet as a scapegoat, and by extension to eliminate the major obstacle to Mahmud's project to gain control over his military and suppress Greek rebels. The removal of Halet, in Mahmud's perspective, would eliminate the horizontal connections of governance that had circumvented Sultan Mahmud and cleared the way for more effective policy making and military victory over the janissaries, who were coming to be seen as irredeemable enemies of the state.[51]

Given the depiction of Halet as the major cause of the conflicts raging in the empire, there seems to have been a general sense of relief after his removal. The British envoy echoed the sentiment of the Ottoman authorities with the following comment in January 1823: "Till lately, the Sultan had his Capodistrias [Halet], who, under the mask of absolute submission to the Sovereign, pursued exclusively his own views and was guided by his own passions . . . fortunately, this dangerous individual was now removed."[52] Now, the envoy continued, the members of the court could "deliver their sentiments without fear," and the sultan would no longer suffer "from the state of ignorance and delusion in which he had been kept by his last Favourite, to tolerate the continuance of a system so fatal to the interests of his Empire."[53]

Without a central military to depend on, loyalists to the Ottoman state were vulnerable, and they seemed well aware of their vulnerability. There were no institutionalized alternative groups at the imperial level, should they be needed, to replace the phanariots and janissaries as diplomatic or military corps with significant capacity, and this was to become a chronic problem during and after the 1820s.[54] As the phanariot house, then the janissary house, came apart, Ottoman leaders employed an ad hoc strategy whereby they attempted to punish the guilty while continuing to use old actors, in particular members of the old phanariot house, for the reconstruction of diplomacy and administration.

The conflicts between thousands of janissaries and forces loyal to sultan Mahmud devolved into another civil conflict in the 1820s, which was "resolved" with street battles in the capital and finally the massacre of thousands of janissaries in June 1826. Even the following cursory consideration of the premeditated, discrete conflict between loyalists to the central state and rebellious janissaries provides a stark contrast to the improvised, drawn out conflict between the same central state and Greek rebels that began in 1821 and continued throughout the decade.

Sultan Mahmud II had apparently prepared for his plan to disband the janissaries from the time of the execution of Halet Efendi in November 1822 through the next four years.[55] He carefully made allies in key centers of power. He began replacing high- and midlevel officials who had supported janissary rebellions in the past, such as those associated with Halet Efendi. He cultivated the allegiance of key sections of the corps itself, such as the artillerymen and bombardiers, "whose loyalty could not be relied upon and who usually acted as accomplices of the Janissaries." Through key appointments and discussion of the issue he won the support of the "critically important *ulema* body, also frequently connected with Janissary risings in the past."[56] And, partly because of the support of the *ulema*, Mahmud hoped that the people of İstanbul would assist the government in breaking the power of the janissaries once conflict broke out.

In 1821 members of phanariot networks had conspired to rise up against the Ottoman state. For the following four to five years the core members of that state were conspiring against (and in fear of) the only nominal imperial military force for the empire in the hopes of reclaiming a monopoly of force that would allow the survival of the Ottoman state. After arranging final alliances in the bureaucracy, military, and Muslim religious establishment, Sultan Mahmud launched an *eşkinci* reform at the end of May 1826 to establish a new, scaled-down, and streamlined military force and, along with that, had the *şeyh-ül-İslam* issue a *fetva* to confirm that the reform was "in accord with Islamic doctrine . . . and that its adoption was a sacred duty for all Muslims in the Empire."[57]

Mobilization of an Islamic establishment—from elite *ulema* down to impoverished theological students—seems to have been central to Mahmud's plan. The *fetva* confirming the *eşkinci* reform was not just a rubber stamp; rather, it was the product of a several-year process of alliance making between Mahmud II and key *ulema* figures. Mahmud had pursued a policy of "rigorous promotion" among the *ulema*, similar to what he had practiced with respect to the Janissary Corps. The aim of this policy was to minimize lateral alliances within the *ulema* and previously the Janissary Corps and to build vertical allegiances to himself among the leadership of those groups. In addition, the *ulema* elites were, according to Uriel Heyd, the "only aristocracy" of the empire and as such had vested interests in preserving the power of the central state, not to mention the power of their relatives and protégés serving as functionaries in the highest secular offices of state.[58]

Mahmud also created incentives for the popular strata of *ulema*—students and teachers of theology—to align with the central state against the janissaries. In his proposed *eşkinci* reform, he had created posts for military imams to be included in each reformed regiment. Thus, the promise of employment likely mitigated the resentment felt by struggling *ulema* of humble origins toward their elite *ulema* counterparts and made them more willing to ally with those elites and the central state against the janissaries.[59] The mobilization of the symbols, personnel, and authority of the Islamic establishment behind the sultan-caliph was hardly a foregone conclusion and, like the larger imperial project in the 1820s, was part of a struggle to establish and maintain strategic alliances and satisfy social groups with divergent and pragmatic interests, such as the elite and popular strata of the *ulema*.

As preparation for the release of the new military reform, Grand Vezir Mehmed Selim Paşa gave a speech to an assembly of over sixty officials from bureaucratic, military, and religious establishments. He explained, "This infidel and sad state of affairs was directly attributable to the insubordination of the Muslim soldiers *who could not even break the feeble rod of the miserable Greek rebels.*" He continued to describe the problems in the Janissary Corps, namely, that "gradually, miserable renegades had infiltrated their ranks. Their pay rolls had become overburdened with names, but among them there remained hardly any true soldiers. *Even Greeks and enemy spies had entered the corps to corrupt it and officers no longer knew how many men would follow them into action.*"[60]

The need for reform was explained not as part of any "Westernization" project but rather as a return to the precepts of Islam. This explanation could have been motivated by a need to attract the support of *ulema,* by a need for *ulema* to convince themselves that their support was more than pragmatic and was aimed at redemption, by a desire on Mahmud's part not to repeat the mistakes of the 1807 reforms of Selim III, which had provoked mass fury, or by any combination of these. The forty-seven points of the reform, under the veneer of a return to the precepts of Islam, were focused overwhelmingly on fiscal matters and the chain of command—timing and organization of pay disbursements, rules for promotions, and division of labor, for instance.[61] The ostensible goal of the reform was to designate approximately one-third of the existing janissaries to be disciplined and trained for an actual fighting force for the imperial state. The dedication of those present at the assembly was sealed with their oath to a *fetva* that was read by the müfti.

The reform and *fetva* were agreed to by over two hundred other janissary officers who remained outside the original assembly, and the next day soldiers for the new reform began showing up at the janissary *ağa's* residence.[62] Two of the janissary officers who had sworn to uphold the reform met on their own and agreed to try to undermine it. They circulated and "sowed doubts in the minds of the Janissaries by asking them surreptitiously and in coffee houses and other places if the new reform was not like the *Nizam-ı Cedid* and similar to infidel military practices."[63]

The first drill of the new *eşkinci* troops occurred in Et Meydanı (Meat Square), the traditional base for janissaries in İstanbul, on Monday, June 12, 1826.[64] Davud Ağa, newly arrived from Mehmet Ali's Egypt,[65] was slated to lead the first drills, for which 5,000 troops (out of a projected 7,650) were registered. The drills were carried out uneventfully, but two days later an uprising began in İstanbul, which precipitated the massacre and abolition of the Janissary Corps.

The final showdown between loyalist troops and rebel janissaries in İstanbul was different in several ways from the upheaval there five years earlier over the Greek insurrections. The sultan and his inner circle of advisers had prepared for a rebellion against their reform, whereas in the case of uprisings in Moldavia they had been caught by surprise. The janissary conflict was more concentrated, both geographically in particular neighborhoods of the city and in time, lasting only three days; in the Greek case, rebellion had occurred in provinces remote from the capital, and yet reprisals could and did happen in any neighborhood, seemingly at any time. In the janissary case, religion and religious authority had to be deployed much more cautiously, for the enemy of the state was not Rum infidels, as had been the case five years earlier, but fellow Muslims and those officially charged since the early days of the Ottoman state with defending the sultanate and caliphate. The deployment of religious authority and the call to loyalty to the sultan would be decisive in gaining the support of the populace of İstanbul against the janissaries and winning them over to the central state.

Mahmud's plan to break down the janissary house in İstanbul had, after much bloodshed, "succeeded" in 1826.[66] But those who were enlisted in the new *eşkinci* corps were in large part veterans of the Janissary Corps, under a different name and formation and with different insignia. As forceful and violent as the leaders of the central state could be, they were forced by dint of circumstances to build a new army out of many of the same men that had made up the old army. According to a contemporary report, "the leaven of the old janissaries remained among the bulk of the [new] troops, and counteracted all [Halil Rıfat's] plans of discipline."[67] In one instance, a "new" recruit showed up for duty and began bragging about how many former units of which he had been in the paybooks.[68] In the same way, when the phanariot house came unraveled in 1821, individual phanariots—such as Stephanos Vogorides—would still be called upon as translators, negotiators, and unofficial functionaries for the imperial state.

Repercussions of destroying the Janissary Corps went far beyond the military life of the empire. As a result of a combination of factors, including the breakdown of the janissary and phanariot houses and the removal of the Ottoman state monopoly of Moldavian-Wallachian grain, specified in the Treaty of Edirne in 1829,[69] a serious crisis emerged for grain provisioning to the Ottoman capital. In 1829, the situation became so desperate that a *ferman* was issued ordering residents of İstanbul to go to the countryside and collect their own grains.[70] The social and political connections necessary to the grain provisioning system, which had been held in place by the phanariot and janissary houses, had broken down. The problems resulting from this change were only compounded by the formal removal of trade restrictions that channeled Moldavian-Wallachian grains to the Ottoman capital.

Within İstanbul, janissaries had performed a range of peacetime municipal and civil duties, such as fighting the frequent fires in the city. After the corps was abolished, the janissary firemen were dismissed, and the Armenian patriarch was called upon to provide ten thousand Armenians from Anatolia to serve as the new firefighting force for the capital city.[71] Two thousand Armenians reported for work within four days and became the new firemen of İstanbul.[72] Just as the phanariot *voyvoda*s had been replaced by Romanian boyars, so janissary firemen were replaced en masse with Armenian subjects.

Even the butchers' profession was affected by the janissary abolition. The butchers' guild, which had been associated with the Janissary Corps, was in effect disbanded, its members sent to enroll as the new military troops. From that point on, "only [Rum] and others not liable for military service were to act as butchers."[73] The corporatist policy of removing entire groups from certain functions and replacing them with other ethnically and religiously defined groups was expedient in the short term for mobilizing manpower. This seems to have been the policy of choice to fill the power vacuum in both the phanariot and janissary cases.

The phanariot house was an—almost—inextricable part and product of Ottoman imperial governance by the turn of the nineteenth century. The Greek Revolution, in the course of which the phanariot house was demolished, was one of several civil conflicts of the 1820s and contributed to the final demise of the Janissary Corps five years later, almost undoing the central state in toto. In these conflicts, the leaders of the central state attempted to negotiate the discontent of groups that had accumulated official and unofficial political power over the previous several decades, as the phanariots and janissaries had. When rebellions broke out and led into civil war, first between Greek partisans and loyalists to the central state, then between janissaries/Bektaşis and defenders of the state and caliphate, the state adopted an ad hoc policy to punish those it perceived as the guilty and their associates. In so doing, the state created a power vacuum in the many areas of politics in which the phanariots and janissaries were involved. These areas included diplomacy (including interpreters and translators), imperial military capacity, economy (grain trade, financing), provincial administration (Moldavia, Wallachia, the Aegean Islands), and religious authority (patriarchate, lower clergy, Bektaşism in the case of the janissaries).

From the Ottoman imperial perspective, both conflicts were part of the central state's struggle, first, to sever itself from groups that had de facto become part of it and threatened to dominate it and, second, to redefine itself and establish a continuity of basic state operations. In both cases, religion—religious symbols, Muslim religious authority, and the identification of the imperial state with an orthodox Islam—was called upon by Sultan Mahmud to bolster his support and mobilize Muslim subject masses in the capital city. Religion was the default structure and language of authority to which Mahmud, as mere sultan, could resort and could therefore stress his role as caliph in addition to sultan.[74] This, combined with the many layers of pragmatic reasons that the elite and popular strata of *ulema* came to support his bid against the janissaries, played perhaps a decisive role in determining the outcome of the civil conflicts of the 1820s.

The initial reactions of the central state to rebellion and to the power vacuum that ensued reveal much about the logic of Ottoman politics and government in the midst of crisis. But the conflicts and policies of the 1820s initiated more prolonged processes of change in political and social relationships. The phanariot investiture ceremony, which had presented a dilemma for the Ottoman state in 1821, survived the outbreak of insurrections in 1822 but was terminated along with the janissaries in 1826. After that date, the two key groups in the phanariot ceremony were officially absent. On a deeper level, the power relations reflected in that ceremony were undergoing a fundamental transformation so as to make the ceremony obsolete.

# Threads

*Let me say something else which might seem paradoxical to those who have had
a different upbringing and have different convictions from us local Christians.*
STEPHANOS VOGORIDES' APOLOGIA

When conflicts broke out in 1821, the position of *voyvoda* must have finally seemed
to Vogorides to be within reach. He was appointed as interim *kaymakam* when his
patron-employer Skarlato Kallimaki fled abruptly to Pisa on the eve of hostilities.[1]
When Greek-hetairist rebellions began in earnest in 1821, the networks around him,
through which he had risen and made his career, began to collapse before his eyes.
This was a moment that Vogorides himself clearly saw as a turning point in his life.
Decades later he described a moment in the course of Greek-hetairist rebellions in
Moldavia when he was faced with a profound dilemma, threatened with attacks by
janissaries in Jassy, Russian armies he thought to be heading for his principality,
and Greek-hetairist rebels he had already repudiated. His choice, as he saw it, was
whether to flee to Russia or to remain in the service of the Ottoman state. Should
he have abandoned the Ottoman state and lived a comfortable life in Russia, or
should he have stayed and risked his life to save the empire? His answer, in the apologia he wrote thirty years later, in 1852, reveals the motivation he derived, perhaps
in retrospect, to remain in the service of the Ottoman state and in effect to resus-
citate phanariot power after the 1820s:

> The moment of decision came one night, when the janissary commanders *[ustas]*
> were assembled to demand money from [me] so as not to report [me] to the Ottoman
> central authorities *for selling their grains to Russia.* Just then, a trusted Greek notable
> arrived, whispering [in my ear] the news that he had brought from Russian army com-
> manders in neighboring Bessarabia, of the following developments; Baron Stroganoff,
> the Russian ambassador, had suddenly left Constantinople, Russian troops were as-
> sembled in St. Petersburg awaiting orders to cross the Pruth River and drive back the
> janissaries and other Ottoman troops in Moldavia, and in such event [I myself], as
> the *kaymakam,* would be in great danger. "The hetairist Greeks that I threw out, ac-

companied by the Cossacks on the road, will cut me up into pieces, and that if I leave with the janissaries they will murder even their own vezirs/commanders in the retreat." As if that were not enough, "the all-powerful Christian-killer in Constantinople, Halet Efendi, was looking for an opportunity to slit my throat." If I were to leave immediately for Russia, they would honor me with the title *général en chef,* of equal status to my title of *kaymakam* bestowed by the sultan in Moldowallachia, and the imperial court [in Russia] will reward and compensate me with land and money.

I, "in a state of great agitation," sent the *ustas* away on a pretext and with great warmth *dans un moment si suprême* "turned to the all-powerful and all-merciful God" and said inside myself that, "if divine Providence had deigned to make me born Russian, then I should have been born in Russia. Since I was created in Turkey [Tourkia], I will owe a great explanation to God if, because of my flight to Russia, I gave a blessed cause for Halet Efendi to murder many Christians, and would justify his anti-Christian and murderous policy, allowing him to allege that, since Stefanaki became a traitor *[haines/hain],* the Sublime Porte should not trust any Christian subject."[2]

Prince Nicholas Soutso, son of Wallachian *voyvoda* Michael Soutso, fled to Transylvania with his family in February 1821, accompanied by his deceased father's corps of thirty Albanian bodyguards.[3] Theodore Negri, a fellow *kaymakam* of Vogorides' in Moldavia, feigned acceptance of his appointment to the Ottoman Embassy in Paris but fled to take part in the Greek Revolution while en route to France. Vogorides, in contrast, stayed on in the imperial service, ostensibly to protect the honor, loyalty, and life of all Christian subjects to their Ottoman critics. He likely also recognized that the flight of so many "spoiled" phanariots from their posts in İstanbul and the principalities would create new opportunities for his advancement, even if in a dangerous and uncertain future.

In the summer of 1822, Vogorides was removed from his position as *kaymakam* in Moldavia, as was his Wallachian counterpart, Constantine Negri. They were arrested and brought, through Silistre, to İstanbul. An uncataloged Ottoman document from the İstanbul file of the Cyril and Methodius National Library's Oriental Collections, in Bulgaria, has Vogorides held in chains in Silistre by a bailiff *(çavuş)* who was awaiting orders of where to deliver him.[4] There were several possible reasons for his removal. A later biographer points to Halet Efendi's accusations of "extortion and oppression" against Vogorides as the reason for his removal, adding that "it was only thanks for the fall of this favorite [Halet] that his head was saved."[5] Vogorides himself, judging from his apologia, seems to agree with this point when he noted that Halet Efendi was looking to slit his throat.[6] Indigenous boyars from Moldavia and Wallachia who were in hiding in Kronstadt (today Braşov), across the border with Transylvania, were negotiating with the Ottoman central government, against Vogorides, to have two of their own installed as *voyvoda*s, thereby wresting those positions from Greek-identified, İstanbul phanariots.[7] And Vogorides' rapaciousness while *kaymakam* had earned him a reputation, even with the British ambassador in İstanbul, who noted in an 1821 dispatch that the Ottoman authorities would surely remove him from his post when the troubles died down.[8] For whatever combination of reasons, Vogorides was taken to İstanbul and exiled to Anatolia for about a year—to Torbalı and İzmit according to some reports, and to Kütahya according to others.[9]

In August of the same year, the first "indigenous" *voyvodas*—Gregorios Ghika for Wallachia and Ion Alexander Sturdza for Moldavia—were appointed from İstanbul.[10] This marked a victory for the native boyars in their attempts to usurp the offices of *voyvoda* and formally dissociate from Greek-identified phanariots.[11] Their victory would be reaffirmed in 1829–30, when the Treaty of Edirne limited eligibility for the offices of *voyvoda* to native-born Moldavians and Wallachians. The formal leadership of the principalities passed out of Greek-identified phanariot hands, but, as will be discussed below, phanariot holdovers would find other ways to maintain a hold on politics in those provinces in the 1830s and 1840s.

A year into the insurgencies, Vogorides had lost the chance to take over directly from his phanariot superiors in Moldavia when native *voyvodas* were appointed there. He had also lost the chance to take up the mantle of the imperial dragoman when Stavraki Aristarchi was executed and the Muslim Yahya Efendi was installed. The patriarchate was surely in disarray at that time—Patriarch Gregorios's replacement, Eugenios, had died just as Vogorides was being brought to İstanbul from Jassy in July—and Vogorides was thus not in a position to recoup power through the Church either. We do not know if he had contact with fellow phanariots in Anatolian exile or if they had contact with Ottoman officials, but it seems that by this moment, the personal networks and political functions of phanariots were profoundly disrupted.

4

# Phanariot Remodeling and
# the Struggle for Continuity

In the immediate wake of violence in the 1820s, phanariot households and families found themselves scattered across long distances and made choices to maxi-
mize their chances of survival. Many members of phanariot *hanedan*s who survived
the immediate İstanbul aftermath of Greek insurgencies in Moldavia were exiled
within Ottoman domains. The *voyvoda* Kallimaki was exiled to Bolu, in northern
Anatolia, where he was subsequently murdered by the governor there.[1] Stavraki
Aristarchi, who has gone down in history as the last phanariot dragoman, was soon
removed from office and exiled with his family to Bolu as well, where he was killed,
ostensibly by "robbers," in 1822 as he was returning from hot springs with his teenage
son Nicholas.[2] Other lesser boyars were exiled with their families to Anatolian towns
such as Zile, Tosya, Bursa, and Kangiri.[3]

Many phanariots escaped abroad. The family of Dragoman Kostaki Muruzi fled
to Odessa and then returned to Moldavia in 1829 with the Treaty of Edirne. Iakovos
Argyropoulo, a.k.a. Yakovaki (who had been imperial dragoman from 1812 to 1815
but was excluded from eligibility for phanariot high offices in the Dynasty of Four
Regulation of 1819), was first exiled to Çorum and then to Ankara until 1825 and
was moved to Bursa in 1829. Upon returning to İstanbul, he was asked to travel to
St. Petersburg with phanariot Stephanos Vogorides to represent the Ottoman Empire in preparatory negotiations for the Treaty of Edirne. Argyropoulo pretended
to accept the proposal but instead escaped to the island of Aegina, then to Athens,
where he lived until 1850.[4]

A significant faction of phanariots of course took part in the Greek Revolution,
and this is the role for which they are most remembered. They settled in the new
Greek capital of Athens and enjoyed a fraught relationship with the coalition of so-

cial groups vying for power in the new Greek state.[5] Alexander Mavrocordato and Kostaki Karaca (son of the former Wallachian *voyvoda*), for instance, had been in Pisa when the Greek rebellions began.[6] They arrived at the site of rebellions in 1821 and immediately began trying to lead the provisional and local governments. They were joined by fellow phanariot Theodore Negri, who had in 1821 just been appointed Ottoman chargé d'affaires to France but, while on the way to his post, defected and joined the Greek insurgency. Mihalvoda (Michael) Soutso (1778–1864), who had been imperial dragoman (1815–18) and was serving as *voyvoda* of Wallachia when Hypsilantis declared uprisings in Moldavia in 1821, joined the revolution (having been a member of the Society of Friends) and was subsequently appointed as head of the Greek legation to Paris, then to St. Petersburg, Stockholm, and Copenhagen.[7]

Once the crisis subsided, phanariots availed themselves of a number of strategies to recoup some of their power within and beyond Ottoman domains. The range of outcomes is clear, even from the six families (the four who were included and the two who were excluded) mentioned in the 1819 Dynasty of Four Regulation. Michael Soutso had been *voyvoda* of Moldavia since 1819. He was inducted into the Society of Friends in late November 1820 (only two months before insurrection started in his principality). After the insurrection failed, he fled with his family to Bessarabia after being excommunicated by Patriarch Grigorios V because of his role in the revolution, then went through Austria to neutral Switzerland. After the establishment of Greece in 1828, the Greek president John Capodistrias appointed Soutso as representative of Greece in Paris. Other branches of the family, also mentioned in the 1819 Dynasty of Four Regulation, remained in Moldavia as Francophiles, like much of the Moldavian and Wallachian local aristocracy. Family members born during and after the 1820s were born in Athens, Odessa, and Paris.

Scarlatos and Ioannis Kallimaki did not survive the first year of the Greek insurrections; they were both exiled to Anatolia and eventually strangled there. The marriages of Scarlatos Kallimaki's daughters, however, indicate a continuity in phanariot alliances: one daughter, Sevasti, married Michael Soutso; another, Smaragda, married Voyvoda Alexander Hançerli; and a third, Maria, married Gregorios Stourza, of a Moldavian boyar family.[8] Another member of the Kallimaki family settled permanently in Paris and served in the Ottoman Embassy there during the mid-nineteenth century. Kostaki (Constantine) Muruzi, the head of the fourth family named in the 1819 Regulation, was killed while serving as grand dragoman in the early days of the Greek insurrections, as mentioned above. His family seems to have fled to Odessa; one son, also named Constantine, studied in France and served in the French navy before settling in Greece in the 1840s; another son, Panagiotis, became a Greek officer in the Russian army, dying in Vienna in 1859 with the rank of general.[9]

The two families who were excluded from eligibility for the top phanariot offices in 1819, Argyropoulo and Hançerli, add to the variety of national and career trajectories. Iakovos Argyropoulo, as mentioned above, was out of office when the revolution erupted and was exiled to Anatolia, where he remained until he fled to Greece. His son Manuel arrived in Greece with his father and was later appointed dragoman of the Greek Embassy in İstanbul, where he served from 1836 until 1849. He was ultimately appointed dragoman of the Russian Embassy in İstanbul and served there until 1863. His younger brother Pericles became a constitutional law professor and ultimately an MP and foreign minister of Greece in the 1850s, just as his brother was serving the Russian Empire in İstanbul. The Hançerli family had long been suspected of Russian sympathies. These suspicions were perhaps not unfounded, because Alexander Hançerli (1759–1854) took refuge in Russia when insurrections began in Moldavia. While in Moscow, he compiled a French-Arabic-Persian-Turkish dictionary and died at the age of ninety-six. The younger generation, exemplified by Grigorios, Dimitrios, and Michael, all of whom were born around the time of the Greek Revolution, were schooled or settled in German states or both, demonstrating yet another possible trajectory.

And then there were families, often of second-tier phanariot status in the period before 1821, who reconstituted a phanariot house in Ottoman territory, albeit on a smaller scale than before and, significantly, without using the term *hanedan*. Stephanos Vogorides and Nicholas Aristarchi are two such examples—the former allied with Britain and the latter with Russia. Using a logic similar to that prior to 1821, both built networks of clientage that connected the Ottoman central state, the emergent Foreign Ministry, the Orthodox Church, Moldavian and Wallachian administrations, and foreign states. New families also emerged, such as the Karatheodori and Musuru families, to be known as "neophanariots."

The dispersal of phanariots took place against the backdrop of the fundamental crises for Ottoman governance and self-definition. The top priority from the perspective of the leaders of the Ottoman imperial state as the decade wore on was the survival of the sultanate along with the continuity of basic operations of governance. This was achieved in the short term by destroying the power of those groups that had grown into multiple areas of governance, but also by reconstituting fragments of administration, court politics, and the military, all the while that the points of engagement between the Ottoman state and international politics were in flux. All of this went on without a large blueprint, proving to be a kind of ad hoc institutionalization.

Before a phanariot house could be reconstructed within Ottoman domains— and before Stephanos Vogorides could step into a meaningful role at the center of Ottoman power—the struggle for basic continuity of governance had to be won. In the context of this struggle, at least three areas of governance were severed from one another in the 1820s: the administrative apparatus at the Ottoman court and the Sublime Porte for translation; the process of Ottoman military policy making at the court; and the language and practices of day-to-day diplomacy in İstanbul in the 1820s. The processes and state projects underway in these three areas illustrate the deeper structural dilemmas that emerged out of several interrelated circumstances: the breakdown of the phanariot house, the disruption in Ottoman diplomacy and foreign relations, and the protracted military conflict with Greek rebels, a conflict inextricably related to both janissary abolishment and the rise of Mehmet Ali as a contender for the Ottoman sultanate.

## OTTOMAN FOREIGN RELATIONS IN THE 1820S

The statement framing the events of this chapter, namely, that Ottoman foreign relations were in flux in the 1820s, demands qualification. In the most immediate sense, many points of contact between the Ottoman and European states were disrupted because of the breakdown in phanariot networks in 1821–22. The personnel at the nodes of phanariot mediating networks—the phanariot imperial dragoman, the dragoman of the fleet, and the two *voyvodas*, not to mention the borderland personnel in the principalities and the merchants living and trading abroad—were formally eliminated from the affairs of Ottoman governance. The Ottoman foreign diplomatic corps, which had been established in the 1790s (and included phanariots as well as nonphanariots), was paralyzed, there were no new diplomatic appointments in the 1820s, and many Ottoman representatives abroad abandoned their posts or returned to an unofficial status.[10]

The domestic preoccupations of Ottoman governance, during the imperial state's encounter with violent discontent from Greek-aligned rebels in the provinces and from the janissaries as its own nominal military in the capital, made sustained attention to foreign relations difficult in the 1820s. Compare this with the Napoleonic period, when the Ottoman central state, although not without major domestic problems, was obliquely involved in Franco-Russian conflicts; particular phanariot families as well as Ottoman officials had cultivated relationships with Napoleon or the Russian tsars or both. In the 1820s, while the imperial governing apparatus was consumed with battling enemies within the empire, the Ottoman Empire had dropped out of this level of involvement in the European alliance system.[11]

Formal diplomatic ties were broken between the Ottoman Empire and France, Britain, and Russia at several points in the 1820s as a result of the conflict with Greek-hetairist rebels. Ottoman-British relations, for instance, reached a low point in October 1824, when Ambassador Lord Strangford left İstanbul after demanding a recall of Ottoman troops from the Danubian Principalities, being told in response that Britain should "disavow the many acts of her subjects in support of the Greeks" and protesting offenses of the dey of Algiers on the British consul there. Ottoman-French relations were also interrupted, from December 1827 until 1829 because of "the Sultan's ire at the result of the Battle of Navarino."[12] Finally, from 1821 until the autumn of 1823, Russo-Ottoman relations were also severed.[13]

From a European perspective, neither was there a consistent or unified policy pursued by France, Britain, or Russia regarding the Greek rebellions, or the Janissary Corps for that matter, for much of the decade.[14] Policy shifts that came with the change of the Russian tsar from Alexander to Nicholas (in 1825), shifts of British foreign policy leaders such as in 1827,[15] hatred between Canning and Metternich, and French waffling between Russia and England all worked to make a united European stance toward the Ottoman Empire and the Greek Question a dream more than a reality until the end of the decade. In that sense, the Ottoman state did not engage (even when invited) in systematic or regular negotiations with the concert of European states, who maintained relations among themselves—however tense at times—but not unanimity about Ottoman-Greek conflicts.

The dynamics of European "balance of power" politics, meanwhile, continued uninterrupted in the 1820s, without the participation of the Ottoman Empire. Paul Schroeder classifies the years between 1823 and 1829 as the "most tranquil of the [European] post-war era," with the "one major crisis in international politics" being the Greek and the Eastern Question.[16] Ultimately, negotiations were conducted between European states regarding the Greek Question from 1826 until 1832 without Ottoman involvement and outside Ottoman territory. And it was because of the continuity in European politics that the years of disruption in Ottoman foreign policy were significant for that empire. Namely, the personnel and the structures of policy making in the Ottoman Empire were changing during these years, as were the dynamics of European politics on their own plane. Thus, when the two worlds—the one of Ottoman politics and the one of intra-European contests for power—met again in İstanbul in 1832, a new fusing began to occur between the two, and a new political culture emerged. In order to understand that encounter, we must consider some of the changes undergone by the Ottoman state when its points of engagement with foreign politics and states were in flux.

While foreign relations existed in the Ottoman 1820s, they were not integrated into the practices and strategies of Ottoman governance, as they would become from 1832 onward. This had much to do with the intertwined crises over Greek secession, janissary abolishment, and, as we shall see, the Mehmet Ali challenge from Egypt. Three areas of governance demonstrate this situation: one that had been part of the phanariot mediating networks of foreign relations but was severed in the 1820s—the Translation Office of the Porte; one that was the preoccupation of governance—domestic military policy making—which was inextricable from the janissary drama but often separate from concerns of foreign relations; and a third—day-to-day diplomatic contacts—an area in which activities continued in the 1820s but were disjointed from the central structures and practices of Ottoman imperial governance. An examination of these three sectors of governance does more than contextualize the institutional changes that took place in the wake of phanariot breakdown. It also begins to explain the reconfigurations that would take place between the military and diplomatic poles of power, a reconfiguration that would in turn facilitate a reconstruction, though a partial one, of a phanariot house.

### TRANSLATION OFFICE

The collapse of the phanariot house brought up several institutional dilemmas for the Ottoman central state. The dilemma of whom to install as the new *voyvodas* in the Danubian Principalities, for one, reflected the larger dilemma for the imperial court of how to ensure continuity of rule in these provinces without sanctioning the power of those perceived as part of the conspiracy against the state. In September 1821, different factions were within the court, one of which advocated the complete removal of Christians from ruling positions in the principalities and the placing of those provinces under the administration of Muslim Ottoman officials.[17] This faction was suppressed, reportedly out of a fear of Russian invasion should the Treaty of Küçük Kaynarca be violated.[18] As a provisional solution, phanariot *kaymakams* (interim governors) were appointed in the principalities until a permanent settlement could be found. In the fall of 1821 the central state found itself between Russian and janissary threats in trying to decide between pulling out Ottoman troops and restoring the *voyvodas* or insisting on Russia's turning over of the many phanariot fugitives.[19] While some thought it in the best interest of the state to back down from the conflict and restore the status quo in the principalities, fear of janissary fury was reported as the major reason for the state's hesitation.[20] Finally, two "local" boyars, Ion Sturdza in Moldavia and Gregory Ghika in Wallachia, who were Greek-speaking and had very much been part of the phanariot complex, were appointed in June 1822, invested on the first of August, and served in those posts until the Russian occupation of the principalities in 1828–29.[21]

After the execution of Patriarch Gregorios, the position of patriarch was yet another that had to be filled early on in the conflicts. The first decision had been to appoint Eugenios, who was said to have been of Bulgarian descent, to replace Gregorios in 1821. When Eugenios died the following year of an ailment, Anthimos III of Chalcedon (Kadıköy) was appointed as his successor.[22] Anthimos was the target of intrigues within the upper clergy in the midst of this upheaval. In February 1823, for instance, janissary commanders who were hired by a Greek priest attacked Patriarch Anthimos.[23] Later that year, "cabals and intrigues" of Greek bishops were aimed at the dismissal of Patriarch Anthimos, but did not sway the Ottoman or British states from their support for him, for he had favored British demands on religious issues in the British-occupied Ionian Islands.[24]

The void left by phanariots at the Ottoman court, however, was particularly difficult for the sultan and his advisers to ignore in 1821–22, first and foremost because the dragoman had been a member of the court and, therefore, someone whose physical absence was palpable to the sultan. The sense of urgency to fill the offices of the Danubian *voyvoda*s, by contrast, was both less intense because of the geographic remoteness of those offices, and more complicated, given the Russian claims to a role in appointing *voyvoda*s. The official function of the dragoman—to translate documents and interpret at official visits—had been necessary, however, for Ottoman communication with European states and had not involved the input of Russia. Add to this the unofficial functions of serving as informant on goings-on at the patriarchate or in the principalities, and the dragoman vacancy must have been all the more debilitating for the central state, especially in a time of civil strife involving Orthodox Christian subjects.

In correspondence between Sultan Mahmud and the grand vezir, discussions about replacing the imperial dragoman went on *after* they had executed Dragoman Kostaki Muruzi. They commented that the need for a replacement was urgent, because *there was no one to read the incoming documents* from foreign states.[25] Although the sultan wrote, "From now on not a single Rum can be trusted," the memo from the grand vezir went on to discuss the possible candidates to replace Muruzi—and most were members of the phanariot Dynasty of Four (Hanedan-ı Erba'a).[26]

Moving outside phanariot circles brought to the fore further problems as the struggle to restaff the Translation Office continued. These problems principally related to a lack of Muslim personnel with the appropriate social station and the appropriate training and language skills or the willingness to use them. Reportedly few Muslims had knowledge of European languages. The court historian Şanizade (Ataullah Mehmet) did, but because he was a scholar and member of the *ulema*, the position of dragoman was thought to be demeaning for him.[27] In the words of Ottoman chronicler Cevdet Paşa, who wrote decades later, "After Kostaki's [Muruzi's] execution, it was determined that a dragoman who was not a phanariot be installed in his place, but one could not be found."[28] The lack of qualified and willing Muslim personnel, one of the most obvious problems Mahmud faced in trying to restaff the office, only makes more vivid the image of the central state's dependence on phanariots before 1821.

Sultan Mahmud dealt with the dearth of qualified and socially appropriate Muslim personnel by replacing, days after the outbreak of Greek rebellions in Moldavia in 1821, then imperial dragoman Kostaki Muruzi with two individuals: an unaligned phanariot, Stavraki Aristarchi, and the Muslim convert Yahya Efendi, who was an aged professor of military engineering.[29] The hope was that the unaligned phanariot Aristarchi could check the work of Yahya Efendi and train him, thereby allowing for continuity in the operations of the office while transitioning the court away from a dependence on potentially traitorous phanariot dragomans. Yahya, who was already quite aged, was joined by his son Ruh-üd-din, who was to replace his father after learning the craft from him. British ambassador Lord Strangford described his visit to the court during Stavraki Aristarchi's tenure as follows:

> The speech of the Ambassador, expressing a desire on the part of his Britannic Majesty to continue the ties of amity and good will between the two powers, was translated to the Sultan by his trembling dragoman; and after a short pause he replied, in a low, but firm, haughty tone, addressing himself apparently to the Vezir, who repeated the speech very badly and hesitatingly to the dragoman, who stammered it out in French to the Ambassador. This unfortunate dragoman's name was Stavrakoglou [sic], not a Greek of the Fanal [sic] but a native of Caramania.[30] He was a tall, cadaverous-looking person, and could not conceal the extraordinary impression of terror under which he laboured. He stood next to me, and trembled so exceedingly as quite to shake me as well as himself, and his nerves were so agitated that he could scarcely see to read the paper he held, which was blotted with large drops of perspiration dropping from his forehead, and more than once nearly fell from his hand. The man had some reason: his predecessor had just been executed, and he had no hope he should escape the same fate.[31]

After one year of sharing the office of dragoman, Aristarchi was indeed dismissed and exiled, and Yahya Efendi was appointed dragoman as well as teacher for a newly formed guildlike school for translation in the court.[32]

With the exile and death of Stavraki Aristarchi, the office of the imperial dragoman passed permanently out of the hands of phanariot-associated Orthodox Christians. From Mahmud's point of view, this was seen as punishment for the disloyalty of the phanariots.[33] Also from the sultan's perspective, installing Yahya Efendi and his sons as replacements was a safe decision, for they had no apparent political leanings and could therefore be depended on as translators and interpreters.[34] An Ottoman account of the transition ran as follows:

> For fifteen or twenty days Bulgarzade Yahya Efendi, of Rum descent and one of the teachers at the School of Engineering, was made to read some documents in Greek [Rumi] and European languages [Frengi] at the Sublime Porte. From this point on he would collate the proceedings of meetings, and explain the subtleties and fine points to the heads of the administration. In addition he was appointed to teach some capable and willing individuals the foreign languages used between states and nations [düvel ve millel]. He was to be given a monthly salary of 500 guruş from an appropriate source. . . . The secret Rum conspiracy was now seen by [the heads of the administration] with their own eyes and a thousand conspiracies of Rum Dragomans who spoke falsely and were blameworthy in many hundreds of years were observed. As a result, from then on, it was intended that the Rum be severed [meczum] from appointment to the post of Dragoman, and that Dragomans should thenceforth be chosen from among the Muslims.[35]

Yahya and his son were outsiders to the social and political networks through which the work of translation and post of dragoman had been integrated into the larger phanariot world of diplomacy and provincial administration. This meant that Yahya Efendi and Ruh-üd-Din, as a teacher and a student at the military engineering school at Kağıthane in İstanbul,[36] lacked the personal and political connections in the same areas of government that their phanariot predecessors had developed over the years, principally because they were "marginal men," as Carter Findley calls them;[37] in the absence of a pool of skilled and socially appropriate Muslim translation personnel, they happened to have independently acquired knowledge of the appropriate languages to serve as translators. Neither were they schooled together with future colleagues, as phanariots had been in the academies, nor were they part of a larger administrative or imperial project before their employment in the 1820s.[38] Thus, unlike the phanariots, they did not have the benefit of a network of acquaintances, informants, and relatives working in politically and commercially strategic locations, such as the Danubian Principalities and the urban centers of central and western Europe.

As they designated individual replacements for phanariot dragomans, Sultan Mahmud and his advisers also grappled with the question of how to structure the office and the system of training for dragoman interns, now that the office was under their direct control, which it had not been before. In tandem with making individual replacements, then, Mahmud also established the new formal entity the Translation Office of the Sublime Porte (Bab-ı Ali Tercüme Odası) shortly after the outbreak of rebellions in 1821.[39] This marked a change in formal status of the dragoman; the dragoman's work of translation and interpretation would no longer belong to the realm of imperial favor and privileges, as it had under the phanariots. Instead, the Translation Office would now be considered an entity independent of its occupants and an official branch of the imperial bureaucracy.[40]

The features of the new Translation Office reflected the divide between the intent to expunge the phanariot house from Ottoman governance, on the one hand, and the limited capacity of the state to build a new house, or framework, to replace the phanariot one, on the other. Language instruction was set up as apprenticeships within the Translation Office (Tercüme odası), which was established as part of the office of the *reis efendi* at the Sublime Porte. In the past, new (phanariot) translators were hired because they had already learned the appropriate European languages, often from a relative employed as a dragoman. Now, instruction would occur under the auspices of the office of the dragoman. In a new chain of command, there would be a dragoman, dragoman *vekili*s (deputies), and *yamak*s (trainees). The financing of salaries for apprentices and teachers would, however, continue to come from the same (phanariot associated) sources as before 1821[41] The employees of the office would be Muslim, with phanariot associates providing unofficial assistance as needed.

The realities of translation work fell short of Sultan Mahmud's intentions for structural revitalization. In September and October 1824, shortly after Yahya Efendi's death, a memo from Grand Vezir Galip Paşa to the sultan in preparation for a *fer-man* declared that Yahya's replacements would be İshak Efendi and one Esrar Efendi, who had been a member of Yahya's retinue of apprentices, and that the income for their salaries would continue to be raised from the same sources as before. Galip Paşa, a long-time man of the pen and former ambassador to London during Selim III's reign, went on to explain the continued lack of qualified personnel; even though "this [was] a prestigious service of the Sublime State," still no one among the new Muslim trainees could both translate *written* documents from the French and *speak* French. Galip then established the goal of having Esrar Efendi, the new dragoman, train five to ten *mütercim,* or translators, and of having these translators come every day to the Sublime Porte and together to function "as a government office" *(kalem gibi),* writing and submitting rough drafts and final drafts and keeping the original documents and draft translations for their records rather than discarding them.[42]

While Mahmud was able to dissociate the work and personnel of translation from phanariots, he was not able to reassociate it with a larger set of people and functions in the 1820s. The establishment of the Translation Office, then, signified a decision about the formal status of the work and the position of dragoman but did little to clarify the ambiguous *functions* of the office of dragoman. Yahya, his son, and a few trainees composed the new Translation Office. State authorities had settled on a system to raise their wages that was very much a continuation of the pre-1821 wage collection system. There, specific sums of money were collected from the areas of former phanariot control: Moldavia, Wallachia, Mt. Athos, the Orthodox patriarchate, the Mora dragoman, and the Ottoman treasury, for instance. In 1824, the year of Yahya Efendi's death and three years after phanariots were removed from the top positions of dragoman and *voyvoda,* the dragomans' wages were collected from these same sources, with the exception that "since the outbreak of the Mora disorders, the monthly totals from that source [Mora dragoman] have not been raised."[43] This structural continuity in the wage collection system for dragomans after 1821 is another indication that the Translation Office had not been structurally reintegrated into a postphanariot Ottoman bureaucracy.

The uncertain functions and the obscurity of the office reflected the uncertainty of a changing imperial and international political context. One example of this is that the dragomans' daily tasks and pedagogical methods were unclear in the 1820s. Carter Findley cites a British observer's report in the following passage:

> M. Chabert called upon [Yahya Efendi] a few mornings ago, and found him surrounded by a number of the young Turks whom the Porte has lately formed into a sort of Collegiate Establishment for the purpose of instruction in the European languages. They had a prodigious pile of Frankfort Gazettes before them, and were busily engaged in translating indiscriminately, by the sultan's positive order, every Article in which the name of the Affairs of Turkey were to be found.[44]

Perhaps poring through European newspapers was merely the method that others had devised for Yahya Efendi to train recruits.[45] Perhaps it was also among the new functions of the Translation Office in a period when the Ottoman state was short on information from the outside world.[46] In either case, this scene reveals that there were changes of a broader order beyond the absence of particular phanariots in the 1820s. The international political landscape was also in flux. Indicative of this is that newspapers were a new source of information, and the Ottoman Empire was a relatively new subject of discussion in those newspapers. They provided Yahya and his pupils with information of a different nature from that which had been gathered by phanariots through their network of informants and partners stationed abroad. Newspaper information on the public realm abroad was at once unmediated (and ideologically unscreened) and more impersonal than the information available through the old phanariot networks. For Yahya and his pupils it was not possible simply to step into the Translation Office and resume the activities phanariots had been engaged in before 1821.

With the removal of the phanariot dragomans and the larger context of domestic preoccupation, the newly named Translation Office of the Sublime Porte dropped into temporary obscurity with respect to Ottoman court politics and international diplomacy. The office was restaffed with men who were deliberately chosen for their lack of political and social connections. Furthermore, the tasks of the dragomans were nebulous, because the kinds of information that needed to be conveyed between the Ottoman court and foreign states were in flux. When substantive relations were initiated between Ottoman and foreign states, the Translation Office was often circumvented altogether. The changes in the Translation Office, when taken together, marked a break with the workings of pre-1821 politics. Before 1821, phanariot dragomans had expanded their role from that of translator to those of diplomat and even autonomous political actors. Their own mechanisms for language training fell outside the purview of the central state, and they had developed their own structure of raising revenue for staff wages, a structure that was dependent on the larger phanariot enterprise. Now, in the 1820s, the task of translating was becoming ever more circumscribed as it became dissociated from the broader tasks of diplomacy and politics. Continuity was achieved in name for the work of translation but was undetermined as yet in substance.

## COURT FACTIONS, MILITARY FORTUNES

The difficulties in rebuilding the translation mechanism for the Ottoman central state resulted from the reality that the Ottoman imperial project in the 1820s was first and foremost a *military* project, not diplomatic or even administrative. The preoccupation of those involved in imperial governance in the 1820s was to secure the continuity of the sultanate, that is, of the imperial state itself, by suppressing internal rebellions and averting outside attacks. This meant that a monopoly of military force had to be reestablished; Greek rebellions were to be suppressed, and the Ottoman military forces—be they janissaries, Albanian irregulars, tribal troops, or forces under the command of Egyptian governor Mehmet Ali—were somehow to be brought back under the control of the central state, even if this allowed only a bare minimum of state operations, including contact with foreign states, in the meantime.

Several decisive turning points occurred in the trajectory of Ottoman military policy making between the breakdown of the phanariot house in 1821 and the reconnection of Ottoman politics with European international politics in 1832. The first was the removal of Halet Efendi. This was not just a transitional event that connected the demise of phanariot and janissary houses. It also set in motion a number of changes in the personnel and structures of Ottoman central leadership. The first changes occurred among Halet's political allies and protégés, who shifted their allegiances just as Halet's power began to wane and contributed to his downfall and death. Halet's absence also created a new space for other factions at the court from the end of 1822. Just as Halet's cronies were exiled at the time of his dismissal, so his former enemies were brought back from banishment and promoted. These included "Hamid Bey (who had been dismissed as Reis Efendi in the summer of 1821), 'Bekgi (chief *ulema*)', Sadik Molla ('distinguished *ulema*') [likely Sıdkızade Ahmed Reşit Efendi], Selim Bey (son of Veli and grandson of Ali Paşa of Yannina), and three surviving brothers of the Armenian Düzoğlu family."[47]

A year after Halet's death, another of his enemies, Galip Paşa, was brought back from his provincial post and named grand vezir.[48] A long-time "man of the pen" and supporter of reform, Galip Paşa was an important interim figure for Mahmud's project to eliminate the janissaries. Interestingly, before his dismissal the following year, Galip Paşa had been told by Mahmud of his plan to eliminate the janissaries and had responded that he, Galip, as a man of the pen, would never be able to realize this plan "because he could not command enough support from the soldiers and other branches of the government."[49] It seems Galip recognized the relationship between military power and success on the one hand and policy making on the other for Ottoman governance. As a man of the pen, he contributed to Mahmud's cause by negotiating and repairing relations with Mehmet Ali, "who had been displeased with Halet's disgrace," and by passing the mantle of grand vezir on to Selim Mehmet Paşa, who had been military commander of Silistre and thus commanded the requisite military authority to realize Mahmud's plan to take on the Janissary Corps.[50]

Halet's removal allowed Sultan Mahmud greater leeway to build his alliances and consolidate strength to oppose the existing Janissary Corps. Among the strategies Mahmud II employed were the promotion of individuals through the ranks of the janissaries and the *ulema* so as to break horizontal relationships in the power structure and the use of popular councils in reclaiming his state from Halet Efendi. Two months after the arrival of Halet's severed head in İstanbul, Sultan Mahmud called a popular council *(meşveret)* together.[51] This council was made up of *ulema,* janissary commanders, and leaders of guilds. The occasion for the meeting was to hasten a policy of reconciliation with Russia, which would allow the Ottoman military to focus on the internal threat of Greek-aligned rebels. In effect, Mahmud was trying to replace Halet not with a new individual favorite but with a consultative assembly that would assist and support policy making. In fact, Sultan Mahmud went beyond meeting with representative councils at his court and took more unusual steps to ascertain popular sentiments about politics and the state in the absence of his court favorite in the 1820s. He at times went out in disguise to coffeehouses of the capital, which were known to be hotbeds of political discussion, to hear popular views on current events and policies.[52] This was another way to circumvent the distortion of reports made to him by one or another faction at court and to form his own opinion about policies.

The immediate changes after Halet's death, then, might appear merely factional—the elevation of his enemies and punishment of his allies—but in fact they opened spaces for more structural alliances that would allow for the state to dislodge the existing Janissary Corps and make dramatic policy changes in the military forces of the empire. In many ways this was analogous to the sudden "amputation" of phanariots from the work of translation. In that case, the space that was opened went far beyond the work of translation and gave way to new, if not immediately exploited, institutional possibilities.

By early 1825 the campaign against Greek rebels was not going well, and the central state did not have the time or money to train troops properly. This meant, first, that Albanian and local feudal troops were to be used again and, second, that Mehmet Ali would be called on for assistance against Greek rebels in the Morea and nearby islands.[53] Ottoman military campaigns were contracted out so that Mahmud could focus on "military and civil preparations to secure his position" in İstanbul vis-à-vis the janissaries, "as he apparently realized that any failure in these areas would mean disaster."[54] Mahmud's struggle for continuity of power and legitimacy at the court and in his capital invited Mehmet Ali's entrance into the Ottoman military conflict with Greek rebels. In this way, military policy and factional crises at the center helped bring about the rise of Mehmet Ali as a new military leader from his provincial base in Egypt. This may have been necessary in the short term, but the rising military might of Mehmet Ali would bring on a series of crises and fundamental changes for the Ottoman central state in the coming years. At the core of these changes was the split that ensued between military power, located in Cairo and commanded by Mehmet Ali, and military policy, based in İstanbul and commanded by Husrev Paşa.

## SPLITTING THE COURT, SPLITTING MILITARY POWER

Husrev Paşa (1756–1855) had been brought to İstanbul from the Abaza subgroup of Circassia, in the Caucasus, as a slave-protégé of *çavuşbaşı* Said Efendi and admitted for service in the palace in the third quarter of the eighteenth century.[55] He had risen through secretarial ranks in the Ottoman navy, serving as chief secretary to the Ottoman admiral against Napoleonic forces in the Battle of Aboukir, in Egypt in 1801, and was appointed governor of Egypt in that year.[56] There, like Stephanos Vogorides, he encountered the young Mehmet Ali (1760s–1849), who had come to Egypt from the Macedonian port town of Kavala along with a detachment of Albanian irregulars to fight Napoleonic forces. Husrev and Mehmet Ali became embroiled in a struggle for power involving factions of the Mamluk and Albanian militaries, out of which Mehmet Ali emerged victorious and expelled Husrev from his post as governor in 1803–4.[57] From this point their careers diverged for over two decades, Mehmet Ali remaining in Egypt and Husrev moving on to a series of provincial and imperial military-administrative posts.[58]

Husrev rapidly changed posts, serving as governor (of Bosnia [1806]; twice of Salonica [1804, 1808]; and of Silistre [1809]), fortress commander *(muhafız)* (of İbrail [1808]), and military commander (of the Tunisian coast [1809]), until being appointed Ottoman admiral in 1811 to fight in the Russo-Ottoman war under way at the time. He returned to İstanbul in 1812 after naval operations in the Black Sea and remained admiral until 1818, when he was appointed governor of Trabzon and soon after, in 1820, military commander of the eastern frontier of the empire, which bordered Qajar Persia. There, his "poor administrative abilities" led to heightened tensions among Kurdish tribes, Ottoman officials, and neighboring Persia. As tensions turned into military conflict, Husrev was removed and reappointed Ottoman admiral, just after Halet Efendi's death in December 1822, to fight against Greek rebellions, which had just broken out on the other side of the empire.[59]

The hallmark of Husrev's long career was his adherence to the system of slavery and patronage in which he had been brought up. According to a contemporary in the 1820s, Husrev had been "for thirty years . . . constantly engaged in buying up children in Georgia and Circassia, to educate them for different offices of the Turkish empire."[60] With no biological children of his own, Husrev built up support for himself by bringing new men into the military and administrative service. This stood in contrast to Halet Efendi's strategy of cementing alliances with already powerful interests and to Mehmet Ali's strategy of gaining political power through military might and strategic alliances at court. Husrev would continue with this strategy throughout the 1820s and, when he reached the uppermost positions, install his slave-protégés in key positions around him in the central government.

In the 1820s, the careers of Husrev and Mehmet Ali intersected again, as they cooperated, reluctantly, to oppose Greek rebels in the Morea. In the two decades since their last meeting, Mehmet Ali had remained in Egypt and attained the post of governor there in 1805 by eliminating competing factions first and gaining the Porte's recognition of his power afterward. Within five years Mehmet Ali had consolidated his military and political power and begun creating and training a new elite to support his rule.[61] He was also working on projects of a broader order to consolidate the economic, military, and political structures of Egypt, for which he would later become known as the founder of modern Egypt.[62] From the imperial perspective, what mattered most was that he was using his new military forces to assist the Ottoman central state, such as against the Wahhabis in Arabia from 1811 to 1818. He had proven his success at reforming the military—for which he used a French model and French personnel—with his success on the battlefield against rebels. For this success, his reforms would even serve as the model for imperial military reform in the wake of janissary abolition in the late 1820s.[63]

With the disarray of the 1820s at the Ottoman court and in the military, Mehmet Ali, although displeased with the downfall of Halet Efendi, focused on his own Nizam-ı cedid (New Order) army, in Egypt. By 1824 he was engaged in negotiations with the Porte, through his agent Necib Efendi and Galip Paşa, regarding the extent of his assistance to Mahmud's campaign against Greek rebels and his compensation for it. He subsequently sent his son, İbrahim, in February 1825 to participate in a joint naval campaign along with Ottoman military commanders, one of whom was Husrev Paşa. They achieved victory over Greek rebels at Mesolonghi in 1825–26 and, in turn, lent Sultan Mahmud the confidence to carry out his plan to abolish the Janissary Corps in the capital.[64]

Mahmud's project to establish continuity of an imperial military in İstanbul following the janissary massacres touched on every aspect of society and governance, reflecting the diversity of functions that had been performed by the nominal military force and the profundity of realignments necessary after the janissaries' removal.[65] In many ways it resembled the phanariot dilemma writ much larger. Beyond the obvious and far-reaching issue of a military force, the activities of firefighting, guilds, religious practices and associations, textile production, ethnic relations, civil administration, and even city planning were involved. As these issues absorbed the attention and treasury of Mahmud and his changing cast of advisers, the center of de facto military power was shifting to Egypt, where Mehmet Ali had years before reorganized his army and administration, which were now at his disposal. Mehmet Ali, although his forces lost to allied European fleets in the October 1827 Battle of Navarino, turning the tide of war in favor of Greek rebels, was still the strongest military leader in the empire and as such continued to amass military (on land) and, by extension, political power from his base in Egypt.

Husrev Paşa returned from the battlefield to seize titular control of the military reform effort one year after the janissary massacres, in May 1827, as *serasker,* the title of the commander for the new imperial military. Ultimately, Husrev Paşa's great influence was won through his military success and involvement in factional power plays in the 1820s. Unlike Halet Efendi, whose career was built on a large patronage network at the interstices of court, bureaucracy, diplomacy, and janissary and phanariot complexes, Husrev rose through the military-administrative ranks and built his power in provincial posts before settling in at the Ottoman court. Husrev's power proved longer-lasting than Halet's. He trained and placed large numbers of protégés in the court, the military, and ultimately the diplomatic corps when that corps was reconstituted in the following decade.[66] He created a pole of power at the imperial center, which would oppose Mehmet Ali's military power based in Egypt; a biographer of Husrev Paşa commented, "The Egyptian crisis, which shook the empire to its foundations for years, appeared on the outside as a continuation of the old rivalry between Husrev and Mehmet Ali."[67]

As a military strategist, Husrev aimed to form sample regiments to present for the sultan's pleasure but to avoid impending military conflict with Russia so as to gain time for reforms. Even seven years later, the Ottoman army, which was sent from İstanbul to oppose İbrahim Paşa's Egyptian forces in Anatolia, was barely present, let alone functional. Stephanos Vogorides, while serving as negotiator for the Ottoman central state in 1833 commented, "It is an illusion to suppose that there is an army—no such thing exists—by the last accounts Rauf Paşa was at Eskişehir and Mehmet Paşa at Kütahya, a few troops remain with them both, the rest are roaming bodies of armed men without order, discipline, or commander."[68] Husrev Paşa's goal seemed to be to build up allies and protégés in the upper echelons of power rather than to rebuild an effective military from the bottom up. He successfully created a new generation of functionaries, whose influence would continue into the following decades and who would go on to combine military positions and court politics with the new ingredient of foreign relations at the end of the 1820s. Husrev's network was a new incarnation of Halet's improvised nexus of interests; Husrev worked with formal or titular authority and reforms, rather than under and against them, as Halet had done. Husrev, for instance, placed scores of his slave-protégés in the officer corps of the new imperial military, regardless of whether it was a functioning military; Halet, in contrast, had inserted himself between potentially conflicting power groups to craft an informal web of power with its center at the court. While Halet's system proved more fragile and, once destabilized, caused his downfall and major structural upheaval in the empire, Husrev waited for reforms and inserted his allies into new official positions of power.[69] In this way, Husrev demonstrated an ability that Halet did not: to adapt to the shifting structures of governance in the 1820s. By the end of the decade, Husrev was able to redeploy his own power and that of his slave-protégés in new directions—such as diplomacy and Russo-Ottoman relations—demanded by changing circumstances of Ottoman governance.

The 1828–29 Russo-Ottoman war and, namely, the Ottoman defeat in 1829 exposed the impotence of the postjanissary Ottoman imperial military forces and, among many other changes, marked the reentry of foreign relations with European states as a major concern for Ottoman governance.[70] And this would usher in new political relationships between Ottoman and European states, leading to further internal transformations in Ottoman governance.

## DAY-TO-DAY DIPLOMACY

The Translation Office of the Sublime Porte and the realm of Ottoman military policy making were two sites of a struggle for continuity that was going on amid the civil crises of the 1820s. These sites constituted the start of separate trajectories in the same struggle, missing the links that the phanariot and janissary houses had provided before 1821. The breakdown of the phanariot networks and the ensuing domestic military preoccupation of the Ottoman government precipitated changes in the individual personnel of both the military and foreign affairs, not to mention changes in the structure, function, and logic of politics connecting the Translation Office, the Ottoman military, and the inner circles of the Ottoman court. This breakdown also coincided with a period of flux in Ottoman foreign relations for the Ottoman state, the causes and repercussions of which went far beyond the phanariot house and the Translation Office.

The day-to-day activities of diplomacy in İstanbul in the 1820s also reflect the domestic preoccupations of Ottoman governance in a time when engagement with the European alliance system was episodic. Many phanariots had engaged in day-to-day diplomatic activities in İstanbul before 1821—as dragomans and secretaries at the palace during official visits, as carriers of information to and from the embassies to the court and abroad, and as negotiators at the side of Ottoman admirals and military commanders on campaign and in the capital. Phanariots had also coalesced into family factions that were aligned with one or another foreign state by the turn of the nineteenth century.[71] The day-to-day relations among foreign representatives in İstanbul became disjointed from larger Ottoman networks and practices of governance—another by-product of the collapse of the phanariot house.

Emblematic of the transformation in diplomatic practice was an event in October 1822, after Aristarchi had been exiled and while Yahya Efendi was serving as dragoman, the Austrian envoy Baron d'Ottenfelt was the first ever to address the sultan directly in Turkish, *without an interpreter*.[72] This was a telling sign that the buffer of phanariot dragomans had been removed from Ottoman diplomatic encounters and that new kinds of relationships were in formation between Ottoman and foreign statesmen. Ceremonies to receive foreign envoys—ceremonies that echoed in many respects the pomp of the phanariot *voyvoda*'s investiture ceremony—continued with the same formalities until the early 1830s, even if the relationships behind the ceremonies were in flux.[73]

Beyond the ceremonial visits of foreign envoys to the palace, European diplomats sought a wider range of contacts in İstanbul. In February 1823, Mahmud II had called a general council to approve a policy of hastening reconciliation, and thereby preventing war, with Russia. The council would be composed of "*ulema,* heads of Janissaries, and the chiefs of the various trades and corporations."[74] Because janissaries and guild members "included a large body of the citizens of Constantinople, they were in some measure the representatives of the people,"[75] and as such the envoy thought it possible to assert his opinions through them.

The British envoy in İstanbul described his strategy to influence the decision of the council as follows: "I will secure support of those on terms of personal friendship with me; or of habitual intercourse with the Embassy, the chief of whom are the new mufti [Yasıncızade Abdulwahhab], the Captain Paşa, Ali Bey (Minister of the Corn Department), Hamid Bey, formerly *Reis* [who had been exiled at Halet's behest and was now pardoned], and "*Bekgi,*" who had been banished during the period of Halet's ascendancy, but who is again restored to his sovereign's favour and confidence."[76] Foreign diplomats followed the internal developments and factional rivalries at the Ottoman Court as best they could. They also tried to gain influence with one or another member of the court in the hopes of affecting policy making. But these foreign diplomats did not operate in a common political field with Ottoman courtiers and ministers, and they did not effect structural change in Ottoman governance. Instead, they sought, through personal relations, to influence specific courtiers on specific policies. This would stand in contrast to the more structured engagement between foreign diplomatic networks and Ottoman governance in the 1830s.

Another channel for contact was opened when Ottoman officials requested unofficial and often secret visits with foreign envoys. In September 1821, İsmael Efendi, who had been one of the "marginal men" to serve in the first generation of the diplomatic corps (London, 1797–1800) and was living in a house adjoining that of Halet Efendi (who had himself just been sent into exile), requested a meeting with Lord Strangford and Mr. Wood (chancellor of embassy), "requesting that no Dragoman be present, and requesting that Mr. Wood be employed to interpret between us."[77]

When visits, official and unofficial, did take place, the goal was for the foreign envoy to glean information about goings-on in the court or to persuade the sultan on one or another policy decision regarding the conflicts under way. In 1821, when Russian intercession had failed to prevent the execution of a phanariot-associated merchant, British intercession succeeded, and the merchant was banished rather than put to death.[78] Again in 1823, for instance, the British envoy described his activities as follows:

> Since my return to Constantinople I have anxiously employed myself in endeavoring to obtain the recall from banishment of some of the chief Greeks [Rum] who were exiled at the beginning of the troubles. This negotiation, which is one of considerable

delicacy and difficulty on account of the personal sentiments of the Sultan towards many of these individuals, begins to wear a very favourable appearance, and I trust that by its complete success I shall have the satisfaction not only of serving the interests of humanity, but of augmenting, in a striking manner, the "série de faits" which has been demanded by Russia.[79]

The issue of Rum in banishment was, admittedly for the British envoy, a proxy issue for the broader Anglo-Russian contest for power. But the outcome of domestic issues such as this was still, in the 1820s, dependent on the goodwill of Sultan Mahmud rather than on the intra-European contest for power, as it would become the following decade.

Ottoman scribal and diplomatic staff who had grown in importance under Sultan Selim III were being sidelined to give central priority to the military concerns of the 1820s. Although the larger story of the Ottoman scribal service and the Nizam-i Cedid of Selim III is outside the purview of this discussion, the fate of the *reis efendi (reis-ül-küttab)* is indicative of the changing relationship between diplomacy and bureaucracy in the 1820s and 1830s. The position of *reis efendi,* or chief scribe, was an old one that had, along with the scribal service as a whole, taken on greater prominence in the seventeenth and eighteenth centuries. By the 1790s, thanks to the Nizam-i Cedid reforms, the *reis efendi* had evolved into a kind of foreign minister (although his title remained "chief scribe"), who, along with the *kahya bey* as quasi–interior minister, served under the grand vezir, himself coming to be the analog of a prime minister, in function if not in name.[80] This chain of command, like the system of Ottoman embassies and diplomatic staff abroad, was not yet formally recognized, however, and as such it was disrupted in the flux of the 1820s. The *reis efendi* did not have a major role to play in military policy making of the 1820s, and yet he would emerge as a key player in diplomacy, and by extension in Ottoman domestic politics, from the early 1830s. This shift only further supports the argument that diplomacy, bureaucracy, and the core—military—concerns of Ottoman governance had become fragmented in the 1820s, only to be rejoined abruptly and in a different configuration the following decade.

Diplomacy in İstanbul in the 1820s was irregular and often unofficial or indirect. Foreign envoys were aware of Ottoman court factions and of the significance of the removal of Halet Efendi, for instance. They saw it possible to capitalize on their contact with one or another faction to advance their views in court. But, with no military force to back up their influence, the inroads they could make into Ottoman politics would remain limited. Contact, when it did occur, was between Ottoman court functionaries and single foreign states. This, as we will see, would shift dramatically in 1832, when governance became subsumed into the multistate arena of European politics. The Ottoman central state had succeeded in tearing down both the phanariot and janissary houses but had yet to replace them with a coherent apparatus for either diplomacy or military defense of the sultanate (let alone for provincial governance, an area that lay between the two poles of diplomacy and defense). Janissaries had been formally eliminated, *ayans* had been systematically silenced, and Mehmet Ali had risen out of the ashes of these conflicts and on the back of the Greek insurrections. Phanariots who remained in the service of the empire, however, were soon to enjoy new relevance when the restoration of Ottoman foreign relations began.

# Persistence and the Old Regime

Even in the 1820s, before the role of diplomatic politics in Ottoman governance expanded, the previous functions performed by phanariot dragomans—negotiations, translation, interpreting, exchange of information within the empire—were at the center of Vogorides' bid to survive and rebuild power. While the central state was focused on military struggles, both within the state (Mahmud II's project to destroy janissary power) and against Greek-identified rebels in the provinces, Vogorides was on hand, like only a very few others, to negotiate. As early as 1823, in the heat of conflict, he was rumored to have been the agent of the Ottoman admiral in negotiations with the Greek insular government.[1]

Vogorides was brought back to politics from his latest exile at the imperial army base in Davudpaşa, İstanbul, in 1828. In a pardon signed by then grand vezir Mehmet Selim Paşa, the "former grand dragoman Yakovaki [Iakovo Argyropoulo] and the Moldavian *kaymakam* Istefanaki" were released from confinement at the imperial army base because of their experience, "loyalty, and moral rectitude" *(sadakat ve istikametlerine mebni).*[2] From there he became involved in heated discussions within the central state regarding reparations to Russia following the 1828–29 Russo-Ottoman war.[3] Arguing for reparations rather than the cession of territory, he would later claim credit for keeping Moldavia and Wallachia, at least nominally, in Ottoman hands.

Vogorides also continued working as negotiator and dragoman: resuming the pre-1821 phanariot mission of *celb-i havadis,* or collecting information from Europe, he submitted dispatches of translated newspaper articles *(Avrupa'dan bu defa tevadir eden gazetelerden tercüme olunup)* and analyses of politics foreign and domestic.[4] He did this, however, on a separate trajectory from that of the newly formed

Translation Office of the Sublime Porte. The decision had been made to exclude phanariots, and Greek-identified Christians in general, from eligibility for the formal office of dragoman. And yet Vogorides, and later other former phanariots, continued to perform the substantive functions of dragoman when the central state needed their expertise.

The tactic of splitting the formal office of dragoman from the informal functions of the office echoed a similar split in military power. There, after the destruction of the janissaries, formal military power had gone to Husrev Paşa, in İstanbul. Military force, however, was concentrated and commanded by Mehmet Ali, in Egypt. Such a split allowed Mehmet Ali to present a formidable challenge to the Ottoman central state throughout the 1830s. The split was also an important catalyst for the fusing together of Ottoman politics and European international politics in the same decade.

A third split between formal and informal power that would affect Vogorides' fortunes emerged at this time. The formal positions of Moldavian and Wallachian *voyvoda* as of 1822 no longer went to Greek-identified phanariots but instead to "indigenous" boyars of those principalities. Despite the dissociation of the top two positions in the principalities from a Greek-identified phanariot system, that system persisted at lower levels of politics.[5] Vogorides' continued connections to Moldavia will be discussed as one such example below.

We do not find Vogorides directly involved in the project or battles to destroy the janissaries in 1826, but he did have a collection of patrons within court factions who were themselves the protagonists of the janissary story, on the side of the central state. We also know that Stephanos was clearly an enemy of Halet Efendi as of the outbreak of the 1821 Greek insurgencies, and perhaps we can presume that he tried to build alliances among Halet's other enemies. Galip Paşa, who was in the Nizam-ı Cedid faction from the reign of Sultan Selim III and took part in Mahmud's plan to destroy the janissaries, was the patron of, for instance, Pertev Paşa, who also "played a 'progressive' role in the abolition of the janissaries and the related attack on the Bektaşi order."[6] Pertev Paşa, in turn, was a patron of Vogorides.[7] Husrev Paşa, furthermore, had been Vogorides' old patron and came in from his military role in the provinces to lead the postjanissary Asakir-e Mansure forces from 1827. If, as is claimed by a biographer, he installed over seventy of his slave protégés to high post in the new officer corps,[8] it would seem to follow that he helped find a place for Vogorides as well. In the 1820s and early 1830s, then, Vogorides seemed not to have sided with one or another rival faction but to have kept contacts in several factions. For someone without a direct role in the military affairs of the empire, this was a wise strategy to pursue in the midst of a conflict with such an unclear outcome and is reminiscent of Photeinos's phanariot account of the 1807–8 conflict over military reform.

# 5

## Diplomacy and the Restoration of a New Order

İstanbul was like a gift in the 1830s, ready to be offered up to one of several possible recipients. In the coffeehouses of the capital, informants exchanged gossip that Husrev Paşa, who had been directing the new Ottoman military, had proposed "turning İstanbul over" to Russia so that he and others in the government would be able to "rest easy."[1] Halil Paşa had reportedly answered that İstanbul would be better turned over to Mehmet Ali Paşa of Egypt, who was a "brother in religion" and already a vezir and subject of the sultan.[2] In a separate coffeehouse conversation, a French diplomat, after explaining to an Ottoman informant why France would keep rather than sell its "share" of İstanbul by allying with Russia, went on to propose that it was Greeks who deserved the Ottoman capital.[3] He likened İstanbul to a house, inherited by a small child from the child's father, then taken away by force from the child. The French statesman continued, "When that child grows up, shouldn't that house go back to the child? In this way, İstanbul used to belong to those of Greek descent. Now this is their father's house, so doesn't it stand to reason that it should go to them?"[4]

There was a range of opinions about whom should "receive" İstanbul already in the 1830s. All seemed to agree that continuity of the Ottoman state could no longer be ensured by Sultan Mahmud II and his government alone and that the Ottoman capital, and by extension the empire, was in any case going to be turned over to someone. Giving İstanbul away was a new issue in the 1830s.[5] Along with that issue, new actors had appeared on the scene since the 1820s; now Russia, France, and even the tiny state of Greece, for instance, were active contenders for İstanbul. This stood in contrast to the 1820s, when power struggles were fought out predominantly among groups involved in Ottoman governance while those in the outside world looked on.[6]

In the end, the recipient of İstanbul was not one or another state or *paşa* but the multistate arena of European foreign politics. The Ottoman Empire rejoined the European alliance system—a process that involved a rebuilding of Ottoman diplomacy—in the early 1830s after several years of flux in its foreign relations. The impetus for this fusing of Ottoman politics and European politics through diplomacy was the resolution of intra-Ottoman crises left over from the 1820s: the Greek Question, resolved with the establishment of a new Greek state, and the Mehmet Ali crises, which saw a more ambiguous resolution. In the process of resolving these crises, the agents of Ottoman politics came face to face with the diplomats and political cultures of several other states. Together they formed a new political landscape in which intra-Ottoman conflicts would be resolved.[7]

The restoration of Ottoman power—after a decade of dissolution—occurred within a new international order, and this had crucial implications on the cultures and structures of court politics, bureaucracy, and diplomacy. Restoration of an Ottoman order hinged on encounters between political actors and traditions, encounters that can be tracked through a series of face-to-face meetings that occurred in İstanbul between Ottoman and foreign representatives from 1832 through 1834. The first meetings had as their aim to make the final arrangements for the independent Greek kingdom and the establishment of Greek-Ottoman relations. The second group of meetings turned to the question of Mehmet Ali and his challenge to the sultanate, a challenge that had been gaining strength in 1831 and 1832. In these meetings we begin to see new and proliferating kinds of political relationships and new processes of policy making and negotiation. These new relationships did not mean simply, as is often assumed in historiography of the Eastern Question, the active British, Russian, and French empires operating on the passive Ottoman state. Instead, the re-fusing of Ottoman internal and foreign politics involved a reorientation within Ottoman politics toward the larger frame of European alliances and rivalries, as well as changing avenues of participation for foreign states in Ottoman politics. These encounters and the new international political realities they represented precipitated further changes within Ottoman politics—the growth of a new order and the possibility to build new houses in such a new framework of governance. This is apparent in the changing structure of factional court politics and the growing significance of the Translation Office in the 1830s.

The aim of the present discussion is not to explain why the relationship between Ottoman governance and international politics changed; the immediate reason for the change was contingent in large part on the military and political outcome of the 1828–29 Russo-Ottoman conflict. Instead, the aim is to explore what those relationships looked like, where diplomatic encounters were beginning to take place in the Ottoman capital, and who was involved in these new political relationships, all of which shed light on the changes that were in turn engendered for Ottoman power relations. The shift from the politics of military and court factions of the 1820s to the politics of international diplomacy in İstanbul was abrupt in the early 1830s, making the two stories seem disjointed from one another. And yet the trajectories of change and the networks of military and political figures from the 1820s are important to understanding how those involved in Ottoman governance encountered and engaged with the shift to diplomatic politics in the 1830s.

## ANSWERING THE GREEK QUESTION IN İSTANBUL

The power to resolve intra-Ottoman conflict was taken in stages by the allied powers of Britain, France, and Russia, starting in 1826.[8] Secret meetings between British and Russian statesmen in St. Petersburg in 1826 over the Greek Question turned into official meetings and offers of mediation later that year.[9] When the Ottoman state refused these offers, meetings among French, British, and Russian representatives continued, in London, and the first Protocol of London was issued in 1827.[10] This first protocol suggested autonomy under Russian or Ottoman suzerainty for Greece and was turned down by the Ottoman state once again. Then, with the Battle of Navarino in October 1827, the fleets of the three allied states intervened, somewhat accidentally but successfully on the side of Greek rebels, against İbrahim Paşa's Ottoman-Egyptian forces.[11] From that point until the 1832 conclusion of the Conference of London, representatives of the three powers met several times, in London, to work out a settlement for an independent Greek state.

Two points demand attention with regard to the progressive involvement of multiple states in an intra-Ottoman conflict.[12] One has to do with the tensions among states—the contest for power among Russia, Britain, and France—going on all the while and driving the "alliance" forward. If one state were to gain a foothold in the Mediterranean and the Ottoman Empire, then the others would have to check that power and establish themselves there as well.[13] This reflected the inherent tensions of the European Restoration with respect to intra-Ottoman conflicts. On the one hand, old regimes—and the Ottoman Empire could be counted as an old regime— were to defend one another against revolutionary movements.[14] On the other hand, the Greek Revolution offered an opportunity (and Greek rebels extended formal invitations) to Russia, then Britain and France, to gain influence in the region at the expense of competing European powers. Thus, when we discuss foreign involvement in Greek-Ottoman affairs we must remember that any action made by one foreign government was closely monitored and responded to by other rival governments. With the onset of the Mehmet Ali crisis, diverging interests of foreign states became ever more decisive in the outcome of events.

The absence of Ottoman representatives in the London negotiations between 1827 and 1832 is another striking feature, given the intensifying involvement of European states in an intra-Ottoman conflict. There were several interrelated reasons for this. The rupture in Ottoman diplomatic personnel and mediating networks in the absence of phanariot networks and in a time of the empire's domestic preoccupation was perhaps the most immediate reason. The Ottoman state had also consistently refused to recognize the Greek-aligned rebels as a political entity or even as official insurgents who could make secessionist or any other demands.[15] As a result of such a policy, the Ottoman state had denied offers of mediation from foreign governments and so did not recognize the Conference of London as having the legitimacy to resolve the Greek conflict until the conclusion of that conference.[16] Thus, although the Conference of London was called to resolve the intra-Ottoman conflict with Greek rebels, it was conducted between 1827 and 1832 in the realm of European international politics, which was still separate from Ottoman politics and geographically remote from İstanbul.[17] This would stand in stark contrast to negotiations over the Mehmet Ali crisis, which would go on in İstanbul and Egypt and would feature the vigorous participation of Ottoman political leaders and factions.

Already the negotiations going on in the Conference of London were novel in the history of Ottoman foreign relations. They were of a different order from the periodic Russo-Ottoman treaties that followed conflicts between the two empires in the 1770s, 1780s, and 1812, for instance. They were even different from the latest round of Russo-Ottoman negotiations in 1829, which were themselves related to the Greek settlement.[18] In those cases, negotiations were carried out between the two (or more, as was the case in the 1780s Russo-Austrian-Ottoman wars) already extant states that had been engaged in military conflict. The losing side, which for several decades had usually been the Ottomans, would cede territory, exclusive trading and navigation rights to the straits, and even rights of protection over Orthodox Christian subjects of the Ottoman Empire, for instance. In this case, however, three powers (sometimes more, when Prussia and Austria were involved) interceded on behalf of a secessionist movement. In affirming and legitimizing the need for secession, the powers did *not* take Greece into their direct sovereignty (as Britain had done with the Ionian Islands after the retreat of Napoleonic armies, more than thirty years earlier, or as Russia had done with Crimea in the eighteenth century). Instead, by February 1830, they created a new, formally sovereign state out of Ottoman territory and acknowledged that Ottoman subjects could, in name at least, form a new, separate government.[19] In setting this precedent and deciding on the propriety of Greek secession from the Ottoman state, foreign powers also implicitly assumed the privilege of deciding, ultimately on their own terms, whether or not future demands for secession would be valid. They would go on to exercise this privilege in the diminutive case of the island of Samos and in the much larger case of Mehmet Ali's territories, not to mention the subsequent cases throughout the Balkans and the Middle East over the course of the next century.

Before international politics returned to İstanbul in 1832, then, representatives of Britain, Russia, and France had already arrived at the settlement for an independent Greek state out of Ottoman territory. When they sent the Treaty of London to their respective courts for ratification, meetings commenced in İstanbul to decide on the execution of the treaty. It was at these İstanbul meetings that diplomats and statesmen, including those from the Ottoman state, met and collaborated on a common project for the first time, signaling in the process new political relationships within and beyond the empire. The location, agenda, and attendance rosters of those meetings all help us understand the emerging arena of multistate diplomacy in İstanbul. This multistate arena would develop and fuse with Ottoman governance to a greater degree in response to the Mehmet Ali crisis.

## INTERNATIONAL POLITICS
### RETURNS TO İSTANBUL, SPRING 1832

In April 1832, meetings among British, French, Russian, and Ottoman officials began to be held in the *reis efendi*'s summer house in the Bosphorus village of Balta Limanı, outside İstanbul. The aim of these meetings was to work out the "details" of the Treaty of London as that treaty was being concluded in Britain by the three signatory foreign states.[20] Such details included the Ottoman-Greek land border,[21] commerce and the use of the Greek flag, reparations to be made to the Ottoman state by the new Greek state, measures to control piracy in the Aegean and brigandage on land, and the question of Samos, an island with a predominantly Greek Orthodox population, which had engaged vigorously in rebellions but was excluded from the borders of the new Greek state.

The space that was allowed to the Ottoman government to participate in these final negotiations, however small at first, became the field of a new politics of diplomacy in İstanbul. The representatives who were active in this field would establish the relationships necessary for further collaboration after the Greek settlement reached its conclusion, and ultimately the diplomacy they initiated would become a fundamental structure of Ottoman governance.

Attendance at the initial meetings in İstanbul indicated, for the Ottoman side, who was involved in a new Ottoman diplomacy after several years of interruption, and for the foreign sides, which foreign representatives would spearhead the fusion of international politics and Ottoman politics. On the foreign side, British statesmen such as Stratford Canning, Mandeville, and later Lord Ponsonby (since May 1833) were often in attendance, as were Russian and French chargés d'affaires and their assistants and dragomans. Often, unnamed "gentlemen" from each embassy attended these meetings, presumably as secretaries or observers.[22] The ambassadors, when they attended such meetings, would report to their foreign ministers in their home states on who from the Ottoman side was in attendance and what was discussed.[23]

On the Ottoman side, the newly appointed *reis efendi* Akif (appointed to this position in 1832) hosted the meetings at his summer house.[24] Akif had entered the palace service almost twenty years earlier (in 1814) with the help of his uncle Mazhar Efendi, who at the time was himself the *reis efendi*. Since then Akif had been climbing the ranks of the bureaucracy in the context of disarray and the crisis of the 1820s: in 1825 he was appointed as *amedçi* (receiver) and in 1827 director of the Office of the Imperial Divan, a post he occupied until his 1832 promotion to *reis efendi*.[25] Akif had survived and prospered in the 1820s, in part through his alliance with Husrev Paşa. Together with Ahmed Fevzi and Halil Rıfat paşas, Akif was among the most successful of Husrev's protégés who were already powerful in the new post-janissary imperial military project and in court politics of the later 1820s.[26]

Other Ottomans in attendance were the chief physician of the palace, who at the time was Abdülhak Efendi; the *amedçi*, Mustafa Reşit Bey; and the director of the Office of the Imperial Divan, Mehmet Nuri Efendi; their unnamed assistants; the official dragoman of the Porte, who was at this time Esrar Efendi; and one Stephanos Vogorides, who was a former phanariot, as we know, and was now serving as an auxiliary or assistant dragoman.[27]

On the Ottoman side, the presence of these particular representatives indicated a growing formality in the chain of command for Ottoman foreign relations. By this I mean that particular duties associated with foreign politics were coalescing in specific formal positions, such as those of the *reis efendi*, who was to become the minister of foreign affairs *(hariciye nazırı)*, the *amedçi*, and the *beylikçi*, and the director of the Office of the Imperial Divan. This stands in contrast to Ottoman foreign politics associated with the phanariot system before 1821, wherein phanariot dragomans, whose official job was to translate documents, and *voyvodas*, whose job was to administer the Danubian Principalities, were also, often unofficially, participating in and administering foreign politics. I do not intend to argue, however, that this formal chain of command constituted the entirety of diplomatic and foreign policy activities. On the contrary, my point is to show that on one level, Ottoman diplomacy was becoming more formalized and institutionalized, while on another level, people continued to use networks of unofficial personnel to convey information and effect changes involving new political actors.

One example of this growing formality is that the *reis efendi* directed the sphere of foreign relations, the *amedçi* was in effect second in command, and the director of the Imperial Divan Office was assistant to the *amedçi*.[28] Furthermore, the presence of the dragoman Esrar indicates a trend toward reintegrating the office of the dragoman into the new politics of diplomacy and balancing the structure and functions of the office. And yet at the same time, the inclusion of Vogorides—a former phanariot—as "auxiliary dragoman" and Abdülhak Efendi, the chief physician and member of the *ulema*, reflects the continuity of holdovers from the previous period. These were men who, despite their being outside a formal chain of command for foreign relations, could bridge the diplomacy of the previous decade with the new meetings taking place and facilitate the reestablishment of diplomatic etiquette and communication for the others. Abdülhak, for his part, represented the *ulema* participation that had been customary at earlier treaty negotiations.[29] Overall, the combination of Ottoman and foreign officials at these 1832 meetings displays a widening sphere of interaction among personnel from several states, both within those states and among them, including new figures as well as men of previous experience in diplomacy.

The location of the meetings also merits attention. These were not official state visits of foreign ambassadors to the Ottoman court. Nor were they official meetings at the Sublime Porte, with the grand vezir in his office.[30] Instead, they were state-sanctioned meetings, presumably of a more casual and less ceremonial nature, held at the summer residence of Akif Efendi, the *reis efendi*. In one light this indicated the minimal importance assigned to the resolution of these matters by the court. This is understandable, considering not only the humiliation the Ottoman central state often associated with Greek independence, but also the situation with Mehmet Ali and İbrahim's forces, which had conquered much of the Levant and were heading into Anatolia for a frontal assault on the sultanate, making that a more pressing priority for the leaders of the central state.

In another light, however, the location, informality, and goals of these meetings point to the broadening scope of diplomatic relationships and mechanisms in İstanbul. A group of foreign statesmen and Ottoman officials worked together to resolve practical issues that arose from the Treaty of London, and they did this outside the physical space of the Imperial Court–Sublime Porte complex. Meetings involving various permutations of these officials would occur with greater frequency and intensity regarding the Mehmet Ali crisis shortly after. Thus the relationships forged in the course of meetings on the Greek Question would continue and would deepen as the Samos issue emerged out of the Greek settlement and the Mehmet Ali negotiations unfolded later that year.

By June 1832, Ottoman ministers had reported to the sultan that only a few matters were left to be resolved, such as a commercial agreement, the terminology of the final treaty, and the status of Samos, but that those issues "could be dealt with by the Dragomans as intermediaries."[31] As such, the auxiliary dragoman Stephanos Vogorides was appointed as the negotiator for the final changes to the treaty in the summer of 1832.[32] Vogorides managed this task in part through direct contact with Sultan Mahmud and earned the gratitude of the British ambassador Stratford Canning, who wrote, "I much question whether we should not still have been forced into another adjournment, if we had not been made acquainted with the conclusive fact, that the Sultan, upon an earnest representation made to him that day before, not by the Reis Efendi or the other Ministers of the Porte, but by Signor Vogoridi *[sic]*, who has greatly contributed to the success of our proceedings, had issued an order for the immediate conclusion of the business agreeably to our demands."[33] Once again, the drive for political expediency created opportunities in the gray area between formal and informal power and between diplomacy and court politics. Vo-gorides, who lacked as yet an official position and was thus operating in this gray area, could nevertheless, through his personal intercession with Sultan Mahmud at the Ottoman court and his personal connection to Canning at the British Embassy, accelerate the resolution of the issues at hand regarding the Greek settlement.

At this stage, the issues relegated to negotiations in İstanbul were considered de-tails. Nevertheless, the individuals and the means they used set a pattern for more crucial issues developing simultaneously, most important the Mehmet Ali crisis. During the Greek negotiations, participants from the Ottoman and three foreign states worked together and earned one another's trust, first by learning one another's agendas. The British diplomatic staff, for their part, were learning the difference be-tween formal audiences with Ottoman officials and achieving their policy objec-tives through unofficial participants such as Vogorides.[34] The Ottoman represen-tatives were assaying the interests and behavior of the British, French, and Russian diplomats to position themselves in emerging factional politics at the court.

In November 1832, meetings of the larger group took place—not just with Vo-gorides, the dragoman of the Porte, and foreign representatives, as in the summer meetings, but again with the *reis efendi,* the *amedçi,* the director of Imperial Divan Office, and the chief physician of the court as well. These meetings happened at the İstanbul winter residence of the *reis efendi.* Their aim was to reach approval of the final settlement that Vogorides had been negotiating in the summer and fall of that year. Vogorides went over the final line edits of the treaty requested by the Ottoman side, and negotiations wound down in December, just as Bavarian prince Otto ar-rived in Nauplion, Greece, to become sovereign of that new state.[35]

In the course of the 1832 negotiations, the question of Samos developed into a separate issue to be resolved. Samians had taken part vigorously in Greek rebel-lions and, although the island had been included in the provisional Greek govern-ment during the revolution, it was, along with Crete, excluded from the borders of the independent Greek state at the 1830 conference of London. Samos was prom-ised an "autonomous" regime at the London meetings, but the details of this regime were left to the later talks in İstanbul.[36]

While the scale of the Samos Question could not compare to the Mehmet Ali crisis or even the Greek Question (Samos was on a trade route of secondary im-portance and had a population of fewer than fifty thousand), the dynamics of the problem and the process of resolving the conflict were similar. Local warlords-turned-political leaders had turbulent relations in the 1820s with the revolution-ary Greek government, of which Samos was a part.[37] Now, they were demanding autonomy from the Ottoman Empire under Great Power guarantee if they were to be written out of the new Greek state. The conflict, then, was between the inhabi-tants of Samos, the central Ottoman state, and the Great Power representatives who were ostensibly mediating the conflict. As was the case with Greece and several times with Mehmet Ali, a continuum of formal administrative options was available to the concert of states involved in negotiations. Samos, like Greece and Mehmet Ali's territory, could be given independence, autonomy, and tributary status or be returned to full submission under Ottoman sovereignty. The formal secession—or reversal of secession—of these territories, great and small, was to be effected by a new constellation of diplomats, from the Ottoman, British, Russian, and French states, in the new political field of diplomacy, often in İstanbul.

A few weeks after the larger Greek-Ottoman issues were resolved, the final settlement for the island of Samos was reached, in December 1832. This settlement, while respecting the demands of the Ottoman state to keep Samos under its sovereignty, gave local autonomy to the island and ordered it to be formed as a principality and administered by a Christian prince (in the name of the sultan), so that the prince would be a coreligionist with the majority Christian population there.[38] Negotiations regarding Samos were yet another opportunity for diplomats of the Ottoman and foreign states to establish relations with one another and to use the new calculus that was developing to determine a political settlement of what had begun as an intra-Ottoman dispute.

Vogorides was chosen and appointed as prince of Samos in December 1832. This decision was made by the British ambassador Canning in concert with Akif and Reşit Mehmet paşas and was the fruit of Vogorides' attempts to earn the trust of both in negotiating the details of the Greek settlement in previous months. From the Ottoman perspective, Vogorides could be trusted to serve the interests of the central state, whereas a native Samian could not. For the British envoy Mandeville, Vogorides was also a known quantity. With the title of prince, Vogorides would in turn claim further legitimacy in the new politics of diplomacy under way, even if he could not claim legitimacy with Samians themselves as their ruler. Vogorides' appointment both reflected and reinforced the growing capacity of diplomatic politics from İstanbul to effect changes in Ottoman governance. He had begun as an unofficial observer and assistant dragoman, earned the task of negotiating the details of the Greek settlement on behalf of the Ottoman state, and received the title of prince of Samos as a result of the relationships he had established in Greece. The significance of this title for İstanbul politics was made clear by the fact that Vogorides always remained in the capital, never resided on that island, and visited it only one time. He continued his involvement and intensified it in unrelated diplomatic and political questions, always using his title as prince of Samos to earn credibility and legitimacy.

We can even trace the significance of official titles in the way that British officials described Vogorides when he was emerging as an unofficial dragoman. In June 1831, he was seen as a disingenuous "Fanariot Greek" seeking Russian and Ottoman support to win the post of *voyvoda* as he "[pretended] to descend from a Wallachian family" and hoped thus to meet the criteria of an indigenous boyar.[39] By April 1832, he was seen in a more neutral light, as just "a Greek of the Fanal *[sic]* who took part in the discussion, rather as an auxiliary to the Dragoman of the Porte than as one of the Turkish Plenipotentiaries."[40] Throughout 1832 he was often referred to simply as Monsieur Vogorides, with no title and no comment other than that he was in attendance at meetings.[41] Early the next year, just after he was "invested with the dignity of Prince of Samos," Vogorides began being referred to in his own right; rather than accompanying the dragoman of the Porte, Vogorides was now accompanied by him, and soon after he was holding his own meetings with Mandeville without the official dragoman altogether.[42] Finally, by May and June, Vogorides was referred to simply as the "Prince of Samos" and was having private tête-à-têtes with Ambassador Ponsonby.[43] By this point, Vogorides' past overtures to the Russians were a fading bad memory; Ambassador Ponsonby wrote, "Your Lordship knows the influence and power of the Prince [Vogorides] with the Sultan and the Porte, and his abilities, and that he was once of the Russian Party, when he hoped, through Russian power, to be made Hospodar, but that end being now out of the question, his interests and opinions turn toward us."[44]

While the issue of Samos may not have been the most consequential for the empire or for European international politics at that moment, it still belonged to the same spectrum of possibilities as the Greek and, as we will see, the Mehmet Ali issues. Furthermore, the manner in which the Samos issue was debated and resolved reflects again the pattern set by the new diplomatic and political community in İstanbul, which involved representatives of several states and was focused on resolving intra-Ottoman conflicts. British attaché David Urquhart drew the connection between Samos and larger issues when he listed a series of questions that demanded resolution through, in his view, a British policy change:

> There is but one way of solving these complications, of uniting France to us—of detaching Austria and Prussia from Russia—of restoring Poland—of solving the Egyptian question—*of maintaining the independence of Greece, which we have effected—of preserving the rights of Samos, we have guaranteed (so leveled are all questions before this, which affects alike a parish and an empire)*—of saving Turkey—of maintaining the *de facto* independence of the Circassians—of defending Persia—of securing India— of preventing another irruption of Northern Barbarians—and that is the presence of England, by her pendants and her guns, on that portion of her own element, from which Russia has ventured too soon, let us hope, to pronounce her exclusion.[45]

Samos, like Greece, Egypt, and indeed the Ottoman Empire as a whole, was, from the British imperial perspective, becoming integrated into the British contest with Russia for supremacy, and in scholarship this is a well-trodden path of the Eastern Question. From the Ottoman imperial perspective, however, the issues of Samos,

Greece, and Mehmet Ali/Egypt were also the occasion for the melding of the Ottoman and the multistate European political systems so as to restore the power of the sultanate. The site of that melding was the field of diplomatic politics in İstanbul.

A crucial result of this new constellation of governance was that diplomacy now had bite, because it carried with it military intervention, both demonstrated, as in the Battle of Navarino, and threatened in intra-Ottoman conflicts by foreign states such as Britain, France, and Russia. The threat of military intervention from Russia, Britain, and France, rather than the threat of a central Ottoman military, would circumscribe Mehmet Ali's military power in Egypt and Syria while the Greek settlement was winding down in the early 1830s. With no Ottoman imperial military to speak of to oppose Mehmet Ali's forces (let alone to oppose Russian forces), it made sense that political discussions on the streets of İstanbul and in the imperial court focused on who the recipient of İstanbul would be. The mechanisms of diplomacy—at the interstices of internal Ottoman politics, military force, and geopolitical rivalries and alliances—expanded in response to Mehmet Ali's gathering threat to the sultanate. The way the Mehmet Ali crisis played out sheds light on the process and implications of this further melding between the Ottoman and European international power structures.

## MEHMET ALI: CONJOINING OTTOMAN
## AND INTERNATIONAL POLITICS

As the 1832 negotiations for the Greek settlement were getting under way in İstanbul, the conflict between Mehmet Ali and his son İbrahim on the one side and the central Ottoman state on the other was already reaching crisis proportions. Mehmet Ali had used his military forces in the defense of the sultanate several times before, most recently against Greek rebels and subsequently European fleets, from 1825 through 1827. Mehmet Ali's "Greek chapter" had in fact been a turning point in his career and in his relations with the Ottoman sultan and central state. According to one of his many biographers, "the Greek episode carried [Mehmet Ali] beyond the sphere of his intended plans for expansion. Rather than portray him in the cloak of a loyal subject to his master, it exposed him as a formidable and dangerous challenger to Ottoman authority."[46] With Mehmet Ali's forces fighting alongside the imperial forces against Greek rebels, Mehmet Ali could gauge his potential strength were he to turn against those Ottoman forces, which he did a few years later.[47]

While the Greek rebellions were certainly one key to Mehmet Ali's transformation from a strong vassal to a contender for the Ottoman sultanate, another key to Mehmet Ali's power was the conflict between janissaries and central state loyalists in İstanbul during the previous decade. Individual reformers and plans for military reform at the imperial center from 1822 on were borrowed from Mehmet Ali's Nizam-ı Cedid army. Mehmet Ali himself had borrowed heavily from French military personnel, engineers, and techniques for his reforms. This created a complex dynamic when reforms were brought to the imperial center, in that they were presented as "Egyptian" (such as uniforms and military drills) so as to make them seem less foreign, and yet were actually French styles and techniques that had been filtered through Egypt. Once strategies for reform were borrowed and the janissaries massacred, the imperial military was crippled until it could train a sufficient number of new troops, leaving the burden of military defense for the empire on Mehmet Ali from his provincial base.[48] As Husrev Paşa usurped formal, titular power over the new imperial military as *serasker* from İstanbul, Mehmet Ali continued to wield de facto military power and to see the potential of that power in gaining him more territory and resources.

From an imperial perspective, the mantle of military leadership had been passed in content to Mehmet Ali and in title to Husrev Paşa. Thus, as scattered Greek rebel forces turned into a formally independent Greek state with the sanction and guarantee of foreign powers in the Treaty of London, the military core of the empire threatened to split in two—the nominal core of military leadership in İstanbul and the substantive core of military power in Egypt. Husrev Paşa and Mehmet Ali, each from his own pole of military power, actively engaged the emerging politics of diplomacy and made the transition from military conflict to international diplomacy.

After returning from the Greek campaign in 1828, Mehmet Ali and İbrahim first made a peaceful request for Syria and Crete as compensation for their services to the Ottoman sovereign and, when shunned, began to prepare for a military campaign of conquest to Syria, thus initiating the "imperial phase" of their careers.[49] This involved, in the military arena, years of campaigns to conquer Syria and much of Anatolia, as well as challenges to the sultanate itself, which turned the rivalry between Mehmet Ali and Sultan Mahmud into an international issue throughout the 1830s.

In 1831 Mehmet Ali's forces, led by his son İbrahim, conquered Syria with the help of local elites there, and in 1832 İbrahim's forces moved on into Anatolia, ostensibly on their way to İstanbul to take over the sultanate. In late 1832, Grand Vezir Mehmet Reşit Paşa, who had led Ottoman forces against İbrahim, was defeated by İbrahim and taken hostage at Konya. This was obviously a humiliating low point for Ottoman imperial military fortunes, and as such it precipitated Sultan Mahmud's request for assistance from foreign states to preserve his sultanate. Sultan Mahmud first appealed to Britain and France, neither of which responded. When he then turned to Russia, at the prompting of advisers such as Husrev and Halil Rıfat paşas, that government, recognizing the opportunity to penetrate and eventually control Ottoman power, responded immediately in the affirmative.[50] These negotiations transpired in January and February of 1833.

The offer and acceptance of Russian naval assistance to the Ottoman state set off a new phase in the standoff between the Ottoman central authority and Mehmet

Ali's forces beginning in January 1833. Namely, the contest for power among Russia, Britain, and France became enmeshed with and superimposed onto the intra-Ottoman rivalry between the sultanate-court and Mehmet Ali. General Muraviev traveled to Alexandria and was promised a cessation of hostilities by Mehmet Ali.[51] Halil Paşa, then Ottoman admiral, followed on his own mission in the same month to negotiate terms of an armistice.[52] It seemed that Mehmet Ali would consider negotiations in response to the promise of Russian assistance to his nominal Ottoman sovereign, and yet because it was his son İbrahim who was physically present and leading the forces in Anatolia, another layer of negotiation between father and son was added, which only increased the uncertainty of the situation. In March 1833, Russian ships entered the Bosphorus and anchored in İstanbul in a symbolic show of Russia's new relationship of "protection" with the Ottoman Porte and court.[53]

The arrival of the Russian admiral and his fleet in the Bosphorus not only alarmed many an Ottoman official, for Russia had been seen overwhelmingly as a threat to rather than a defender of the Ottoman state in the past decades, but also alarmed the British and French governments, whose leaders lived in fear of Russian domination of their trade routes and colonies. The offer of Russian aid to the sultanate thus prompted further involvement of British and particularly French statesmen as "mediators" to discourage this Russo-Ottoman alliance and at the same time to diffuse the intra-Ottoman conflict between Mehmet Ali and the central Ottoman state by the end of 1832. If Mehmet Ali's conquest of Syria initiated the "imperial phase" of his career in 1831, the alliance between the Russian and Ottoman empires in 1833 bound the internal politics of the Ottoman Empire more closely than ever before to the European power struggles of the day. This in turn intensified the relationships and politics of diplomacy operating out of İstanbul, a phenomenon visible in the meetings that are the centerpiece of this discussion. Negotiations reached a new intensity throughout the spring of 1833, as French and British diplomats sought ways to diffuse the conflict with Mehmet Ali so as to remove the Russian pretext for settling its fleet indefinitely on the Bosphorus. The Peace of Kütahya was reached later that spring (May 1833), which established an uneasy truce between Mehmet Ali and the central Ottoman state. When the Ottoman representatives Husrev (as imperial military commander), Akif (as *reis efendi*), and Ahmed Fevzi (as the Ottoman admiral) signed a defensive pact, the Treaty of Hünkar İskelesi, with Russia, this was taken as an affront by Mehmet Ali, who then refused to pay his tribute as promised, and tensions rose once again in the fall of 1833.

## CRITERIA FOR SECESSION: STRATEGIC AND MORAL

The differing perception in Europe of the Ottoman conflict with Mehmet Ali as opposed to the Greek Question colored the realities—and outcome—of negotiations that would ensue regarding a settlement with Mehmet Ali. Whereas resolution of the Greek Question had precipitated a concerted effort among several foreign states, and ultimately with representatives of the Ottoman state, the Mehmet Ali crisis was, simultaneously, cleaving the unity of interests among Britain, France, and Russia with regard to Ottoman affairs. This came in part from the broader contest for power and resources among Russia, Britain, and France: the foreign power that could gain control of Egypt and Syria would dominate the trade routes to India, thereby either safeguarding (if that power were British) or breaking (if France or Russia) the British hold on India. Mehmet Ali's attempt to formally break away from, or take over, the Ottoman center contained the temptation for the three foreign states of gaining this crucial territory, whereas the territory slated for Greece, while important as a foothold in the region, was less tempting for the larger power struggles under way.

In the European press, discussions of why Greece should have been allowed to secede but Mehmet Ali should not reveal another dimension of politics that coexisted with geostrategic realities and contests for military superiority. While the practical successes of Mehmet Ali's reforms did not go unacknowledged, his identity and claims as a Muslim seemed to prevent Europeans from seeing him as leader of a potential successor state while they searched for principles of secession.[54] They could imagine him only in a zero-sum game with Sultan Mahmud, either as his potential successor or as returning to vassal status with some special privileges in Egypt. There was also speculation, especially on the part of the French, that Mehmet Ali did not honestly intend to secede but was using this possibility or scenario as a bargaining chip to gain more privileges and resources.[55] In short, the Mehmet Ali conflict, despite Mehmet Ali's demonstrated projects and successes for reorganizing his military, social structure, and economy, was perceived in the context of a greedy vassal trying to push the limits of his power against a weak central state.

The Greek case, by contrast, had not only struck the chord of philhellenism, particularly in Britain, but fit more closely the European template of a "nation" demanding freedom. Despite the discomfort such a popular movement inflicted on Restoration Europe, it was nevertheless a recognizable movement for European observers, and above all a movement of Christians against Ottoman (and, more important in the minds of Europeans, Muslim) rule. Urquhart reflected this logic with his comparison of the two cases:

> The annals of the empire, for a long series of years, are filled with the rebellions of Pashas, who, with more or less means, for a longer or shorter period of time, have withdrawn their provinces from the control of the Porte—have invaded other provinces—have formed foreign alliances—have been regarded abroad as founders of new dynasties, but who have all, without a single exception, been in the end destroyed ... the only exceptions to this rule are to be found in Greece and Servia. *In Greece, however, no Pasha arose against his sovereign, a people arose. The Greeks fought for their indepen-*

*dence, and achieved it: it may be of little value to them, it may be precarious, thanks to European theories; but it was obtained against the whole weight of the Ottoman power, because the whole population thought itself interested in the struggle.*[56]

However tempting the location and the demonstrated military successes of Mehmet Ali may have been then, his bid for power could not be seen in the same category as the Greek Revolution in the eyes of European statesmen or public opinion. Therefore, the issue for competing foreign powers was one of how, where, and to what extent to prop up Ottoman governance and military power at the center and, in the most drastic scenario, whether to replace Sultan Mahmud with Mehmet Ali. When Russia made the first move to come to the military defense of the sultanate, France and Britain were prompted to deeper engagement in the politics of diplomacy between İstanbul and Alexandria so as to prevent a Russian takeover of the Ottoman sultanate.

Returning to the Ottoman political context, we see that Husrev Paşa pursued a strategy for the survival of the sultanate despite military weakness by favoring an alliance with Russia. This alliance, if it meant that Russia would actively defend the central Ottoman state, would overpower Mehmet Ali, on the one hand, and bring in the involvement of the Russian rivals, France and Britain, who had been trying to keep a safe distance once again from what they perceived as an intra-Ottoman power struggle, on the other. Mehmet Ali, in contrast, drew French diplomats into his bid for power by requesting mediation in his feud with the central state.[57] This further strengthened his engagement with France as well as French sympathy for Mehmet Ali's project. While foreign states had their own incentives to become involved in the standoff between Mehmet Ali and the Ottoman central state, Ottoman actors on both sides of the standoff were for their part encouraging, indeed requesting, this involvement so as to gain leverage against each other in the already intricate politics of the court and the military.

The conflict between Mehmet Ali and the central Ottoman state was inseparable from individual European states. Those states—Britain, France, and Russia— were emerging as supporters of one or the other side and ultimately became actors in their own right in the intra-Ottoman conflict. But this conflict was also inextricable from the totality of strategic political alliances and rivalries among those individual foreign states, that is, from the European state system. This was exemplified not only by the tone and content of debates in Europe regarding the conflict but even by reports of conversations in İstanbul coffeehouses. In a newly opened Beyoğlu coffeehouse, "near the Asmalı Mosque," the merchant and Greek citizen Gianni Hrisodilo (Christodoulou?) put it succinctly, if crudely, when he told an Ottoman informant, "There is a lot of tumult among all the states. And all of them are preparing for war. And Mehmet Ali is also preparing for war. Let's see on whose head the pumpkin will burst."[58] From both the Ottoman and the European perspectives, this conflict was not simply between Mehmet Ali and the Ottoman sultan, with foreign states as mediators, but "all the states" were involved in the tumult, and all stood to lose or gain from the outcome. From the Ottoman perspective, imperial governance and intra-Ottoman power relations were becoming subsumed into international politics; diplomacy was thus expanding into a more crucial area of governance than ever before. It was in this context that negotiations, often informal, took place in İstanbul between 1832 and 1834.

## NEGOTIATIONS: IDEALS AND REALITIES

The acute phase of negotiations and tensions went on in 1833, when Russian diplomats and warships had arrived in the Bosphorus in the defense of the Ottoman sultanate, and all parties were uncertain of the intentions of others. An agreement in the spring of 1833 between the Ottoman-Egyptians İbrahim Paşa and Mehmet Ali and the central Ottoman state entailed the cession by the central state of four Syrian *paşalık*s and, soon after, the cession of Adana as well to Mehmet Ali in exchange for annual tribute to the Porte. By July 1833 the Treaty of Hünkar İskelesi, a defensive pact between Russia and the Ottoman Empire, was signed. This was taken as an affront by Mehmet Ali, who rightly presumed that the defensive pact was made with him in mind.[59] The following September, after further rounds of negotiations, the amount of tribute to be paid to the Porte for these provinces—thirty thousand purses—was agreed, and troops were withdrawn from Anatolia. The historian Dodwell summed up the outcome: "The Syrian [crisis] was thus ended to the satisfaction of no one. The Sultan had suffered the vexation of defeat by a contumacious pasha; [Mehmet Ali] had secured neither the independent status nor a controlling influence at the Porte; the western powers were annoyed at the opening which İbrahim's victories had offered to the Russians; while the Russians were disappointed at having been unable to entrench themselves more securely at Constantinople."[60] Mehmet Ali and İbrahim stayed in Syria, agreed to pay tribute to the Porte, and agreed not to continue their march toward the capital. The broader international alliance that had precipitated this intra-Ottoman truce—namely, Russia's arrival to defend the Ottoman central state—had further repercussions on British and French policy toward the Ottoman state and added another layer of complexity to the already tension-fraught "resolution."

The resolution to the elaborate crisis over Mehmet Ali and Syria demonstrated, among other things, the unfinished process of melding between Ottoman politics and European international politics at this time. Conflicting interests that had brought about the crisis—both within and beyond the Ottoman Empire—continued in conflict after the formal resolution. The aspect relevant for this discussion, however, is that of the encounters that went on among Ottoman and foreign statesmen in the course of negotiations in İstanbul. The day-to-day realities of diplomacy regarding the Mehmet Ali crisis reflected the emergence of diplomacy as a structure of imperial governance, out of the years of domestic preoccupation and sporadic diplomatic engagement in the 1820s.

If İstanbul negotiations for the Greek settlement occasioned the first encounter between Ottoman politics as a whole and the European state system as a whole after years of separation, then the Mehmet Ali case took that encounter a step further and involved the mutual dismantling and melding of Ottoman and European international politics. The goal here is not to detail all of the many rounds of meetings that went on in İstanbul but to give a sample of the range of who could be involved in meetings relevant to the Mehmet Ali crisis, what could be discussed at these meetings, and what these meetings signified in the larger pattern of diplomatic politics. The ways information was passed between the Ottoman center and the court of Mehmet Ali in Egypt incorporated foreign, particularly French, diplomats. Interestingly, former phanariots such as Vogorides still had a space to maneuver—and serve the empire—in this emerging structure of diplomatic politics.

In contrast to the Greek talks, during which representatives of several states met together, the Mehmet Ali case involved a dizzying array of meetings between one or another small group of Ottoman officials and one or another foreign representative or among foreign representatives independent of Ottoman officials. In February 1833, the French admiral Roussin first met with Reis Efendi Akif to warn him that if Russian ships were to arrive in Turkey the ensuing events (involving French and British military response) would "erase Turkey from the map of Europe." A few days later, when Russian ships did arrive, Stephanos Vogorides and his associate M. Blaque rushed to Admiral Roussin to convey the "terror and desperation of the members of the Divan" and to say that he and Blaque "had been charged by them and by the sultan himself and the *serasker* [the imperial military commander Husrev Paşa] to solicit the support of France, which would allow them to renounce Russian support formally and immediately" if the French ambassador would guarantee a peace on the conditions offered earlier by Halil Paşa on his mission to Mehmet Ali. On a separate occasion a few months later, Admiral-Ambassador Roussin met three times with the British ambassador Ponsonby in the first three days after the latter's arrival in İstanbul. The subject of the meetings was how to immediately remove the Russian pretext for its military presence in the capital city.[61]

While meetings with Admiral Roussin and various combinations of Ottoman officials dealt with France's stance toward the Ottoman Empire and Russia in the Mehmet Ali crisis, other meetings with de Varenne, the French chargé d'affaires in İstanbul at the time, were focused more on conveying information between the Ottoman central state and Mehmet Ali's court in Egypt. In October 1832, "de Varenne verified that the *reis efendi* (Akif) was not at all frightened by the idea of seeing France interfering with a view to finding a settlement; de Varenne furthermore counseled the viceroy, through M. Mimaut as an intermediary, to indicate his terms for a compromise."[62] By December 1832, Mehmet Ali made use of de Varenne by sending a letter to the Porte through him, offering his submission in exchange for all of Syria. He called "upon M. de Varenne to employ his best endeavors to engage the Porte to accept his proposals."[63] In contrast to the British ambassador's attempts to effect his own policy goals through members of the Divan in the 1820s, Mehmet Ali, an Ottoman vassal, now used the French chargé d'affaires to further his policies from Egypt.

Meetings involving further combinations of officials (and some who were not officials) illustrate the kaleidoscope of Ottoman diplomatic politics at this moment. The British report of this communication, mentioned above, from Mehmet Ali to the *reis efendi* through de Varenne, was made possible by a separate meeting between the *reis efendi* and the British ambassador. Furthermore, the statement by de Varenne to the *reis efendi*, that he, de Varenne, "was merely the channel through which [Mehmet Ali] has thought proper to make his proposals to the Porte, and that there has been no desire expressed on the part of the French *chargé d'affaires* that France should be the mediator between the Sultan and Mehmet Ali," was made at a meeting between the *reis efendi* and de Varenne, which was also attended by Stephanos Vogorides (who reported this to the British ambassador).[64] De Varenne, then, had contact with Mehmet Ali through correspondence (likely mediated by the French consul Mimaut in Alexandria), with the *reis efendi*, who himself was also in direct contact with the British ambassador Mandeville, and with Stephanos Vogorides, who at this point had not been appointed as prince of Samos and so still had no official position but was, as shown above, in direct contact with Sultan Mahmud and many others at the court.

From the Ottoman perspective these meetings, and the reports they generated, were crucial to gleaning the intentions and goals of the relevant foreign powers. An extensive Ottoman report from 1832 detailed a series of conversations: first, a "secret" *(baş örtülü)* conversation with the Russian ambassador, and second, a conversation involving Reis Efendi Akif, Stephanos Vogorides, Abdülhak Efendi, who was the chief physician on the Ottoman side, and the French dragoman Lapierre.[65] The question for the Ottoman government was how to set up a "proper framework for discussions with Russia given the current Ottoman alliance with Britain." The three Ottoman officials mentioned above were assigned to study and consider this question, and in doing so, Vogorides met "by chance" *(tesaduf ile)* with Lapierre.[66] As was popular at this time, the two envisioned potential scenarios of how the conflict between Mehmet Ali and the Ottoman central state could play out if one or another foreign power were to intervene.[67] Lapierre informed Vogorides that, if Mehmet Ali were besieged by Russian forces in Anatolia, for instance, then France would be forced to come to Mehmet Ali's aid, and then the Greek government, too, would get involved on the side of Mehmet Ali, and the conflict would continue to escalate.[68] Several other factors were discussed: the Serbian Question, the "matter of autonomy" *(serbestiyet maddesi),* the caution that needed to be taken in formulating Ottoman policy against Mehmet Ali so as not to encourage other "traitors" to follow his example and challenge the central state, and the necessity for trust between the Ottoman and Russian states. Most telling about these meetings and the Ottoman report generated from them is that the Ottoman central state exerted great effort to understand the calculus of politics from the French, Russian, and British perspectives at the same time as from the perspective of Mehmet Ali and other "potential" Mehmet Alis within their domains. The calculus of imperial governance was coming to include consideration beyond the empire on an equal footing with considerations of possible scenarios within the empire's borders. Foreign relations, then, were on par with imperial administration in the struggle to maintain operations of governance.

Even coffeehouse "intelligence" (better known as *dedikodu,* or gossip, in Ottoman documents) collected by informants for the sultan at this time was part of the growing field of diplomatic politics. In memos written to the central authorities, conversations regarding the Mehmet Ali crisis were reported between anonymous informants and an anonymous French diplomat, a Greek merchant, and even one Mehmet Efendi, a clerk at the headquarters of the imperial military command (Seraskerate).[69] Those in the Ottoman central state (in particular Sultan Mahmud himself) seemed desperate for information, both on the goings-on within their own ranks and on the opinions and intentions of foreign states at this moment.[70] As a result, the state sponsored and monitored a range of encounters that, if they had gone on in the 1820s, had not been integrated into the affairs of governance, as became the case in the 1830s.

These examples clearly demonstrate that multiple levels of contact had been initiated and sustained between the Ottoman and foreign states in the early 1830s. Although, aside from the coffeehouse intelligence, the meetings were carried out in formal and quasi-formal contexts and often involved the formal personnel of diplomacy, the substance of the meetings made it increasingly difficult to differentiate between foreign relations and Ottoman policy making. This stood in stark contrast to the politics of domestic preoccupation in the 1820s, when Ottoman military fortunes and court politics, to the relative exclusion of foreign relations, drove policy making. The changes in the political landscape since the 1820s are clear in the attempts of one more diplomat to participate in Ottoman and international politics—this time a diplomat who tried to enter the circles of diplomacy in İstanbul when they were already in formation, in late 1833.

When Baron de Boislecomte arrived in İstanbul, the Mehmet Ali crisis was formally over. Boislecomte, already an experienced diplomat and high-ranking official in the French Foreign Ministry, had been sent from France on a special mission to solidify the shaky reconciliation between Mehmet Ali and the Ottoman central state and, by extension, to remove the Russian military presence from İstanbul. Boislecomte traveled first to Egypt and spent several months there, with Mehmet Ali, and then in Syria and Anatolia before moving on to İstanbul. In İstanbul his goal was to convey his intelligence to the French Embassy and ascertain the perspective and strategy of the Porte regarding Mehmet Ali during a time when an official but tension-fraught settlement had been reached between the two.

Even Boislecomte's arrival in İstanbul was made difficult by the political situation. The Russian envoy de Butenev had secured an alliance with Sultan Mahmud and nurtured the latter's fear of Mehmet Ali.[71] As such, his goal was to keep Boislecomte, a potential mediator and assuager of the sultan's fears of Mehmet Ali, out of the capital. Through the mediation of the dragoman of the Porte, permission was requested from the *reis efendi* (Akif Paşa) for the boat Boislecomte was in to pass through the Dardanelles. The *reis efendi* gave permission on the condition that Boislecomte would not ask for an audience at the court or Porte.[72] The French envoy was then relegated to informal channels of diplomacy when he reached the capital.

Unable to meet directly and formally with members of the Ottoman court, Boislecomte worked through "various channels" to get his message through to the Porte; through Lord Ponsonby, the British ambassador, through the French ambassador Admiral Roussin, through the Austrian and Prussian envoys, and all of their dragomans.[73] Based on a strategy to decrease Ottoman dependence on Russia, his message was that Mehmet Ali should not be feared and thus that the British and French representatives' policy should be to downplay such fears when speaking to the sultan: "Perhaps, Monsieur le Duc, it would be a good policy for the ambassadors of France and England to combat the fears spread by [Russian] agents, but instead they partake personally in those fears, and it would clash with the loyalty of their characters to try to inspire in the Porte a confidence that they themselves do not have."[74] The French envoy went on to give the example of Lord Ponsonby, who "went even further" than the others and even set a date for Mehmet Ali's attack on the sultan, predicting, "Before the end of November you will see Mehmet Ali in Constantinople."[75] Surely, according to Boislecomte, statements like these were only pushing the sultan and his advisers further into the arms of Russia. "How can one at once reveal such a fear and engage His Highness to abandon Russian protection?" Boislecomte asked.[76]

After trying to convey his message that Mehmet Ali was not to be feared through a range of political and diplomatic personnel that had proliferated in the Ottoman capital in recent years, Boislecomte was finally allowed unmediated contact with Ottoman officials one evening. He was taken by the French ambassador to a fête given by the sultan for the diplomatic corps in the Kağıthane quarter of İstanbul. The very fact that the sultan hosted a formal social gathering for the "diplomatic corps" indicated the changes that were under way in the culture and mechanisms of diplomacy from the previous decade.[77] Whereas in the 1820s, foreign envoys had struggled to maintain contacts with one or another Ottoman official and had made infrequent visits to the court, in the 1830s a critical mass of individuals had developed, from several states, who could and did gather together, even at times under the auspices of the sultan for a social gathering.[78] This was, according to Boislecomte, the perfect opportunity to see what effect his "language taken to the Divan through different channels had produced there."[79]

At the fête, the French ambassador introduced Boislecomte to the "principal personages" of the empire, who all treated him "with as much kindness as reserve," avoiding "with a sort of affectation" any discussion of the current political events.[80] Despite the formal snub Boislecomte received from Ottoman officials as someone trying to undermine current Ottoman policy—both the alliance with Russia and the policy toward Mehmet Ali—the French envoy located yet another informal channel through which to voice his message: the assistant dragoman of the Porte and prince of Samos, Stephanos Vogorides. Vogorides approached Boislecomte at the fête and requested a private meeting at his residence, a request that, although seeming unofficial, was understood by Boislecomte, in the context of this new politics of diplomacy, to have been authorized by Vogorides' superiors.

Boislecomte introduced Vogorides as "one of the most willing agents employed by the Porte in diplomatic affairs," who "himself requested to be presented to me and immediately begged me to tell him what time and what day I would be able to receive him at my home." He continued, "*I was already too familiar with the reserve and discretion that are imposed on the agents of the Porte not to see in this demand a démarche authorized by the government of Her Highness.* It seemed that if I could not seek communication regarding the situation with Turkish ministers, I should no longer rebuff this demand, and I responded to M. Vogorides that, since I was residing in the countryside and was coming often into the city, it seemed more comfortable for both of us for me to come to his home."[81]

Vogorides and Boislecomte had a frank discussion, which indeed took place in Vogorides' home in Phanar, regarding Mehmet Ali's intentions toward the sultan and France's intentions toward the Ottoman Empire and toward the Mehmet Ali crisis in general. Boislecomte assured Vogorides that Mehmet Ali was fully occupied with his exploitation of Syria and Egypt and had no interest in further expanding the territory under his control, and that therefore the settlement made with the Porte was sincere and would be lasting. The two went on to discuss the language used by France when dealing with Mehmet Ali, as a way of reassurance to Vogorides and the Ottoman central state that France was not plotting an alliance against the Porte. Finally, Vogorides, likely following orders given to him by his (non-Russian-aligned) superiors, conveyed the view that the Ottoman central state would favor a rapprochement with Mehmet Ali, which would strengthen the empire and its resistance to Russian influence. Boislecomte went immediately to the French ambassador, who in turn sent word to Mimaut, the French consul in Egypt, that a démarche for rapprochement be drawn up and given to Mehmet Ali.

Shortly after this first meeting, Boislecomte paid another visit to Vogorides to learn what had become of the plan for reconciliation. Vogorides responded that everyone at the Sublime Porte sincerely desired a reconciliation with Mehmet Ali, but, he added, "Everyone is so afraid that no one would dare to give this counsel to the sultan."[82] He requested that perhaps Boislecomte could help by persuading the French ambassador to broach the topic confidentially to the *reis efendi* and explain the motives that have made Mehmet Ali refuse to pay his tribute. Boislecomte responded that *without an official title he could not have access to the Turkish ministers* and that Vogorides should gather the courage to bring this issue to the sultan himself, to which Vogorides replied that he would assign one Monsieur Blaque the role of intermediary.[83]

Alexandre Blaque was a French-Belgian Levantine who had been a lawyer in İzmir, had published the first newspaper in the Ottoman Empire (in French) in 1821, and subsequently, in the late 1820s, had moved to İstanbul. Once in İstanbul, he became the editor of the first official Ottoman newspaper, which first saw publication in 1831 and was published in two simultaneous versions—in French as *Le Moniteur Ottoman* and in Turkish as *Takvim-i Veka'yi*. Blaque was quite involved in Ottoman foreign relations, and Vogorides claimed him as a close friend. Mandeville, the British envoy, upon learning of the new gazette to be published by Blaque, wrote that he was "a person of extreme liberal principles and not likely to remain uninfluenced by the French Embassy here, and whose object would not perhaps always be to cultivate a continuation of harmony and good understanding between the Porte and Russia."[84] In terms of the conceptual scheme put forth here regarding formal and informal power in the new Ottoman diplomacy, Blaque was comparable to what Findley dubbed the "marginal men" who stepped forward in the 1820s; without having been expressly trained in or for an Ottoman political career, Blaque happened to have had the desired skills and acquaintances to serve an important function in İstanbul politics and to initiate publication of the official newspaper.

In the end, however, the intermediary for these negotiations was the French ambassador, who delivered Mehmet Ali's response to Consul Mimaut's démarche that had requested a rapprochement. The French ambassador, upon receiving this response, passed it on to the grand vezir, Rauf Paşa. Rauf Paşa replied that those of the Porte were afraid to even mention the name Mehmet Ali to the sultan, who had said, "What do I care about the empire? What do I care about İstanbul? I would give İstanbul and the empire to he who would bring me the head of Mehmet Ali!"[85] The grand vezir then begged the French dragoman to thank the French ambassador for his advice, to tell him that the Porte entirely shares his opinion and his will on this issue, but that the sultan had said he would cut off the head of the first man who would speak to him in favor of Mehmet Ali.[86]

By the time of Boislecomte's visit to İstanbul in 1833, a whole gamut of personnel had developed who were involved in negotiations that were at once domestic and diplomatic. French ambassadors, chargés d'affaires, dragomans, and special envoys met with Ottoman officials (and some who were not officials, such as those in coffeehouses) who spanned from the *reis efendi* and grand vezir to Vogorides, the prince of Samos, as well as with British diplomats. Russian diplomats (such as Butenev), for their part, met with the sultan and other high officials in the court, and the Russian admiral even enjoyed guided tours of the imperial mint and received jewels from Sultan Mahmud.[87] British diplomats followed developments on all sides closely, often through their Ottoman allies, such as Vogorides himself.[88] So many points of contact proliferated between Ottoman politics and European international politics, and so many channels through which to convey information from one actor to another, that distinguishing between domestic and diplomatic politics in Ottoman governance was becoming more and more difficult.

At the same time, constraints that existed on both sides prevented the two systems—the Ottoman and the international—from merging completely. This was principally the result of the conflicting interests inherent in the discrete, sovereign states of the European system. In addition, although at times the Ottoman polity appeared in danger of being wholly subsumed by one state or a combination of states, the decision to maintain the territorial integrity of the empire also entailed maintaining the formal structure, or "integrity," of Ottoman politics and political culture.[89] Regardless of how deeply involved the British, French, and Russian envoys were in one or another court faction or in one or another Ottoman policy decision, they were forced to respect the outward trappings of Ottoman power—the issuance of *fermans*, the ranks, titles, and honors of Ottoman officials, and the personal power dynamics within the court and Porte. The fusing, then, between Ottoman and international politics would not be completed, but it did help to form a new political landscape in which diplomacy saw an increased complexity and capacity that eclipsed the capacity of military power within the empire and became a crucial area of Ottoman imperial governance.

## DIPLOMATIC POLITICS AND OTTOMAN POWER RELATIONS

The implications for this growing field of diplomatic politics on Ottoman power relations extended to both the military and the bureaucratic realms. Military force that was provided by a combination of Great Power states to back up diplomatic politics worked to limit the significance of the military force that was once used to fight out intra-Ottoman power struggles. When deadlocks between Ottoman forces and Greek rebels could be broken by Great Power fleets, or the superiority of Mehmet Ali's forces over those of the sultanate could be trumped by a Russian army, the calculus of imperial governance had to be transformed. At the same time this new politics of diplomacy had a double effect on the bureaucratic life of the empire both by shifting the orientation of Court factions and by expanding the political potential of mediating structures such as the Translation Office. Below is a brief discussion of the military and then the bureaucratic repercussions of the changing politics of diplomacy in İstanbul.

Mehmet Ali and İbrahim, who seized the military void in Ottoman governance in the 1820s, also had to cope with the repercussions of the new politics of diplomacy they had helped precipitate with their challenge to the sultanate. Mehmet Ali's military prowess and successes against Ottoman forces, in the context of a geostrategic calculus, were now only two of many factors that went into political decision making. What power could Mehmet Ali have in the context of Ottoman power relations, when Russian forces could overrun him, on behalf of the Ottoman central state, at any time? For British, French, and Russian policy makers and diplomats, intra-Ottoman conflicts were read simultaneously within the framework of Ottoman power relations and as proxy issues for interstate power struggles. The process of deciding which rebels deserved to secede from the Ottoman Empire shifted to the realm of diplomacy, which greatly circumscribed the significance of military contests made manifest within the empire. Greek rebels, for instance, were losing the military battle against Mehmet Ali on behalf of the sultanate but were eventually granted statehood. Mehmet Ali, who was acknowledged by all to have the military resources to take over the sultanate, was retained as a vassal and eventually, by 1841, marginalized politically and militarily (even if granted hereditary rule in Egypt). Both of these decisions were made in the realm of diplomatic politics, and both demonstrated the diminishing role of domestic military contests in determining outcomes in Ottoman politics in the early 1830s.

The marginalization of Ottoman military power as a deciding factor in conflict resolution and policy making stood in contrast to the tremendous expansion of diplomacy as a factor in Ottoman court politics and the bureaucratic realm. Diplomacy rose in importance, as the decisions of whether or not to enact territorial changes in response to intra-Ottoman conflicts moved into the realm of multilateral negotiations and international political calculus. Those who still occupied positions of official power in the Ottoman government, then, adapted their relationships to fuse Ottoman politics, as they knew it, to European international politics. This fusion did not immediately transform the structures and relationships of Ottoman politics and diplomacy wholesale. Rather, it formed yet another layer of relationships within court politics. It also set in motion changes in the hierarchy of functions within the bureaucracy, exemplified by the new significance for diplomatic offices and operations.

The state most prepared to take advantage of Ottoman military vulnerability was Russia, whose forces invaded in 1828 in order to force Ottoman concessions on Greek independence and a settlement for the Danubian Principalities (and Serbia). From that point, Husrev Paşa, who had been appointed *serasker* in 1827 and so knew the state of the Ottoman military, and his protégés became involved in negotiations with Russia and advocated a conciliatory policy toward that state. These protégés included Halil Rıfat Paşa, who in 1836 replaced Husrev as *serasker,*[90] as well as Ahmed Fevzi and Akif paşas, both of whom ascended the ranks of power in the late 1820s. As mentioned above, Halil Rıfat, who would later be appointed *tophane müşiri* (marshal of the imperial arsenal) went on several diplomatic-political missions to Mehmet Ali; Ahmed Fevzi Paşa was the *kapudan paşa;* and Akif Efendi went from receiver (1825) to director of the Imperial Divan Office (1827) and ended up as *reis efendi* (1832) during the Greek and Egyptian negotiations.

These three men—Husrev (as military commander), Ahmed Fevzi (as Ottoman admiral), and Akif (as *reis efendi*)—signed the defensive Hünkar İskelesi pact with Russia in the summer of 1833. Their group became aligned with Russia, preferring its takeover to a Mehmet Ali takeover, in part because of Husrev Paşa's visceral hatred of Mehmet Ali. As a result of the realities of the Ottoman military situation, then, one group at the court made the transition from military to diplomatic functions so as to achieve an alliance with Russia. Another group, which had included Galip Paşa and, after his death in 1829, his protégés, such as Pertev Paşa and Mustafa Reşit Paşa, came to identify with British interests and diplomatic personnel. Galip Paşa was the eldest of this group and was one of the Ottoman officials who had served abroad during the reign of Selim III and maintained relations the British in the 1820s. Pertev Paşa (who was also the tutor of Abdülmecit, who himself would take over the sultanate while still a young boy in 1839, presiding over the first round of Tanzimat reforms) and Mustafa Reşit Paşa were Galip's protégés who were most involved in diplomatic politics. They lacked the military background of Husrev and Ahmed Fevzi paşas and had opposed Russian involvement in the Ottoman state. Partly as a result of earlier connections with British diplomats and partly as a result of the preexisting dynamics of factional rivalries, these men developed closer ties to Britain and France in the early 1830s.

During this reorientation of court politics, rivalries developed between officials who had worked together in the late 1820s. Pertev and Akif, whose rivalry would mark Ottoman politics of the mid-1830s and help demarcate the Russian and British factions at the court, were one such example. Although, according to Carter Findley, their respective patrons, Galip Paşa and Mustafa Mazhar Efendi, had been rivals a generation before,[91] Akif and Pertev had worked together in the course of their ascent to power; in 1828, for instance, at the request of Sultan Mahmud they had worked together to draft a response countering a conciliatory policy toward Russia and the cession of territory to Greek rebels. Interestingly, they located a basis in Islamic law for their claims that Ottoman territory must not be ceded, and they used those claims against a member of the *ulema,* Keçecizade İzzet Molla, and the chief physician Behcet Efendi, who were advocating compromise with Russia and Greek rebels.[92]

Pertev, although serving as *kahya bey,* or interior minister, had established important connections in the areas of foreign and military affairs. Mustafa Reşit Efendi (Paşa) is an important example of one of Pertev's connections, because he was a protégé of Pertev even though he had served as receiver under Akif. Pertev's son-in-law, Vassaf, was a secretary at the palace and a favorite of the sultan. Furthermore, Pertev's brother, Emin, was the supervisor of military supply *(mühimmat-i harbiye nazırı).*[93] Pertev, with former diplomatic experience and well-placed allies in the domain of his rival Akif, helped intensify preexisting frictions between the two.

As these political realignments took place in the early 1830s, new kinds of conflicts reflecting this new layer of diplomatic politics occurred within court politics. One famous incident illustrating how factional politics had become entwined with diplomatic politics was known as the Churchill incident and was precipitated in June 1836 by a British subject who mistakenly wounded a Muslim child while hunting outside the capital city.[94] Akif Paşa, as *reis efendi,* ordered the arrest of the British subject, Churchill, who was held in the Bagno, as the İstanbul prison at the naval arsenal was called.[95] The British ambassador Ponsonby then called his friend, Kahya Pertev Paşa, and expressed his outrage at the imprisonment of a British subject. Pertev looked into the incident and, finding that Akif had ordered the arrest, himself ordered Akif's dismissal as *reis efendi* and the release of the prisoner, all without the consent of the sultan. Akif's supporters attempted to get Ponsonby removed as ambassador, and Ponsonby responded by attempting to have Admiral Ahmed Fevzi dismissed. Akif and his supporters then notified the sultan that Pertev had made these unilateral decisions and, after a long series of events, caused Pertev's arrest, exile, and ultimately execution the following year.[96]

The Churchill incident demonstrates the added layer of diplomatic politics that was now grafted onto court politics in the 1830s. Surely the rivalry between Pertev and Akif had predated this incident and had likely been a factor in their alignments with opposing foreign states. The Churchill incident no longer had to do with military success against rebels, as had feuds of the 1820s, or even directly with any decisive matter of government. It was, however, an opportunity for competing high officials to undermine each other's reputation to the sultan under the guise of foreign relations. It also illustrated the deepening involvement of foreign diplomats in Ottoman factional and personal struggles. In this way, as the sphere and capacity of diplomatic politics in İstanbul widened, this politics was becoming incorporated into preexisting factional politics at the court.

The Translation Office of the Sublime Porte was another site where changing Ottoman power relations were played out. In the 1820s, the attempt to fill the void left by phanariot dragomans went on in a context of uncertainty over the significance and day-to-day realities of foreign relations. The office, although restaffed, was marginal to the process of Ottoman policy making and the episodic diplomacy that went on in that decade. In the 1830s, by contrast, the ability to communicate directly with French, Russian, and British representatives took on a new significance, because those representatives were now actors in Ottoman political struggles and policy making. Carter Findley has noted, "In the tense interlude between the defeat of the Ottoman armies by the Egyptians at Konya (December 1832) and the conclusion of the Russo-Ottoman Treaty of Hünkâr İskelesi (July 1833), the Translation Office . . . came under renewed scrutiny. The employees of the office received sizable increases in salary and were joined by three young men from the Important Affairs Section of the Office of the Imperial Divan."[97] The staff of the office grew from the handful of men in the 1820s to thirty civil servants by 1841.[98]

In addition to the increasing wages and the growing size of the Translation Office, the prestige and location of the office in the larger context of Ottoman politics and bureaucracy shifted in the 1830s. Future grand vezirs, such as Aali and Keçecizade Mehmed Fuat, as well as other important figures of the next generation, such as Mehmet Namık Paşa and Ahmet Vefik, who was the grandson of the "marginal" dragoman from the 1820s Yahya Efendi and the son of Ruh-üd-din Efendi, entered the translation service in the 1830s.[99] A knowledge of French was becoming necessary for an Ottoman political-bureaucratic career; thus, the work of translation no longer seemed demeaning for educated Ottomans, as it had during the phanariot ascendancy. "The main source from which a scribal official could acquire this knowledge [of French] was the Translation Office of the Porte."[100]

At the same time, in order to facilitate the fusing of Ottoman and diplomatic politics, further institutional changes were made to Ottoman bureaucracy to render the apparatus of Ottoman foreign relations more analogous to those of relevant foreign states. In 1836, the reis efendi, whose official title, as we've seen, meant "chief scribe" but whose functions had evolved to encompass matters of foreign relations, was renamed hariciye nazırı, or foreign minister.[101] In November of the same year, the office of müsteşar, or undersecretary for foreign relations, was created. Again in the same year, the kahya bey, whose official title had meant steward but who had come to be the chief of domestic affairs, was renamed first mülkiye nazırı (civil service minister) and then shortly after dahiliye nazırı (interior minister),[102] thus delineating the spheres of domestic and foreign politics just as the two were de facto blurring together. In 1834, even the calendar for new appointments to offices was changed to the month before Ramazan, rather than the month after, and the annual renewal ceremonies for all high officials was changed so that appointments would be made as needed.[103] Finally, a system of ranks and medals was created in the mid-1830s and refined by the end of the decade to consist of four ranks, and the foreign minister was one of the officials of the first rank.[104]

Together with these internal changes to the structure, personnel, and functions of Ottoman diplomacy and the translation service, new protocol was established for the reception of foreign ambassadors. In March 1832, just before İstanbul negotiations over the Greek settlement would commence, Stratford Canning noted,

> The fatiguing and in some respects humiliating, ceremonial, formerly observed on the presentation of Ambassadors, was superseded in this instance by an Audience more similar to what is now practiced in the Courts of Christendom: and the Reis Efendi has informed me that the Sultan does not intend to return in future to the antient [sic] etiquette. . . . On landing from the Bosphorus, I was received by an officer of the Imperial Guard, and subsequently by the Dragomans of the Porte, who introduced me into one of the saloons of the Palace, where I found the Sultan's favourite, Mustafa, the Syr-Kiatib [serkatip, a new name for reis efendi], and Ahmet Pasha, commander of the fortresses on the Bosphorus, with two or three more officers of rank.[105]

Compare this low-key reception to the elaborate and lengthy ceremony described by Rev. Robert Walsh, who enjoyed an audience with the sultan in 1821. Walsh and the British ambassador experienced many of the same customs that phanariot voyvodas had before 1821: the day before their visit to the sultan they met with the grand vezir in his quarters; they set off before dawn on Tuesday (the "day of the divan"), supplied with "richly caparisoned horses," and passed lines of janissaries on either side all along their way, then set off on boats to the same dock, where they stopped and smoked pipes with Turkish officials who were waiting for them; they dismounted their horses, as the voyvodas had, at the second gate of the palace and proceeded to the Divan, where they ate a ritual meal with the council members; and finally, they were seized by the collar and shuffled into their audience with the sultan.[106] In the 1830s, in contrast, etiquette had been made more analogous to the conventions of Britain and other "Courts of Christendom."

In addition to the changes to Ottoman diplomacy at home, the Ottoman foreign diplomatic corps was resuscitated in the early and mid-1830s, again to make that body more analogous to the structures that brought foreign ambassadors to İstanbul. In the 1820s no Ottoman ambassadors were serving in posts abroad. Even by 1832, only one representative, J. Mavroyeni (a phanariot affiliate from long before 1821), was reappointed as a permanent diplomatic envoy in Vienna, following an Austrian request.[107] In 1834, Mahmud appointed Mustafa Reşit Bey (made paşa in 1838) to the permanent Paris Embassy and by 1836–37 had appointed staff to London as well. According to Findley, with the exception of Mustafa Reşit Paşa, who took Ruh-üddin with him to Paris as translator, other appointees still chose Orthodox Christians (Rum) to accompany them abroad as secretaries and dragomans.[108]

To sum up, the fusing of Ottoman politics and international politics, demonstrated by the proliferation of diplomatic personnel in İstanbul and the frequency of face-to-face meetings involving subsets of that personnel, had a number of repercussions for Ottoman power relations in the 1830s. Most profoundly, the relative significance of military and diplomatic power within the Ottoman Empire was inverted from the 1820s to the 1830s. This meant a marginalization of the military power commanded directly by the Ottoman central state as a deciding factor in intra-Ottoman political conflicts and the growing importance of diplomatic politics as a field in which intra-Ottoman power struggles would be worked out. As a result, factional politics at the court underwent a reorientation so as to align with the international rivalries and alliances that subsumed Ottoman governance. The prestige and capacity of the Translation Office were bolstered, and the office was reorganized along with the Ottoman Foreign Ministry and the Ottoman foreign diplomatic corps in response to the growing significance of diplomacy for Ottoman governance, making the Translation Office the nucleus of a new Muslim reforming elite. And finally, conventions of Ottoman diplomacy were reconfigured so as to correspond with those of European courts. These "pre-Tanzimat" reforms were not merely a spontaneous move to imitate European ways but rather were prompted by a deeper shift in the configuration of Ottoman governance. İstanbul was indeed given over to international politics in the 1830s, changing the political landscape of the capital and of the imperial government. Despite all of these changes, Stephanos Vogorides and his phanariot cronies and rivals were able to carve out a new a niche for themselves at the epicenter of Ottoman diplomacy, which was itself ever more central to the task of Ottoman governance. From that epicenter they would experience act one of the Tanzimat project in 1839. This first act was not so much a revolution for them as the 1820s were or the 1850s would be, but it did provide an abundance of new materials, which, combined with the old phanariot materials, enabled them to build new houses for themselves.

# The Second Ascendancy

*Prince Vogorides, Also Known as Istefanaki Bey*

As the horizons of Ottoman diplomacy began to expand again in the later 1820s, Vogorides became involved, as translator, secretary, and negotiator, in successive treaty negotiations with Russia.[1] He traveled several times to St. Petersburg—first in 1826 to negotiate the Treaty of Akkerman (presumably on a kind of furlough from his internal exile), then in 1828–29 for the preparatory negotiations of the Treaty of Edirne, and some sources place him there again in 1833 to negotiate reparations from the 1829 conflict—with Halil Rıfat Paşa, a military-turned-diplomatic figure under the protection of Husrev Paşa.[2] The 1833 trip to St. Petersburg was not as successful as the earlier ones;[3] Stephanos and Halil Rıfat were called back to İstanbul and replaced by Ahmet Fevzi, another Husrev protégé (and son-in-law of the sultan), and Nicholas Aristarchi. This occurred not only because of Halil Rıfat's "incompetence" at negotiating treaties but also because of Stephanos's apparently obvious pro-British actions that were not well-received in St. Petersburg.[4] One can only conclude that Husrev Paşa played a decisive role in these appointments; not only had Stephanos long been a member of his retinues, but also both Halil Rıfat and Ahmet Fevzi belonged to his faction at court. Vogorides was still without an official position since his removal as *kaymakam* of Moldavia in 1822, and he depended on the state's ad hoc demand for his skills and connections when negotiations arose in the later 1820s.

While Vogorides' successes as negotiator and translator-interpreter in the new politics of diplomacy in İstanbul were the mainstay of his reputation with both Ottoman and British-French statesmen, he branched out beyond diplomacy at the earliest opportunity. Using the credibility he had built up in İstanbul, he created a role for himself in the new provincial administration of the island of Samos, in factional politics in the Ottoman court, and in Church politics at the İstanbul and Jerusalem patriarchates, as well as in provincial Church and administrative politics in areas such as Moldavia. Taking each of these realms in turn, we clearly see that Vogorides at once reconstituted phanariot power from before 1821 and adapted it to a new political context in the 1830s and after.

Vogorides was present at virtually all of the new sites of diplomatic politics: at the palace, at the fêtes for the diplomatic corps, at the houses of the *reis efendi,* at the ambassadorial residences; even his own household was among the new sites of politics. At this time, he used his previous phanariot identification to gain entry and credibility at the multistate negotiations under way in İstanbul.

The first formal position granted to Vogorides after 1822 was that of prince (bey) of the autonomous polity of Samos, a polity that had emerged out of the settlement for an independent Greek state in 1832. He was officially given the title in December 1832, in large part because he was not a local Samian and had, from İstanbul, earned the favor and trust of the British ambassador Canning and Sultan Mahmud in facilitating the conclusion of Greek-Ottoman negotiations. His absentee administration of Samos on behalf of the sultan, however, was not accepted by Samians until the summer of 1834, when Kostaki (Constantine) Musurus, the Vogorides-appointed governor of the island, traveled personally to each of the island's seventeen villages to negotiate with and gain the acceptance of the headmen there.[5]

As a creature of the pre-1821 phanariot house, Vogorides saw in Samos a chance to re-create the administration in which he had participated in Moldavia, and yet the tension-fraught realities of his "rule" in Samos reflected the new political circumstances of the 1830s. He had negotiated a seven-year term for taxes, similar to the tax regime in Moldavia and Wallachia under phanariot administration, and had set the tribute according to the same formula that had been used in those principalities.[6] Again as had been the case in Moldavia, he had attempted to create an administrative structure reminiscent of the phanariot *voyvoda*ship by calling himself *hegemonas* (the Greek term for *voyvoda*) and appointing a *kaymakam* (G. *topoteretes*), or governor, to represent him on the island. His first appointee to the position of *kaymakam* was his son Yanko (Ioannis) Vogorides, then in his twenties, along with one Eustathios Nicolaides.[7] Yanko, who was later declared mentally disturbed, was not successful in negotiating with the Samians, so was called back and replaced by Kostaki (Constantine) Musurus.[8] From that point on, the list of governors and tax collectors under Vogorides' Samos administration reads like a roster of his emerging patronage network; Alexander Photiades (1837–38), Gabriel Krestides (1847–50), the tax collector Demetrios Ioannides (1834–50), and Ioanni Adamantides (1849–50) would be the most striking examples.[9]

In Samos, Vogorides also tried to replicate the pre-1821 involvement of phanariot *voyvoda*s in the Church affairs of their provinces. In the case of Samos this meant changing the status of autonomous monasteries by bringing them under the direct authority of the patriarchate (which made them *stauropegeion*) and changing the status of the archdiocese of Samos and Ikaria to a metropolitanate.[10] Metropolitan Theodosios negotiated with Vogorides after he was exiled from Samos to the Iviron Monastery on Mt. Athos in order to get his possessions back, finally agreeing never to visit Samos again in exchange for their return.[11] It is clear that Vogorides, as absentee prince, sought involvement not only in the tribute arrangements of his principality but also in the Church and monastic affairs and in the local politics that had long predated him on the island.

The similarities of Vogorides' administration to the old phanariot system in Moldavia and Wallachia were not lost on the local population, some of whom had had direct experience in phanariot and patriarchate retinues in those provinces before 1821. In the course of local conflicts that ensued under Vogorides' administration, the faction that supported the İstanbul leadership was dubbed *phanariotiscos,* or "little phanariots."[12] The island's communities had experienced membership in the provisional Greek polity in the 1820s and had expressed their desire for self-rule, whatever their conception of that was. While some worked with Vogorides' regime, that regime, precisely for its phanariot resonances, elicited strong reactions, which in turn further polarized the already fractured politics on the island.[13]

Vogorides retained his title through seemingly endless rounds of tense negotiations, several gubernatorial appointments and removals, and more than one attempt on his life. At one point Constantine Stamatiades, a French-educated lawyer from Samos known for his Frankish clothes and hats, had traveled to İstanbul and reportedly tried to assassinate Vogorides, who in turn had Stamatiades put in the Bagno in İstanbul. Keeping this enemy from Samos under close watch in the İstanbul prisons, Vogorides also used Samos as an open-air prison for enemies from other areas, such as Georgi Mamarchev Buyukli, a fellow Kotel native who set up a Bulgarian detachment to fight on the Russian side in 1828–29 Russo-Ottoman hostilities.[14]

Rebellions in Samos in 1849–50 finally forced Vogorides to step down. Even then, he saw to the appointment of his fellow phanariot Alexandros Kallimaki, who refused to leave his post at the Ottoman Embassy in Paris to take up such a position. Georgios Konemenos was finally appointed as the governor for Kallimaki, who nevertheless received the title of prince of Samos without ever having to leave Paris. The principality of Samos had begun as part of Vogorides' project to reconstitute a provincial base for phanariot power, and it continued, with varying success, as a stronghold for "neophanariots" until it was joined to the Greek state in 1912.[15]

## COURT-PORTE POLITICS IN THE 1830S: ISTEFANAKI BEY VERSUS LOGOFET BEY

While Vogorides liked to think of Samos as his domain of absolute power, albeit a diminutive domain, he was also entrenched in more consequential factional politics at the Ottoman court–Sublime Porte. As Vogorides' involvement intensified, Nicholas Aristarchi, grand *logothete* of the patriarchate from 1824 until the 1850s, emerged as Vogorides' adversary in almost every quarter of the latter's activities. As court factions took shape and aligned with foreign states and local controversies, Vogorides and Aristarchi lined up along opposing axes on questions of international, ecclesiastical, provincial, and court politics.

Nicholas Aristarchi had had fewer years of experience than Vogorides in the pre-1821 phanariot house but nevertheless used the logic of that system to adapt to new political opportunities. He was born a generation after Vogorides, in 1799, and was the son of Stavraki (Stavro) Aristarchi, who had been the last Rum imperial dragoman in 1821. At eighteen, in 1817, he was appointed *mühürdar,* or keeper of the seal, for the Wallachian *voyvoda* Alexandros Soutso.[16] Nicholas was a young man of twenty-three, then, when he was exiled along with his father to Bolu, Anatolia, in 1822. His father was killed there shortly after their arrival, reportedly on the order of Halet Efendi, and Nicholas returned to İstanbul. His mother, Sophia Aristarchi, who remained in the capital, was the daughter of Manol (Emmanuel) Ağa, a prominent banker of influence in patriarchate politics and reportedly with the Ottoman central state before 1821.[17]

Like Vogorides, Nicholas Aristarchi was active in politics even during the tumult of the 1820s. In 1824 he was appointed *logothete,* or intermediary between the patriarchate and the Ottoman central state. In 1828, he was said to have been a "secretary" to Mahmud II and "first translator at the imperial palace."[18] By the 1830s Nicholas was the private French tutor for the future sultans Abdülmecid and Abdülaziz, which illustrates the favor he must have enjoyed with Sultan Mahmud.

As Vogorides and Aristarchi emerged out of the 1820s and built anew their personal and political alliances, they were portrayed by others as men of distinct characters and prejudices who nevertheless pursued the same favor in the Ottoman central state, at the patriarchate, and with foreign envoys in İstanbul. An Ottoman informant conveyed the comments of a French diplomat in the 1830s on the difference between Vogorides and Aristarchi, whom he depicted as the two poles of Christian-Ottoman power in İstanbul. He said that, while Vogorides was a "Muslim soul" (*Müslüman ruhu*) and would therefore remain loyal to the Ottoman state in opposition to Greece and Russia, Aristarchi, whom he called "Logofet bey," was "a Christian. He is a political man. With politics he uses both sides [Ottoman and Russian]."[19] Another Ottoman informant reported the contents of a passionate (and to the Ottomans, seditious) speech given by an unnamed cleric to the Holy Synod in 1832–33, on the tenth anniversary of the death of Nicholas Aristarchi's father, wherein the cleric condemned the Ottoman politicians and politics that he saw as responsible for the murder of Nicholas' father and called for vengeance.[20] Nicholas Aristarchi reportedly stood alongside the cleric and concluded the speech by affirming that vengeance would one day be theirs.

Regardless of the different career paths and sentiments of Vogorides and Aristarchi, they were perceived more and more as equal and opposite agents at all levels of politics emanating from İstanbul. In the early 1840s, the British statesman Layard noted that the two were engaged "in a constant struggle for influence in the palace and at the Porte," and, while their success varied, Vogorides was believed to have "exercised the more solid influence over the Turks, and was the more esteemed of the two, and especially by the Sultan."[21] For our discussion, Vogorides—Istefanaki Bey—and Aristarchi—Logofet Bey—took part, from different starting points, in the same project to reconstitute the phanariot system in which they had been created before 1821. We trace here the areas in which the two men sought power in light of the pre-1821 phanariot system: in the politics of court and Porte factions, in Church politics, in provincial administrative and Church affairs, and in the new institution of the Foreign Ministry by the late 1830s.

Vogorides, for his part, aligned at once with the British Embassy and with the Pertev faction at the court in the mid-1830s. In serving as a "secret communication link between Pertev, the sultan, and the British ambassador, Ponsonby,"[22] Vogorides aligned simultaneously *against* the Russian–Akif Paşa–Aristarchi faction. This dynamic would play out on a grand stage in the first Mehmet Ali crisis of 1832–34; namely, Vogorides was unofficially put in charge of facilitating negotiations with French mediators, who were in turn working toward a settlement between the Ottoman central state and Mehmet Ali. Such a settlement would, if successful, weaken Russian influence as well as the influence of the court factions in the process of aligning with Russia against Mehmet Ali.

Nicholas Aristarchi, in contrast, assumed a position in the Russian-aligned palace faction of Ahmet Fevzi Paşa (the Ottoman admiral), to whom he was named special counselor in 1833, and of Akif Paşa, who was foreign minister through much of the 1830s.[23] Some even believed that Husrev would use Aristarchi to gain influence with Akif Paşa and simultaneously use Vogorides to gain influence over Akif's rival, Pertev, in the 1830s.[24] The Russians, for their part, had put Aristarchi on their payroll, no doubt finding him a useful contact in both court politics and politics of the patriarchate, where he enjoyed the official rank of *logothete*.[25]

As court and diplomatic politics spread from the matter of secession regarding Greece and Egypt to the matter of autonomy under Ottoman rule for Samos and Moldavia-Wallachia, new opportunities arose for both Vogorides and Aristarchi as Orthodox Christians at the center of Ottoman governance. We have already seen how Vogorides acquired the title and privileges of the autonomous principality of Samos, partly because of the informal trust he had earned from the British ambassador and Ottoman sultan. But another reason Vogorides was a suitable candidate for the new position of prince of Samos was that he fulfilled the criterion—set by European states—as a "coreligionist" prince for the Christian population of the island. The principle that a Christian population within the Ottoman Empire should have a Christian administrator—now to be called prince—opened up a new category of positions for Vogorides and Aristarchi, as it did for Prince Milosh Obrenovitch in Serbia in the 1830s.[26] In the realm of diplomatic politics, once the decision had been made to maintain the formal integrity of the Ottoman Empire, it must have looked to European diplomats like a comfortable compromise: if the Christians of the Ottoman Empire could not be given independence from their Muslim rulers for the chaos that might ensue, according to European logic, then *at least* they could be allowed a coreligionist administrator. To have a coreligionist administrator, then, was seen, from the outside, as inherently less oppressive than to be ruled over directly by a non-Christian sultan or *paşa*. From the inside, it was a chance for Vogorides to adapt phanariot politics to new provinces.

BEYOND DIPLOMACY:
POLITICS AT THE PATRIARCHATE

At the same time that they were regaining power in the Ottoman central state and provincial administration, Vogorides and Aristarchi were important players in patriarchate politics. While the dragomanates and *voyvoda*ships could be taken away from phanariot control by the Ottoman central state, the patriarchate, located in the Phanar quarter, could hardly have been wrested from Greek-identified notables, who were a definitive feature of that institution.[27] Manuel Gedeon, the late nineteenth-century Church historian, for instance, gives a picture of continuity in personalities and lay-cleric relationships in the 1820s and 1830s: one Marki (Markos) Kalfa, an architect-builder who had restored the Sublime Porte complex in 1802 and built the Rum hospital in Galata in 1818, went on to become a member of the Community Council established at the patriarchate in 1824, at the height of Greek-Ottoman conflicts in the provinces.[28] A contemporary of his, Hacı Nikoli (Nicholas) Nikitaides,[29] hailing from the island of Leros and a relative of the (Leran) metropolitan of Heracleia Meletios, had been a palace architect in İstanbul before 1821 and was also responsible in the 1830s for rebuilding many of the churches that had been damaged in the previous decade. Nikitaides was apparently a favorite of Sultan Mahmud II and used to entertain Rum notables *(prokritoi tou Genous)* as well as Athanasios, the patriarch of Jerusalem, in his Phanar home the 1830s.[30] This is just one example that shows, although the ruptures in the larger phanariot system affected the administration of the Danubian Principalities and the offices of dragoman, they did not put an end to the many layers of personal connections operating in and around the patriarchate.[31]

Politics at the patriarchate in the 1820s was no less complicated than it had been before, despite the removal of a significant bloc of influential phanariots from the scene. This politics was in general conducted between lay and clerical factions before, during, and after the 1820s, featuring not only prominent bankers and merchants but also Rum guilds of İstanbul, representatives of which served on the Community Council. These guilds included the architects' and furriers' guilds.[32] Financial matters of the patriarchate, many of the large monasteries elsewhere in the empire, and patriarchal and metropolitan appointments were decided by this mixture of lay and clergy interests.[33]

Both Aristarchi and Vogorides inserted themselves into the complex politics at the patriarchate and integrated that politics into their involvement in the Ottoman Porte and court and with foreign embassies. In 1824, Aristarchi was appointed grand *logothete* of the patriarchate, making him responsible, on the side of the patriarchate, for patriarchate-Ottoman state relations.[34] On the one hand, this was an honor inherited from his father, Stavraki, who had also been known as "Logothetis."[35] On the other hand, in the new political circumstances, his formal position at the patriarchate made him an appealing ally to Russian statesmen. Aristarchi was, after all, appointed *logothete* during the first patriarchate of Anthimos III (July 1822– July 1824), who was known to have been Russian-aligned and to have resisted British attempts to limit his power.[36] Aristarchi's official role as *logothete* in the patriarchate administration likely aided in turn (and was facilitated by) his alignment with Russian interests, as the patriarchate was one of the avenues through which the Russian Empire sought to increase its influence within the Ottoman Empire. By 1839, the British ambassador Ponsonby wrote, "I have to inform your Lordship that the present Patriarch [Gregorios VI] is the tool of Mr. Aristarcki, a Greek, who is a paid agent of the Russian Government and the instrument constantly employed to work upon the Ottoman Ministers and others."[37]

Aristarchi found a way, through his connections with Church administration, to expand his activities to an Aegean island, if not to Vogorides' Samos. In patriarchate correspondence, Aristarchi was mentioned as "exarch" of several villages in northern Chios, an island near Samos but with a far more illustrious phanariot past, as early as 1830.[38] The title of exarch was associated with the office of grand *logothete* and brought with it income from the relevant villages and associated monastic holdings.[39] Aristarchi worked in the capacity of exarch with the high clergy and monasteries of the island, as well as with "Misé Yannis" (Ioannis) Psychares, a local Chiot who had established himself in İstanbul as the intermediary to the Porte for Chios.[40] While Vogorides had attained his position as prince of Samos through his influence in the Ottoman central state and with British diplomats, Aristarchi was appointed exarch of Chios through his deeper involvement in Church administration. Though not a new, modern-sounding autonomous principality with the potential for political independence, the exarchate of Chios provided an income and a further boost in status for Aristarchi in patriarchate circles, as Chios was the wealthy island birthplace of many phanariots before 1821.

Vogorides' residence was still in the Phanar quarter, just between the İstanbul patriarchate complex and the *metochion* (dependency) of the Jerusalem patriarchate, which served as a kind of İstanbul embassy for that patriarchate. While there is no evidence of Vogorides' direct involvement in Church politics in the midst of upheaval in the 1820s, there is evidence that he maintained his connections in the Phanar and became involved in patriarchate politics. An example of the former is that one Smaragda, daughter of physician Stephanos Karatheodori and his wife, Loukia Alexandrou Mavrocordato, was baptized in Vogorides' Phanar house in August 1831 and named Smaragda after her maternal grandmother, Princess (Domnitsa) Smaragda Mavrocordatou née Muruzi.[41] These were all members of pre-1821 phanariot families still associating with one another, and with Vogorides, in Phanar.

Following phanariot tradition, Vogorides had also become involved in patriarchate appointments and politics, albeit without an official position in the patriarchate administration. In 1830, Vogorides collaborated with Alexander Photiades (as we've seen, the eventual father-in-law of Vogorides' daughter) to lead a lay movement that ousted Patriarch Agathangelos and replaced him with Constantios I, who had been archbishop of the monastic community of St. Catherine's of Mt. Sinai.[42] This move accelerated the trend toward involvement of the "lay element" in Church administration, illustrated as well by the change in the source of the patriarch's salary; he was now to be paid out of the Community Treasury, which would presumably make him more accountable to the lay community.[43]

Vogorides even left evidence of his attempted involvement in Greek-identified craft guilds in İstanbul. These were an important bloc in communal politics, but presumably this element was an area, like that the larger one of patriarchate politics, in which he enjoyed limited success. One story places Vogorides at a meeting of the İstanbul furriers' guild and other lay and clergy in 1835, perhaps as he was trying to garner support for his candidate for patriarch. In the course of the meeting, one Zagano, head of the guild, responded abruptly to Vogorides' comments by saying, "Enough already! Why should we listen to you, you old Bulgarian!"[44]

Vogorides' activities to promote certain candidates for patriarch ran up against Aristarchi's efforts to support opposing candidates in 1835, expanding their rivalry beyond the Ottoman Palace and Porte to the sphere of Church affairs. Aristarchi, it seems, worked with the Jerusalem patriarch Athanasios and Aristarchi's brother-in-law, Sotirios Kalliades,[45] for the patriarchal election of Gregorios, the metropolitan of Serres, who also happened to be a Russophile. Vogorides worked again with Alexandros Photiades for the election of Paisios, metropolitan of Caesareia (Kayseri), who presumably enjoyed British support. Historians have noted that the victory of Gregorios, Aristarchi's candidate, demonstrated the significant influence of guilds in İstanbul, which had played a decisive role in Gregorios's elevation.[46] For our discussion, Gregorios's elevation to patriarch in 1835 also demonstrates the expanding power of foreign and court alliances beyond the sphere of diplomacy and into Church politics, which were themselves becoming entwined in new ways with lay institutions, such as guilds, in İstanbul.

By the 1840s, Vogorides' and Aristarchi's involvement in patriarchal appoint-ments, like their involvement in foreign and Ottoman court and Porte politics, had solidified into two opposing camps. Vogorides was behind the appointment of Pa-triarch Anthimos VI Koutalianos,[47] who reigned twice in the 1840s and 1850s. Aristarchi supported Anthimos III, who reigned intermittently from the 1820s to the early 1850s, and Germanos III, who also split his rule between the 1840s and 1850s, in their bids for the patriarchate. Vogorides' and Aristarchi's stake in Church politics went beyond patriarchal appointments. A recent student of patriarchate pol-itics goes so far as to say that "all of these prominent neophanariots [Vogorides, Aristarchi, Photiades, Psychares] had created and controlled a network of ap-pointments and transfers of metropolitans in exchange for exorbitant payoffs."[48] Church historian Gedeon implied that in 1848, during the tenure of an opposition patriarch, Vogorides came up with the idea to carve out his own institutional niche from the patriarchate and become *hegemonas,* or prince, of the Bulgarians, as Milosh Obrenovitch, "the former pig merchant," had become prince of Serbia.[49]

Vogorides' efforts to gain influence in Church affairs by proxy, whether because of his Bulgarian descent, his closeness to the Porte, or his pro-British alliances, were perhaps less successful than Aristarchi's direct efforts from within the patriarchate and with pro-Russian alliances. By the late 1840s, however, the Holy Synod had lodged a formal complaint with the Ottoman central state regarding both Vogorides' and Aristarchi's involvement in metropolitan elections and submitted a petition to have the accounts of former patriarch Anthimos VI's (Vogorides' crony) audited.[50]

## MARRIAGE, STATUS, AND
## OFFICIALDOM IN THE PROVINCES

From involvement in court politics, diplomacy, and patriarchate politics in İstan-bul, both Vogorides and Aristarchi expanded their activities to provinces beyond their island fiefdoms of Chios and Samos. The most important in their phanariot memory were the principalities of Moldavia and Wallachia. Neither man was eli-gible for appointment as *voyvoda* any longer, although Vogorides had tried his luck by claiming Moldavian or Wallachian descent or both in the 1820s. As *kapıkahyas* from İstanbul, however, they maintained the phanariot legacy as well as political relations, personal alliances, and material connections in the principalities. The sta-tus of the principalities vis-à-vis the Porte from 1821 until the late 1840s allowed them space to cultivate personal connections, even as formal Ottoman sovereignty there was fading.

Gregorios Ghika and Ion Sturdza, the princely appointments in the 1820s, were "small" boyars and thus considered indigenous and distinct from the Greek-phanariot imports from İstanbul. By the fall of 1827, it must have seemed like stability was being restored, for the "grand" boyars began returning to their estates from their exile in Kronstadt (Braşov).[51] The following spring, however, Russian forces arrived and drove Prince Sturdza out of Moldavia, installing a military government in both provinces, with General Kiselev and Russian consul de Minciaki. The Treaty of Edirne the following year (1829) ended hostilities, but the Russian military regime remained until 1834.[52] During that time, the Règlement Organique,[53] a system of laws and statutes, was drawn up under the supervision of Kiselev. This system devised a procedure to elect princes, established administrative autonomy, legal process, and checks and balances, created a gendarmerie, lowered the tax and tribute burden for peasants, and proclaimed the rights and interests of Moldavians and Wallachians "for the first time in two hundred years."[54] By 1831 in Wallachia and 1832 in Moldavia, the Règlement had been submitted by a commission from the two principalities and revised by the Russian court, then modified and passed by the general assemblies that had been set up, and finally, since the provinces were still formally under Ottoman rule, confirmed in a *hatt-ı şerif*.[55]

The twin principalities of Moldavia and Wallachia were formally returned to Ottoman rule in 1834, although the new regulations for administrative and legal autonomy, as well as free trade outside the Ottoman Empire, would remain in place. This represented, on one level, a significant distancing of the Moldavian and Wallachian regimes from the central Ottoman state and, as such, rupture from the ancien régime of the phanariot *voyvodas*. On another level, however, there were provisions that allowed the maintenance of personal ties between native boyars and foreigners, such as former phanariots. Namely, the right to "native" status in the new Règlement of the principalities was, as had been customary, to go to those who had married native boyars. With indigenous status, one was in turn eligible for public employment.[56]

Behind the changes in formal status and official political relations between the principalities and the Ottoman central state, the connections between "native" boyars and İstanbul-based phanariots continued in the 1830s and 1840s.[57] Even the provisional *voyvodas* of the 1820s, who were said to have been from petty boyar families and thus more a part of the native aristocracy, had connections abroad and to the previous phanariot administrations. Gregorios Ghika had been a *ban*, a position of midrank in phanariot-run Wallachia.[58] His brother was working for Russia and living in Vienna, and his sister was married to M. Valarmi, who was in the personal service of Emperor Alexander, as had been other phanariots before 1821. Ion Sturdza, for his part, was married to the sister of the phanariot prince Alexandros Muruzi.[59] Nicholas Soutso, mentioned above for his marriage alliance to the Wallachian native Cantacuzeno family, assimilated into the Moldavian provincial government in the late 1820s. *Postelnik* from 1832 to 1839, he was given the "guardianship of the fountains" and the "pavement commission" and other public works positions from 1840 until his appointment to the Department of Justice in 1846. Even after the removal of Michael Sturdza in 1848, this "Romanianized" phanariot continued in high state offices through the mid-1850s.[60]

By the 1830s, when a settlement for the legal and administrative status of the twin principalities was under negotiation between the Russian and Ottoman states, Vogorides and Aristarchi adapted to the new regime (which they had in fact helped bring into being with their role in the Russo-Ottoman negotiations) and located a place for themselves within it.[61] Aristarchi had reportedly passed through Jassy in early 1834, on his way back from St. Petersburg with Ahmet Fevzi Paşa, and there confirmed the choice of Michael Sturdza, a Russophile, as the new *voyvoda* of Moldavia.[62] Sturdza, it was pointed out by rival Nicholas Soutso, also enjoyed "the support of his presumptuous father-in-law in İstanbul," none other than Stephanos Vogorides. Vogorides had had his daughter Smaragda (b. 1816) married to Michael Sturdza, thereby ensuring his own rights as a "native" boyar in that principality.[63] The alliance he made was not only in keeping with the phanariot system into which he had been assimilated in 1812–13 with his marriage to Voyvoda Kallimaki's relative Ralou, but also was still an effective strategy for maintaining a political hold on Moldavia in the new political circumstances and in the absence of the broader phanariot system. Aristarchi, who was not yet married, took this opportunity to marry Maria, the daughter of the Moldavian grand *postelnik* Gregorios Mano, in 1833, and thus used a similar strategy to gain entry into the "native" boyar class.[64]

Out of their marriage alliances to native boyars in Moldavia, Vogorides and Aristarchi staked their claim on the one position that bound each principality to the Ottoman central state: *kapıkahya,* or agent at the Porte for the *voyvoda*s. Vogorides, although he had established a reputation already as an Anglophile, was appointed *kapıkahya* to his son-in-law, the Russophile Moldavian *voyvoda* Michael Sturdza. Aristarchi, married to the daughter of another native boyar, was appointed *kapıkahya* (1833–66) to the Wallachian *voyvoda* Alexandros Ghika.[65] As *kapıkahya*s, they maintained fragments of the pre-1821 phanariot system, exemplified by their ceremonial role in postphanariot investitures; in 1834, for instance, the former phanariot Nicholas Soutso delivered the invitation to Michael Sturdza, which had been given to him by Logothete Aristarchi, to come to İstanbul for Sturdza's investiture.[66]

Their activities as *kapıkahya* became, by the 1840s, extensions of their İstanbul intrigues and involvement in Russo-Ottoman relations. In 1847 Aristarchi engaged in a secret correspondence with Nicholas Soutso, who was receiving information from his son, a member of the Divan in Moldavia, about the wrongdoings of Voyvoda Sturdza. For his part, Vogorides had corresponded with his son-in-law Voyvoda Sturdza and others to glean evidence to undermine the rule of the Wallachian prince Ghika, who was toppled from power in the early 1840s.[67]

Out of these marriage alliances, Vogorides and Aristarchi achieved the formal titles of *kapıkahya* from the Porte to their respective *voyvoda*s, as well as a foothold into the provincial government, politics, and economy of those regions.[68] They would also remain active in the material affairs of the Church in Moldavia and Wallachia—the affairs between the İstanbul patriarchate and the principalities, as well as among those of the large monastic complexes of the empire. It was possible for Vogorides and Aristarchi to be involved in Church matters only because they had already achieved formal positions, as *logothete* in the Church and, in Aristarchi's case, in Wallachia and, in Vogorides' case, at the Porte and in Moldavia.

Church and monastic holdings in Moldavia and Wallachia long predated the phanariot networks of the eighteenth century.[69] Still, phanariots had distinguished themselves by their patronage of the patriarchate and the large monasteries of the Ottoman Empire as they donated land and built churches and monasteries in the Danubian Principalities in the eighteenth and early nineteenth centuries. When their formal hold on the principalities was lost to "native" boyars in the 1820s and after, however, the formal administration in the principalities began to diverge from the formal Church administration in Phanar and elsewhere.

In the 1830s, the financial matters of monasteries and monastic holdings were mediated by the *voyvoda*'s regime and the İstanbul patriarchate; the *voyvodas*, and sometimes the Holy Synod in İstanbul, adjudicated financial disputes between boyars and abbots regarding proceeds from the monastic lands.[70] The proceeds from the vast holdings of the larger monastic complexes and patriarchates outside the principalities, however, had remained in the possession of those institutions.[71] In the late 1840s, as boyars mobilized into a movement with claims to unification and nationhood, they demanded the expropriation of those monastic and patriarchal lands. The course of the Romanian unification and independence movement is outside the scope of this discussion. Of concern here is the ongoing struggle in the 1840s and 1850s, between the native landowning nobility on the one hand and the Orthodox religious institutions in the Ottoman Empire with a claim to the land and proceeds of their monastic holdings in the principalities on the other.

In 1848, when the revolutionary regimes of the principalities demanded expropriation, the authorities of the Christian Holy Sites of Palestine (Church of the Holy Sepulchre), the patriarchate of Jerusalem, and Mt. Athos launched a protest against the "temporary administration of Vlachobogdania [Wallachia-Moldavia], the new constitution of which had among its 23 articles the statement that "the Wallachian people will render unto God what is God's, and will receive from the Pharisees that which is not of the Pharisees so as to give it to the poor."[72] This meant they intended to expropriate the monasteries there and remove them from the authority and material ties to these holy places.

With the new institutional arrangements for monasteries in Moldavia and Wallachia in the 1830s and 1840s went new personnel appointments in the provincial regimes to administer monastic holdings; Vogorides chose to maintain a hold on the material affairs of Moldavian monasteries through marriage alliances to this new personnel. In 1848, Kostaki (Constantine) Konaki, a leading local boyar, was made "*epitropos*" of the *metochia* (dependencies) of Haghia Savva in Jassy, which belonged to the Church of the Holy Sepulchre in Jerusalem.[73] Vogorides, for his part, arranged a marriage for his son Nikolaki (Nicholas) with a member of the Konaki family. (Nicholas subsequently went by the name Vogorides-Konaki.)[74] In 1850, Vestiar Laskaraki (Laskaro) Cantacuzeno, another son-in-law of Vogorides', was also involved in "monastic politics"—in the financial affairs of the Three Hierarchs monastery in Moldavia in 1851.[75] Even as the material connections between İstanbul—both the central Ottoman state and the Orthodox Church establishment centered in İstanbul—to the Danubian Principalities dwindled, Vogorides used the tactic of marriage alliances to conserve his personal connections to Moldavia.

Vogorides' and Aristarchi's involvement in Church politics meant that their influence transcended İstanbul and the Balkans and extended into the Arab provinces of the empire, with their significant Orthodox Christian populations and sites. Since the issues of privileges and possession at the Christian Holy Sites in Palestine in particular grew out of so many political trajectories, there were several avenues, all of which Vogorides and Aristarchi were already involved in, to these politics; through the Jerusalem patriarchate, through the Church of the Holy Sepulchre (both of which had *metochia* and personnel in İstanbul), through foreign powers who increasingly felt they had a stake in the Holy Sites, and through the Ottoman central state, which found itself in the middle of many conflicting interests regarding the Church of Bethlehem and the Holy Sepulchre. In 1846, Nicholas Aristarchi and Vogorides were both asked by the Ottoman foreign minister—in a request sent through the İstanbul patriarchate—to give their opinion regarding the matter of the keys to the outer door of Bethlehem, which was going to be given to the Armenians, and the matter of appointing an Ottoman guard for the Church "like the one at the Holy Sepulchre."[76] Vogorides, for his part, was a representative for the financial affairs of the Jerusalem patriarchate in İstanbul and as such was responsible for negotiating the forgiving of debts owed by that patriarchate to the Ottoman state.[77]

### THE OTTOMAN FOREIGN MINISTRY:
### A NEW HOME FOR AN OLD PHANARIOT

Vogorides' personal friendships and patronage relationships with the British ambassador Canning and Mustafa Reşit Paşa were a crucial prerequisite for his activities in the new foreign politics. Mustafa Reşit Paşa had been a fellow protégé of Pertev Paşa until the latter's death in 1838. As Mustafa Reşit continued his ascent to power with his appointment as foreign minister in July 1839, Vogorides had already begun to build a base of protégés within the Foreign Ministry and would continue to do so with the sanction of Mustafa Reşit and others in his "political system."[78] In January 1844, Vogorides acknowledged the importance of Reşit Paşa to his plans when he instructed Kostaki Musurus in Athens to write occasional letters to Reşit Paşa (who was then the Paris ambassador and whom Vogorides called "our Reşit Paşa Efendi"), not only because Reşit Paşa was Musurus's "financial patron," but also because Reşit Paşa had *"tôt-ou-tard avenir brilliant"* in Turkey.[79]

With important British and Ottoman patrons, Vogorides cultivated his own protégés below him, who included many of those who had worked for him in Samos: Kostaki Musurus, his sons Yanko (Ioannis), Aleko (Alexandros), and Nick-olai (Nicholas), Gabriel Krestides, later Yanko (Ioannis) Photiades, and Alexandros Kallimaki. While Vogorides' Samos project had its purposes for his larger ambi-tions, the expansion of his patronage network in the foreign diplomatic corps and Foreign Ministry at home held the greatest potential power for him. From 1839, Vogorides began his project to appoint his protégés to diplomatic posts abroad, beginning with Kostaki Musurus, to whom Vogorides had recently married his daughter Annika (Anna). The newlyweds took up Musurus's post in Athens, where they would stay almost a decade. The other protégés set off for posts as secretaries and chargés d'affaires in Paris, London, Berlin, and sometimes Vienna.

In İstanbul, the day-to-day operations necessary to maintain the positions of Vo-gorides' protégés and augment their formal status in the bureaucracy and foreign service included making at least weekly visits to the palace, or *mabeyn* as he re-ferred to it, keeping up with events and intrigues there, and personally conveying the dispatches he had translated from his far-flung contacts.[80] In January 1845, for instance, Vogorides wrote despairingly that he had been ill and bedridden for a month and so had been unable to visit the sultan for that unusually long period of time. He had, however, managed to translate the dispatches he had received from Musurus and had sent them to the ministry with his son Aleko.[81] In this way his role was reminiscent of a *kapıkahya* for pre-1821 *voyvoda*s; he served as their agent to the Porte—conveying strategic information in both directions. He adapted the functions, however, to fit the new circumstances of foreign affairs, wherein written dispatches from the diplomatic corps were an important channel of information to the Ottoman central state. As such, Vogorides mediated and translated those reports back and forth, not only because the dispatches were often in Greek and needed to be translated into French or Ottoman, but also because Vogorides' pro-tégés, such as Musurus, did not know Ottoman Turkish and were therefore unable to communicate directly with those ministers who still did not know French.[82]

Vogorides' İstanbul activities to promote his protégés also involved composing and submitting the formal petitions requesting promotions in ranks and granting of formal honors, as well as facilitating the physical production of the medals through his connections at the imperial mint (Darphane), while his protégés served in their foreign diplomatic posts.[83] He did this for his sons, who were working at the Paris, London, and Berlin embassies in the 1840s, and for his sons-in-law, their relatives, and the occasional cleric, as well as for one Osman Efendi, a member of

Musurus's diplomatic staff Athens. This system of ranks (established in 1835) was, as Findley pointed out, an important new feature of the Foreign Ministry–Sublime Porte and of the civil service as a whole.[84] Vogorides participated in this institutionalization by securing ranks and medals for himself and his protégés through whatever means necessary in the 1830s and 1840s.

Another of Vogorides' functions reflected the institutionalization in progress at the Foreign Ministry in the 1830s and 1840s—facilitating the payment of salaries for his men who were stationed abroad. Still in the 1840s, salary payments were hardly systematized. He would procure the money, through a *politsa,* or loan, from Greek banker Baltazzi or from Vogorides' other son-in-law, the *voyvoda* of Moldavia (Michael Sturdza),[85] and send it by steamship to Musurus in Athens, then London when Musurus was promoted to the Ottoman Embassy there.

Kostaki Musurus was perhaps Vogorides' greatest creation and contribution to the new Ottoman foreign politics. In addition to being Vogorides' son-in-law, as mentioned above, Musurus also seemed to have been his closest confidant among his protégés. Musurus became a statesman and diplomat in his own right, continuing on as Ottoman ambassador in London long after Vogorides' death, in 1859. The two engaged in almost daily correspondence throughout the 1840s and 1850s, while Kostaki was in Athens, then Vienna, and then London, and Vogorides was manning the İstanbul headquarters of their network. They corresponded on personal and familial matters, events in Samos, Greece, rebellions in the Balkans, and court intrigues, especially those involving "Satan" (Ho Satanas) as Vogorides liked to refer to Logothete (Nicholas) Aristarchi by the 1850s.[86]

A letter from Vogorides (in İstanbul) to Musurus (in Athens) in November 1844 is a typical example of the variety of topics included in their correspondence: After discussing the reception of Musurus's last dispatch by the *amedçi,* Vogorides mentions the matters that needed to be resolved pertaining to Greek refugees from the islands of Psara and Crete, as well as from Macedonia and Larissa, Thessaly. Then, according to Rıfat Paşa's letter to foreign diplomats, Vogorides announces that the *paşa* had been removed from his post at the Foreign Ministry in a "peaceful and humble way," and in his place "our" Şekip Efendi was appointed. Vogorides recommends that Musurus write a "congratulatory letter" to Rıfat, for the goodwill he had shown toward Musurus during his time at the ministry and to congratulate him for his new post as a member of the Meclis-i Vala-yı Ahkam-ı Adliye.[87] Vogorides states that this appointment of Şekip was necessary, "so as to use the right tone in conversations with and requests to ambassadors *and to realize the independence of our ruling kingdom.*"[88] Vogorides then moves on to talk about Mr. Canning's insistence on certain matters regarding "African Tripoli" and specific articles of the (Anglo-Ottoman) Commercial Agreement. He finally mentions the esteem for the Ottoman ministers expressed by Metternich through Prokesch. He ends his letter with some confidential gossip about future appointments mixed in with the practical matter of Musurus's salary arrangements:

> Confidentially, one night when His Highness deems it appropriate, he will receive and approve the renewal of the ministry and the dismissal of Fethi Ahmet Paşa from the presidency of the Ahkam-ı Adliye and of Rıfat Paşa as minister of foreign affairs, both men known to be *moderés*. Until today I still have not received your monthly salary, but I will do as you say, on this matter, and I will make sure to supply it as well as the memo on the ecclesiastical press you requested. Sarım Efendi has been appointed ambassador to London in place of Ali Efendi, and this appointment is already provoking intense undercurrents from the losing political system.[89]

From afar, he orchestrated public relations between his protégés and the Ottoman state, such as when he directed Kostaki Musurus, while ambassador to Athens, to "have an '*illuminazione*'" and a "'bright soirée' at your embassy in honor of the birth of Ottoman heir Sultan Abdülhamit, son of His Most Serene Highness," in 1842. In 1847–48, in fact, Vogorides himself was the host of an official banquet at his home one Sunday evening for twenty-five of the highest-ranking Ottoman functionaries in the Foreign Ministry and military, including the military commander, imperial admiral, and several Muslim members of the diplomatic corps.[90] The purpose of the banquet was to discuss the "Greek events," namely, the falling-out that had occurred between Kostaki Musurus, as the Ottoman ambassador in Athens, and the Greek king Otto over the extradition of fugitives from Greek territory who were Ottoman subjects.[91] Vogorides had remade himself from the secret agent of the Ottoman authorities to negotiate with Mehmet Ali through the French envoy Boislecomte in 1833 to the host of an official state banquet and sponsor of an official discussion of foreign policy by the late 1840s—all still without an official position at the Foreign Ministry. The process of reconstitution of the pre-1821 phanariot system and the adaptation to new circumstances from the 1820s through the end of the 1830s lay at the core of Vogorides' life experience and career trajectory as he saw it. To Vogorides, "the most treacherous waves" were the ones he had to traverse in these years.[92]

___

# In the Eye of the Storm

*I wonder what the Duke of Wellington, that man rare in history for his moral and military virtue, who completed duties of the utmost importance for England, and who was esteemed and honored by his ethnos in life and in death, I wonder what he would do in my place, if he were serving an anti-Christian ethnos, which looks with suspicion on the loyalty [T. sadakat; G. sadakati] of a Christian, which is envious and disbelieves that a Christian can be both most obedient [phronemoteros] and most faithful before the Sublime Porte. I ask, would the Duke of Wellington endure the situation or would he try to save [Moldavia and Wallachia, or] Turkey [as such,] from all the misunderstandings and the inroads of fanaticism or not?*

CLOSING LINES OF STEPHANOS VOGORIDES' APOLOGIA

A Christian statesman serving the Ottoman Empire in 1852 would have had a number of reasons to invoke the career of the Duke of Wellington. The recently deceased Wellington was Anglo-Irish and yet rose from that disadvantaged background to become a military and diplomatic leader defending the British Empire in India and against Napoleon.[1] Representing Britain at the Congress of Vienna, Wellington was conservative in a time of changes and challenges for England and for the European system of politics. Wellington had apparently managed to reconcile the contradictions and challenges of his position and earn a shining reputation in life and in death as a defender of the British Empire. Stephanos Vogorides, the Ottoman Christian statesman who invokes Wellington here, was almost an exact contemporary of his. (Wellington lived from 1769 to 1852; Vogorides, from ca. 1772 to 1859.) He encountered perhaps even more profound challenges than Wellington, struggling to no avail to reconcile his position as an Orthodox Christian serving not the Russian or even Greek state but the Ottoman state, in the midst of the conflicts growing more intense by the day in the early 1850s.

The decade of the 1840s, or the opening years of act one of the Tanzimat, had brought Vogorides a number of opportunities to expand his reach into Ottoman governance. Domestically, he built up and circulated his network of protégés among Samos, the island he governed from İstanbul, Moldavia, for which he was *kapıkahya*, and the Ottoman capital. He served as the bey, or prince, of Samos in an attempt to emulate his phanariot predecessors in Moldavia and Wallachia as well as his Serbian contemporary Milosh Obrenovich, whom he greatly admired. On the foreign politics front, he remained close to Elçi Bey, or Stratford Canning, the hugely influential British ambassador in İstanbul, as well as to his Ottoman patrons Husrev and Mustafa Reşit paşas, and cultivated his protégés when they received appointments as Ottoman envoys in European capitals from Berlin and Paris to London. Finally, he maintained close if turbulent relations with the Orthodox patriarchate, still firmly embedded in the land and administration from Moldavia to Sinai and Palestine.

Indeed, the ambiguities of Ottoman governance post-1839, when political equality of Ottoman subjects regardless of religion was officially declared, but the legal and political frameworks were not yet developed to realize this declaration, held nearly limitless potential for Vogorides and other powerful Ottoman Christians. In this context, new projects could be imagined and begun, new arguments based on the principles of the Tanzimat used, all the while as old mechanisms of patronage and hierarchy could remain in place. In many ways the 1840s were the heyday of Vogorides' career.

Two affairs that absorbed Vogorides' energy as the 1840s drew to a close involved the uprisings among Moldavian notables (boyars) that came on the heels of the Paris and Vienna revolutions in 1848 and the movement to establish a Bulgarian church in İstanbul, which came to a head in 1849. In the first instance, Vogorides found himself, as one of the few with personal and political ties that still bound Moldavia to the Ottoman center, battling Moldavian upstarts who were demanding a constitution and further autonomy. In the second, he was the agent chosen by Ottoman ministers such as Mustafa Reşit Paşa to co-opt the Bulgarian movement, allowing for an officially Bulgarian-speaking parish and church building down the street from the ecumenical Orthodox patriarchate in Phanar.

Given these immediate and now decades-old tensions involving ethnicity and political secession, Sultan Abdülmecit's gesture of preparing to attend the November 1851 wedding of Vogorides' daughter Maria to Ioannis Photiades—the first time an Ottoman sultan would attend a ceremony in a Christian Church—was all the more momentous. Turning down Vogorides' offer to build the sultan a special *kafes* (royal cage) for the occasion, the sultan asked what he could offer as a wedding gift. Vogorides responded that he would never dare to have the presumption to ask for a gift beyond his *iltifat*, or the favor of the sultan's presence, and that instead, for the sultan, he had composed the verses to what he called "Our Marseillaise," to commemorate this event.[2]

With the "goal of blessed sympathy and integration of Muslim and Christian countrymen," he had named his Ottoman anthem "Gayret Edup İleri Gidelim," or "Let's Do Our Best and Go Forward." He explained to Sultan Abdülmecit that he took his inspiration for the poem from the hadith "Hubb ul-watan min el-Iman," or "Love of the Fatherland Is a Part of Faith."[3] The sultan praised Vogorides for his efforts and ordered him to take the poem to Donizetti, the Swiss-Italian Ottoman court composer at the time, and have him put it to music. Vogorides then translated the verses into Greek and looked forward to presenting the poem to "Ottomans and Christians." While we do not know if this was ever done, we do know that more than a decade before the hatching of Ottomanism as an official ideology, Vogorides, in his own way, made strides in imagining how an Ottoman commonwealth should look and in preventing the political fragmentation of Orthodox Christians along ethnic lines, all the while carving a niche for himself and his descendants in Ottoman governance. Vogorides was, incidentally, also grappling with far more mundane dilemmas, such as how to pay his debts of 484,000 *guruş* to the Greek banker Baltazzi and 400,000 more *guruş* to the *esnaf*, or guilds, who had recently built his new house in Arnavutköy on the Bosphorus. He maintained that by day he was "under siege" in his own home from the *esnaf* demanding their money.[4]

Through the 1830s and 1840s, then, Vogorides had been working, quite successfully, to reconcile (and exploit) his allegiances and connections to several arenas of Ottoman governance, Orthodox Christian institutions and patronage circles, and multiple ethnic-political categories, among them Moldavian-turning-Romanian, Bulgarian, and Greek. Operating at the increasingly blurry interface between imperial governance and multistate negotiations, he had the ear of both the British ambassador and the Ottoman sultan and monitored the goings-on in the Ottoman capital and far beyond so as to be able to "swim through so many dangers" that could come his way at any moment.

What he could not have been prepared for was the profound shift in the nature of his predicament that occurred just as the 1850s dawned. The most dramatic moment in Stephanos Vogorides' life, and one of the most complicated moments in Ottoman governance of the nineteenth century, did *not* revolve around the threat of secession based on ethnic nationalism or even Muslim-Christian tensions. Instead, it was the Orthodox–Latin Catholic split over custodianship of specific objects and sites of religious significance in Ottoman Palestine that opened out to a web of conflicting loyalties, alliances, and policies within and beyond Ottoman territories. The Ottoman central state found itself the arbiter of a dispute that tethered its own Orthodox Christian Church and Christian subjects to Russian and French spiritual and territorial claims and, by extension, to the multivalent world of Great Power politics.

I argue that, while Vogorides and so many others who were involved in Ottoman governance managed to survive and adapt to the myriad changes of the first half of the century, the controversy around the Christian Holy Sites in Ottoman Palestine represented a new kind of breach—and challenge. This breach was political, diplomatic, and perhaps most important it brought with it an epistemic shift for Ottoman

Christians, caught at this moment in the crosshairs not of nationalisms but of empires. Faced with a series of discursive attacks from Ottoman, French, and Russian actors, Vogorides chose this moment to articulate a remarkable set of responses to the immediate political intrigues of the day but also to the much larger dilemmas they reflected.

After setting the scene for this moment in 1852 with historical background and a discussion of relevant historiographical debates, I take up the series of Vogorides' revealing reactions to the crisis developing around him. Fortunately for us, he documented his arguments, explanations, and the apologia that has figured so prominently in the present study. He sent them—in secret code—to his son-in-law Kostaki Musurus in London, hoping he would pass on the appropriate information to the British authorities so actively involved in Ottoman governance by the 1850s. The Tanzimat was promulgated in close proximity to the Treaty of Paris, which itself marked the end of the Crimean conflict. In analyzing Vogorides' discursive responses to the betrayals, crises, and impasses just before military conflict erupted, one cannot help but be struck by the links between his thinking and that of both "anti-reform" Muslim statesmen who preceded him and the next generation of Muslim Young Ottoman reformers. Moreover, Vogorides' responses allow a glimpse into a vision of Ottoman governance alternative to the one that eventually emerged out of the other side of the Crimean War.

## AT THE CROSSHAIRS OF EMPIRES AND HISTORIES

The controversy over the Christian Holy Sites in Ottoman Palestine was the cause of the crisis that would engulf Vogorides and many of his fellow statesmen in 1852. On its most literal level, the controversy was between Greek Orthodox and Latin Catholic monks over the custodianship of the keys and star of the Church of the Nativity in Bethlehem and of the rights to use and repair the altar, cupola, and main entrance of the Church of the Holy Sepulchre in Jerusalem.[5] At issue were the sites where Jesus is said to have been born and buried, respectively. Given their foundational significance to Christianity, both Christian sects (in addition to the Armenian Church, which was left out of the larger controversy, as it was not tethered to a specific Great Power) could and did hold spiritual, and therefore physical, claim to these sites.

Furthermore, as Ottoman governance had become ever more entangled with Great Power politics since the 1830s, the conflict took on the potential to engage the French government on the side of the Catholic monks and the Russian government on the side of the Orthodox monks, as well as the many Russian Orthodox pilgrims who were resident in Jerusalem by this time. The fact that Britain, concerned more about the threat of an expanding Russia than about Latin Catholic or Orthodox possession of Christian Holy Sites, was the power that was most involved of all in Ottoman governance by this point only added another layer of complexity to the issue.

For decades, Ottoman governance had been fused with multistate politics. Because of this, even the arena in which the conflict would be resolved was ambiguous. Was this a domestic affair, involving Ottoman Christian subjects on Ottoman territory, or a matter for international negotiations by dint of its implications for the Latin Catholic and Orthodox Christian faiths? Would a *ferman* from the Ottoman sultan carry sufficient legitimacy, or would the matter have to be resolved in the sphere of international treaty negotiations? If so, would it follow the precedents already established in the previous century with Catholic France, or those with Orthodox Russia? The Holy Sites issue was fast becoming a thorn in the side not only of a precarious system of Ottoman governance but also of an equally precarious European state system, lacking a consensus as to what procedure and outcome would constitute a legitimate resolution.

## OTTOMAN CHRISTIANS: A HISTORICAL VORTEX

Historians have generally interpreted the Holy Sites issue as merely a pretext and a kind of proxy issue for the "real," ongoing turf battles between the expanding British and French empires, to some extent the Austrian Empire, and the Russian Empire in the wake of the political upheaval of 1848. For example, R. W. Seton-Watson, the renowned British historian, claimed that the Holy Sites issue was the "spark and not the powder magazine" that ignited the Crimean War. He commented, "It is humiliating to reflect that the rival claims of Greek and Latin monks for the custody of the Holy Places in Jerusalem and Bethlehem should have been magnified into a struggle for political influence, in which Napoleon III and Nicholas I became their respective champions and voiced the hostility of the Roman and Orthodox Churches."[6] As humiliating as it might have been, the controversy dragged on for years and absorbed the energies of countless statesmen and secretaries in no fewer than five of the largest Eurasian states of the era. It also led quite directly, along with conflicts over Montenegro, Moldavia-Wallachia, and Bosnia, to the greatest military conflict Europe would experience between the Napoleonic Wars and World War I.

The seeming disconnect between the lack of significance attributed to the issues that led to the Crimean War and the military and political significance of the war itself can be explained in part by the role of Ottoman Christian subjects. From the perspective of Ottoman governance, Ottoman Christians were at the center of many disputes that led to the Crimean War. The Holy Sites dispute, in which they were crucial claimants to religious and political privileges, was but one of a series of flashpoints that led to multistate military conflict.[7] Others in the series involved issues of ecclesiastical jurisdiction and political sovereignty in Christian-administered

Montenegro and in the autonomous Christian principalities of Moldavia and Wallachia, which were fought out between Austria and Russia, and the treatment of Christians in Bosnia. All along, the British for their part called for "equality" among Ottoman subjects regardless of religion, implying that the status of Ottoman Christians should be raised and they should receive more privileges and rights.

Despite the ubiquity of Ottoman Christians in the episodes leading up to the Crimean War, in English- and French-language histories of the Crimean War written up to the present, the perspective of Ottoman Christians, and to a lesser extent the perspective and dynamics of Ottoman governance as a whole, are rarely given center stage. In the context of European history, the Ottoman Empire is the passive battleground, and Ottoman Christians the helpless pawns in the "game" of Great Power conflict.[8] The predicament of Ottoman Christians and the positions they took in these complex imperial and international disputes are ignored, in part because of the primacy given to official state actors in political and diplomatic history. Did Ottoman Christians have a vision for change that was separable from Russian and British (and Greek) designs on the empire or from the Ottoman Empire itself? Did they see their religious and political identity as related to the Ottoman state, to Islam, or to the territory where they lived? We have little sense of the answers to these questions if we read the conventional political and diplomatic histories, so often written from the British and French perspectives.[9]

From modern scholarship on the Ottoman Empire we also glean next to nothing about the perspectives of Ottoman Christians on the eve of the Crimean War. Far more interest has been generated around the application of the Tanzimat reform program, first announced in 1839 and then begun in earnest after the Treaty of Paris that concluded the Crimean War in 1856. This issue is certainly relevant to the predicament of Christian populations in the empire, because a major implication of legal equality among all the sultan's subjects (to become Ottoman citizens in 1856) was that such equality would raise the status of Christians and, it was assumed by many, formally incorporate them into the sphere of Ottoman governance. If we look at this period from such a new perspective, the Tanzimat begins to look not only like a cause of change but also like the outcome of political tensions and transformations over the previous decades.

Questions of historical agency for Christian populations in the Ottoman Empire, absent from the Tanzimat narrative, are normally relegated to the narrative of Balkan national movements. Nationalism was indeed important in this era, not only in the wake of 1848 in Europe, but also in the middle years of the process of the Ottoman Empire's dissolution into states based on a national principle, when the Greek kingdom was in its infancy and the Serbian, Romanian, and Bulgarian national movements were in the process of formation. Ottoman Christians, we can all too easily believe, were busy determining when, where, and how they could secede and to which nation-state—Greece, Romania, Bulgaria, or Serbia—they would belong.

Yet, controversies such as the Holy Sites dispute occurred on a different plane from the national one.

Neither was the Holy Sites dispute national, nor did it hinge on Muslim-Christian relations. Rather, on its face this was an intra-Christian dispute—between Latin Catholic and Orthodox—and yet it brought to the fore the tensions and dangers of Ottoman Orthodox Christians aligning with and coming under the official protection of their coreligionist Russian Empire, or the possibility, as we will see, of Ottoman Christians uniting with their fellow Muslim Ottoman subjects against outside powers. In other words, this is hardly a moment in which modern assumptions about the alignment of religious and political affinities will explain the motivations and behavior of the actors involved. Rather, as we will see below, the issue for Ottoman Christians such as Vogorides in 1852 was one of political survival and self-definition *within* the confines of Ottoman governance.

The Crimean conflict that ensued (1853–56) would further complicate the position of Ottoman Christians because of the multiple ways it transformed the Ottoman Empire.[10] It engendered military and cultural encounters wherever British and French troops fought side by side with Ottoman troops.[11] It precipitated the building of crucial infrastructure in the Balkans and eastern Anatolia. As a result of the war a tremendous influx of Muslim refugees arrived from Crimea and the Caucasus to virtually every part of the Ottoman Empire, and these populations would have profound political and economic effects on the Ottoman Empire through the following decades of the empire's existence.[12]

I do not intend to dispute the feelings of humiliation of R. W. Seton-Watson or, for that matter, to argue the importance or lack thereof of the Holy Sites controversy or the Crimean War for the European empires that were involved in it. Rather, I intend to pursue here the question of why the Holy Sites controversy of 1852–53 was so protracted by calling attention to a different dimension of the conflict—the predicament and agency of Orthodox Christians through a phanariot lens and in their broader context of Ottoman governance—and to bring to the fore some of the underlying contradictions that were exposed, for Vogorides and doubtless many others, as the controversy unfolded.

## HOLY SITES IN THE CAREER OF VOGORIDES

Stephanos Vogorides, already an elder statesmen with more than half a century of service to the Ottoman sultanate by 1852, is uniquely qualified to provide us with the crucial perspective that has been missing from discussions of the Holy Sites controversy and its implications. As discussed above, the pre-1821 phanariot repertoire had long entailed involvement in the material and administrative affairs of the Orthodox institutions in the Holy Sites and had continued to be part of the repertoire of men such as Vogorides and his nemesis Aristarchi Bey in the 1830s and after. They were involved through the Jerusalem patriarchate, through the İstanbul-based personnel and landholdings of the Church of the Holy Sepulchre, through the foreign powers becoming increasingly involved in the politics surrounding the Holy Sites, and of course through the Ottoman central state, itself increasingly an arbiter among these diverse and conflicting interests. Vogorides, for his part, was a representative for the financial affairs of the Jerusalem patriarchate in İstanbul and, as such, was responsible for negotiating the forgiving of debts owed by that patriarchate to the Ottoman state in the 1840s.[13] His vantage point on the Holy Sites dispute is also significant by dint of his being neither a member of the Orthodox clergy proper nor an Ottoman statesman of the highest rank but of being informally involved with the İstanbul and Jerusalem patriarchates, the Ottoman central state, and the British Embassy in İstanbul.

Vogorides was, even by his own standards, unusually, even desperately, prolific on the issue of the Holy Sites and surrounding controversies in 1852 and 1853. In addition to the series of messages he sent in secret code to his son-in-law Kostaki Musurus, Ottoman ambassador in London at the time, Vogorides also sent a series of briefs to Stratford Canning and, we presume from his correspondence to Musurus, to Reşit, Fuat, and Aali paşas, each of whom served as foreign minister during this period, and delivered at least one pamphlet to Sultan Abdülmecit related to this issue. A review of some of his comments, schemes, and views during 1852 and 1853 brings into sharp relief the multiple dimensions in which he was forced to function and the vision that emerged in response to the crisis he experienced.

In sifting through the overwhelming amount of detail contained in Vogorides' writings, we see the emergence of the twin issues of predicament and agency—indeed, the constituent parts of what we now refer to as "identity"—for those Orthodox Christian Ottoman subjects who were politically engaged on the side of the Ottoman state. In the labyrinth of dilemmas and contradictions around him, Vogorides was most preoccupied with explaining his position, differentiating it from the position of a "Russified" Ottoman Christian, and advancing strategies and arguments to defend his existence as an Ottoman Christian loyal to the Ottoman sultanate and to his own Orthodox Christian faith.

## THE CRISIS

Two of the issues that most deeply embroiled and alarmed Vogorides were, first, the status of the *ferman* for Orthodox (as opposed to Latin Catholic) rights to the Holy Sites in 1852 and, second, the broader question of political status and belonging for Ottoman Orthodox Christians. The *ferman* was released to the Orthodox patriarch to grant rights of custodianship of the Holy Sites to the Orthodox clergy in Palestine but was never read aloud and therefore never enacted.[14] Instead, Fuat Efendi and Aali Paşa, young francophile leaders of reforms in the Foreign Ministry, made a separate deal with the French to affirm the claims of Latin Catholics to the Holy Sites, based on the 1740 Capitulation granted to the French by the Ottoman state, conceding to them the key to the Church of the Nativity in Bethlehem.[15]

The central issue that concerned Vogorides, that of the status of Orthodox Christian subjects of the Ottoman Empire, loomed behind the narrower question of the Holy Sites. Tsar Nicholas and his envoys seemed to equate Orthodox custodianship of the Holy Sites with Russian custodianship and, by extension, with a Russian protectorate over all Ottoman Orthodox Christians.[16] The British, for their part, at strategic moments and places advanced the position that the Russian tsar was the natural leader of Orthodox Christians within and beyond the borders of the Russian Empire.[17] On this issue, Vogorides formulated intricate plans to gain acknowledgment of an Ottoman Orthodox Christian political-spiritual entity, separate from the Russian (and Greek) state and Church.

Judging from the memos he drafted to Musurus, we can see that Vogorides seemed to perceive the issue of the Holy Sites *ferman* on the one hand and the issue of Ottoman Christians as a political entity on the other as a series of interrelated crises that were occurring in concentric circles around himself. The crisis of the most immediate circle around him involved his own honor and reputation. He felt an urgent need to prove to his fellow Ottoman statesmen and to the British authorities that his defense of the Orthodox claims, both for the Holy Sites and at large, did not mean that he was "turning to the Russian side."[18] In order to prove this he wrote the apologia, elaborating a kind of epistemic framework for his loyalty and listing all the moments in his more than fifty-year career when he could have defected to the Russians but instead stayed loyal to the Ottoman sultan and his Christian *reʿaya*. With the apologia he would maintain his credibility with the two audiences—Ottoman and British statesmen—that he felt he needed most to legitimize his existence as a Christian loyal to the Ottoman sultanate and to realize his vision of reforms.

Vogorides explained his predicament by portraying himself as steeped in the values and doctrines of Christianity, all the while adapting his vision of Christianity to fit—and legitimate—his milieu of Ottoman governance. Responding to those of his generation who heralded an anti-clerical, revolutionary Enlightenment, he began by asserting that he, too, was "enlightened," but, "by the theory of the Evangelical Logos." This logos "commands us to render unto Caesar that which is Caesar's *(idol worshipers though they were then)*." Adapting the famous biblical verse, "Render unto Caesar that which is Caesar's and to God that which is God's," Vogorides inserted his own parenthetical remark, implying that just as Jesus, the quintessential embodiment of Christian morality, had served the Roman caesar, who was not a Christian, so Vogorides could be the best of Christians while serving a non-Christian sovereign, in this case a Muslim. Vogorides went on to adapt Christian values to a Muslim Ottoman milieu by referring to the doctrine to "love one's neighbor as oneself," regardless of whether one's neighbor is a Samaritan or one "who does not glorify the resurrection as we Christians do." Again, loving one's non-Christian neighbor who does not glorify the resurrection (read a Muslim) was part and parcel of Christian values à la Vogorides. This implies that functioning within the framework of Muslim Ottoman governance was not in contradiction to living a good Christian life. The message so far was that Vogorides would feel no obligation of loyalty to Russia superior to that which he felt to the Ottoman sultan merely by dint of his being an Orthodox Christian.

Instead, the essence of Christian values, according to Vogorides' version of the doctrine of the Evangelical Logos, is to "avoid anything that brings about scandal, abnormality, or disorder to human society, where divine Providence deigned to form us out of nonbeing, I have thus always been bound not to give occasion for discord, for responsibility and accusations of suspicion against Christians of the Ottomans (under whom God has subjected us for our sins)." Indeed, Orthodox Christians were placed (by God) under the rule of the Ottomans for a reason, and that was to punish them for their sins. But the situation of Christians living under Ottoman sovereignty was not something to be changed or questioned; rather, it was to be accepted toward the greater Christian goal of submission.

Having established the religious-moral framework for Orthodox Christianity in an Ottoman Muslim milieu, Vogorides then explained his own role in the larger scheme of (Christian) religion and (Ottoman Muslim) state: "I am shamed to give my fellow Christians an example of submission and forbearance, so that our most holy Christian religion not be blasphemed by the exploitation of some other Christians. I never failed to take care in executing the political duties that were incumbent on me, nor to be bought out by or take advantage of the circumstances of the day that come with this awareness."

And it was the circumstances of the day that were the greatest challenge to Vogorides' modus vivendi. Immediately following the apologia, in which he explained his position and elaborated on his record of loyalty to the Ottoman state and his service to and protection of his fellow Ottoman Christians, Vogorides enclosed a series of coded memos detailing the specific intrigues and dilemmas in which he was embroiled.

Vogorides went on in these coded memos to portray his actions as part of the larger conflict between his own faction and enemy factions. These enemy factions were within the Orthodox Christian elite and included his archrival, the *logothete* Aristarchi, the Russian dragoman (former phanariot Hançerli), and candidates for patriarch who belonged to this clique. Factional enemies could also be found among his Muslim Ottoman colleagues. This group was perhaps more threatening, because they had power to make policy without the approval or knowledge of Vogorides and other Ottoman Christians. When Fuat Efendi and Aali Paşa made the secret agreement with the French to honor the 1740 Capitulation Agreement and Latin Catholic claims to the Holy Sites, Vogorides considered this a profound personal betrayal above all else. He wrote in a coded letter from November 23, 1852:

> I don't see how our [Foreign] Ministry, run by Fuat Efendi, who is part of the same "system" [faction] as Aali Paşa, could have deceived us and preferred the French system when they already issued the royal *ferman* to the Romans [the Rum or Greek Orthodox] validating our old privileges to the Holy Sites. . . . Aali Paşa, secretly and without informing our patriarchate or the Russian Embassy, gave a note to the French ambassador that the key to the Church of Bethlehem be given to the French . . . such a note indicates bad faith and his inability to explain himself.

When Vogorides attempted to confront the prime minister (Grand Vezir Mustafa Reşit Paşa), he was thwarted:

> Yesterday I deliberately went to the Prime Ministry (Porte) to give my regards, and I found the *logothete* [Aristarchi Bey] there. The prime minister (Fuat Efendi) said, "Oh, I had intended to invite you as well to tell you the latest on the Jerusalem Question and that the key to Bethlehem had been given to the French, and that the requests of others for it is insignificant."

Feeling himself in an awkward position with his enemy Aristarchi Bey within earshot, Vogorides wrote,

> I couldn't fully explain myself in front of the *logothete,* so I only told him that since the sultan, may he live long, had written his promise to the Russian emperor that he would maintain the current regime [in favor of the Orthodox] and would send a copy of the *ferman* in favor of the Orthodox, this latest move in favor of the French damages the esteem of the sultan and undermines the emperor's trust in the royal character.[19]

The question of credibility and personal intrigue that permeated Vogorides' telling of the intricate story—the sultan's credibility, Aali and Fuat's disrespect, Reşit Paşa's failure to notify Vogorides and others of the double deal, and the *logothete*'s dubious motives for hanging around the Prime Ministry—were crucial to the way he experienced this dispute. But, according to him, these were acts of betrayal, because they indicated profound disrespect for the sultan and for the Orthodox Church, the two pillars, it seemed, of Vogorides' world.

The next concentric circle around Vogorides had to do with structures: institutions, such as the Orthodox patriarchate, states (Ottoman, French, Russian, British), and even discursive categories (Christian, Byzantine or Roman, Catholic, Muslim, Turkish, Ottoman). These discursive categories were crucial to the strategies Vogorides formulated to win back concessions when it looked as if the French and Latin Catholics would emerge victorious.

Important to keep in mind is that individuals on all sides of the Holy Sites issue formulated arguments to serve their personal loyalties and states' interests, but they did so in a discursive field with common modes of explanation. These modes of explanation featured the use of historical precedent. The French argued their point on the basis of the 1740 Capitulation Agreement. Russian statesmen put forward the Treaties of Küçük Kaynarca (1774) and Hünkar İskelesi (1833) to support their claims of protection over Ottoman Christians. And in response the Orthodox patriarchate offered *fermans* issued in earlier centuries.

Vogorides responded to the historical precedent argument regarding Ottoman permission and the argument about the inherent significance of the Holy Sites with his own arguments.[20] As we explore these arguments, we will see that a core issue here for an insider like Vogorides was the delineation between domestic and international power: the Holy Sites were on Ottoman territory and were therefore an internal matter in which foreign powers should not interfere. This domestic-international question was at play in other senses as well—the relative legitimacy of the 1740 Capitulation, the 1774 international Küçük Kaynarca Treaty, and Ottoman *fermans* that had been granted to the Orthodox Church in the Ottoman Empire were all at stake. In the arena of multistate negotiations, on the one hand international treaties were considered more legitimate than internal agreements between the Ottoman state and the Orthodox Church, while on the other hand foreign states were involved in the procedural intricacies of Ottoman governance so as to secure a *ferman* to their liking, which would apparently signal the final resolution of the matter.

THE RESPONSE

Vogorides' discursive response to Russian and French incursions on his political territory and betrayal on the part of his fellow Ottoman statesmen was multitiered. He first reacted with an argument about precedents, countering Russian and French claims with Orthodox Christian claims. He then elaborated a series of strategic arguments that would be made to Ottoman, Russian, and British authorities to persuade them of the need to maintain the status quo of Orthodox supremacy at the Christian Holy Sites in Palestine. Third, he laid out the procedural means necessary to arrive at an Orthodox victory over both French and Russian claims. And finally, he used this crisis as a springboard to discuss broader social criticisms and, I argue, his burgeoning ideology of reforms in an Ottoman-Islamic framework.

The argument of precedents put forth by Vogorides was at once the simplest and the most telling of his responses. He could trump claims based on agreements from one hundred years earlier (in the case of France) and from seventy-five (in the case of Russia) with the argument that the Orthodox Church had a history of harmony and treaties with Muslim rulers going back to the time of Muhammad. In his words, "From the beginning . . . privileges [were] extended to the Greeks [*eis tous* Graikous], first from Muhammad to [the monastery at] Mt. Sinai, and later by Omer Hatab [Caliph 'Umar] to the holy grotto and Holy Sepulchre [in Jerusalem], and later from the caliphs of Syria and Egypt and Baghdad, and subsequently from the predecessors of our current king [sultan] in Constantinople."[21] Indeed, this must have seemed an obvious argument to advance for the Orthodox Church: in a later memo to the British ambassador Canning, Vogorides emphasizes, "Russia did not even exist on the world scene when the privileges and immunities enjoyed until today by the Orthodox Church were granted by the predecessors of the sultan."[22] While Russia may have been claiming the mantle of the Roman and Byzantine empires, it was the Orthodox Church, still alive *within* the framework of Ottoman governance, that was the literal descendant of those empires. Logically, and absent the calculus of Great Power politics, this should have nullified Russia's claims over the Holy Sites and the Orthodox Church per se.

We see from Vogorides' argument that what matters is not the symbolic importance of the Holy Sites as the birthplace of Christ so much as it is the pacts that had been made in Palestine with the Byzantine-cum-Ottoman Orthodox Church long before the emergence of European states, whether those states be France, England, or Russia. The institution of the Church is the surrogate for a state for Ottoman Christians, and as such it overshadows the question of which religion has a stronger claim to the legacy of Jesus himself. Thus Vogorides' historical-religious arguments are both a response to and a more intricate version of the French and Russian claims.

After trumping French and Russian arguments based on precedents, Vogorides employed a strategic argument to play on prevalent fears of popular rebellion among Ottoman subjects, should the Holy Sites dispute be solved in a way unfavorable to the Ottoman masses. While others had used the idea of an empirewide Muslim uprising against possible Russian (Orthodox) success, Vogorides urged the French that "the crying voice of so many million *reaya*—16 million in all, 5 [million] Moldo-Wallachian, 1 [million] Serbian, 4 [million] Bulgarian, 1 [million] Bosnian, and 3 [million] Armenian—[would have to] be silenced so as to avoid a terrible domestic apostasy" should the issue be decided in favor of French-backed Latin Catholics.[23]

A third common mode of argument had to do with foreign involvement in the internal affairs of the Ottoman Empire. Vogorides argued in a (July 1853) memo to Canning, shortly after the fraught visit of the Russian envoy Prince Menshikov, that if Russia were granted what Menshikov was demanding, its claims of protection over Ottoman Christians would amount to a Russian protectorate, not only over the twelve million *reaya* of the Greek rite, but also over the three million Armenians in the Ottoman Empire, whose spiritual head had always been based in Hedjmiazin, in Russian territory.[24] But Vogorides' last comment twists this argument in a new direction; he writes, "Once the principle of foreign involvement in the internal affairs of a state has been accepted, this involvement, if the state that permits it is the weaker one, cannot but amount to a complete predominance, and it remains only at the discretion of the state that possesses this right, to interpret the facts as they wish and to deal with issues according to their importance to that state's own views and plans."[25] This is none other than an invitation to England to be that protecting power, for Vogorides had written before that it was not only his perception but also that of Reşit and Fethi Ahmed paşas that, if England did "not see to it to guarantee the successful implementation of reforms in the Ottoman Empire, we're all done with."[26]

After establishing three discursive responses to Russian and French arguments, Vogorides went on to describe the procedural *means* he would use to effect an outcome favorable to the Ottoman Christians, and these means, like his discursive arguments, were a mirroring of those put forward by the Russians and French, as well as a continuation of customary encounters between Orthodox Christian groups and the Ottoman state. The Russians, for instance, not satisfied with the international commission that had been called to resolve the matter, had demanded an Ottoman council *(meşveret)* earlier in 1852, to be made up principally of *ulema* and Ottoman statesmen, to arbitrate on the Holy Sites issue. With this demand, they had hoped to increase their chances of a favorable outcome, assuming that the traditionalist Muslim religious elite could be counted on to side with the *zimmi* Orthodox Christians over the more foreign Latin Catholics.[27]

In response to the double deal that was made between the French and the Ottomans, Vogorides formulated the intricate means to convey his arguments to win back concessions for Ottoman Orthodox Christians. He recounted to his son-in-law Musurus, "When I returned from the hot springs of Bursa (12 Dec. [1852]) and learned of the Jerusalem proposals of Russia on the one hand and France on the other, I said to the prime minister Reşit Paşa that it is not in the interest of the Sublime Porte to spread the notion among the Christian subjects that Russia or France is defending the Holy Places against the anti-Christian Turk, because that would always benefit the Russifying tendencies among us [Ottoman Christians]."[28] Clearly for Vogorides, this issue needed to remain a domestic one.[29] In order for that to happen, customary Ottoman procedures would have to be used to resolve the conflict, thereby preserving the internal integrity and legitimacy of Ottoman governance. Specifically,

the patriarchate, I argued to Reşit, should prepare a "national petition" *[arz-ı mahzar]* and submit it through the patriarchate to the (advisory) council *[meşveret]* that had been assembled at the Sublime Porte and consisted of *ulema* and high state officials. This national petition would explain [the privileges granted to Greeks from the time of Muhammad until now]. *This petition we should submit to the Sublime Porte in the presence of the Şeyh-ül-İslam . . . and the ulema,* and we should rely on the Islamic shari'a, which we *re'aya* have always respected and submitted to since the beginning, on the basis of the religious privileges bestowed upon us by the shari'a. This review/ retrospective and our taking refuge in the shari'a (along with the political power of our king) will mean the bringing together of about fifteen million, or five [million] Moldo-Wallachians, one [million] Serbians, four [million] Bulgarians, one [million]

Bosnians, and three [million] Armenians. We will tell them that the strength of these *[en to kefalaio tou]* will be in agreement with you.[30]

Finally, Vogorides advised Reşit Paşa that "he should show the French Embassy that the Sublime Porte has an imperative to quell the crying voice of so many millions of Her *re'aya* and to prevent the outbreak of a terrible domestic apostasy." Only in this way, by using the Russian-inspired and customary Ottoman means of a royal *meşveret* to unite the Muslim learned elite and the Orthodox Christian interests of the Ottoman Empire, could the French be intimidated to back off their claims for fear of a massive rebellion of both Muslims and Christians. Clearly, Ottoman Christians did not constitute a force to be reckoned with on their own, but they could still manipulate an alliance with a more powerful actor than Russia—in this case Muslim Ottoman subjects—to gain some agency.

## EMERGENT IDENTITY, BURGEONING IDEOLOGY?

The problem Vogorides faced was clearly more immediate than the Holy Sites dispute itself or even than the brewing international military conflict. He faced the growing paradox of his own political existence and grappled with it by formulating even broader arguments and an incipient ideology about his place as an Orthodox Christian in the Ottoman polity. Vogorides' argument about the intimate relationship between Muslims, including Turks, and Byzantine-Orthodox Christians was not just a convenient response to Great Power arguments. In the midst of this crisis Vogorides also began to articulate more encompassing ideas about the history, culture, and future of Muslims and Christians in the Ottoman Empire.

Shortly before the double deal that Fuat Efendi made with the French, Vogorides complained of his suspect behavior, adding, "Fuat Efendi [on September 23, 1852] gave to the [French] ambassador a diplomatic *dîner* [meal] to which I was also invited, and he avoided any contact with me under the pretext of my old age."[31] Vogorides used this snub from the young francophile reformist Fuat Efendi as a springboard to explain the more systemic problem of this new generation of European-educated Turks. He writes, still in secret code, "This is why today I prefer the old Turks, religious and capable, being of the same culture [as ourselves], who have been brought up stage by stage [inch by inch] . . . seed of their own old legal system of the caliphs of Baghdad and Andalusia . . . today's Byzantine Turks, to those who have had their European tour and have taken their moral and political lessons from there. The one group has scorned their own religion, and the other are descendants of the Byzantine ethos."

Aside from the new generation of Europeanized Turks, the empire was host also to more structural ills, which were a kind of replay of late Byzantine history, according to Vogorides. He went on to explain to Kostaki Musurus, "A few days ago, a document of many pages appeared before His Benificence [presumably written by Vogorides himself], which demonstrated to his Excellency the culture of the old Muslims and the wretched and foul state of the second Byzantine Restoration, [noting that] the paralysis of our [Byzantine] administration [caused] ... the old inhabitants of the Byzantine state, hearing of the lenient justice and laws of their [Muslim] forefathers, [to seek] refuge in Bursa and [leave] deserted the city of Byzantium [Constantinople]." Vogorides is likely referring to the final years of Byzantium, when the Ottoman emirate had established its first capital in Bursa (in the 1330s), implying that Christian residents of Constantinople voted with their feet and chose to migrate to Ottoman Bursa.[32]

Vogorides goes on to relay the latter-day phenomenon: "[Likewise recently] (from the one side like Jonas) the Christians saw the bad [Ottoman] administration and left for Trieste and to Austrian lands, and others left to Odessa and Russia, and that way the enemies of the Ottoman kingdom were strengthened." Here he refers to the migration of Orthodox Christian merchants from Ottoman lands in the late eighteenth and early nineteenth centuries, to port cities that were on the Adriatic and Black Sea coasts and were beyond Ottoman control. From the national perspective, it was these middle-class merchants that helped amass the capital and arms to launch the Greek insurrections-turned-revolution in the 1820s.[33] From Vogorides' perspective, these merchants (among whom were his classmates, brother Athanasios, and colleagues in the phanariot administration of Moldavia and Wallachia) were simply repeating the actions of fourteenth-century Constantinopolitans by fleeing a deteriorating state (the Ottoman, rather than the Byzantine) and seeking better conditions for themselves (in Europe and Russia, rather than in the Ottoman emirate).

After this historical and social analysis, Vogorides goes even further and articulates his vision for the future: "My goal and wish is for civilization to be fully realized in Turkey but with the names and paradigms of the Muslim legal system, guarding the unity of Ottomanism and of the Ottoman ethnos and the need for fusion, diffusion, and intermixing and equality before the law [isonomia] of the Christian reáya." Despite Vogorides' anglophile leanings, this vision was a far cry from British notions (specifically those of Stratford Canning) of reform and secularization in the Ottoman Empire, notions that entailed a wholesale restructuring of law and polity rather than an accommodation of any Ottoman Islamic tradition.

A pamphlet of Vogorides was, on the order of the sultan, to be sent and explained to Mr. Canning by Kostaki Musurus in London. It contained what was yet again a familiar argument turned inside out: rather than the internal "decay" of the empire causing the current problems, it was the paralysis of administration that caused Christians to leave and in turn strengthen the empire's enemies. Furthermore, Vogorides broadens and reroutes the concept of civilization from the European equation of civilization with Western Christianity and Christian notions of secularism when he calls for civilization with a Muslim structure and the fusion of Christians and Muslims.

This is quite distinct from the British-inspired vision of reforms that prevailed after the Crimean War, in which a quota system of political and legal representation further entrenched differences and competition between Christians and Muslims throughout the empire. And yet it was more than a flimsy defense of the "traditional" order; instead, it was an attempt, in the throes of a grave crisis of political (and personal) survival, to articulate the relevance and the feasibility of adapting the old structure to the ever-shifting landscape of Ottoman governance.

From our perspective in the twenty-first century, we may find it initially puzzling to ponder Vogorides' larger historical and cultural arguments that link Ottoman Christians to Islamic civilization, link Turks to Byzantium, all the while as he is trying to convey these arguments to both the sultan and the British so as to secure support for his own vision of reforms. Vogorides formulated several different arguments for the many audiences with which he had to contend, using a combination of fear mongering, historical precedent, and appeal to shari'a to prove how deserving Orthodox Christians were to keep political power as such within the Ottoman Empire. He even formulated, I argue, a nascent ideology and historical justifications for his position and sought to sell those to Canning in the hopes of continuing his vision of reforms with British guarantee.

The constellation of Ottoman governance in place since the 1830s gave primacy to the politics of multistate diplomacy over domestic military strength. This had been demonstrated by the successive encounters with Mehmet Ali and with several domestic challenges involving the Balkans; in these cases it was the calculus of multistate diplomacy, not the monopoly of force commanded by the Ottoman central state, that determined the outcome of conflicts and rebellions. With the Holy Sites issue and the other flashpoints that led to the Crimean War, the Ottoman military, even in its postjanissary incarnation, hardly commanded the same force that was available to British, Russian, French, and even, indirectly, to Ottoman diplomats. Out of the tense diplomacy of the 1830s and 1840s emerged the military conflict of the Crimean War, wherein the Ottoman military was aided if not revived by British and French allied forces against Russia. And out of that "hot" war another new order of Ottoman governance emerged.

Vogorides was part of an invisible tradition of service to the Ottoman sultanate by 1852—the tradition of phanariots serving that sultanate *as Christians*. Nicholas Mavroyenis's military service to the sultanate had soon after been rendered virtually invisible, as had the 1819 Dynasty of Four, the actions of phanariots who opposed the "Greek apostasy" in the 1820s, and the service of several top phanariot diplomats in the 1830s and 1840s. Because such figures and episodes remained invisible (or unaccounted for even if they received a passing mention) in the official Ottoman record and in the national frameworks that were developing around phanariots from the 1830s, they had not been forced to articulate a justification for their service beyond the generic language of loyalty and servitude. The discursive attacks against Vogorides as custodian of "Ottoman Christians" in the early 1850s, however, prompted a desperate attempt to articulate such a justification.

From Vogorides' struggle through the 1830s, the 1840s, and the controversies of the early 1850s, it becomes clear that the Tanzimat reforms that came out the other side of the Crimean War in 1856 were as much the result of these conflicts as they were the first cause of another set of changes for the Ottoman government and its subject populations. It also becomes clear that Vogorides' multiple loyalties as an Ottoman Orthodox Christian statesman at this moment—to the sultan, to the Orthodox Christian faith and Church, to the British—which he had managed to balance for over two decades, were ultimately irreconcilable. Furthermore, Vogorides' predicament was only an exaggerated version of the predicament of the sultanate he served—caught between opposing camps and without the ability to defend his position through force of arms.

# Afterlives

Stephanos Vogorides died in August 1859, just as act two of the Tanzimat project was beginning in earnest. His son-in-law Constantine Musurus, however, went on to serve the Ottoman Empire as its London representative for more than twenty-five years after Vogorides' death. Operating as a Tanzimat-era statesmen, Musurus served the empire within the confines of his official position, unlike Vogorides, whose de facto role in governance had dwarfed his official title. Musurus helped negotiate the loans from the British to the Ottoman state and the establishment of the Ottoman Bank, mediated for Ottoman subjects living in Britain, and even was granted the title of *paşa* in 1867. A Renaissance man (in all senses of the word), toward the end of his long career Musurus also decided to translate and publish one work of literature. And that was Dante's *Inferno*.

The first edition was published in 1882, while Musurus was still in London. (He would return to İstanbul and enter into retirement three years later.) In his prologue, dated mid-October 1881, he modestly explains the adjustments he was forced to make to the iambic meter of the original Latin as he translated into Greek and expresses a debt of gratitude to Sir Frederick Pollock (1815–88), the British scholar whose translation of Dante into English (in 1854) he had benefited from when composing his own translation. He does not go into the reasons that may have prompted him to publish his translation of *The Inferno* at this moment in time.[1] It is, however, tempting to surmise today that there was a looming subtext that he preferred not to make explicit.

Musurus watched from afar in May 1876 as the first coup d'état to depose a sultan since the Nizam-ı Cedid events of 1807-8 took place. This effected the removal of Abdülaziz followed by his suspicious death, the installation first of Sultan Murad V (a constitutionalist but traumatized and mentally ill) and then, after three months, the sultan who would rise to power as a constitutionalist but quickly thereafter proudly wear the label of neoabsolutist, Abdülhamit II. Interestingly, two key figures who carried out the coup that removed Abdülaziz were Hüseyin Avni, the minister of war, and Süleyman, the director of the military academy—a harbinger of a renewed primacy of military force over foreign politics to come in the internal calculus of Ottoman governance.[2]

The tumult in İstanbul prompted open rebellion in Serbia and Montenegro, and according to a historian of the Tanzimat, Roderic Davison, "the Turks [sic] began to rouse themselves for a real struggle, which began to look like a religious as well as a national war."[3] The military effort in the area that had become known as the Balkans blurred together in the minds of many with the fight against Russia, as Ottoman Muslim groups increasingly resented Russia's brutal treatment of that empire's own Muslim populations. In the midst of this, Midhat Paşa and others deliberated on the form a constitution would take, drafting a version that had "among its basic principles . . . complete equality of Christians and Muslims, eligibility of Christians for all offices including that of grand vezir, a chamber of elected deputies—sixteen from İstanbul and four from each vilayet, a ministry responsible to the chamber, the admission of Christian testimony against Muslims in the courts, and security of tenure of judged and civil officials."[4]

The short-lived Ottoman constitution, in many ways the fruit of two decades of the Tanzimat program, was approved and promulgated in late December 1876. The chamber of deputies convened for two sessions (March–June 1877 and December 1877–February 1878) before being dissolved and the constitution suspended for another thirty years. And in the midst of these events came the Russo-Turkish War of 1877–78, which began with Russian intervention to support uprisings and protect what they saw as victimized Christian populations in the Balkans and ended with military engagement through that region as well as the Caucasus.

By 1881, perhaps Musurus also had in mind not just the political polarization leading up to the Russo-Turkish War but the horrible violence of the war itself, including its deployment of irregulars to carry out large-scale civilian massacres, not to mention the implications, first, of the Treaty of San Stefano and, then, of the Congress of Berlin. Called by Otto von Bismarck, the Berlin Congress's object was to take back Russian gains from the first treaty and put an end to the war. Such implications included the first border changes since the Crimean War: the establishment of the independent states of Romania, Serbia, and Bulgaria, the British annexation of Cyprus (1878), and shortly thereafter the establishment of British "protection" over Egypt (1881). They also included the ratcheting up of ethnic and confessional violence from Macedonia to eastern Anatolia, which would reach a nightmarish crescendo in the Balkan Wars and World War I. Perhaps Musurus also felt dread associated with the Ottoman Empire's visible shift away from alliance with

Britain after the "Bulgarian Horrors" of 1876, opening the way for a future alliance with the new player on the stage of Great Power politics, Germany.

Taken together, these developments must have seemed ominous, to say the least. And for Musurus, who, like his father-in-law, had staked his life and career on advancing the interests of the Ottoman state, one could even begin to imagine the rationale behind his translation and evocation of Dante's nine circles of hell. Christian populations in the Ottoman Empire had less and less possibility of asserting political agency as Christians within the realm of Ottoman governance without being assumed to harbor sympathies for Russia and, by extension, to be working for national secession and the dissolution of the empire. And yet given the failure of the constitutional movement, neither could they hope to efface confessional difference within a "secular" vision of governance. The impasse Vogorides had faced in 1852 had grown into a full-blown crisis along with so many others by the 1880s: the dilemma between remaining loyal to the sultanate and fleeing to the Russians (Russifying), which blurred together with becoming a nationalist. Suddenly remaining loyal entailed walking on a knife's edge, remaining Christian but not overstepping the formal political boundaries for Christians, even if those boundaries were said to be expanding. The suspicion and paranoia that permeated Abdülhamit's reign no doubt had reached all the way to Musurus's London embassy.[5]

Practicing Ottoman governance after the Crimean War, and particularly after 1878, had become an entirely different undertaking from what it had been in the first half of the nineteenth century. While it may have seemed at first glance that the realities and horizons of governance for Orthodox Christians had changed dramatically for the worse in 1821 and only improved with the Tanzimat discourse and promise of political equality in 1856, in actuality a different narrative seems to have been more accurate when viewed from the perspective of Vogorides and his contemporaries. Certainly, the years immediately following 1821 were dangerous and volatile, but from the early 1830s restoration until the 1850s there was a fluidity at the top echelons of governance that made it possible for Vogorides, his protégés, and his rivals to make and sustain a career for themselves at the edge of the center. They were rarely required to articulate a justification or ideology to back up their actions, beyond the common discourse of loyalty they shared with their Muslim counterparts.

With the new discursive framework of the second round of the Tanzimat—which was welcomed, along with British (rather than Russian) protection—the space for unofficial, unarticulated service to the state grew tighter for those Christians at the top. Musurus, as ambassador in far-off London, perhaps did not have to confront this reality, but two of Vogorides' sons did. Nicholas Vogorides had been put forward by his father back in 1857 to be *kaymakam* of Moldavia.[6] Nicholas was technically born in Moldavia (in 1821 while father Vogorides was *kaymakam*) and did own land in the principality, thereby fulfilling two requirements for inclusion in the burgeoning national government. He even married into a prominent Molda-vian family, the Conaki family, in classic phanariot style.[7] And yet, the local boyars seemed to view him as a carpetbagger, capitalizing on his tenuous ties to Moldavia to gain undeserved power and status.

A tragicomic effort to keep the twin principalities separate from each other and tethered to the Ottoman Porte ensued, involving flagrant electoral fraud in the course of a Great Power–mandated plebiscite. The father-son Vogorides effort ended in fail-ure and in the union of the principalities, showing not only that Stephanos had lost his finesse for Ottoman governance but also concomitantly that circumstances had changed, no longer permitting his behind-the-scenes tactics. It also showed that Nicholas's only opportunity for inclusion in Ottoman governance could come by cap-turing a formal position, and this he failed to do. He went on to become an "Otto-man general" in 1860 and died shortly thereafter, in 1862, in Bucharest.[8]

Vogorides' other son, Alexander (Aleko, 1825–1910), although slightly more for-tunate, was still another example of the same shift. After a career of his own in the Ottoman foreign service and stints in Berlin, London, and Vienna, he resigned in 1877 in the course of the Russo-Ottoman war that ended the following year. Ac-cording to a biographer, he claimed in his resignation letter that "his Bulgarian ori-gins and the traditions of his family no longer permitted him to serve the Porte."[9] When the province of Eastern Rumelia was created at the Congress of Berlin, Aleko was appointed governor by Russia, with the agreement of the other powers and sub-ject to the nomination of the sultan. He was thus promoted to the rank of *paşa* and nominated to that position by Abdülhamit II in January 1879. He served in that post until 1884, when Eastern Rumelia was finally removed from Ottoman sover-eignty and united with independent Bulgaria. Once again, the space for an autono-mous polity, still tethered and loyal to the Ottoman sultanate (if under the guar-antee of Russia and the other Great Powers) but run by a Christian administrator (examples of which included the autonomous *beylik* of Samos, the *mutasarrifiya* of Mt. Lebanon, and later Crete), was being snuffed out. And yet without that post, Aleko could not have a share in Ottoman governance. Upon union of Eastern Rumelia with Bulgaria, Aleko retired to Paris, where he died.

Ironically, options for already-elite Ottoman Christians dwindled as the discourse of political equality became predominant. The option they had enjoyed for almost a century, of staying tied to both reformists and nonreformists at the Ottoman center (as phanariots had managed to do in the wake of 1807–8 and 1826), was in-creasingly complicated. This was because reforms after 1856 were directly targeted at changing the status of non-Muslims and were apparently aimed at the formal political integration of Muslims and non-Muslims. These efforts were of course un-dermined by the tactic of using a quota system to achieve non-Muslim represen-tation at all tiers of government, a policy that only further institutionalized con-fessional difference.[10] The efforts to change the status of non-Muslims were also complicated by the increasing presence of national movements in which Orthodox Christian Ottoman subjects were eligible for involvement. And a further complication was, from the Hamidian period, the increasingly robust Ottoman military, fast becoming the ground for a reassertion of reform by force. Military force, which had taken a back seat to diplomacy for the resolution of intra-Ottoman conflicts since the 1830s, would, by the Young Turk Revolution of 1908, come to replace it at the top of the Ottoman calculus of governance.

My aim in this study has not been to portray the fluidity of Ottoman governance before the Tanzimat as utopian. Fluidity, after all, often resembles anarchy and was experienced by Vogorides as a sea in which dangerous waves could drown him at any moment. Such fluidity required a state of constant vigilance and information from all directions in order to keep abreast of developments in İstanbul, diverse provinces, and several foreign states—and faith in Divine Providence to protect him from the threatening waves. Even if life and governance before the Tanzimat were not without their dangers, clearly a different level of violence was wrought by the Tanzimat—discursive violence and ultimately physical violence, set in motion by the late 1870s.

In this book I have argued that the phanariot ascendancy, which has been effectively buried by the Tanzimat and successive waves of nationalism and versions of national history, from Greek in the 1820s to Turkish in the 1920s, offers important insights into Ottoman governance in the age of revolutions—from the 1769–74 war with Russia, which prompted a revolution in phanariot horizons, to the 1807 Ottoman civil war, the 1821 Greek Revolution, the 1826 self-imposed revolution in governance, and the 1839 and 1856 proclamations of a new discursive basis for governance. The case of phanariots before 1821 exposes the possibilities of political integration without a concomitant ideology or a fully elaborated imagination of integration. This turns the binary opposition between secular and religious, as well as the long-held assumption that Christians would inevitably support a secular basis of government, on its head.

Phanariots who stayed in the Ottoman Empire after the 1820s provide a different vantage point as well. From their perspective, the inversion in relative capacity between diplomacy and military force was crucial and actually allowed them, in smaller numbers, to augment their power by rebuilding a new house out of many of the pre-1821 materials. While confessional lines hardened and military service became less possible than it had been in Mavroyenis's time, military participation also became less desirable, and in the final analysis it became unnecessary to achieving a place in Ottoman governance. If from the edge of the center one could engineer appointments to ambassadorial posts (from which their occupants could exert significant influence on policy) and engineer solutions to territorial disputes—

autonomy, independence, and everything in between on this spectrum—why would the hazards of military involvement be necessary?

Mehmet Ali Paşa was a contemporary as well as a friend and rival of Stephanos Vogorides. His career and legacy played out in a very different way from Vogorides', but they shared the same world of governance. Both were born in Rumelia around the early 1770s and were shaped by their experiences in the Napoleonic era. Both also went on to carve out the largest possible niche for themselves given the shifting constraints and possibilities of Ottoman governance in their day. Mehmet Ali did so by accumulating unprecedented military strength at the territorial margins of the empire. Vogorides did so by accumulating power and information in İstanbul, which was the Ottoman center and the interface between the Ottoman state and European states and was increasingly the locus of power for Ottoman governance.

Mehmet Ali's challenge to the Ottoman central state, in part because he was a Muslim, was not seen on the outside or the inside in the same light as the Greek Revolution; instead, from the outside it was assumed he was merely a rebellious vassal in a zero-sum game with Sultan Mahmud II. In this game, in which the outside world of diplomacy began to matter as much as the inside dynamics of governance by force, Mehmet Ali would either be allowed to take over the sultanate from within or remain a regional magnate with significant concessions. Likewise Vogorides, precisely because he was a Christian, has confounded students of Ottoman history who would expect him to be nationalist and therefore disloyal to the Ottoman sultan.

Furthermore, the memory of Mehmet Ali that has been constructed in the service of modern Egyptian nationalism has made him out to be far more important than Vogorides, who had all but disappeared. Mehmet Ali is to this day credited (and faulted) as the father of the Egyptian nation and was indeed the founder of the dynasty that ruled Egypt until Nasser's ascent to power in the 1950s. Vogorides, in sharp contrast, is the father of nothing, a historical dead end, given the available frameworks of imperial and national histories.

In September 1955, Stephanos Vogorides and Constantine Musurus surfaced again, quite literally. In the course of urban riots in İstanbul directed against the Rum residents and establishments of the city, a group that can be described only as a mob broke into the crypt of the Taxiarchon Church in the Bosphorus village neighborhood of Arnavutköy, where the two men had been buried since the previous century.[11] The rioters disinterred the remains of the two men, strewing them about the church courtyard, according to an eyewitness to the events still resident in the neighborhood.[12]

While certainly one of the more grisly acts of the September 6–7 events, it is also a fascinating and very telling symbol of both the living legacy and the failure to remember the pre-Tanzimat world at the height of the modern, nationalist era. The Ottoman Empire was no more, having been succeeded by the Republic of Turkey in 1923. And Orthodox Christians had been forcibly removed from Ottoman-turned-Turkish territory, as had Muslims from Greek territory, with the sole exceptions of Orthodox Christians in the city of İstanbul and Muslims in Greek Thrace. The riots in 1955 were prompted by tensions between the modern states of Greece and Turkey brought about by the British decolonization of the island of Cyprus, adding a layer of irony to the violence. Britain had originally colonized the island, of course, in the wake of the Congress of Berlin in 1878, just as Musurus was presumably embarking on his translation of Dante's *Inferno*.

Even in Musurus's wildest imagination he could not have foreseen that his remains would be disinterred as part of a response to the end of that island's colonization. Given the beginnings of mass violence that he witnessed in the Hamidian era, however, this might not have come as such a surprise to him. Likewise, the rioters that night could hardly have appreciated these levels of irony; perhaps to them Vogorides and Musurus represented the threat of a foreign, non-Turkish element, making them stand-ins for a Greek state encroaching on what they saw as the rightful Turkish territory of Cyprus. So effectively buried had the legacy of Vogorides' and Musurus's world become that it may have been impossible for these rioters to imagine that a world of governance had existed where these two Christians had spent their lives working to protect the Ottoman sultanate.

# Genealogies of the Vogorides, Musurus, and Aristarchi Families

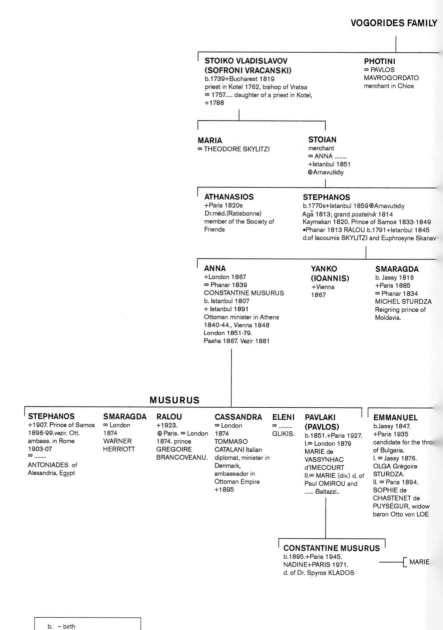

FIGURE 4. Genealogy of the Vogorides and Musurus families. Adapted from Sturdza, *Dictionnaire historique et généalogique des grandes familles de Grèce, d'Albanie, et de Constantinople*, 466–67.

```
┐
...........(son)
b. Bucharest 1803
+after 1815


┐
        YORGO(?)
```

| CHARICLEIA | NIKOLAKI (NICHOLAS) | ALEKO (ALEXANDROS) | MARINGKO (MARIA) |
|---|---|---|---|
| b.1828 +Naples 1860. I. ∞ Jassy 1847 LASKARAKI CANTACUZENO Pascanu (div.) II. ∞ MAXIMILIAN NYSSON Danish painter. | b. Jassy 1821 +Buc. 1862 Mavroyeni Church. *Kaymakam* of Moldavia 1857. Ottoman general 1860. ∞ 1844 Tiganesti (Mold) CATHERINE KONAKI rem. to prince Ruspoli of Poggio-Sussa, mayor of Rome | b. Istanbul 1823. +Paris 1910 attorney (Paris) Ottoman minister of Public works in Vienna. prince - governor of Rumélie (pasha) 1879-1884. ∞ ASPASIA BALTAZZI+1899. | ∞ Phanar 1851 YANKO PHOTIADES bey. Ott. minister in Athens 1860-70, Rome 1886. Gov. of Crete.+1892. |

**PHOTIADES**

| ONSTANTINE | MARIA | LOUKIA | STEPHANOS | CLEOPATRA | ALEXAN-DROS | RALOU |
|---|---|---|---|---|---|---|
| 849 ∞ Rome 94. LAURA SPOLI of the nces de Bisignano rvieto 32. | b.1851. +⊛Jassy 1931. ∞ Jassy 1872.PIERRE count of ROME. | b.Jassy 1855. +Jassy 1938. ⊛Stînca (Jassy) I. ∞ Jassy 1875. NICHOLAS ROSETTI ROZNOVANU II. ∞ Jassy 1894. DÉMÈTRE GRECIANU minister of justice for Romania. pres. of the Senate+murdered Buc. 1920. | b.Istanbul 1854 +Athens 1918 bey Ottoman I. ∞ HELENE BALTAZZI II. ∞ PENELOPE CHOREMI of Alexandria, Egypt. | ∞ CONSTANTINE KARATHEODORI prince of Samos 1908 | b.Istanbul 1858 +Athens 1933 | b.Istanbul 1852 +Athens 1923 |

| SMARAGDA | EVANGELOS | CONSTANTINE | ALEXANDROS | GEORGIOS | VASSILIOS |
|---|---|---|---|---|---|
| b.1879.+1940 Catholic nun. (MADELEINE) | b.1880.+1916. | b. 1882. +Paris 1949. professor at Sorbonne, writer. ∞ IRENE SOUTSO (div.) | b. 1890. professor of Physics at Polytechnic in Athens ∞ Paris 1921. IRENE SOUTSO | b.1897.+1929. | b.Athens 1901.+Paris 196.. painter/writer, rep. of Greece to UNESCO. ∞ IRÈNE AVIOLAT. |

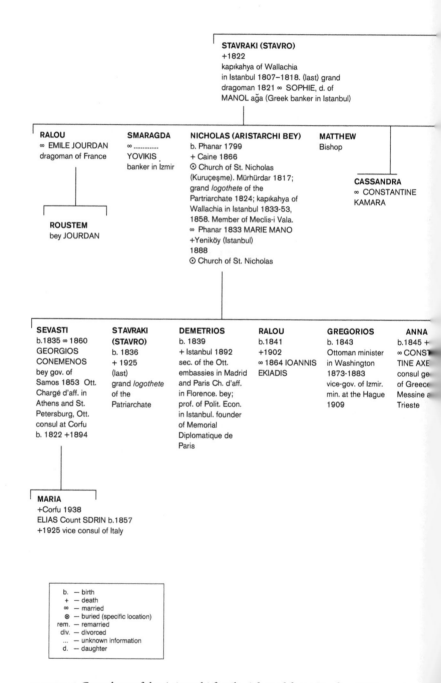

STAVRAKI (STAVRO)
+1822
kapıkahya of Wallachia
in Istanbul 1807–1818. (last) grand
dragoman 1821 ∞ SOPHIE, d. of
MANOL ağa (Greek banker in Istanbul)

RALOU
∞ EMILE JOURDAN
dragoman of France

SMARAGDA
∞ .............
YOVIKIS
banker in İzmir

NICHOLAS (ARISTARCHI BEY)
b. Phanar 1799
+ Caine 1866
⊙ Church of St. Nicholas
(Kuruçeşme). Mürhürdar 1817;
grand *logothete* of the
Partriarchate 1824; kapıkahya of
Wallachia in Istanbul 1833-53,
1858. Member of Meclis-i Vala.
∞ Phanar 1833 MARIE MANO
+Yeniköy (Istanbul)
1888
⊙ Church of St. Nicholas

MATTHEW
Bishop

CASSANDRA
∞ CONSTANTINE
KAMARA

ROUSTEM
bey JOURDAN

SEVASTI
b.1835 ∞ 1860
GEORGIOS
CONEMENOS
bey gov. of
Samos 1853 Ott.
Chargé d'aff. in
Athens and St.
Petersburg, Ott.
consul at Corfu
b. 1822 +1894

STAVRAKI
(STAVRO)
b. 1836
+ 1925
(last)
grand *logothete*
of the
Patriarchate

DEMETRIOS
b. 1839
+ Istanbul 1892
sec. of the Ott.
embassies in Madrid
and Paris Ch. d'aff.
in Florence. bey;
prof. of Polit. Econ.
in Istanbul. founder
of Memorial
Diplomatique de
Paris

RALOU
b.1841
+1902
∞ 1864 IOANNIS
EKIADIS

GREGORIOS
b. 1843
Ottoman minister
in Washington
1873-1883
vice-gov. of Izmir.
min. at the Hague
1909

ANNA
b.1845 +
∞ CONST
TINE AXE
consul ge
of Greece
Messine a
Trieste

MARIA
+Corfu 1938
ELIAS Count SDRIN b.1857
+1925 vice consul of Italy

b.  — birth
+  — death
∞  — married
⊛ — buried (specific location)
rem. — remarried
div. — divorced
... — unknown information
d.  — daughter

FIGURE 5. Genealogy of the Aristarchi family. Adapted from Sturdza, *Dictionnaire historique et généalogique des grandes familles de Grèce, d'Albanie, et de Constantinopl*
221.

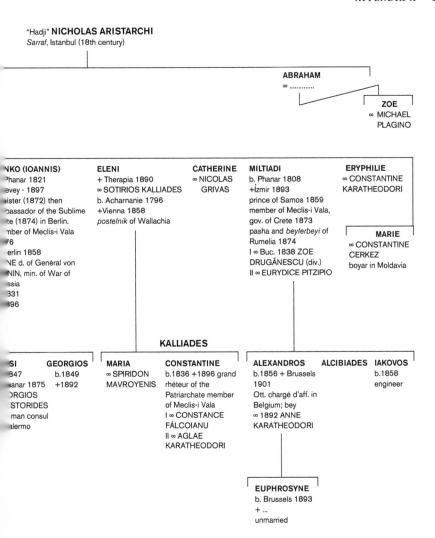

"Hadji" **NICHOLAS ARISTARCHI**
*Sarraf*, Istanbul (18th century)

**ABRAHAM**
∞ ...........

**ZOE**
∞ MICHAEL
PLAGINO

**NKO (IOANNIS)**
Phanar 1821
evey - 1897
ister (1872) then
bassador of the Sublime
te (1874) in Berlin.
mber of Meclis-i Vala
76
erlin 1858
NE d. of Genèral von
NIN, min. of War of
ssia
331
896

**ELENI**
+ Therapia 1890
∞ SOTIRIOS KALLIADES
b. Acharnanie 1796
+Vienna 1858
*postelnik* of Wallachia

**CATHERINE**
∞ NICOLAS
GRIVAS

**MILTIADI**
b. Phanar 1808
+İzmir 1893
prince of Samos 1859
member of Meclis-i Vala,
gov. of Crete 1873
pasha and *beylerbeyi* of
Rumelia 1874
I ∞ Buc. 1838 ZOE
DRUGĂNESCU (div.)
II ∞ EURYDICE PITZIPIO

**ERYPHILIE**
∞ CONSTANTINE
KARATHEODORI

**MARIE**
∞ CONSTANTINE
CERKEZ
boyar in Moldavia

**KALLIADES**

**SI**
847
anar 1875
ORGIOS
STORIDES
man consul
alermo

**GEORGIOS**
b.1849
+1892

**MARIA**
∞ SPIRIDON
MAVROYENIS

**CONSTANTINE**
b.1836 +1896 grand
rhéteur of the
Patriarchate member
of Meclis-i Vala
I ∞ CONSTANCE
FÁLCOIANU
II ∞ AGLAE
KARATHEODORI

**ALEXANDROS**
b.1856 + Brussels
1901
Ott. chargé d'aff. in
Belgium; bey
∞ 1892 ANNE
KARATHEODORI

**ALCIBIADES**

**IAKOVOS**
b.1858
engineer

**EUPHROSYNE**
b. Brussels 1893
+ ...
unmarried

# Phanariot Dignitaries in the Four High Offices of Dragoman (Grand Dragoman; Dragoman of the Fleet) and *Voyvoda* (of Wallachia and Moldavia), 1661–1821

|  | Dragoman of the Fleet | Imperial Dragoman | *Voyvoda* of Wallachia | *Voyvoda* of Moldavia |
|---|---|---|---|---|
| Panagiotes Nikousios | | 1661–73 | | |
| Alexander Mavrocordato | | 1673–1709 | | |
| Ioannakis Porphyrites | 1701–10 | | | |
| Constantine Ventoura | 1713–31 | | | |
| Nicholas Mavrocordato | | 1689–1709 | 1715–16, 1719–30 | 1711–15 |
| Yanaki Mavrocordato | | 1709–17 | 1716–19 | 1743–47 |
| Constantine Mavrocordato | | | 1730, 1731–33, 1735–40, 1744–48, 1756–58, 1761–63 | 1741–43, 1748–49 |
| Michael Rakovitsa | | | 1730–31, 1741–44 | 1715–26 |
| Gregorios Ghika (II) | | 1717–27 | 1733–35, 1748–52 | 1726–33, 1747–48 |
| Georgios Ramadani | 1731–43 | | | |
| Matthaios Ghika | | 1751–52 | 1752–53 | 1753–56 |
| Nicholas Ioannis Mavroyeni | 1744–50, 1756–59 | | | |
| Constantine Rakovitsa | | | 1753–56, 1763–64 | 1749–53, 1756–57 |
| Skarlatos Ghika | | | 1758–61, 1765–66 | 1757–58 |
| Stephanos Dimakes | 1762–63 | | | |

| | Dragoman of the Fleet | Imperial Dragoman | *Voyvoda* of Wallachia | *Voyvoda* of Moldavia |
|---|---|---|---|---|
| Stephanos Rakovitsa | | | 1763-64 | |
| Ioannis Kallimaki | | 1741-50, 1752-58 | | 1758-61 |
| Gregorios Kallimaki | | | | 1761-64, 1767-69 |
| Alexander Ghika | | 1727-40 | 1766-68 | |
| Gregorios Ghika (III) | | 1758-64 | 1768-69 | 1764-67, 1774-82 |
| Georgios Karaca | | 1764-65 | | |
| Constantine Muruzi | 1764-65 | 1774-77 | | |
| Alexander Mavrocordato | | | | |
| Stephanos Mavroyeni | 1765 | | | |
| Nicholas Rosetti | 1765-67 | | 1770-71 | 1788-89 |
| Manuel Argyropoulo | 1767-68 | | | |
| Manuel Rosetti | | | | |
| Scarlatos Karaca | | 1765-68, 1770-74 | | |
| Nicholas Soutso | | 1768-69 | | |
| Alexander Hypsilanti | | 1774 | 1774-82, 1796-97 | 1786-88 |
| Nicholas Karaca | | 1777-82 | 1782-83 | |
| Alexander (Firari) Mavrocordato | | 1783-85 | | 1785-86 |
| Michael Soutso (I) | | 1782-83 | 1783-86, 1791-93, 1801-2 | 1793-95 |
| Nicholas Mavroyeni | | 1786-88 | | |
| Alexander Kallimaki | | 1785-88, 1794-95 | | 1795-99 |
| Manuel Karaca | | 1788-90 | | |
| Alexander Muruzi | | 1790-92 | 1793-96, 1799-1801 | 1792, 1802-6, 1806-7 |
| Constantine Hançerli | 1790-97 | | 1797-99 | |
| Georgios Muruzi | | 1792-94, 1795-96 | | |
| Constantine Hypsilanti | | 1796-99 | 1802-6 | 1799-1801 |
| Alexander-Nicholas Soutso | 1797-99 | 1799-1801 | 1819-21 | 1801-2 |
| Ioannis-Nicholas Karaca | 1799-1800 | 1808 | | |
| Ioannis Karaca (II) | | 1807-8, 1812 | 1812-19 | |
| Ioannis Kallimaki | 1800-1803 | 1818-21 | | |
| Panagiotes Muruzi | 1803-6 | 1809-12 | | |
| Michael Hançerli | 1806-7, 1810-11 | | | |
| Skarlatos Kallimaki | | 1801-6 | | 1806, 1812-19 |
| Alexander Hançerli | | 1806-7 | | 1807 |

| | Dragoman of the Fleet | Imperial Dragoman | *Voyvoda* of Wallachia | *Voyvoda* of Moldavia |
|---|---|---|---|---|
| Alexander-Michael Soutso | | 1802–7 | | |
| Demetrios Muruzi | | 1808–12 | | |
| Jacob Argyropoulo | 1809 | 1812–17 | | |
| Constantine Mavroyeni | 1811–16 | | | |
| Michael Soutso (II) | | 1817–19 | | 1819–21 |
| Michael Mano | 1816–18 | | | |
| Nicholas Muruzi | 1818–21 | | | |
| Constantine Muruzi | | | 1821 | |
| Stavraki Aristarchi | | | 1821 | |

SOURCES: Sturdza, *Dictionnaire historique et généalogique*, 157; Soutzos, *Mémoires du prince Nicolas Soutzo*, 304–5; Stamatiades, *Biographiai ton hellenon megalon diermeneon*, 191; Zeynep Sözen, *Fenerli Beyler: 110 yılın öyküsü (1711–1821)* [Phanariot princes: 110-year story] (İstanbul: Aybay Yayıncılık, 2000), 187–90; Sphyroeras, *Hoi dragomanoi tou stolou*, 174.

# NOTES

## ABBREVIATIONS

AMAE    Archives du Ministère des affaires étrangers
ASB     Archivele Statului București
BOA     Başbakanlık Osmanlı Arşivi
CML     Cyril and Methodius Library, Orientalia Collection
EI2     *The Encyclopaedia of Islam*, 2nd ed.
EPI     Archive of the Ecumenical Patriarchate of İstanbul
İA      *İslam ansiklopedisi*
IJMES   *International Journal of Middle East Studies*
MHE     *Megale hellenike encyclopedia*
MP      Musurus Papers
PRO     FO: Public Records Office, Foreign Office papers
TKSA    Topkapı Sarayı Arşivi

## PREFACE

1. See Bernard Lewis, *The Emergence of Modern Turkey* (London: Oxford University Press, 1968).

2. To date there is no book-length study in English of Mahmud II's reign, and only one book on Sultan Selim III's reign—Stanford Shaw's *Between Old and New: The Ottoman Empire under Sultan Selim III, 1789–1807* (Cambridge, MA: Harvard University Press, 1971).

3. Timothy Mitchell, "Society, Economy, and the State Effect," in *State/Culture: State Formation after the Cultural Turn*, ed. George Steinmetz (Ithaca, NY: Cornell University Press, 1999), 77.

4. Ibid., passim.

5. Rifa'at 'Ali Abou-El-Haj, *Formation of the Modern State: The Ottoman Empire Sixteenth to Eighteenth Centuries,* 2nd ed. (Syracuse, NY: Syracuse University Press, 2005); Cemal Kafadar, *Between Two Worlds: The Construction of the Ottoman State* (Berkeley: University of California Press, 1995).

6. *Hetairist* refers to the secret society, known in Greek as the Philike Hetaireia (Society of Friends), that initiated the Greek secessionist uprising.

7. James Scott, *Seeing Like a State: How Certain Schemes to Improve the Human Condition Have Failed* (New Haven, CT: Yale University Press, 1998).

8. Roderic Davison, *Reform in the Ottoman Empire, 1856–1876* (Princeton, NJ: Princeton University Press, 1963), 93.

9. See R. J. Crampton, *A Concise History of Bulgaria* (Cambridge: Cambridge University Press, 1997), 46 ff.

10. See Roderic Davison's characterization of the Tanzimat project in *Reform in the Ottoman Empire.* See also Pars Tuğlacı, *Bulgaristan ve Türk-Bulgar ilişkileri* [Bulgaria and Turkish-Bulgarian relations] (İstanbul: Cem Yayınevi, 1984).

11. Michel Foucault: *Discipline and Punish: The Birth of the Prison* (New York: Vintage Books, 1979); *The Order of Things: An Archaeology of the Human Sciences* (New York: Vintage Books, 1994); and "On Governmentality," in *The Foucault Reader,* edited by Paul Rabinow (New York: Pantheon Books, 1984).

12. On *ayan*s, see Yuzo Nagata, *Tarihte ayanlar: Karaosmanoğulları üzerinde bir inceleme* [Ayans in history: A study on the Karaosmanoğlus] (Ankara: Türk Tarih Kurumu Basımevi, 1997); and Bruce McGowan, "The Age of the Ayans," in *An Economic and Social History of the Ottoman Empire,* vol. 2, ed. Suraiya Faroqhi, Bruce McGowan, Donald Quataert, and Şevket Pamuk (Cambridge: Cambridge University Press, 1994). On households, see Metin Kunt, *The Sultan's Servants: The Transformation of Ottoman Provincial Government, 1550–1650* (New York: Columbia University Press, 1983); Leslie Peirce, *The Imperial Harem: Women and Sovereignty in the Ottoman Empire* (New York: Oxford University Press, 1993); Jane Hathaway, *The Politics of Households in Ottoman Egypt: The Rise of the Qazdaglis* (Cambridge: Cambridge University Press, 1993); and André Raymond, *Le Caire des janissaires: L'apogée de la ville ottomane sous 'Abd al'-Rahman Katkhuda* (Paris: CNRS Éditions, 1995).

13. On the question of the Sunni Muslim identity/character of the formal Ottoman state, see Cornell Fleischer, *Bureaucrat and Intellectual in the Ottoman Empire: The Historian Mustafa Ali (1541–1600)* (Princeton, NJ: Princeton University Press, 1986). Halil Inalcik and others have brought to light the phenomenon of non-Muslims (even bishops) being granted *timar*s and, we presume, serving as *sipahi*s in the Ottoman cavalry in the fifteenth century (Halil Inalcik, "Timariotes chrétiens en Albanie au XVe siècle d'après un register de timars Ottoman," *Mitteilungen des Osterreichischen Staatsarchivs* 4 [1951]: 118–38).

14. Mehmet Ali Paşa of Egypt is of course the major exception to this, as an *ayan* who survived (and in fact was instrumental to) the crises and transformations of the 1820s and 1830s. See Khaled Fahmy: *All the Pasha's Men: Mehmet Ali, His Army, and the Making of Modern Egypt* (Cambridge: Cambridge University Press, 1997); and *Mehmet Ali,* Makers of the Muslim World series (New York: OneWorld Press, 2008).

15. To name a few: Carter Findley, *Bureaucratic Reform in the Ottoman Empire: The Sublime Porte, 1789–1922* (Princeton, NJ: Princeton University Press, 1980); Şerif Mardin, *The*

*Genesis of Young Ottoman Thought: A Study in the Modernization of Turkish Political Ideas* (Princeton, NJ: Princeton University Press, 1962); Paschalis Kitromilides, *The Enlightenment as Social Criticism: Iosipos Moisiodax and Greek Culture in the Eighteenth Century* (Princeton, NJ: Princeton University, 1992); Fahmy, *All the Pasha's Men;* Virginia Aksan, *An Ottoman Statesman in War and Peace: Ahmed Resmi Efendi, 1700–1783* (Leiden: Brill Academic Publishers, 1995); and İlber Ortaylı, *İmparatorluğun en uzun yüzyılı* [The empire's longest century] (İstanbul: Alkım, 1983).

16. George Steinmetz, *Regulating the Social: The Welfare State and Local Politics in Imperial Germany* (Princeton, NJ: Princeton University Press, 1993), introduction; and Steinmetz, ed., *State/Culture,* especially pp. 8–9.

17. For a related discussion of archives and authority, see Brinkley Messick, *Calligraphic State: Textual Domination and History in a Muslim Society* (Berkeley: University of California Press, 1993).

18. More common sources from Ottoman officials are chronicles from court historians *(vaka'nüvis)* such as Şanizade (Tarih-i Şanizade) and later the Tanzimat statesmen-historians Cevdet Paşa (Tarih-i Cevdet) and Lütfi Paşa (Tarih-i Lütfi). Even *risales* (letters) such as that of "Koca Sekbanbaşı" (actually Ahmed Vasıf Efendi) regarding the New Order reforms seem to be an effort to disseminate an official argument for reforms. See appendix 1 of William Wilkinson, *An Account of the Principalities of Wallachia and Moldavia: With Various Political Observations Relating to Them* (London: Longman, Hurst, Rees, Orme, and Brown, 1820), for a translation of Koca Sekbanbaşı's *risale* (letter); and Kemal Beydilli, "Sekbanbaşı risalesinin müellifi hakkında" [Regarding the author of the Sekbanbaşı *risale*], *Türk kültürü incelemeleri dergisi* 12 (2005): 221–24. Such histories are helpful in ascertaining the official stances of the Ottoman central state, but rarely do they provide candid glimpses of the day-to-day experience of governance.

19. Mihail-Dimitri Sturdza, *Dictionnaire historique et généalogique des grandes familles de Grèce, d'Albanie, et de Constantinople* (Paris: M.-D. Sturdza, 1983), 448. All translations are mine unless otherwise noted.

20. See Christine Philliou, "The Paradox of Perceptions: Interpreting the Ottoman Past through the National Present," *Middle Eastern Studies* 44, no. 5 (September 2008): 661–75.

21. Stanford Shaw, "The Origins of Ottoman Military Reform: The Nizam-ı Cedid Army of Sultan Selim III," *Journal of Modern History* 37 (1965): 292.

## STEPHANOS VOGORIDES' APOLOGIA

1. "The Evangelical Logos" refers to the New Testament.

2. *Apostates* refers to the Greek insurgents/partisans.

3. MP, Musurus-Vogorides correspondence, IX: 69, Constantinople, November 1852.

## 1. THE HOUSES OF PHANAR

1. Thomas Hope, *Anastasius, or Memoirs of a Greek Written at the Close of the Eighteenth Century* (1819; London: John Murray, 1836), 1: 52–53.

2. The island of Chios, for instance, was the birthplace of prominent phanariots such as

Panagiotis Nicousios in the seventeenth and eighteenth centuries, as well as large-scale mercantile families such as the Rallis and Argentis in the eighteenth and nineteenth centuries.

3. For structural analyses and typologies of Greek mercantile diaspora firms, see Gelina Harlaftis, "Mapping the Greek Maritime Diaspora from the Early Eighteenth to the Late Twentieth Centuries"; Ioanna Papelasis-Minoglou, "Toward a Typology of Greek Diaspora Entrepreneurship"; and Maria-Christina Hatziioannou, "Crossing Empires: Greek Merchant Networks before the Imperialistic Expansion"; all in *Diaspora Entrepreneurial Networks: Five Centuries of History,* ed. Ina Baghdiantz-McCabe, Gelina Harlaftis, and Ioanna Papelasis-Minoglou (Oxford: Oxford University Press, 2005); Olga Katsiardi-Herring, "He hellenike diaspora: He geographia kai he typologia tes" [The Greek diaspora: Its geography and typology], in *Hellenike oikonomike historia 150s–190s aionas* [Greek economic history, fifteenth to nineteenth centuries], ed. Spyros I. Asdrachas (Athena: Politistiko Hidryma Homilou Peiraios, 2003), 237–47; and Gelina Harlaftis, *History of Greek-Owned Shipping: The Making of an International Tramp Fleet, 1830 to the Present* (London, New York: Routledge, 1996).

4. Benjamin Braude, "Foundation Myths of the Millet System," in *Christians and Jews in the Ottoman Empire: The Functioning of a Plural Society,* 2 vols., ed. Bernard Lewis and Benjamin Braude (New York: Holmes and Maier Publishing, 1982).

5. Access to more systematic records of marriage and godparentage alliances is also limited because the lion's share of the Archive of the Ecumenical Patriarchate (EPI)in İstanbul is not open to researchers. Passing mentions of marriages, baptisms, and financial-property matters do find their way into the outgoing correspondence from the patriarchate to metropolitan sees, which is the one section of the archive that is available to researchers.

6. Ioanna Papelasis-Minoglou, among others, has noted the similarly "amorphous" structures of Greek merchant coalitions. See her article "The Greek Merchant House of the Russian Black Sea: A 19th-Century Example of a Traders' Coalition," *International Journal of Maritime History* 10 (1998): 61–104.

7. Halil Inalcik, "Centralization and Decentralization in Ottoman Administration," in *Studies in Eighteenth-Century Islamic History,* ed. Thomas Naff and Roger Owen (Carbondale: Southern Illinois University Press, 1977), 27–52; Rifa'at Ali Abou-El-Haj, "The Ottoman Vezir and Pasha Households, 1683–1703: A Preliminary Report," *Journal of the American Oriental Society* 94 (1974): 438–47; Abou-El-Haj, *Formation of the Modern State.*

8. See Virginia Aksan, "Ottoman Political Writing, 1768–1808," *IJMES* 25, no. 1 (1993): 53–69; and Bernard Lewis, *The Muslim Discovery of Europe* (New York: W. W. Norton, 1982).

9. Rifa'at Ali Abou-El-Haj, "The Formal Closure of the Ottoman Frontier, 1699–1703," *Journal of the American Oriental Societies* 89 (1969): 467–75.

10. Nicholas Mavrocordatos (1599–1649) was the first to move from his native Chios to İstanbul, becoming prominent in the lay service of the Orthodox Church there. Alexander *ex aporiton* (minister of secrets) the grand dragoman (1636–1709) was his son, and Nicholas (1670–1730), the *voyvoda* of Moldavia and Wallachia, his grandson.

11. Sir Stephen Runciman, *Great Church in Captivity: A Study of the Patriarchate of Constantinople from the Eve of the Turkish Conquest to the Greek War of Independence* (New York: Cambridge University Press, 1968).

12. Sanjay Subrahmanyam and C. A. Bayly, "Portfolio Capitalists and the Political Econ-

omy of Early Modern India," *Indian Economic and Social History Review* 25, no. 4 (1988): 401–24.

13. Ibid. See also the world-systems-inspired literature on comprador bourgeoisies in the Ottoman Empire, predominantly focusing on port cities such as İzmir in the eighteenth and nineteenth centuries. Reşat Kasaba, *The Ottoman Empire and the World Economy: The Nineteenth Century* (Albany: State University of New York Press, 1988).

14. See Kunt, *The Sultan's Servants*.

15. For the *ulema*, see Madeline Zilfi, *Politics of Piety: The Ottoman Ulema in the Post-classical Age (1600–1800)* (Minneapolis: Biblioteca Islamica 1988). For the bureaucracy, see Findley, *Bureaucratic Reform in the Ottoman Empire*. For Egypt, see Hathaway, *The Politics of Households in Ottoman Egypt*.

16. The term *ayan* varies in meaning between the Arab and non-Arab Ottoman provinces. In the Arab provinces, *ayan*s were an "urban elite that occupied the top stratum of local society and acted as mediators between the population and the government. [They] existed as an identifiable group as early as the ninth century, and its formation was closely linked to the evolution and functioning of the city in Islamic society and the distinctive political structures in which it was embedded" (Margaret Meriwether, *The Kin Who Count: Family and Society in Ottoman Aleppo, 1770–1840* [Austin: University of Texas Press, 1999], 31). In non-Arab provinces, the term *ayan* signifies a new class that came to power in the late seventeenth century and came to combine formal office and military power and to constitute a threat to the power of the central state by the late eighteenth century.

17. For discussions of the range of factors that led to the systematic adoption of phanariots as dragomans in the eighteenth century, see Damien Janos, "Panaiotis *[sic]* Nicousios and Alexander Mavrocordatos: The Rise of the Phanariots and the Office of Grand Dragoman in the Ottoman Administration in the Second Half of the Seventeenth Century," *Archivum Ottomanicum* 23 (2005): 177–96"; and Christine Philliou, "Worlds Old and New: Phanariot Networks and the Remaking of Ottoman Governance, 1800–1850," PhD diss., Princeton University, 2004, chapter 1.

18. This became ever more important in the eighteenth century, after 1765 interruptions in supply from Egypt and the 1783 loss of Crimea to Russia. M. M. Alexandrescu-Dersca-Bulgaru, "Les rapports économiques de l'Empire Ottoman avec les principautés Roumaines et leur réglementation par les Khatt-i Sérif de privilèges (1774–1829)," in *Économie et sociétés dans l'Empire Ottoman (fin du XVIIIe—debut du XIXe siècle)*, ed. Jean-Louis Bacque-Grammont and Paul Dumont (Paris: Éditions du Centre national de la recherche scientifique, 1983), 317–26.

19. The grand dragoman was "the only Ottoman official to pay formal calls on European diplomats" by the turn of the nineteenth century. See Findley, *Bureaucratic Reform in the Ottoman Empire*, 78. In the period under discussion, the principalities were supplying one-third of the grain for İstanbul. Tevfik Güran, "The State Role in the Grain Supply of Istanbul, the Grain Administration, 1793–1839," *International Journal of Turkish Studies* 3, no. 1 (1984–1985): 27–41.

20. See Johann Strauss, "The Millets and the Ottoman Language: The Contribution of Ottoman Greeks to Ottoman Letters (19th–20th Centuries)," *Die Welt des Islams* 35, no. 2 (November 1995): 189–249.

21. On the dragoman of the imperial army, see MP, Ottoman file II.2.18; BOA, HAT: 11633. On the dragoman of the Morea, see Dimitris Stamatopoulos, "Constantinople in the Peloponnese: The Case of the Dragoman of the Morea Georgios Wallerianos and Some Aspects of the Revolutionary Process," in *Ottoman Rule and the Balkans, 1760–1850: Conflict, Transformation, Adaptation* (Rethymno, Greece: University of Crete Press, 2007), 148–67. By the turn of the nineteenth century, phanariots such as the former grand dragoman Karaca Manolaki were also teaching French at the military engineering school in İstanbul. BOA, HAT: 10925 (A.H. 1211; M. 1799–1800). (In temporal notations, "M." abbreviates "Miladi," signifying the Christian year.)

22. Photeinos died sometime between 1821 and 1824 in Bucharest. We find in February 1824 one Vasilios Dimitriou Photeinos, "nephew of the deceased Serdar Dionysios Photeinos," receiving seventeen hundred florins from a member of the Balasa (Balche) family for a property of Dionysios's in Wallachia. EPI: codex IE', 116.

23. David Goldfrank, *The Origins of the Crimean War* (London: Longman, 1994), 42; Shaw, *Between Old and New*, 22.

24. Dimitrie Cantemir, *Dimitrie Cantemir, Historian of South East European and Oriental Civilizations: Extracts from "The History of the Ottoman Empire,"* edited by Alexandru Dutu and Paul Cernovodeanu; translated from the Latin by N. Tindal (Bucharest: Association internationale d'études du sud-est européen, 1973). Cantemir's original work was completed shortly before his death in 1723. Dimitri Cantemir (1673–1723) was a pivotal figure for the phanariot and Moldo-Wallachian story. It was his flight to Russia while serving as *voyvoda* of Moldavia that prompted the Ottoman decision to shift from indigenous boyars to İstanbul-based phanariots for the positions of *voyvodas* for the principalities.

25. Kritovoulos, *The History of Mehmed the Conqueror*, translated from the Greek by Charles T. Riggs (Princeton, NJ: Princeton University Press, 1954), prologue, 11.

26. The use of *philomousos* suggests a connection to the Philomousos Hetaireia, founded sometime during 1811–12. This has been seen as the overt, cultural wing of the Philike Hetaireia secret society. Apostolos E. Vacalopoulos, *Nea hellenike historia 1204–1985* [Modern Greek history 1204–1985] (Thessaloniki: Vania, 1993), 157.

27. *Postelnik* was analogous to foreign minister: see "Ο Μέγας Ποστέλνικος—Ούτος είναι καθ' αυτό του ηγεμόνος μινίστρος των εξωτερικών υποθέσεων" (Dionysios Photeinos, *Historia tes palai Dakias ta nyn Transylvanias, Wallachias, kai Moldavias ek diaphoron palaion kai neon syngrapheon syneranistheisa para Dionysiou Photeinou* [History of the former Dacia, the current Transylvania, Wallachia, and Moldavia compiled from various old and new sources by Dionysios Photeinos], 3 vols. [Vienna: Typ. Io. Varthol. Svekiou, 1818–19], 3: 485).

28. Traian Stoianovich, "The Conquering Balkan Orthodox Merchant," *Economies and Societies: Traders, Towns, and Households*, vol. 2 of *Between East and West: The Balkan and Mediterranean Worlds* (New Rochelle, NY: A. D. Caratzas Publishers, 1992).

29. Sturdza, *Dictionnaire historique et généalogique des grandes familles*, 245–47.

30. Ibid., 297.

31. See Metin Kunt, "Ethnic-Regional *(cins)* Solidarity in the Seventeenth-Century Ottoman Establishment," *IJMES* 5 (1974): 233–39.

32. Ibid.

33. We should keep in mind that in many cases these name changes did not constitute

an irreversible and complete change of identity (since many shifted the endings of their names depending on the context, reverting to Slavic when in a Slavic milieu, et cetera). But it is clear that a phanariot-dominated arena existed wherein names not of Greek origins were altered to fit the context.

34. See Evangelia Balta, *Karamanlidika: Nouvelles additions et compléments* (Athens: Centre d'études d'Asie mineure, 1997).

35. Regarding Garabed amira Balyan's role in the Dolmabahçe Palace, see Pars Tuğlacı, *Osmanlı mimarlığında batılılaşma dönemi ve Balyan ailesi* [Westernization and the Balyan family in Ottoman architecture] (İstanbul: Yeni Çığır Bookstore, 1990), 5.

36. "Kaymakam Paşa: Bu günlerde Fenarlı takımı kendu meramlarını terviç içün gunagun eracif ve havadis ve mülgatlar neşr eyledikleri mesmu'm oldu. Bunların bu hareketi devletime müzir oluyor. Niçün sen ve sair memurin buna dikkat edüp def'ine say etmiyors[un]uz? Bu kafirlere hiç bir şey tesir etmez mi acaba? Hançerlioğlu ibret olmadı mı? Böyle şeyler Eflak ve Boğdan takımından çıkar lakin bunlar benim gayet intikal edeceğim şeyidir. İşte bu fesadın def'i suçlu suçsuz bu kafirlerin ekserini katl ile öldür. Bundan sonra bir şeyi işitmeyeyim. Bila-iman cümlesini katl ederim. Bunlara sen iyice tenbih ile gözlerini açsunlar sonra kendüleri bilur." BOA, HAT: 13375 (undated). One wonders whether this was written at the same time as another sultanic note to his grand vezir (A.H. 1222; M. 1807), wherein Selim refers to "Hypsilanti the swine" and the spies all over İstanbul. He finally orders that those of the *"millel-i selase"* (Rum, Yahudi, Ermeni) and of Islam who are doing such things, whoever they are, should be removed *(harice çıkarıp)* and that he should be informed about them. BOA, HAT: 7562 (A.H. 1222; M. 1807).

37. BOA, HAT: 13745-A.

38. See Findley, *Bureaucratic Reform in the Ottoman Empire.*

39. Ibid.

40. BOA, HAT: 13645 (A.H. 1216; M. ca. 1801).

41. Ibid.

42. BOA, HAT: 23768 (A.H. 1225; M. 1810–11): "Rusya taraftarlığı ile ittiham ederler: Muruz Aleksandiri Bey dört defa beyliklere. . . . Fransa taraftarlığı ile muştehirdir: Suçu Aleko hala Eflak Voyvodasında olarak; Rusya taraftarlığı ile ittiham ederler: Moruz Bey'in ikinci karandaşı Dimitreşko al-yevm ordu-yu Hümayun tercümanıdır."

43. See, for example: BOA, HAT: 13662, for Muruzis's report from Paris ca. 1803; BOA, HAT: 2443 (A.H. 1209), for a translation of the Spanish consul's *(maslahatgüzar)* dispatch on the events involving Robespierre (Robzpiyer *nam şahs*) and others in Paris in the summer of 1794; BOA, HAT: 12565 (A.H. 1232; M. 1816–17), for Moldavia Voyvoda "İskerlet's" reports gathered by his spies about goings-on across the banks of the Pruth River, in Russian territory; and BOA, HAT: 13081 (A.H. 1212; M. 1797–98), for news regarding the French Revolution conveyed by Wallachian Voyvoda Alexander.

44. BOA, HAT: 13754-A.

45. Photeinos, *Historia tes palai Dakias,* 3: 422.

46. Quotation from BOA, HAT: 13745-A (A.H. 1216). On the travel document confirmation, see BOA, Ahkam defterleri: Boğdan and Eflak, various.

47. This seems to have been similar to the pre-1783 arrangement the Ottomans had with the Crimean khans, although not with the Egyptian households and the *ayans.* See Athana-

siou Komnenou-Hypsilantou, *Ekklesiastikon kai politikon ton eis dodeka biblion H', Th' kai I' etoi ta meta ten Alosin (1453–1789), ek cheirographou anekdotou tes hieras mones tou Sina,* ekdidontas Archim Germanou Afthonidou Sinaitou [Ecclesiastical and political events from after the fall (1453–1789), in twelve books from an unpublished manuscript in the Monastery of [St. Catherine's of] Sinai, published by Archimandrite Germanos Afthonides of Sinai] (Athens: Bibl. Note Karavia, 1972), 417.

48. The term *kapıkahya/kapıkethüda,* meaning "steward" or "scribe," was originally a guild office *(kahya/kethüda).* Guild terminology permeated many areas of Ottoman governance: note references to the Rum *ta'ifesi* above.

49. See Marc-Philippe Zallony, *Essai sur les fanariotes, où l'on voit les causes primitives de leur élévation aux hospodariats de la Valachie et la Moldavie, leur mode d'administration, et les causes principales de leur chute; suivi de quelques réflexions sur l'état actuel de la Grèce* (Marseille: A. Ricard, 1824), for an explanation of this system.

50. BOA, HAT: 13745-A.

51. On ceremonies, see Eric Hobsbawm and Terence Ranger, eds., *The Invention of Tradition* (Cambridge: Cambridge University Press, 1983); on Ottoman ceremonial, Gülru Necipoğlu, *Architecture, Ceremonial, and Power: Topkapi Palace in the Fifteenth and Sixteenth Centuries* (Cambridge, MA: MIT Press, 1991); Selim Deringil, "The Invention of Tradition as Public Image in the Late Ottoman Empire, 1808–1908," *Comparative Studies in Society and History* 35, no. 1 (1993): 3–29; and Hakan Karateke, ed., *An Ottoman Protocol Register Containing Ceremonies from 1736 to 1808: BEO Sadaret Defterleri 350 in Prime Ministry Ottoman State Archives, Istanbul,* Ibrahim Pasha of Egypt Fund Series (Istanbul: Royal Asiatic Society/Ottoman Bank Archive and Research Centre, 2007).

52. For a later description of an earlier ceremony (that of Nicholas Mavroyenis in 1786), see Théodore Blancard, *Les Mavroyènis: L'histoire d'Orient,* 2 vols. (Paris: E. Leroux, 1909), 1: 169–79.

53. BOA, HAT: 13745-A (A.H. 1216).

54. The ceremony had changed and grown in complexity over time. The version depicted here is from Dionysios Photeinos's *Historia tes palai Dakias* and likely reflects the 1812 investiture ceremony. This may have been particularly elaborate, since it marked the Ottoman state's retaking of the principalities from Russian control between 1806 and 1812. For descriptions and analysis of earlier investiture ceremonies, see Philliou, "Worlds Old and New," chapter 1; Radu G. Paun, "Sur l'investiture des derniers princes phanariotes: Autour d'un document ignoré," *Revue des Études Sud-Est Europeennes* 35 (1997): 63–75; Wilkinson, *An Account of the Principalities of Wallachia and Moldavia;* and Zallony, *Essai sur les fanariotes.*

55. Confirming Photeinos's description, Sultan Selim III ordered in a note to his grand vezir that if Aleko, the son-in-law of the reigning Moldavian *voyvoda* and the current *kapıkethüda* of Moldavia, was to be appointed dragoman of the fleet, then the following evening an "inviter" should be sent to him, and the following day the ceremony should commence. BOA, HAT: 7872.

56. Photeinos, *Historia tes palai Dakias,* 3: 418.

57. Alexandrescu-Dersca-Bulgaru, "Les rapports économiques de l'Empire Ottoman," 317–26.

58. Photeinos, *Historia tes palai Dakias,* 3: 419–20.

59. For an example of a *telhis,* see BOA, HAT: 5530 (A.H. 1216; M. ca. 1801–2).

60. "Killeri Hümayunum, dikkat eylen *[sic]* rabıtasını senden matlub olunur. Avrupa tarafından havadis yetiştiresin, Eflak voyvodalığı menküli Serbestiyet üzere Sana nasp olundu, sadakatin matlup olunur." Photeinos, *Historia tes palai Dakias,* 3: 422. (Rather than translating in the corresponding text passage, I've transliterated into English directly from the Greek letters, thus conserving the grammatical variations and mistakes in the Greek author's Turkish.) The investiture with a *kaftan,* or robe, was common to all Ottoman high officials. See, for instance, Karateke, *An Ottoman Protocol Register.*

61. Ibid., 483.

62. Ibid., 446–47.

63. Albert Hourani, "Ottoman Reform and the Politics of Notables," in *The Beginnings of Modernization in the Middle East: The Nineteenth Century,* ed. William R. Polk and Richard L. Chambers (Chicago: University of Chicago Press, 1968), 41–68; McGowan, "The Age of the Ayans"; Deena Sadat, "Urban Notables in the Ottoman Empire: The Ayan," PhD diss., Rutgers University, 1969; Deena Sadat, "Rumeli Ayanlari: The Eighteenth Century," *Journal of Modern History* 44, no. 3 (1972): 346–63.

64. See works by Yuzo Nagata, such as *Muhsin-zade Mehmed Paşa ve Ayanlık Müessesesi* [Muhsinzade Mehmed Paşa and the *a'yan* institution] (Tokyo: Institute for the Study of Languages and Cultures of Asia and Africa, 1976).

65. On the decentralization or privatization, see Ariel Salzmann, *Tocqueville in the Ottoman Empire: Rival Paths to the Modern State* (Leiden, Boston: Brill, 2004).

66. See Fikret Adanir and Suraiya Faroqhi, eds., *The Ottomans and the Balkans: A Discussion of Historiography* (Leiden, Boston: Brill, 2002), chapter 9, "Coping with the Central State, Coping with Local Power: Ottoman Regions and Notables from the Sixteenth to the Early Nineteenth Century," 351; Ehud Toledano, "The Emergence of Ottoman-Local Elites, a Framework for Research," in *Middle East Politics and Ideas,* ed. Ilan Pappe and Moshe Ma'oz (London and New York: I. B. Tauris, 1997), 145–62, for a typology of provincial elites in the eighteenth and nineteenth centuries.

67. Other *ayan*s, particularly those in Arab provinces and to some extent in Bosnia, had different origins, including in the indigenous Muslim landed elite.

68. Robert W. Zens, "The Ayanlık and Pasvanoglu Osman Pasha of Vidin in the Age of Ottoman Social Change, 1791–1815," PhD diss., University of Wisconsin, Madison, 2004, 40.

69. Salzmann, in her *Tocqueville in the Ottoman Empire,* points out that non-Muslims frequently circumvented this prohibition by teaming up with a Muslim who would be the official holder of the *iltizam.*

70. Note, for instance, the Armenian phanariot affiliate Düzoğlu referred to as the "*Darphane İfraz mukataası mutasarrıfı*" in the 1790s. BOA, HAT: 11418 (A.H. 1205; M. ca. 1792).

71. Sergiu Columbeanu, *Grandes exploitations domaniales en Valachie au XVIII-e siècle* (Bucharest: Editura Academiei Republicii Socialiste Romania, 1974).

72. BOA, HAT: 9799 (A.H. 1212; M. 1799/1800?).

73. For the two merchants, see BOA, HAT: 8839 (A.H. 1211; M. 1798–99).

74. BOA, HAT: 12550-A: "Senede bir defa Eflak ve Boğdan voyvodaları taraflarından nakit olarak Enderun-e Hümayuna irsali emr-i Hümayun buyurulan: kuruş 30,000." The *kuruş* was suffering severe devaluation at this time (post-1760). About ten or eleven *kuruş* were

worth one Venetian ducat in 1810. See Şevket Pamuk, "Evolution of the Ottoman Monetary System," part 5 of *An Economic and Social History of the Ottoman Empire*, vol. 2, *1600–1914*, ed. Halil İnalcık with Donald Quataert (Cambridge: Cambridge University Press, 1999), 945–80. Providing some comparative perspective on the value of 30,000 *kuruş*, Salzmann notes that "a governor from Aleppo spent 126,830 *kuruş* for ten months in office over the years 1781 and 1782" (Salzmann, *Tocqueville in the Ottoman Empire*, 111).

75. BOA, HAT: 14731 (A.H. 1210; M. 1795–96). For an even more comprehensive list of "Bayram peşkeş" given by the *voyvoda* to the Ottoman Palace in the 1780s, see Athanasiou Komnenou-Hypsilantou, *Ekklesiastikon kai politikon ton*, 793–96. *Kamaraş* was the name of a rank in the phanariot administration; *tuğsuz* means one without a horsetail *(tuğ)*, which was another indicator of rank.

76. BOA, C., Hariciye: 6632.

77. BOA, HAT: 7560: "Dün söylediğim gibi Kalimaki Beyi şimdilik Boğdan Voyvodası namiyle Mustafa Paşa maiyyetine irsal olunması bana münasib görünuyor. Mülahaza eyliyüb münasib ise irsal edesin."

78. See Francis Joseph Steingass, *A Comprehensive Persian-English Dictionary including the Arabic Words and Phrases to Be Met with in Persian Literature* (1892; London: K. Paul, Trench, Trubner and Co., 1930), 443.

79. BOA, HAT: 13745-A.

80. The fascinating point here is that their status as a kind of landed aristocracy was used to argue for their appointment as resident Ottoman ambassadors to European or Christian states. The writer of the document argues that European societies have always respected aristocratic descent *(hanedanzadelik)* (implying that this is not so much the case in the Ottoman context), and since ambassadors who would command respect in Europe should be appointed, phanariots were the best candidates for the embassies. Ibid.

81. Citation from a document ibid.

82. See Hathaway, *The Politics of Households*, for the Caucasian slave and Anatolian janissary origins of Egypt's eighteenth-century households.

83. Meriwether, *The Kin Who Count*, 43.

84. Ibid., 44.

85. Ibid., 50–51.

86. See Abou-El-Haj, "The Ottoman Vezir and Pasha Households," for the same phenomenon among Muslim grandees of the late seventeenth and early eighteenth centuries.

87. Hathaway, *The Politics of Households*, 110.

88. See Michael Herzfeld, *The Poetics of Manhood: Contest and Identity in a Cretan Mountain Village* (Princeton, NJ: Princeton University Press, 1985); and John K. Campbell, *Honour, Family, and Patronage: A Study of Institutions and Moral Values in a Greek Mountain Community* (Oxford: Oxford University Press, 1970). See also, in EPI, various codices, for mention of godparentage among prominent phanariots, even in the midst of the conflicts of the 1820s.

89. See Vasile Dragut, "Le monastere de Vacaresti: Expression des relations artistiques roumanogrecques," in *L'Époque phanariote*, 265–94; Ierom. Iustin Marchiş, *Stavropoleos* (Bucharest: Stavropoleos, PriceWaterhouseCooper, 2005).

90. Tülay Artan, "Architecture as a Theater of Life: Profile of the Eighteenth-Century Bosphorus," PhD diss., Massachusetts Institute of Technology, 1989.

91.  See Findley: *Bureaucratic Reform in the Ottoman Empire;* and Carter Findley, *Ottoman Civil Officialdom: A Social History* (Princeton, NJ: Princeton University Press, 1989).

92.  The section heading relates to Cemal Kafadar, "Janissaries and Other Riffraff of Ottoman Istanbul: Rebels without a Cause?" in *Identity and Identity Formation in the Ottoman Empire: A Volume of Essays in Honor of Norman Itzkowitz,* ed. Baki Tezcan and Karl K. Barbir, 113-34 (Madison: University of Wisconsin Press, 2008).

93.  Ibid., 124.

94.  Ibid.

95.  Such connections occurred as multiple offensives in the 1660s: in Moldavia, Transylvania, and Slovakia (against the Habsburg Empire) and in Crete (against the Venetians). See Rhoads Murphey, *Ottoman Warfare 1500-1700* (New Brunswick, NJ: Rutgers University Press, 1999), 57. Murphey makes the point that from the sixteenth to the early eighteenth century, the proportion of janissaries stationed at provincial garrisons rose more dramatically than the threefold increase of janissaries in İstanbul.

96.  See Mert Sunar, "Cauldron of Dissent," PhD diss., State University of New York, Binghamton, 2004, for a statistical breakdown of janissary titleholders.

97.  See Howard Reed, "The Destruction of the Janissaries by Mahmud II in June, 1826," PhD diss., Princeton University, 1951, 183.

98.  Eunjeong Yi, *Guild Dynamics in Seventeenth-Century Istanbul: Fluidity and Leverage* (Leiden: Brill, 2004).

99.  Janissaries had, since the sixteenth century, engaged in artisanal occupations and guilds (Murphey, *Ottoman Warfare*). In the eighteenth century, however, more and more were listed in the official pay registers, and fewer and fewer were showing up for campaigns (Virginia Aksan, "Whatever Happened to the Janissaries? Mobilization for the 1768-1774 Russo-Ottoman War," *War in History* 5, no. 1 [1998]: 26-27).

For definitions and history of Bektaşism, which was a variety *(tarikat)* of Sufism and was at times condemned as heretical by the Sunni establishment, see R. Tschudi, "Bektashiyya," *EI2,* vol. 1; F. W. Hasluck, *Christianity and Islam under the Sultans,* vol. 2, ed. Margaret M. Hasluck (New York: Octogan Books, 1973); and Butrus Abu Manneh, *Studies on Islam and the Ottoman Empire in the 19th Century (1826-1876)* (İstanbul: Isis Press, 2001).

100.  On the relationship of the craft guilds, see Onur Yıldırım, "Transformation of Craft Guilds in Istanbul during the Seventeenth and Eighteenth Centuries (1650-1826)," *Revue des Études Sud-Est Europeennes* 37 (1999): 91-109; Engin Akarli, "Gedik: Implements, Mastership, Shop Usufruct, and Monopoly among Istanbul Artisans, 1750-1850," *Wissenschaftskolleg Berlin Jahrbuch* (1986): 223-31; and Cemal Kafadar, "Yeniçeri-Esnaf Relations," MA thesis, McGill University, 1981, 27-41. On the widespread connections among janissaries, commerce, and craft guilds, Rhoads Murphey notes that janissaries were mentioned as artisans and tradesmen in peacetime even in fifteenth-century İstanbul, soon after the city's capture by Ottoman forces. He goes on to conclude that "this dimension of Janissaries' activities cannot be regarded as an aberrant behavior associated with the decline of the Janissary fighting force in the 18th century" (Murphey, "Yeni Çeri," *EI2,* 327). It is suggested here, not that the mere involvement of janissaries in artisanal trade was "aberrant" or a cause of their decline, but instead that perhaps the intensity and significance of guild politics were changing in the eighteenth century, so that their continued involvement in economic and

political affairs was eclipsing their military potential in a period of prolonged peace. See also Molly Greene, *A Shared World: Muslims and Christians in the Early Modern Mediterranean* (Princeton, NJ: Princeton University Press, 2000).

101. "The [Bektaşi] order's political importance was due to its connexion with the Janissaries; the latter had been from the beginning, in the same way as all other early political institutions of the Ottomans, under the influence of religious corporations. In the second half of the 9th/15th century at the latest the Bektashis acquired exclusive authority among them. . . . The destruction of the Janissaries in 1241/1826 by Mahmud II affected also the order to which they were linked; many monasteries were destroyed at that time" (Tschudi, "Bektashiyya," 1: 1162).

102. This was also the case with provincial dragomans, or *beratlı*, attached to foreign embassies in port cities such as Salonika and İzmir.

103. Reed, "The Destruction of the Janissaries," 279; Kafadar, "Janissary and Other Riffraff of Ottoman Istanbul."

104. Large, permanent janissary regiments (mixtures of *yerli*, or local, and imperial troops from İstanbul) were also stationed in the provinces—in Baghdad, Belgrad (Belgrade), Kandiye (Herakleion, Crete), Halep (Aleppo), and Salonika, for instance, as well as İstanbul janissaries sent to various provinces on rotations of two to three years. Although these groups constituted the numerical majority of janissary troops in the empire as a whole, the focus in this discussion is on the janissaries' presence and activities in İstanbul and their relationship vis-à-vis the central state. For one thing, it was in the capital that their guild and political-religious activities came into direct contact, and ultimately conflict, with the central state; and for another, their development and expansion in İstanbul enable the following comparative discussion involving phanariots, for whom İstanbul also constituted a base of power and significant points of contact with the central state.

In regard to janissaries' role, Robert Mantran notes, "The role of the police consisted not only of assuring order in the capital day and night but also of inspecting the souks, bazaars, and markets, which the janissary *ağa* would do once a week with the grand vezir, and the other officers would do two or three times a week; and with the title of inspector, these officers had the right to fine and punish guilty merchants or artisans" (Robert Mantran, *Istanbul dans la seconde moitié du XVIIe siècle: Essai d'histoire institutionelle, économique, et sociale* [Paris: A. Maisonneuve, 1962], 148).

105. Mantran notes that the janissary *ağa* was responsible for policing some quarters, while other military officials, such as the *bostancıbaşı, cebecibaşı, topçubaşı*, and *kapudan paşa*, were responsible for policing other quarters; "so the police of the city was not assured by a specialized corps, but by certain military groups" (ibid.). A. de Juchereau de Saint-Denys, resident in İstanbul for the 1807–8 rebellions, writes, "*Tulumbacı*, or firemen formed a corps to fight fires and are stationed throughout İstanbul in four *odas* of 200 men each. They adhere to the corps of the janissaries, from which they were chosen, and are dressed as artillerymen" (A. de Juchereau de Saint-Denys, *Les révolutions de Constantinople en 1807 et 1808, précédés d'observations générales sur l'état actuel de l'Empire Ottoman*, 2 vols. (Paris: à la librairie de Brissot-Thivars, 1819), 1: 80.

106. Mantran, *Istanbul dans la seconde moitié*, 159–60: "In case of fire in İstanbul, the

*bostancıbaşı* accompanied the janissary *ağa* to make sure the fire did not spread to the sultan's properties and, if it did, to take the necessary measures."

107. Esad Efendi (1826), member of the *ulema* and court historian, listed the range of functions that janissaries performed in order to condemn them for straying from their intended purpose, in his very loyalist treatise on janissary abolition, Üss-i Zafer (Foundation of Victory) (Mehmed Assad Éfendi, *Précis historique de la destruction du corps des janissaires par le sultan Mahmud en 1826* [Paris: Firmin Didots Frères, 1833], 220). The Fifty-sixth Orta of the Janissary Corps, for instance, while charged with looking after the provisioning of the capital, had taken over the fruit (at Çardak) and vegetable (at Eminönü) commerce, charging ships and farmers from the city's environs exorbitant customs fees for entering the capital. Even coffee grinding was the monopoly of janissaries (at the "public establishment called Tahmis," according to Esad Efendi; see ibid., 225). Janissary "kitchen-masters" oversaw the coffee grinding and diluted the coffee grounds with other materials so as to increase their profits.

108. See Greene, *A Shared World*, 91, for examples of local janissaries in Crete, local Christians who enjoyed patronage and protection of janissaries, and janissaries rotating through Crete from İstanbul in the eighteenth century and early nineteenth century. Customarily it was the *kadı* of İstanbul who was in charge of coordinating the grain supply for İstanbul. See Mantran, *Istanbul dans la seconde moitié*, 187.

109. See Güran, "The State Role in the Grain Supply of Istanbul, the Grain Administration, 1793–1839," *International Journal of Turkish Studies* 3, no. 1 (1984–85): 29, for the list of official functions of the Grain Administration. The Grain Administration was abolished at the end of the Nizam-ı Cedid, or New Order (1807–8); it was reinstated and continued to function until 1839. See also Lynn Marie Thompson Şaşmazer, "Provisioning Istanbul: Bread Production, Power, and Political Ideology in the Ottoman Empire, 1789–1807," PhD diss., Indiana University, 2000.

110. While in the 1790s the *rayic* system began to supersede the *miri* system, in 1807 the *miri* system was officially reinstituted (ibid.). This is perhaps an indication that the janissary interests, which had won out in the civil conflicts against Selim III in 1807, preferred the *miri* system and had been threatened by the *rayic* system, as with other measures of the Nizam-ı Cedid.

111. Ibid., 35; specifically, 32.5 percent of the city's total grain supply on average for the period from 1793 to 1839.

112. Regarding Kapan merchants, see BOA, HAT 5476. One Alexander Yanakizade wrote an extensive memo to İstanbul describing the famine going on in Moldavia and the inability of producers to supply any grain in 1797–98. He mentioned that over the past eight years he had served twice as the (provincial) dragoman for the Moldavian *voyvoda* so as to demonstrate his loyal service to the Ottoman state. From his comments it is clear that he was in charge of organizing the grain collection and thus responsible for explaining why there was no grain collection that year.

See BOA, Ahkam defterleri: Boğdan: 80/4: 282, for travel permit documents, lists of names, and other affairs relating to Kapan merchants traveling to Moldavia and phanariot officials there. See especially p. 371 for a list of all merchants residing at Bal kapanı in İstanbul in the 1790s, a list that includes both Christian and Muslim names. Some were Muslim names (such as Süleyman Alemdar) with Christian partners (Sofuli zimmi ve şeriki Savva zimmi), others were Muslim names with origins from the Black Sea coast of the Balkans (such as Silistreli el-hac Süleyman Efendizade), and some had recognizable janissary, religious, and guild titles (such as Salim beşe, the partner of Molla Mehmet and Ali Usta).

113. G. G. Angelopoulos and G. P. Angelopoulos, "Anecdotos ekthesis episemou kai autoptou omogenous" [Unpublished official account of an eyewitness Greek], in *Ta kata ton aiodimon protathleten tou hierou ton hellenon agonos ton Patriarchen Konstantinopoleos Gregorios ton V* (Athenai: Ethnikon typographeion, 1865–66), 126.

114. See Mantran, *Istanbul dans la seconde moitié*, 190, for discussion of *yasakçı*, who arranged the maritime traffic between provincial port cities and İstanbul. Pompiliu Eliade states that, after the 1783 loss of Crimea, Moldavia, and Wallachia became the "granary of İstanbul" and that, in place of a cash tribute, those provinces paid tribute in kind. "Twice a year, agents would come, furnished with a *ferman* to 'buy' provisions. *They were, in spring, the 'capenlei' [kapanlı], Greek merchants* who would buy livestock at prices fixed in advance by the Sublime Porte (free to be altered by them in connivance with the functionaries of those provinces), *and in summer, the Turkish janissaries, who would load up a fixed quantity every year of grain and maize at Galatz and Ibrail*" (Pompiliu Eliade, *De l'influence française sur l'esprit public en Roumanie: Les origines, étude sur l'état de la société roumaine à l'époque du règne phanariote* [Paris: E. Leroux, 1898], 12, my emphasis). Mantran states that wheat was unloaded at Un Kapanı and remitted directly to bakers or millers charged with establishing a reserve, according to the orders of the *kadı* or *muhtesib* (market inspector). He writes that wholesalers *(matrabaz)* probably existed but does not provide evidence for this (Mantran, *Istanbul dans la seconde moitié*, 190).

115. Ibid., 162

116. Salih Aynural, *İstanbul değirmenleri ve fırınları, zahire ticareti (1740–1840)* (İstanbul: Türkiye Ekonomik ve Toplumsal Tarih Vakfı, 2002), 119, citing BOA, HAT: 16066 (A.H. 1204; M. 1790). According to Aynural, although "the majority of the bakers in İstanbul were non-Muslim . . . [and] the majority [of those] were Armenian," he continues that, "as for the Muslim bakers, the majority were Albanian, and they were at the same time also janissaries."

117. See A. Salzmann, "Governance in the Vernacular," in *Tocqueville in the Ottoman Empire.*


BIOGRAPHY OF AN EMPIRE I

Epigraph source: Stephanos Vogorides, MP, Musurus-Vogorides correspondence, IX: 69.

1. For a brief but pioneering article on Vogorides' life, see Maria Todorova, "Stefan Bogoridi: A Bulgarian Phanariote in the Ottoman Empire" (in Dutch), in *Oost-Europa in het verleden: Liber amicorum Z. R. Dittrich,* ed. A. P. van Gouoever (Groningen: Wolters-Noordhoff/Forsten, 1987), 177–87.

2. Sturdza, *Dictionnaire historique et généalogique,* 448. See also his autobiography: Sofroni Vracanski, *Vie et tribulations du pecheur Sofroni: Introduction traduction et notes établies par Jack Feuillet* (Sofia: Sofia-Presse, 1981).

3. Little research in English exists on these local conflicts; for a Bulgarian study, see Vera

Mutafcieva, *Le temps de Kirdjalis* (in Bulgarian) (Sofia: Izd-vo na Bŭlgarskata akademiia na naukite, 1993).

4. Irena Peneva, "Neizvestia biographia na Stephan Bogoridi ot Neofit Hilendarski (Bozveli)" [Biography of Stephanos Vogorides by Neophytos Hilendarski], in *Studia in honorem Professoris Verae Mutafcieva*, ed. E. Radushev et al. (Sofia: Amicita, 2001), 293–300. Arbanasi was also known as Arvanitochori (G.) and Arnavutköy (T.). See also multiple references in Sofroni's autobiography *(Vie et tribulations)* to his children living in Arbanasi in the early 1790s.

5. On the identity and service of Muruz Bey (1740–88), see Epameinondas Stamatiades, *Viographiai ton hellenon megalon diermeneon tou Othomanikou kratous* [Biographies of the Greek grand dragomans of the Ottoman state] (Thessaloniki: Ekdoseis P. Pournara, 1973), 142.

6. Sphyroeras, *Hoi dragomanoi tou stolou*, 113–15.

7. See Peneva, "Neizvestia biographia na Stephan Bogoridi," 295.

8. Sofroni must have also known Greek, since he was active in Church politics, the language of which was Greek. In addition to his professional familiarity with the Greek language and his apparent desire to hellenize his grandchildren by changing their names and sending them to a phanariot academy, he was also the author, in 1806, of the first published work in vernacular Bulgarian. The work was an anthology of religious treatises translated from Greek and Slavonic. See Sturdza, *Dictionnaire historique et généalogique*, 448. In Bulgarian national(ist) historiography, Sofroni is portrayed as a "pioneer of the Bulgarian national renaissance" (ibid.).

9. Peneva, "Neizvestia biographia na Stephan Bogoridi."

10. Ariadna Camariano-Cioran, *Les Académies princières de Bucharest et de Jassy* (Thessaloniki: Institute of Balkan Studies, 1974), 300.

11. See ibid., 46, for subjects and organization of the schools. On page 47 the social composition of students receiving scholarships is described as follows: "The students had to be sons of boyars [indigenous Romanian land-owning elites] who had lost their charge, sons of merchants or artisans, or sons of poor foreigners," not sons of indigenous peasants.

12. Ibid., 54.

## 2. VOLATILE SYNTHESIS

Epigraph source: Shaw, "The Origins of Ottoman Military Reform," 292.

1. Virginia Aksan, in her recent *Ottoman Wars, 1700–1870: An Empire Besieged* (London: Pearson-Longman, 2007), 169, confirms the designation of this period as a prelude by noting, "Selim III's reign is most often characterized as the period when attempts at military reform failed. I think it more correct to view the years after 1793 as the prelude to the complete overhaul of the Ottoman system of governance, not just the military."

2. This problem cuts to the heart of modern orientalism, which by all accounts originates with Napoleon's attempted conquest of Egypt in 1799—in the midst of the Nizam-i Cedid experiment. See, for instance, Edward Said, *Orientalism* (New York: Pantheon Books, 1978); and Timothy Mitchell, *Colonising Egypt* (New York: Cambridge University Press, 1988).

3. See Aksan, *Ottoman Wars*, chapter 5, "Selim III and the New Order," for a fuller description of the period.

4. Aksan notes, "The tumult which exploded in 1807 delayed further implementation of reforms for two decades" (ibid., 205).

5. The Hypsilanti family was Russian-aligned, and members of the family would go on to spearhead the Greek rebellions in 1821, first in Moldavia and then, after the failure there, in the Morea, where the rebellions eventually succeeded. See Sturdza, *Dictionnaire historique et généalogique*, 468–73; and Mihai Tipau, *Domnii fanariotii in Tarile Romane*, 94–105.

6. The office of *ispravnik* was akin to that of regional governor—according to Photeinos's description, something between a *voyvoda* and a *kadı* "in Turkey." Photeinos, *Historia tes palai Dakias*, 3: 509.

7. Stephanos was made dragoman of the fleet in 1765 and died the following year. According to biographer Vasilios Sphyroeras, Stephanos and his brother Petros had fled the Morea in 1715 when the Ottomans took it back from Venice. They moved to Paros, buying much land and accumulating wealth, which allowed Stephanos's influence in İstanbul when he moved there. Petros stayed behind and had two sons, one of whom was Nicholas (Sphyroeras, *Hoi dragomanoi tou stolou*, 115–16).

8. Ibid., 124; Blancard, *Les Mavroyènis*, 2: 45. Haci Nikolaki, as Cevdet Paşa tells us in his history, was Gazi Hasan's accountant *(sarraf)* and was Grand Dragoman Stavraki (Aristarchi)'s father (Ahmed Cevdet, *Tarih-i Cevdet* [Dersaadet (İstanbul): Matbaa-yi Osmaniye, A.H. 1309; M. 1893], 5: 63). If this is true, it would mean that Haci Nikolaki was the father of the last phanariot dragoman, Stavraki Aristarchi, and the grandfather of Aristarchi Bey, a major Russophile phanariot in the 1840s and 1850s. It would also support the hypothesis that the Aristarchis were hellenized Armenians, as Armenians were often *sarraf*s of high officials. See Hagop Levon Barsoumian, "Armenian Amira Class of Istanbul," PhD dissertation, Columbia University, 1980.

9. Three close relatives, however, had already held the office of dragoman of the fleet between 1744 and 1765, indicating that in the early phase of the phanariot ascendancy the networks surrounding the naval administration were to some extent separate from those involving the imperial court and the Danubian Principalities (Sphyroeras, *Hoi dragomanoi tou stolou*, 124).

10. Nicholas Mavroyeni has been the object of fascination and admiration also for several of his contemporaries and subsequent writers. See, for instance, Hope, *Anastasius;* and Blancard, *Les Mavroyènis*.

11. Virginia Aksan notes the split between pro-war Koca Yusuf Paşa and cautious Cezayirli Hasan Paşa over this war, the goal of which from the Ottoman perspective was to recapture the Crimean Peninsula from Russia (Aksan, *Ottoman Wars*, 161).

12. Photeinos, *Historia tes palai Dakias*, 2: 359. Tanzimat-era Ottoman chronicler Cevdet Paşa also refers to Petraki (as Darphane *sarrafı* Petraki) in his chapter on "Mavroyani Bey" (entitled, "Sabıken Eflak voyvodası Mavroyanı Bey'in katl ve idamı"), and although he refrains from calling Petraki the most powerful personage in the empire, he does specify that he was an opponent of Mavroyani and a supporter of Mihal Bey (Soutso), a rival claimant to the throne of Wallachia at the time (Cevdet, *Tarih-i Cevdet*, 5: 65). The united front of Cezayirli Hasan Paşa and Koca Yusuf Paşa is interesting, in that they were ordinarily rivals

but, if Photeinos's assertion is correct, seem to have joined forces to effect Mavroyeni's appointment.

13. In regard to the expression "crude islanders," islanders were known as "rabbits," or *tavşan (taousanedes)*, according to Photeinos. Cevdet confirms that Petraki's head was severed on the day Mavroyeni was appointed *voyvoda* ("Petraki'nin başı kat' olunup Mavroyani Eflak Beyi olduğu gün . . . ") (Cevdet, *Tarih-i Cevdet*, 5: 65). The entire episode is confirmed by Thomas Hope in his *Anastasius*, originally published the same year as Photeinos's history.

14. Photeinos, *Historia tes palai Dakias*, 2: 360–61.

15. We find several orders to and requests from Mavroyeni to the Ottoman central state regarding military operations at this time. For memos regarding the sending of provisions and specialists to the front in areas such as Özi, see BOA, C., MTZ: 927 (A.H. 1201). See BOA, C., MTZ: 1000 (A.H. 1203), for a statement on the loyalty Mavroyeni showed in protecting Wallachia from enemies. See BOA, C., MTZ: 818 (A.H. 1203), for Mavroyeni's petition to the Porte to promote one İbrailli Yakub Ağa to the rank of *mirimiran*. See also BOA, C., Askeriye: 657 (A.H. 1202) for a *hüküm* ordering Mavroyeni to provide lumber from Wallachia for the repair of emplacements for the moat at Rusçuk Kalesi.

16. See BOA, C., Hariciye: 1039 (A.H. 1202), for an order (with the seal of Yusuf Paşa, then *kaptan-ı derya*) to send five thousand janissary troops from the imperial army to aid Mavroyeni's effort to liberate the *kasaba* (town) of Jassy: "ordu-yu humayundan beş bin nefer olmak üzere kırk iki bayrak (girinde) yeniçeri askeri ifraz." Interestingly, Yusuf Paşa puts the *mutasarrif* of Alaiyye (Alanya), one Bicanzade Ali Paşa, in charge as *mirimiran* of these troops and refers to Ali Paşa as "bizim Kapudan Paşa pederimizin çirağı," or the apprentice of Yusuf Paşa's father, and therefore an ally.

17. Photeinos, *Historia tes palai Dakias*, 2: 360–61.

18. For a smaller-scale example of Christian heroism in defense of the sultanate, see Aksan, *Ottoman Wars*, 152. The *ban* of Craiova, one Manolaki, defended Craiova from Russian troops with the help of Albanian irregulars and troops from Vidin after the *voyvoda* of Wallachia, Gregory Ghika, had fled to Russia.

19. See ibid., 182, for descriptions of the mutinies but no mention of Mavroyeni's role. We have confirmation of these events involving Mavroyeni in contemporary Ottoman chronicles such as Cabi Ömer Efendi's *Cabi Tarihi* ([Ankara: Türk Tarih Kurumu Basımevi, 2003], 1: 22), in later Ottoman histories such as Cevdet's *Tarih-i Cevdet* (5: 63 ff.), and in the early twentieth century history of Blancard, *Les Mavroyènis*. There is even a fictionalized contemporary account of Mavroyeni's life that makes up most of Thomas Hope's *Anastasius*. Mavroyeni receives passing mention in the works of Stanford Shaw and Nicolae Iorga, but modern historians of Ottoman history have for the most part neglected the entire episode.

20. This Çelebi Hasan Paşa Rusçuklu, took over the Grand Vezirate after Cezayirli Hasan Paşa and before Koca Yusuf Paşa, serving in that office between April 1790 and February 1791. See Tipau, *Domnii fanariotii in Tarile Romane*, 190.

21. Contemporary chronicler Cabi Ömer Efendi states simply that "Mavroyan Bey's" execution was carried out on a pretext ("nihayet mesfur Mavroyan Bey'i cüz'i bahane ile katl edüp") (Ömer Efendi, *Cabi Tarihi*, 1: 23).

22. Photeinos goes on to praise Mavroyeni, reminding the reader that he could have

sought refuge in one of the European kingdoms at any time and lived with honor and esteem, as many of his advisers had urged him to do. But, "so as not to bring derision on the
*genos* of the Christians and have the Turks think that all of the *voyvodas* are disloyal and
scheming, he didn't do it" (Photeinos, *Historia tes palai Dakias*, 2: 373). Note the similarity
between this language and that which Stephanos Vogorides would later use in his apologia
of 1852.

23. Ibid., 372.

24. A century later, Mavroyeni's life had blurred with legend. Late nineteenth-century
Church historian Manuel Gedeon asserted that prominent phanariots were members of janissary regiments and gives the example of Nicholas Mavroyeni. Gedeon notes that after
Mavroyeni was "killed for betraying the interests of the state," his wife appealed to his janissary regiment to prevent his possessions from being confiscated, which would have left her
and Mavroyeni's young son indigent. Leaders of his janissary regiment then appealed to "Sultan Abdulhamit I" (the sultan at the time would have been Selim III) one day when "he was
on his way back from praying in Eyüp" and convinced him to reverse the order to confiscate
Mavroyeni's belongings (Gedeon, *Mneia ton pro emou,* 402).

25. For Mavroyeni's *vakfiye* (*vakıf* records), see BOA, C., Evkaf: 24427. For matters con-
cerning his property and debts, see, for instance, BOA, C., MTZ: 528 (A.H. 1205); BOA, HAT:
11170 (A.H. 1204); and BOA, HAT 11363 (A.H. 1205); and for an *irade* ordering that his
house and *yalı* (seaside mansion) in İstanbul and house in Rhodes be given to his nephew
after Mavroyeni's severed head and *yafta* (tag, containing the explanation for his execution)
were brought to İstanbul, see BOA, HAT: 11674 (A.H. 1204).

26. Zens, "The Ayanlik and Pasvanoglu Osman Pasha," 160.

27. Cooperative *ayans* were often used to neutralize janissaries in the provinces. See
Sunar, "Cauldron of Dissent," 176.

28. Photeinos, *Historia tes palai Dakias,* 2: 382 fn.

29. See Rossitsa Gradeva, "Osman Pazvantoğlu of Vidin: Between Old and New," in *The
Ottoman Balkans, 1750–1830,* ed. Frederick Anscombe (Princeton, NJ: Markus Wiener Publishers, 2006), 115–62.

30. Photeinos's lengthy description of Pasvanoğlu is of tremendous value and has hardly
ever been used by scholars researching this highly significant personage. (Nicolae Iorga is
an important exception, using Photeinos's account for factual information in his *Osmanlı
İmparatorluğun Tarihi/Geschichte des osmanischen reiches* [Turkish translation, İstanbul:
Yeditepe Yayınevi, 2005], although he does not discuss in any depth the fascinating perspective the account represents.) Until now, research has been based on French officer
Meriage's biography, a Slavic translation of a Greek-language text written by one Kuzikos,
and various European consular reports, as well as scattered Ottoman documentation. See
Gradeva, "Osman Pasvantoğlu of Vidin," esp. fn. 5, for a summary of primary sources and
modern scholarship on Pasvanoğlu. See also Robert Zens, "Pasvanoglu Osman Pasha and
the Pashalik of Belgrade, 1791–1807," *International Journal of Turkish Studies* 8 (Spring 2002):
88–114, which likewise makes no mention of Photeinos's history as a source for Pasvanoğlu's
reign. Stanford Shaw, in his *Between Old and New* (458 fn. 54), discusses sources for Pasvanoğlu, focusing primarily on Meriage's account, and also does not mention Photeinos. It
is likely that Photeinos witnessed firsthand the latter half of Pasvanoğlu's reign (arrived in

the principalities ca. 1799) and had access to information from many of his contemporaries regarding Pasvanoğlu's background.

31. As Gradeva points out, there is still much discussion about Pasvanoğlu's origins. Synthesizing two opposing theories (based on Meriage's account on the one hand and historian Vera Mutafcieva's work with Ottoman sources on the other), Gradeva puts forward the hypothesis both that Pasvanoğlu was of Bosnian (Slavic and Christian) origin and that his family was already entrenched in Vidin landholding circles and politics at the time of his rise (Gradeva, "Osman Pazvantoğlu of Vidin," 120–21). Photeinos's account is consistent with this hypothesis. Stanford Shaw claims that Osman's grandfather Pasvan Agha "was given two villages near Vidin in return for services in the recently concluded war against Austria" and that his father, a janissary, inherited these villages and became a "minor notable," but when he was executed, Osman lost that status and land and was merely one of many roaming brigands by the conclusion of the 1787–91 war. See Shaw, *Between Old and New*, 237.

32. Photeinos, *Historia tes palai Dakias*, 2: 382. This only confirms Pasvanoğlu's janissary origins. The more commonly used term, *serdengeçti*, meaning one who is willing to give up his life, was indeed an honorary title given to janissaries who volunteered for risky service in time of war. It would have been around this time in the eighteenth century that it began to be used as a general term for janissary volunteers for a campaign. See Sunar, "Cauldron of Dissent," 165.

33. This is also consistent with Gradeva's findings, which include Osman's father having been exiled back to Belgrade and Osman returning to Vidin once again by the end of the Russo-Austrian-Ottoman war of 1787–91. His continued connections to Belgrade are well-known, as he made Vidin into a refuge for janissaries who had escaped from Belgrade and a center more generally for those in opposition to the central authorities.

34. Gradeva, "Osman Pazvantoğlu of Vidin," 122.

35. Photeinos, *Historia tes palai Dakias*, 2: 387–88. This number of troops is likely an exaggeration. Nicolae Iorga confirms it was the naval force under the command of Kaptan-ı Derya Küçük Hüseyin Paşa that approached via the Danube but claims only forty thousand men were involved. Stanford Shaw gives an estimate of a hundred thousand men who were amassed on land, in addition to the naval troops who arrived via the Danube, bringing the number closer to, but probably still well below, two hundred thousand (Shaw, *Between Old and New*, 238).

36. Gradeva asserts twenty-four *paşas* rather than seventeen surrounded Vidin (Gradeva, "Osman Pazvantoğlu of Vidin"). Gradeva also notes that this second campaign was a strange one, involving these *paşas* slowly circling and surrounding the area of Vidin.

37. Photeinos, *Historia tes palai Dakias*, 2: 388.

38. In this they echoed the actions of "all the notables of the area" who signed pardons of Pasvanoğlu on at least two occasions. See Aksan, *Ottoman Wars*, 220.

39. Photeinos, *Historia tes palai Dakias*, 2: 382.

40. Ibid., 2: 386.

41. Ibid., 2: 382.

42. Ibid., 2: 385.

43. Pasvanoğlu was reportedly close to Righas Pheraios Velestinlis, whose Balkan anthem and call to arms, "Thourios," includes an evocation of Pasvanoğlu. See Rossitsa Gradeva, "Se-

cession and Revolution in the Ottoman Empire at the End of the Eighteenth Century: Osman Pazvantoğlu and Righas Velestinlis," in *Ottoman Rule and the Balkans, 1760–1850: Conflict, Transformation, Adaptation,* ed. Antonis Anastasopoulos and Elias Kolovos (Rethymno, Crete: University of Crete, Department of History and Archaeology, 2007), 73–94.

44. See Mutafcieva, *Le temps de Kirdjalis.*

45. See Sturdza, *Dictionnaire historique et généalogique,* 339, for genealogical and biographical information.

46. Photeinos, *Historia tes palai Dakias,* 2: 493.

47. We do have some Ottoman accounts of the 1807–8 conflict, such as Koca Sekbanbaşı *risalesi* (whose author seems to have been Ahmed Vasif Efendi; see Beydilli, "Sekbanbaşı risalesinin müellifi hakkında," 221–24). The major problem with these is that they are laden with state rhetoric and are tracts designed to "sell" the reforms or to defend the interests of the central state or both. An alternative Ottoman source, which is also used here, is *Cabi Tarihi.* The author, reportedly one Cabi Ömer Efendi, seemed to have been a midlevel functionary of the Ayasofya Mosque in İstanbul, making his perspective a Muslim counterpart to Photeinos's.

48. For a French eyewitness account, see Juchereau de St. Denys, *Les révolutions de Constantinople.*

49. Photeinos, *Historia tes palai Dakias,* 2: 508.

50. Ibid., 2: 509.

51. Ibid., 2: 510.

52. Manouk's is a fascinating and largely untold story. He went on to Bucharest, where, known as Manouk Bey, he was a prominent merchant and dragoman for the phanariot *voyvodas.* It was in his *han* (Hanul Manuc, still standing and newly restored), next to the old palace in Bucharest, that the Treaty of Bucharest was negotiated in 1812. Soon after, he fled to Bessarabia and died on his estate there. For Ottoman documents regarding Manouk Bey, see BOA, HAT: 24611, for a note (April 1813) from the Russian consul of Bucharest to Wallachian prince Karaca, stating that Manouk Bey was a Russian subject and granting Manouk the consul's permission to move with his family to Russian territory. BOA, HAT: 45405, discusses Manouk's association with Ramiz Paşa, an Ottoman figure who had been executed for conspiring with Russia, and the fact that Manouk, because he was Armenian *(ermeni cinsinden),* was often mistaken for a Russian. See also Mihail Guboglu, *Catalogul documentelor turcesti,* vol. 1 (Bucharest: Academy of Sciences, 1960), doc. no. 817, for reference to an Ottoman document housed in the Historical Museum of Bucharest (inventory no. 43377) from November 1807, in which Sultan Mustafa IV accords privileges to "Dragoman Manouk and his *ex aporiton [omul san de incredere]* Magardic *[sic]."*

53. Photeinos, *Historia tes palai Dakias,* 2: 522.

54. The dragoman at the time was Ioannis Karaca, although in December 1808 he was replaced by Dimitrios Muruzi. Galip Efendi and Muruzi would go on to negotiate for the Ottomans at the Treaty of Bucharest in 1812. Muruzi would then be executed for his performance there, and Ioannis Karaca would resume that office in June 1812, only to be followed three months later by Iakovos Argyropoulo. See Ismail, "The Making of the Treaty of Bucharest."

55. Photeinos, *Historia tes palai Dakias,* 2: 516.

56. Ottoman historian Frederick Anscombe commented in the introduction to the volume he recently edited, *The Ottoman Balkans, 1750–1830* (Princeton, NJ: Markus Wiener Publishers, 2006), that none of the contributions of the volume addresses the period between 1808 and 1830—"between the fall of Selim III and the formal recognition of an independent Greece" (7–8), reflecting a large lacuna in scholarship.

57. Aksan portrays Halet as the "instrument of Mahmud II's will," although the reality seems more complicated. See Aksan, *Ottoman Wars,* 285–86.

58. He was *mühürdar yamağı* to Rikab-ı hümayun reisi Mehmet Raşid, then attached himself to the Rumeli *valisi* Ebubekir Sami Paşa, and thus secured a position in the service of Ohrid mir-i miran Ahmed Paşa before becoming himself the *naib* of Yenişehir Fener (Ş. Tekindağ, "Halet Efendi," in *İA,* 5: 123).

59. Regarding Galip Dede, see A. Gölpınarlı, "Şeyh Galib," in *İA,* 11: 462–67. Mehmed Esad Şeyh Galib (nicknamed Galip Dede) (1757–99) at age twenty-four, in 1781, entered the office of the *beylikçi* (director of Office of the Imperial Divan) and was well-liked by Sultan Selim III even before he became a *şeyh* in 1791. See Tekindağ, "Halet Efendi."

60. Wilkinson, *An Account of the Principalities of Wallachia and Moldavia,* 119: "Meanwhile hostilities commenced between France and Russia, and the Porte, having evinced a resolution of remaining neutral, unwilling to give umbrage to either of the contending powers in the choice of the new hospodars, resolved to fix upon two individuals whose political principles had never been connected with foreign parties. A great number of candidates offered their services, but none of them being qualified for the appointments, their claims were rejected. Halet-Efendi, intimate counselor of the Sultan, was instructed to make a choice, and he fixed it on the prince Charles [Skarlatos] Callimaki for Moldavia, and Yanco Caradja [Karaca] for Wallachia."

61. See Enver Ziya Karal, *Halet Efendi'nin Paris Büyük Elçiliği (1802–1806)* [Halet Efendi's Paris Embassy] (İstanbul: Kenan Basımevi, 1940).

62. BOA, HAT: 7153 (A.H. 1219; M. ca. 1804), refers to both Halet in Paris and Yakovaki in Berlin.

63. See Ömer Efendi, *Cabi Tarihi,* 1: 151, 165, and 552 for references to and stories about Halet as *reisülküttab* and for his exile to Kütahya.

64. Aksan, *Ottoman Wars,* 286; drawn from BOA, HAT: 20896 (A.H. 1225; M. 1810); also cited in Tom Nieuwenhuis, *Politics and Society in Early Modern Iraq: Mamluk Pashas, Tribal Shayks and Local Rule between 1802 and 1831* (The Hague: Martinus Nijhoffs, 1982), 62–68. See also Dina Rizk Khoury, *State and Provincial Society in the Ottoman Empire: Mosul, 1540–1834* (Cambridge: Cambridge University Press, 1997), 60, for a description of an 1813 transaction between a Jalili governor in Mosul and Halet Efendi's Baghdadi Jewish banker, Haskel. A payment of fifteen hundred *guruş* was remitted to Halet through Haskel, for securing the office of vezir for the governor. Khoury cites BOA, C., Dahiliye: 9295. On page 114, Khoury specifies that "Khwaja Hezekiel" (Hoca Haskel) was the "Jewish banker" of Saʿdullah Paşa al-Jalili of Mosul. If that was the case, it would mean that Halet Efendi shared the same (Baghdadi) banker with the Mosuli governor.

65. See Tekindağ, "Halet Efendi," for biographical information; and Cevdet, *Tarih-i Cevdet,* 11: 153, for reference to Halet's relationship to phanariots and janissaries.

66. See Cevdet, *Tarih-i Cevdet,* 11: 152, for a description of Halet's removal of Yakovaki

Argyropoulo and installation of Mihal, Yanko Karaca's son-in-law, as well as Halet's role in the appointment of İskerletzade Kallimaki's brother, Yanko, from Moldavian *voyvoda* to imperial dragoman.

67. Keçecizade İzzet Molla was also the father of Keçecizade Mehmed Fuat Paşa (1815–69), who, along with Ali Paşa, succeeded Mustafa Reşit Paşa as leading Tanzimat statesmen in the later 1840s and dominated Ottoman foreign policy making in the 1850s and 1860s. See A. H. Bayat, *Keçecizade Mehmed Fuat Paşa'nın nesirleri şiirleri nükteleri hakkında şiirler* (İstanbul: Türk Dünyası Araştırmaları Vakfı Yayınları, 1988).

68. The 1812 Treaty of Bucharest ended Russo-Ottoman hostilities for the time being and ushered in almost a decade without large-scale rebellions or foreign wars.

69. See Camariano-Cioran, *Les Académies princières*, who discusses these codes as Code Callimache and Code Caradja.

70. Photeinos, *Historia tes palai Dakias*, 2: 447.

71. See Vassilios Sphyroeras, "O Kanounnames tou 1819 gia ten ekloge ton phanarioton stis hegemonies kai thn dragomania" [The Kanunname of 1819 for the election of phanariots to the principalities and the dragomanate], *Ho Eranistes* 11 (1974): 568–79; and Andrei Otetea, "La désagrégation du régime phanariote," in *Symposium l'époque phanariote 21–25 octobre 1970* (Thessaloniki: Institute for Balkan Studies, 1974), 439–47.

72. BOA, Name-i Hümayun defteri: no. 989.

73. See Andrei Pippidi, "Jean Caradja et ses amis de Geneve," in *Symposium l'époque phanariote 21–25 octobre 1970* (Thessaloniki: Hydrima Meleton Chersonesou tou Haimou 145, 1974), 187–208.

74. ASB, Soutso family archive: no. 25.

75. Informality of power was key to Halet's role in Ottoman politics. In 1821, the Spanish ambassador attempted to get an audience with the grand vezir without bringing the requisite gifts and, when he failed, proceeded to Halet Efendi's residence to ask his assistance. The British consul at the time noted, "There is nothing which Halet Efendi dreads so much as having his power over the Sultan placed *en evidence*—and M. de Zea's visit, for the avowed purpose of soliciting an exercise of it, was in the highest degree, unwelcome" (PRO: FO, 78/101, October 25, 1821).

76. Ibid.

77. Guboglu, *Catalogul documentelor turcesti*, vol. 1, no. 1316.

78. See MP, Musurus-Vogorides correspondence, microfilm no. 29: ca. 1849.

79. For an English translation of the Sened-i İttifak, see Ali Akyıldız and M. Şükrü Hanioğlu, "Negotiating the Power of the Sultan: The Ottoman Sened-i ittifak (Deed of Agreement)," in *The Modern Middle East: A Sourcebook for History*, ed. Camron Michael Amin, Benjamin Fortna, and Elizabeth Frierson (Oxford, New York: Oxford University Press, 2006), 22–30. See also Salzmann, *Tocqueville in the Ottoman Empire*; and Mardin, *The Genesis of Young Ottoman Thought*, chapter 1, for a discussion of the document.

80. For the latest expression of this notion, see Akyıldız and Hanioğlu, "Negotiating the Power of the Sultan," 22–30, the preface to which states, "Some scholars compare the Sened-i İttifak to England's Magna Carta of 1215, while others are of the opinion that the constitutional movement in Turkey started with this document. They even argue that the Sened-i –İttifak was a kind of basic constitutional draft and the first step towards democracy" (22).

## BIOGRAPHY OF AN EMPIRE II

1. Blancard, *Les Mavroyènis*, 2: 560.

2. Bakirtzes, "Vogorides, Stephanos," 443.

3. AMAE: Correspondance diplomatique, tome 21, doc. 43, 56.

4. Sturdza, *Dictionnaire historique et généalogique*, 448; for the rise of Mehmet Ali and factional conflicts involving Tahir Paşa, see Afaf Lutfi al-Sayyid Marsot, *Egypt in the Reign of Muhammad Ali* (Cambridge: Cambridge University Press, 1984); and Henry Dodwell, *The Founder of Modern Egypt: A Study of Muhammad Ali* (Cambridge: Cambridge University Press, 1967).

5. Mustafa Refik Efendi had been a member of the Rusçuk Committee (Rusçuk Yaranı), a group in favor of the Nizam-ı Cedid at the provincial headquarters of Bayraktar Mustafa Alemdar, in opposition to the "conservative" forces and janissaries who took over İstanbul in rebellion in 1807–8. When Sultan Mahmud II took the throne in 1808, several members of the Rusçuk Committee were accepted back into the imperial service. Mustafa Refik was one example when he became lieutenant to the grand vezir *(kethüda)*. See Avigdor Levy, "Military Policy of Sultan Mahmud II, 1808–1839," PhD diss., Harvard University, 1968. MP: Ottoman file (uncataloged), II.2.18: "In the end of the reign of Sultan Selim, [Your Humble Servant [I] was working as a translator for the imperial army for Mustafa Refik Efendi, who was himself the principal *kethüda* in the imperial army during negotiations with Russia [presumably the 1808 negotiations which collapsed into war the following year]."

6. Sturdza, *Dictionnaire historique et généalogique*, 448.

7. Ibid.

8. See F. Ismail, "The Making of the Treaty of Bucharest, 1811–1812," *Middle Eastern Studies* 15, no. 2 (1979): 163–92.

9. This was one of the newly created positions of the phanariot administration in Moldavia, dated by Dionysios Photeinos to the 1760s (Photeinos, *Historia tes palai Dakias*, 2: 509).

10. Sturdza notes that the title *ağa* was, from the seventeenth century until 1856, conferred on boyars in the Danubian principalities when they were appointed chief of police in Bucharest or Jassy (Sturdza, *Dictionnaire historique et généalogique*, 637).

11. Ralou was born in 1791 and died, in İstanbul, in 1845. She was the daughter of Iacoumi Skylitzi and Euphrosyne Skanavi (ibid., 466). Vasileos Sphyroeras mentions that one Demetrios Skanavi was an official servant to the dragoman of the fleet in 1809 (Sphyroeras, *Hoi dragomanoi tou stolou*, 59). He would have been working for Theodoros Rizos (who was dragoman of the fleet between December 1807 and January 1809 and then again from October 1809 to September 1810) or for Jacob Argyropoulo (February 1809—October 1809) or for both (ibid., 157–63). The position of servant, or *anthropos*, of the dragoman included duties of a messenger of money and documents to and from the Aegean Islands. This places the Skanavi family, aside from their familial connections to Voyvoda Kallimaki, directly in the orbit of phanariot dragomans around the time Stephanos married Ralou.

12. See Georgios Kioutouskas, "He voulgarike paroikia sten Konstantinoupole os ta 1878," in *He parousia ton ethnikon meionoteton sten Konsantinoupole ton 190 aiona* ["The Bulgarian Colony in Constantinople until 1878," in *The Presence of Ethnic Minorities in Istanbul in*

*the 19th Century*] (Athens: Syndesmos ton en Athenais Megaloscholiton, 1997), on Vogorides' granting of his land in Phanar to the Bulgarian community in 1849.

13. By his own recollection, Vogorides worked on drafting the law codes with Iakovaki Rizos, who moved to Athens after the establishment of the Greek state (MP, Musurus-Vogorides correspondence, X: 15).Vogorides refers to the pamphlet he wrote, titled *He tetrarchia sten Moldovlachia* [The quadruple dynasty in Moldavia and Wallachia], and claims authorship of it (MP: Musurus-Vogorides correspondence, X: 15).

14. Regarding Vogorides as "Hatman Istefanaki Vogori," see BOA, Name-i Hümayun defteri: no. 989: 245. Those who served as *hatmans* "commanded the defense of the borders." See N. Soutzos, *Mémoires du prince Nicolas Soutzo, grand logothete de Moldavia (1798–1871)* (Vienna: Gerald and Cie, 1899), 96, for a summary of duties for the top positions in the principalities before the 1820s.

15. R. W. Seton-Watson, *A History of the Roumanians: From Roman Times to the Completion of Unity* (Cambridge: Archon Books, 1963), chapter 8.

16. I qualify the term *foreign relations* with quotation marks because Moldavia was not a formally independent polity but a semiautonomous province or principality, which nevertheless featured a minister of foreign affairs *(postelnik)* and engaged in quasi-diplomatic relations with Wallachia, other provinces, and foreign states.

## 3. DEMOLITIONS

1. PRO: FO, 78/101, September 25, 1821, dispatch from Strangford.

2. Other types of ceremonies were tethered to janissary customs as well. In October 1822, the British interim envoy Hamilton noted, "Foreign ministers are generally only admitted to the presence of the Sultan when Janissaries receive their quarterly pay" (PRO: FO, 78/111).

3. Words frequently used in reference to rebels in this period were *hain* (traitor) and *asi* (insurgent/rebel), with *fesad* (intrigue) and *hiyanet/ihanet* (treachery) often used in reference to the rebellion. The word *ihtilal* (revolution, uprising) was used to refer to particular uprisings.

4. The rule established in 1819 with the Dynasty of Four regulation was already in disarray in early 1821. Prince Karaca had fled Wallachia to Pisa in 1818, and his successor, Wallachian prince Aleko Soutso, fell ill and died in January 1821. (See Soutzos, *Mémoires du prince Nicolas Soutzo*, 38.)

5. See John A. Petropulos, *Politics and Statecraft in the Kingdom of Greece: 1833–1843* (Princeton, NJ: Princeton University Press, 1968).

6. The account was published several decades later in a Greek literary journal, *He Pandora* (published in Athens by Ch. A. Doukas from 1850 to 1872), as well as in a volume of documents relevant to the life and martyrdom of Patriarch Gregorios V. Quotations here, taken from the accounts of 1821–22 events in İstanbul, are from *He Pandora* (July 15, 1863): 199–205; and Angelopoulos and Angelopoulos, "Anecdotos ekthesis episemou kai autoptou omogenous," unless otherwise noted.

7. Angelopoulos and Angelopoulos, "Anecdotos ekthesis episemou kai autoptou omogenous," 126. This referred to the massacre of eighty Turkish merchants, perpetrated by the hetairists, in Galatsi. See Seton-Watson, *A History of the Roumanians*, 195.

8. Ibid., 129. This is likely a reference to the Kapan merchants.

9. BOA, C., Dahiliye: 10747 (A.H. 1236), describes the unfolding of the rebellion, first with "Eflaklı Todori's" (Vladimirescu's) uprising followed by *"firari voyvoda İpsilandi'nin oğlu Aleksandır,"* and then with the massacre of Muslim merchants in Kalas *("Kalas'ta ehl-i İslam tüccarını katleylediklerinden . . . ").*

10. Angelopoulos and Angelopoulos, "Anecdotos ekthesis episemou kai autoptou omoge-nous," 125: "They [Turks] stormed into their [the *kapıkahyas'*] houses; that is to say, they confiscated *[tous confiscarisan]* them outright."

11. Ibid., 132.

12. In the eyewitness source, although the language of the source is Greek, the word used for "populace" is the Italian *"popolo."*

13. The choice of terminology or names—Byzantium and Chryssopolis, for instance—indicates the layers involved in this narration. A Greek-speaking Christian author is reporting the sultan's order, wherein the sultan warns of a plot to take over the seat of the imperial government. The author uses the Greek words, however, to refer to the seat of government *(Byzantium)* and to the return of the imperial city, which would be referred to in Ottoman Turkish with a number of phrases *(dersaadet,* for instance), to Christian control, which would mean, in effect, a return to *Byzantium.*

14. Janissaries had frequently been setting fire to neighborhoods in İstanbul to show their discontent toward the state, which makes this an interesting accusation on the part of Sultan Mahmud.

15. Other sources (Spyridon Trikoupes, *Historia tes Hellenikes Epanastaseos,* 4 vols. [Athens: Ek tou typographeiou tēs "Hōras," 1888]; Mehmet Ataullah Efendi Şanizade, *Tarih-i Şanizade* [İstanbul: Ceride-i Havadis Matbaasi, 1290 (M. 1873)]) refer to a *ferman* or the Hatt-ı Hümayun that ordered Muslim residents to arm themselves, but they do not provide details, thus do not refer to the perceived plot to set fire to the Asian shore of the Bosphorus that is given in the anonymous eyewitness report.

16. BOA, C., Dahiliye: 3650 (A.H. 1236).

17. Angelopoulos and Angelopoulos, "Anecdotos ekthesis episemou kai autoptou omoge-nous," 135.

18. Rev. Robert Walsh, *A Residence in Constantinople, During a period Including the Commencement, Progress, and Termination of the Greek and Turkish Revolutions* (London: Richard Bentley, 1838), 1: 313.

19. Angelopoulos and Angelopoulos, "Anecdotos ekthesis episemou kai autoptou omoge-nous," 135.

20. The *postelnik* was based in the principality, not in İstanbul, as was the *kapıkahya.*

21. The Skanavi family was from Chios and had long been involved in mercantile activities and in the networks of the phanariots and Danubian Principalities. They were allies (and marriage partners) of the Kallimaki family in Moldavia and, by extension, of Stephanos Vogorides.

22. Walsh also describes the mayhem that ensued on the streets of İstanbul (*A Residence at Constantinople,* 1: 313): "There were now many thousand fellows of all descriptions completely armed, in addition to the populace of the town, going about with loaded pistols, which they discharged in mere wantonness at every object that presented itself, so

that day and night we were disturbed by a succession of reports." See also BOA, C., Askeriye: 236 (A.H. 1236).

23. Angelopoulos and Angelopoulos, "Anecdotos ekthesis episemou kai autoptou omogenous," 135. The eyewitness account of Rev. R. Walsh confirms this. See Walsh, *A Residence at Constantinople*, 1: 313.

24. According to Ottoman chronicles, Ali Paşa was the grand vezir for a matter of days at this point and was replaced by Hacı Salih Paşa. Hacı Salih Paşa was reportedly a nominee of Halet Efendi and was appointed on May 1, 1821, following the nine-day tenure of Ali Paşa of Bender: "Ali Paşa had outraged Greek and European public opinion by his hasty hanging of the Greek orthodox Patriarch Gregory, in Istanbul on April 22, 1821. He had also failed to cooperate with Halet Efendi, so lost power in a few days" (Reed, "The Destruction of the Janissaries," 58; see also Cevdet, *Tarih-i Cevdet*, 11: 162–65).

Indeed, numerous directives went out from the central state ordering the disarming of subjects in İstanbul at this time: see, for instance, BOA, C., Askeriye: 159 (A.H. 1236), for an order for a "Muslim watchman" *(Müslüman nazır tayin edilmesi)* to be appointed to every *han* and for arms to be given up in exchange for money at all the *hans* in İstanbul. See also BOA, A.DVN. 863–70 (A.H. 1236), for registers containing lists of *"reaya"* and *"rum milleti"* who had their weapons confiscated *(silah bulundurmayacakları; silah toplanılması; toplanan silah)* and signed guarantees of one another's character *(kefalet)*.

25. The Greek eyewitness report claims the peace lasted four days; Ottoman chronicler Şanizade and Reed ("The Destruction of the Janissaries"), who uses Şanizade's account, claim it lasted for nine days. Regarding the reinstatement of Musa Paşa, other reports state that Benderli Ali Paşa was deposed after an eight-day tenure as grand vezir and replaced by Hacı Salih Paşa (Walsh, *A Residence at Constantinople*, 1: 345).

26. Angelopoulos and Angelopoulos, "Anecdotos ekthesis episemou kai autoptou omogenous," 127. In addition to the registers mentioned in the text, registers were also compiled at this time to appraise the value of the "houses, shops, churches, and mills" that were dependencies of monasteries of Mt. Athos. See BOA, A.DVN.KLS.930 (A.H. 1237).

27. The incident is described differently by a British eyewitness (Walsh, *A Residence at Constantinople*, 1: 308).

28. The next year, in October 1822, the census project was expanded when the patriarchate was ordered to "open a register in which the names of all the Greek residents at Constantinople, with those also claiming foreign protection, are to be inserted" (PRO: FO, 78/111).

29. Muruzi's wife, Rallou, née Mavrocordato, and their children escaped to Odessa in 1821 and lived there until 1829, when they returned to Moldavia. Several versions of the details surround Muruzi's death; another version involves his being ordered to translate a letter from Alexander Hypsilanti, and, failing to translate the passage stating that all Greeks were involved in the uprisings, he was killed for disloyalty (Stamatiades, *Biographiai ton hellenon megalon diermeneon*, 184; Florin Marinescu, *Étude généalogique sur la famille Mourouzi* [Athens: Kentron Neoellenikon Ereunon, Ethnikou Hidrymatos Ereunon, 1987], 93–95).

30. Angelopoulos and Angelopoulos, "Anecdotos ekthesis episemou kai autoptou omogenous," 127.

31. Regarding Antonaki Tsiras, see ibid., 119. The merchant Paparrigopoulos was likely

the Russian consul of Patras and the father of Greek national historian Constantine Paparrigopoulos. Paparrigopoulos was the author of *Historia tou ellenikou ethnous apo ton archaiotaton chronon mechri ton neoteron* [History of the Greek nation from Ancient to modern times], 5 vols. (En Athenai: Ek tou typographeio N. Passare, 1865–74), which established a canonical version of Greek national history and the "continuity" of Hellenism thesis. Ağa Alexander Ralli was a member of the Ralli merchant family from Chios.

32. Although Muruzi had been ordered to compose a systematic register of Greek phanariots, it appeared, to our eyewitness, that the sultan opened the register each day and picked names at random (Angelopoulos and Angelopoulos, "Anekdotos ekthesis episemou kai autoptou omogenous," 127).

33. Stavraki had served as the chief *kapıkahya* to Voyvoda Aleko Soutso but had not gotten along with any of the Dynasty of Four and so was considered neutral by the sultan and grand vezir at this moment (Cevdet, *Tarih-i Cevdet,* 11: 231–32).

34. Two reasons were given for the execution of Gregorios: he had sheltered Constantine Muruzi's family after Constantine's execution and had later aided their escape to Odessa; and he was a native of Kalavrita, the town in the Morea that had recently exploded in insurrection, and thus Gregorios was considered a co-conspirator and supporter of that revolt. (See Şanizade, *Tarih-i Şanizade;* Cevdet, *Tarih-i Cevdet;* and Trikoupes, *Historia tes Hellenikes Epanastases.*)

35. While five bishops and Patriarch-elect Anthimos III were in prison the following February 1822, Stavraki, as ex-dragoman and their "great patron and friend," was smuggling the notes written by the British ambassador, Lord Strangford, to the Porte, requesting their release (PRO: FO, 78/109). The first name put forward as a possible successor to Patriarch Gregorios was apparently one Archbishop Gregorios, but since he was outside the city it would take him time to reach the capital, and the nomination would be delayed. Consequently, it was decided to nominate someone among the Holy Synod who was already at the patriarchate, and thus Eugenios was chosen (Walsh, *A Residence at Constantinople;* Trikoupes, *Historia tes Hellenikes Epanastases*).

36. Angelopoulos and Angelopoulos, "Anekdotos ekthesis episemou kai autoptou omogenous," 137. The ceremony to appoint a new patriarch was not as problematic as the investiture ceremony for Danubian princes, which would present the state with a dilemma five months later. The ceremony for the patriarch was less problematic because it was humbler, limited in its geographic location, did not represent a granting of near-royal power to Christians, and was part of the punishment of the former patriarch and therefore could be seen in the service of justice.

37. Şanizade, *Tarih-i Şanizade,* 4: 30.

38. Walsh, *A Residence at Constantinople,* 1: 370.

39. Angelopoulos and Angelopoulos, "Anekdotos ekthesis episemou kai autoptou omogenous," 121.

40. Ibid., 135–36.

41. Uriel Heyd, "The Ottoman Ulema and Westernization in the Time of Selim III and Mahmud II," *Scripta Hierosolymitana* 9 (1961): 72.

42. Their anger could also be directed at their titular chief as part of the central state,

even during the Greek rebellions, when a united Islamic front against the "infidel traitors" might have been expected; in December 1821 "many hundreds of softas demonstrated before the palace of the Şeyh-ül-İslam, demanding the liberation of one of their professors who had been condemned to exile because of his anti-government speeches. The Grand Vezir was compelled personally to assuage the angry and dangerous crowd" (Heyd, "The Ottoman Ulema and Westernization," 73). Unfortunately, Heyd does not specify what sentiments the anti-government speeches contained.

43. Ibid.

44. On Ali Paşa, see Fleming, *The Muslim Bonaparte*; and Dennis Skiotis, "The Greek Revolution: Ali Pasha's Last Gamble," in *Hellenism and the First Greek War of Liberation (1821–1830): Continuity and Change*, ed. Nikiforos P. Diamandouros (Thessaloniki: Institute for Balkan Studies, 1976).

45. Reed, "The Destruction of the Janissaries," 47.

46. Ibid., 47.

47. "Yesterday evening his two houses were sealed up and his Jew Broker, Haskel [Hezekiel], was sent to the Bostandgi Bashi's Prison, together with his son, his cash-keeper and two others employed by him. Halet 's Greek physician [and spy, Asimaki] has shared the same fate. This Haskel's brother is at Baghdad and a man of some consequence in that city—it is surmised that the Tartar dispatched yesterday to the Pasha of Baghdad conveyed orders for the seizure of his Person." PRO: FO, 78/111, November 26, 1822.

48. Halet Efendi reportedly made one last attempt to reenter the good graces of the sultan and janissaries in the spring and early summer of 1822, when he lobbied for a *ferman* to order subjects to donate all their silver and jewels for the state to produce more arms against the Greek rebels. This was interpreted as only another sign that the people were being impoverished at the expense of the state, and Halet Efendi was deemed responsible. "His plan was miscarried and during the summer of 1822 numerous fires in Istanbul served as a sign of discontent and a warning against the unpopular policies of the government" (Reed, "The Destruction of the Janissaries," 58).

49. The label attached to Halet's nose read as follows: "The man generally accused of being the cause of all the present distresses of the Empire" (PRO: FO, 78/111).

50. PRO: FO, 78/111, December 6, 1822.

51. Janissaries had been seen as enemies of the state before this, particularly since the 1807–8 Nizam-ı Cedid rebellions, when they violently attacked the palace, Sultan Selim III, and Grand Vezir Mustafa Bayrakdar.

52. Capodistrias was the Greek native of the Ionian island of Corfu (Kerkyra), who entered the service of the Russian tsar in the early nineteenth century and, after the establishment of the ill-fated Greek Republic in 1827, became the president of that polity. Presumably the British envoy is referring to Capodistrias's ostensible loyalty to the Russian tsar while working for the goal of Greek revolution and independence.

53. PRO: FO, 78/114, January 25, 1823. The envoy had also written, "The representations of the Allied Missions will now by conveyed to His Highness' knowledge; and I cannot think that they will be altogether without effect, seconded as they will now be by the advice of those wise and enlightened Members of the Council, who, during the period of Halet's influence, never dared either to utter their own sentiments or to support those of the Chris-

tian powers. We shall now, in fact, be represented in the Divan, an advantage which for many years we have not enjoyed."

54. Attempts had been made to raise a new kind of army, with troops known as *levend*, in the eighteenth century (Aksan, "Whatever Happened to the Janissaries?"). In emergencies, the Ottoman state had for generations used a combination of Albanian irregulars and tribal or feudally raised troops from Anatolia and more recently had turned to Mehmet Ali in Egypt as a defender.

55. In a wider sense, Mahmud had been planning to destroy the janissary system since he took power in 1808. See Shaw, *Between Old and New*; and Levy, "The Officer Corps in Mahmud II's New Ottoman Army, 1826–1839," *IJMES* 2, no. 1 (1971): 21–39. Some assert that Mahmud was earnest in his attempt at *eşkinci* reform (Levy calls it the "final attempt at gradual reform"), arguing that the janissaries rebelled of their own volition. Others (such as Reed, "The Destruction of the Janissaries") imply that the *eşkinci* reform (see n. 57) was nothing but a ruse to precipitate the janissary rebellion and thus justify the sultan's destruction of the corps. I argue that other possibilities come to the fore when the 1826 events are extracted from the *longue durée* of Ottoman reforms. Thus, the particular events of the 1820s— the Greek rebellion and phanariot breakdown—were certainly contributing factors to the volatility and to Mahmud's decision to adopt drastic measures to do away with the imperial military. Rather than see the 1826 events as an epilogue to the 1807-8 and a prologue to the Tanzimat, we will find it more useful for this discussion to consider the specificities of governance in the 1820s, and one such specificity was Mahmud's knowledge of the mistakes and fate of his predecessor, Selim III, and thus his intention, likely long-held, to devise a strategy to destroy the janissaries, maintain the sultanate, and preserve his own life.

56. Reed, "The Destruction of the Janissaries," 105. See Heyd, "The Ottoman Ulema and Westernization"; and Avigdor Levy, "The Ottoman Ulema and the Military Reforms of Sultan Mahmud II," *Asian and African Studies* 7 (1971): 13–39, especially 15, for the role of *ulema* elites in Mahmud's reform program and for details of Mahmud's aggressive appointment policy aimed at installing submissive *ulema*.

57. Reed, "The Destruction of the Janissaries," 113. "His [the sultan's] final preliminary moves were: first, to check once more with the former Janissary Ağa, Hüseyin Paşa; next, to assure once again the cooperation of the senior Janissary officers; and finally, to obtain the formal, public cooperation of religious, civil, and military leaders whose backing would be vital in assuring success to his reform plans" (ibid., 112). *Eşkinci* was the name of archaic Ottoman troops; see H. A. R. Gibb and Harold Bowen, *Islamic Society and the West: A Study of the Impact of Western Civilization on Moslem Culture in the Near East* (London: Oxford University Press, 1957), vol. 1, part 1, 50. The word was resuscitated for the sultan's new corps, the members of which were chosen from current janissary troops and specially trained.

58. Heyd, "The Ottoman Ulema and Westernization," 83.

59. Ibid.; Levy, "The Ottoman *Ulema* and the Military Reforms of Sultan Mahmud II."

60. Reed, "The Destruction of the Janissaries," 126; my emphasis in both quotes.

61. BOA, A.DVN.Kanunname-i Askeri 1 (A.H. 1241; M. 1826).

62. Reed, "The Destruction of the Janissaries," 158.

63. Ibid., 170. See also Cengiz Kırlı's "The Struggle over Space: Coffeehouses of Ottoman Istanbul, 1780–1845," PhD diss., State University of New York, Binghamton, 2001.

64. Et Meydanı was located near today's Vatan Caddesi, near the Aksaray quarter of İstanbul; see N. Sakaoğlu, "Etmeydanı," in *Dünden bugüne İstanbul ansiklopedisi*, vol. 3 (İstanbul: Kültür Bakanlığı ve Tarih Vakfı'nın ortak yayınıdır, 1993–).

65. This is significant, because much of the substance of the military reform had come from Mehmet Ali Paşa, who had set an example for military reform and discipline. See Fahmy, *All the Pasha's Men*.

66. In the following days, janissary strongholds such as Edirne and Bosnia were sites of conflict. Thousands of janissary prisoners were brought from İstanbul to Trabzon, where the Janissary Corps was also disbanded.

67. Walsh, *A Residence at Constantinople*, 2: 524 (appendix 7).

68. Conspiracies among the new troops were discovered months after the abolition of the old corps. They were "blamed on former Janissaries who had managed to infiltrate the new troops. Some 75 gunners and over 200 infantrymen were arrested, 8 of their ringleaders and 9 civilian accomplices were strangled, and the remainder exiled" (Reed, "The Destruction of the Janissaries," 338).

69. One of the provisions of the 1829 Treaty of Edirne was that private sale of grains from Moldavia and Wallachia was to be allowed beyond the borders of the Ottoman Empire.

70. Aynural, *İstanbul değirmenleri ve fırınları*, 58.

71. The Greek patriarch's cooperation was also ordered. In his case he was to "order all Greek cloth merchants who were supplying material for uniforms, bedding and tents to the government, to make only a three per cent gain on each transaction" (Reed, "The Destruction of the Janissaries," 335).

72. Ibid., 296; Cevdet, *Tarih-i Cevdet*, 13: 175.

73. Reed, "The Destruction of the Janissaries," 339.

74. See Selim Deringil, *The Well-Protected Domains: Ideology and the Legitimation of Power in the Late Ottoman Empire, 1876–1909* (London: I. B. Tauris, 1998), for a discussion of Sultan Abdülhamit II's instrumentalization and ottomanization of shari'a later in the nineteenth century.

## BIOGRAPHY OF AN EMPIRE III

1. According to Blancard, Vogorides arrived in Bucharest on February 20, 1820, on a mission as *postelnik* of Moldavia, along with Spathar Constantine Negri and Postelnik Ioannis Samurkassis, all representing Skarlatos Kallimaki, to negotiate a peace with Tudor Vladimirescu. Finding things there "in a piteous state," he soon came under the protection of Mehmed Selim Paşa, military commander of Silistre, and was named interim governor *(kaymakam)* of Moldavia in 1820 (Blancard, *Les Mavroyènis*, 2: 560). According to Sturdza, Vogorides was the *kaymakam* of Moldavia from February 1821 (when hetairist insurgencies began) until July 1822 (Sturdza, *Dictionnaire historique et généalogique*, 448).

2. MP, Musurus-Vogorides correspondence, IX: 69, November 1852; my emphasis. I have paraphrased Vogorides' words (after decoding and translating from Greek) and used quotations marks within the paraphrasing for exact quotations.

3. Soutzos, *Mémoires du prince Nicolas Soutzo*, 39.

4. CML, Ottoman documents: İstanbul dossier. Neofit Hilendarski's biographical sketch

of Vogorides describes the moment when Mehmed Selim Paşa, the military commander of Silistre at the time, almost had Vogorides executed on suspicion of involvement with the hetairist conspiracy. According to Neofit, a group of notables *(çorbacı)* from Vogorides' hometown happened to be in Silistre for business, and, by swearing that they knew Vogorides and that he was Bulgarian and not Greek and therefore not part of the conspiracy, they saved him from execution (Peneva, "Neizvestia biographia na Stephan Bogoridi ot Neofit Hilendarski"). This report conflicts somewhat with Bakirtzes, who claims that Vogorides enjoyed the protection of Selim Mehmet Paşa, who had appointed Vogorides to the position of interim governor of Moldavia the previous year, but it is possible that Selim Mehmet changed his opinion about Vogorides by the time of the latter's arrest (Bakirtzes, "Vogorides, Stephanos").

5. Blancard, *Les Mavroyènis,* 2: 562.

6. MP, Musurus-Vogorides correspondence, IX: 69.

7. Seton-Watson, *A History of the Roumanians,* 201. Kronstadt (Braşov) was a city in Transylvania under Austrian control. Soutzos notes, "We left Wallachia, but not the Wallachians. Emigration had transported to Kronstadt all of society that had had relations with my family" (Soutzos, *Mémoires du prince Nicolas Soutzo,* 40–41).

8. PRO: FO, 78/109. In June 1822 Strangford wrote, "Ali Bey is still uncertain who will be named Hospodar *[voyvoda]* of Moldavia—but he does not think that the appointment will fall upon any of the Moldavian Deputies now here. The Porte had the intention of naming one of those individuals, but was deterred from it by the consideration that he was the near kinsman of the Caimakam *[sic]* Stephanaki Vogorides, whose maladministration of the Province confided to him, and whose tyrannical oppression of the Inhabitants, have excited the anger of the Sultan, and will probably, as soon as the Prince who is to succeed him shall have been installed, lead to a severe examination of his conduct."

9. Regarding the Torbalı and İzmit report, see Blancard, *Les Mavroyènis,* 2: 563. Regarding the Kütahya report, see Sturdza, *Dictionnaire historique et généalogique,* 448.

10. The British envoy in İstanbul, for his part, saw Ghika's appointment in a positive light, noting that Ghika's arrival in Wallachia met with "crowds joyful and thankful to the Sultan for having delivered them from the oppression and rapacity of the Greeks of Constantinople" (PRO: FO, 78/111). Paun, "Sur l'investiture des derniers princes phanariote," 69 n. 18.

11. It is also seen as such in retrospect by nationalist historians; see Kurt W. Treptow, ed., *A History of Romania* (Iaşi: Center for Romanian Studies, 1997), 242–43.

### 4. PHANARIOT REMODELING AND THE STRUGGLE FOR CONTINUITY

1. Sturdza, *Dictionnaire historique et généalogique,* 247.

2. Nicholas Aristarchi would return to İstanbul two years later and start a long career as grand *logothete* for the Orthodox patriarchate and Russian-aligned Ottoman court favorite.

3. BOA, C., Hariciye: 148 (evasit-e Muharrem 1236; November 1820). These lesser boyars were associated with İskerlet (Skarlatos) Kallimaki, the *voyvoda* of Wallachia who fled just before insurrections broke out.

4. Stamatiades, *Biographiai ton hellenon megalon diermeneon,* 165–66.

5. See Trikoupes, *Historia tes Hellenikes Epanastaseos,* 2: 110–11, for the dissatisfaction of mainland Greeks after encountering their phanariot potential leaders in 1821.

6. Ibid., 2: 108 and passim.

7. Others escaped in the early days of the conflict and returned only two years later. In June 1823 the British consul reported, "Many Greeks who had fled to Odessa are now returning to Constantinople and Smyrna [İzmir]" (PRO: FO, 78/114).

8. G. D. Koromelas, "Kallimaches," in *MHE*, 13: 572.

9. Th. Vellianites, "Mourouzes," in *MHE*, 17: 426.

10. See Findley, *Ottoman Civil Officialdom*, 132: "The chargés and consuls of the time being Greek, by and large, the outbreak of the Greek Revolution in 1821 led to the abolition of the diplomatic service for the time being. In the case of the consular service, the break may have been less decisive, perhaps only a revision to the nonofficial status of the eighteenth century. Still, there would be no more diplomatic appointments until the early 1830s; no more consular ones until the middle of that decade."

11. This is not to say that no military conflicts occurred between the Ottoman Empire and other states in the 1820s: the decade opened with hostilities on the border with Persia (1821–23) and closed with another Russo-Ottoman war (1828–29), which turned out to be decisive for the Ottoman state's recognition of an independent Greece and compromise on the status of Moldavia, Wallachia, and Serbia, for instance.

12. Reed, "The Destruction of the Janissaries," 76–77.

13. Paul Schroeder, *The Transformation of European Politics, 1763–1848* (Oxford: Clarendon Press, 1994), 638.

14. Ibid. France, Britain, and Russia did become involved in 1827 with the Conference of London and the Battle of Navarino, but even then there was little consensus about how to resolve the Greek Question.

15. Schroeder mentions that "when Liverpool resigned in ill health in February 1827, Canning defeated Wellington in the contest for premiership, whereupon Wellington, who disapproved of Canning both on general grounds and for his recklessness on the Greek question, resigned from the cabinet, leaving Canning to run foreign policy through Lord Dudley as titular foreign secretary" (ibid., 649).

16. Ibid., 637. I qualify the term *balance of power* with quotation marks because, although it has been a term used most often to describe the principle of European politics in the nineteenth century, Paul Schroeder has offered compelling arguments as to the inadequacy of this term for the politics of that period. See his "Did the Vienna Settlement Rest on a Balance of Power?" *American Historical Review* 97, no. 3 (1992): 683–706.

17. "I am not ignorant of the fact that there exists a strong party in the Divan, which is not only opposed to the Project of removing the [Ottoman] troops [from Moldavia and Wallachia] but which carries its distrust of the Greeks so far as to recommend that none of the Rayah *[sic]* Subjects of the Porte should henceforward be employed in Wallachia and Moldavia, and that the Government of those Provinces should be confided to Turkish Paşas" (PRO: FO, 78/101, September 10, 1821).

18. PRO: FO, 78/101.

19. PRO: FO, 78/101, August 1821. A September 1821 meeting was held between İsmael Efendi and Lord Strangford, at which the former (who was out of office but a frequent visitor and counselor of the sultan, according to the report) informed the ambassador that there

was a split in the imperial council over whether to pull Ottoman troops out of the principalities and restore the *voyvoda*s or to keep troops there and insist on Russia's turning over the fugitives, who included Michael Soutso.

20. In a discussion between the sultan and İsmael Ferruh Efendi (who had been Ottoman ambassador in London [1797–1800] and was "frequently summoned to the Divan to give his opinion . . . but . . . constantly refused the dangerous honor of being officially employed by the Sultan"), the sultan "did not shrink from avowing that the Fear of the Janissaries was such, that this Government was obliged to temporize, and to do many things contrary to its judgment and intentions, for the sake of keeping them in good humor—that the Porte thought it better to content herself with this sort of limited and imperfect authority over them, than to drive them to open insurrection, and perhaps to introduce revolution and anarchy, by opposing their wishes—that one of the points the Janissaries would not listen to reason, was the giving up of the fugitive traitors" (PRO: FO, 78/101). In October 1823, Beyzade Kostaki, son of the *voyvoda* of Wallachia, and Beyzade Yanko, son of the *voyvoda* of Moldavia, were received at the Porte but were sent home to Phanar to await further instructions (PRO: FO, 78/111).

21. Nicolae Iorga, *A History of Roumania: Land, People, Civilization.* Translated by Joseph McCabe. (London: T. F. Unwin, 1925): 217. Sturdza and Ghika reportedly "obtained their thrones by the aid of the smaller boyars who, on their side, declared in favor of a broader oligarchy, composed of all the holders of dignities and titles of honor" (ibid., 219). In October 1827 the Treaty of Akkerman was signed, which fixed the terms for *voyvoda*s at seven years. The administration of Ghika and Sturdza was interrupted by Russian occupation of the principalities from 1829 until 1834. In 1834, Alexander Ghika was appointed *voyvoda* of Wallachia and Michael Sturdza was appointed his counterpart in Moldavia. Their tenure lasted until 1842 and 1849, respectively (ibid., 272–23).

22. Gregorios V reigned in 1797–98, 1806–8, and 1818–21. Eugenios II reigned only in 1821–22, and Anthimos III reigned only in 1822–24.

23. PRO: FO, 78/114, February 28, 1823.

24. PRO: FO, 78/116, August 25, 1823. Anthimos's successor, Chrysanthos, was, like Eugenios in 1821–22, of Bulgarian descent, born in Grammatikov in Macedonia. See Manouel Gedeon, *Patriarchikoi Pinakes: Eideseis hisotrikai biographikai peri ton patriarchon Konstantinopoleos, apo Andreou tou Protoletou mechris Ioakeim III tou apo Thessalonikes, 36–1884* [Patriarchal portraits: Historical and biographical information on the patriarchs of Constantinople] (Constantinople: Lorenz and Keil, 1890), 687–78. Chrysanthos was at the center of his share of scandals; see TKSA, Evrak 4268, for a detailing of his attempts to abscond with the monies of the Orthodox community's poor relief fund in time of famine and to hide the evidence on his *"fahişe"* and the son born out of wedlock to her. He was removed in 1826, presumably in the midst of the janissary crisis in İstanbul.

25. Şanizade mentions, for instance, that there were documents that could not be translated at this time, not only in French, but also in Greek (T. *Rumi ül-ibare*) (Şanizade, *Tarih-i Şanizade*, 4: 33).

26. Cevdet, *Tarih-i Cevdet*, 11: 152–53. "Sultan Mahmud was also reported to be greatly pleased to receive a translation of the regulation for French infantry to which had been ap-

pended many drawings showing the new troops in every position of the manual of arms. This translation had been prepared by a son of the late Yahya Efendi, former Dragoman of the Porte" (Reed, "The Destruction of the Janissaries," 350–51).

27. Findley, *Ottoman Civil Officialdom*, 133. Şanizade was the court historian from 1819 to 1825 and was succeeded by Esad Efendi, who served as court historian from 1825 until his death in 1848.

28. Cevdet, *Tarih-i Cevdet*, 11: 231: "Çünkü ber-veche bala Kostaki'nin idamından sonra yerine Fenerlulardan olmamak şartiyle tercüman araştırıldı bulunamadı."

29. Findley notes that Yahya Efendi's epithet was Bulgarzade and hence that he was of Bulgarian Christian descent (Findley, *Ottoman Civil Officialdom*, 133); see also AMAE, Consular correspondence from the cities of the Ottoman Empire: Constantinople, file B: 243 (1822). Şanizade describes him as "Bulgarzade Yahya Efendi of Rum descent," illustrating the ambiguity between Rum as Greek Orthodox of Greek-speaking origins and Rum as Greek Orthodox not of Greek-speaking origins (Şanizade, *Tarih-i Şanizade*, 4: 34). Hacı İshak Efendi, a convert of Judaism and hailing from Arta, was another professor at the military engineering school who entered the Translation Office. See Levy, "The Ottoman Ulema and the Military Reforms of Sultan Mahmud II," 34.

30. The Aristarchi family was said to have been from Zimiske, near Trabzon (formerly Trebizond) on the Black Sea coast, not from "Caramania," which is today considered a separate region in central Anatolia. See E. R. Rangavi, *Livre d'Or de la noblesse phanariote et des familles princières de Valachie et de Moldavie* (Athens, 1892), 22.

31. Quoted in Walsh, *A Residence at Constantinople*, 1: 361 (May 1821).

32. Aristarchi was murdered in exile, in September 1822. See PRO: FO, 78/111. Yahya, in addition to his knowledge of languages, was also fluent in the ceremonial customs of his new office. In October 1822, Baron d'Ottenfelt (a Prussian envoy) was "the first minister that has arrived since the office of Dragoman of the Porte has been filled by a Turk, [so] some curiosity was excited on the occasion; however it appears that the Turk had been so well schooled and had rehearsed his part so often, that he acquitted himself of his share in the ceremony much better than was expected—and he accepted the present offered him without any embarrassment" (PRO: FO, 78/111).

33. See Şanizade, *Tarih-i Şanizade*, 4: 33–34.

34. According to the court historian Şanizade, Yahya's loyalty was tested and he was approved by the imperial council (ibid., 35).

35. *Meczum* means literally "amputated." See ibid., 33–34: "On beş yirmi günden berudur Bab-ı Ali'de Rumi ve Frengi ül-ibare bazı evrak kiraat ettirilmekte olan mühendishane hocalarından Rumi ül-asl Bulgarzade Yahya bundan sonra dahi o makule tercümeleri mukabele ve evrak-ı müzakereye nazar ederek lazım gelen dakaiki evliyayı umura ifade ve tefhim ve bazı mustaid heveskarlara düvel ve milel beyninde mütedavil olan elsine-i ecnebiyeye talim eylemek hususlarına me'mur kılınması ve bir münasib mahalden kendüsüne (olki zi hak-ı haka) lazım sınca mahiye beşar yüz guruş maaş tahsis olunması. . . . evliyayı umurun fitnei hafiye-i Rum bu defa re'y'ül-ayn malumu ve erbab-ı hark ve iltiyamın Rum tercümanların nice yüz senelerden beri derkar olan *hezar fesadları bil-müşahede* meczumu olmaktan naşi fima'bad tercümanların ehl-e İslamdan olmasına niyet olunup" (emphasis added).

36. Levy, "Military Policy of Sultan Mahmud II," 35–36. Levy notes that one Mehmed

Ruh-üd-din Yahyazade (meaning "son of Yahya") was translating military treatises from French at the engineering school as of 1807 (36).

37. Findley, *Bureaucratic Reform in the Ottoman Empire*, 131.

38. Yahya Efendi had been a professor of mathematics at the *"mühendishane"* (school of military engineering) before 1821. This school had been established during the reign of Selim III, and it provided training for military translators.

39. Findley states that the Translation Office of the Sublime Porte was officially established in response to the Greek rebellions and "general attack on the Phenariot *[sic]* elite," but he does not give an exact date for the formal establishment of the office (Findley, *Bureaucratic Reform in the Ottoman Empire*, 132-33). Bernard Lewis claims this change happened in 1833, but the court historian Şanizade notes that, because of ambitious people, in 1821 the work of translation was put under a new rule and in a new office within the Sublime Porte (Lewis, *The Emergence of Modern Turkey*, 88; Şanizade, *Tarih-i Şanizade*, 4: 34).

40. The French government had formed language schools to train translators in the late eighteenth century. Their express motivation was to decrease their dependency on phanariots and Levantines, who had been serving as dragomans in İstanbul and provincial consulates (AMAE, Mémoires et correspondances diverses: tome 30, doc. 29, June 11, 1797).

41. BOA, HAT: 2134. After the "purification from employment of infidels" in the dragoman's office, apprentices, or *yamaks*, were Esrar Efendi and Sami Efendi, and the dragoman was İshak Efendi after the death of Yahya Efendi. Wages would still come from the imperial fisc (6,000), Greek patriarchate (5,000), Mt. Athos monasteries (9,175), Wallachia (10,000), and Moldavia (5,000).

42. BOA, Name-i Hümayun defteri, no. 989: 326-27.

43. Ibid., 326.

44. Findley, *Ottoman Civil Officialdom*, 134.

45. There had been an informal system of training in place among phanariots before 1821 (recall the example of Todoraki Tuğsuz Kamaraşoğlu), but by the time trainees were admitted into the office of the dragoman, they already had knowledge of Western languages and translation skills.

46. In 1831 (A.H. 1247) "Stefanaki" (likely Stephanos Vogorides) was still submitting summary translations of newspaper reports he deemed relevant to Ottoman affairs, such as reports of *"hayli fesadlar,"* or "many conspiracies," underway at the Greek border or of the wives of the Russian tsar's younger brother Michael and Count Nesselrode visiting London and their dealings with King William IV. Stefanaki punctuated his report with heartfelt laments about how difficult it was to find decent men in state service at that time ("Ah efendim ah, on eşref-i devlet-i aliye'den hiç bir mahalde bir adem bulunmaması mucip te'essufumdur") (TKSA, Evrak: 5163).

47. PRO: FO, 78/114, February 10, 1823.

48. This occurred on December 1823. See Reed, "The Destruction of the Janissaries," 71.

49. Ibid., 80; Cevdet, *Tarih-i Cevdet*, 12: 99.

50. Cevdet, *Tarih-i Cevdet*, 12: 92-93. Benderli Selim Mehmet Paşa "had begun his career as a simple Janissary and had risen to a high rank, had commanded troops in Varna, Damascus, Tunis," and most recently in Silistre, where he had been coordinating the military forces against rebels in the northern Balkans (Reed, "The Destruction of the Janissaries," 82).

51. Heyd discusses *ulema* participation in the state council (Encümen-i Meşveret or Meclis-i Şura) and refers to both the "new councils" set up by Selim III and Mahmud II to enact their reform program and the permanent councils set up in the late 1830s by Mahmud II (Heyd, "The Ottoman Ulema and Westernization," 83–84). Presumably, then, the popular council called in 1823 by Mahmud II was not a permanent one but was assembled for the occasion.

52. See Ralph Hattox, *Coffee and Coffeehouses: The Origins of a Social Beverage in the Medieval Near East* (Seattle: University of Washington Press, 1985); and Kırlı, "The Struggle over Space." Also, Heyd cites page 65 in Es'ad's *Üss-i Zafer*, which refers to the "imams of the various quarters of İstanbul who were instructed by the cadi of the capital to act against any criticism of the new military institutions expressed in coffee-houses and other places" in 1826 (Heyd, "The Ottoman Ulema and Westernization," 63–96 ). And finally, Levy notes that, in 1808, coffeehouses, which were packed at night during Ramadan, became the scene of calculated incitement against Mustafa Bayraktar Alemdar, the member of the Rusçuk *ayans* who was a leading proponent of the Nizam-ı Cedid reforms (Levy, "Military Policy of Sultan Mahmud II," 64).

53. Reed, "The Destruction of the Janissaries," 86; Cevdet, *Tarih-i Cevdet*, 12: 105.

54. Reed, "The Destruction of the Janissaries," 90. See also Cevdet, *Tarih-i Cevdet*, 12: 84.

55. Çavuşbaşı translates as "chief baliff." See Findley, *Bureaucratic Reform in the Ottoman Empire*, 70, for a discussion of its significance.

56. Halil Inalcik, "Husrev Pasha," in *İA*, 5: 610.

57. Tahir Paşa, a fellow Albanian of Mehmet Ali, was instrumental in expelling Husrev Paşa but was later eliminated by Mehmet Ali in the latter's rise to power in Egypt. See Dodwell, *The Founder of Modern Egypt*, 11; Toledano, "Muhammad Ali Pasha," in *EI2*, 7: 423–31; and İnalcik, "Husrev Pasha," 610, for the same events from Husrev's perspective.

58. See Fahmy, *Mehmet Ali,* for more on the rivalry between Mehmet Ali and Husrev Paşa.

59. İnalcik, "Husrev Pasha," 611.

60. Walsh, *A Residence at Constantinople,* 2: 523 (appendix 7).

61. Toledano, "Muhammad Ali Pasha."

62. According to a biographer, he was building "strong and well-equipped land and sea forces, a solid and prosperous economic base, an effective administrative structure and a network of social services capable of maintaining and reproducing the governing elite" (ibid., 424). See Fahmy, *All the Pasha's Men,* for a review and critique of Mehmet Ali's place in Egyptian nationalist historiography.

63. Levy, "The Officer Corps in Mahmud II's New Ottoman Army," 22, 24, 32.

64. See Levy, "Military Policy of Sultan Mahmud II," 172, for the political background to the June 1826 events; and Reed, "The Destruction of the Janissaries," 111–12.

65. The repercussions of janissary abolition in society and governance are often taken for granted by historians, such as Lewis, whose argument is that the janissaries were finally "safely out of the way" in 1826 (Lewis, *The Emergence of Modern Turkey,* 80), and Findley, whose focus is on formal bureaucratic institutions (Findley, *Bureaucratic Reform in the Ottoman Empire*). This oversight occurs because formal institutions in the nineteenth-century Ottoman Empire are often taken at face value; that is, janissaries were a problem because

they had strayed from their formal purpose and functions, and bureaucracy and administration are assessed as formal structures.

66. Levy estimates that between seventy and eighty of Husrev's slaves attained the highest ranks in the postjanissary army of the late 1820s and 1830s. He points out that, while "this group was outnumbered by the graduates of the Court Battalion (a special unit which included 'young slaves from the Sultan's household and free-born Muslim youths, usually the sons of grandees who were in training at the Court'), Husrev's slaves held the more prominent positions during the period of his ascendancy, particularly in the regiments of the Mansure" (Levy, "The Officer Corps in Mahmud II's New Ottoman Army," 29).

67. İnalcik, "Husrev Pasha," 611: "Böylece imparatorluğu yıllarca temelinden sarsan büyük Mısır buhranı, zahirde, Husrev ile Mehmed Ali arasındaki eski rekabetin bir devamı gibi görünür."

68. PRO: FO, 78/221, January 13, 1833, Mandeville to Palmerston (quoting Vogorides' comment to Mandeville).

69. See Levy, "Military Policy of Sultan Mahmud II," 178, and his "Officer Corps in Mahmud II's New Ottoman Army," for discussions and lists of new positions created in the postjanissary imperial military.

70. Heyd, "The Ottoman Ulema and Westernization," 92: "The shattering victories of the Russians in this war, their occupation of Adrianople (Edirne) and threat to Istanbul brought about a deep change. With the Peace of Adrianople of 1829 a completely new era opened in Ottoman relations with Europe. Now the Turkish leaders understood that without maintaining very close relations with at least one major Christian Power the Empire was lost." Heyd also comments, "The Ottomans had a foretaste of such a predicament when they had to enter anti-French alliances with Russia and England at the time of Napoleon's invasion of Egypt," in 1799.

71. BOA, HAT: 23768 (A.H. 1225); Seton-Watson, A History of the Roumanians, 156.

72. PRO: FO, 78/111, October 25, 1822.

73. See Walsh, A Residence at Constantinople, 1: 345–63, for a very detailed description of his audience with Sultan Mahmud in May 1821. See also a note from Stratford Canning regarding the recent change in ceremonials at the presentation of ambassadors to the court, so as to conform to the "Courts of Christendom" (PRO: FO, 78/209, March 17, 1832).

74. PRO: FO, 78/114, February 10, 1823.

75. Walsh, A Residence at Constantinople, 1: 395.

76. PRO: FO, 78/114, February 10, 1823.

77. PRO: FO, 78/101, September 25, 1821; see BOA, C., Hariciye: 6632, for a reference to İsmael Ferruh Efendi as patron for phanariot Manolaki circa 1802.

78. This, too, was motivated by a British desire to remove the pretexts for Russian discontent and possible invasion regarding these issues. See Walsh, A Residence at Constantinople, 1: 367–68.

79. PRO: FO, 78/114, February 10, 1823.

80. See Findley, Ottoman Civil Officialdom, 113, for discussion of Selim III's reforms and Mahmud II's early reforms. Findley does not provide discussion of the 1820s except to say that the position of Greek phanariots in the diplomatic corps had become untenable as a result of the Greek Revolution.

BIOGRAPHY OF AN EMPIRE IV

1. PRO: FO, 78/115, June 10, 1823.

2. TKSA, Evrak: 9241 (A.H. 1244).

3. BOA, HAT: 43189-A; BOA, HAT: 43200 (A.H. 1247; A.H. 1248).

4. TKSA, Evrak: 5163 (A.H. 1247). In this dispatch he records who has been helping him in his task: "Akdemce gönderilen evrak kimin yazısıyla olduğu sual buyurmuş: Ekser-i evrak-ı mursule-i mesbuka oğlum kölelerinin kalem ile ve ikisi bulgar cinsinden . . . sabık Patrik Katibi Vasilaki namında bir bendelerinin yazısıyla yazılmıştı."

5. See Soutzos, *Mémoires du prince Nicolas Soutzo*, 62–63, for a description of how all of Wallachian society that had had dealings with phanariot *voyvoda* Aleko Soutso returned from self-imposed exile (in Kronstadt, Hermannstadt, and Cernowitz) in early 1827.

6. Findley, *Ottoman Civil Officialdom*, 71 n. 98; Butrus Abu-Manneh, "The Naqshbandiyya-Mujaddidiyya in the Ottoman Lands in the Early 19th Century," *Die Welt des Islams* 22, no. 1 (1982): 21, 27–28, 33.

7. Pertev was also the patron of Mustafa Reşit Bey-Paşa, who would go on to shape Ottoman politics through the Crimean War.

8. Levy, "The Officer Corps in Mahmud II's New Ottoman Army."


5. DIPLOMACY AND THE RESTORATION OF A NEW ORDER

1. BOA, C., Dahiliye: 12037.

2. Ibid.

3. The word used in reference to the Greeks is *yunani*, which was the term used for Greeks of the Greek state, in contradistinction to "Rum," for Greek Orthodox subjects of the Ottoman Empire.

4. BOA, C., Hariciye: 2500.

5. Secret plans had been made before, such as that between the French king Charles X and Russia, to divvy up the empire. In the 1830s, however, the topic was openly discussed, even by members of the central state itself, as cited above.

6. Russian leaders had long seen themselves as contenders for the Ottoman Empire (since the reign Catherine the Great in the later eighteenth century), but the difference now was that other parties, including the Ottomans themselves, acknowledged and debated this possibility.

7. The relationship between European powers and the Ottoman Empire has traditionally been referred to as the Eastern Question. See, for example, M. S. Anderson, *The Eastern Question 1774–1923: A Study in International Relations* (New York: St. Martin's Press, 1966); and Philip E. Mosely, *Russian Diplomacy and the Opening of the Eastern Question in 1838 and 1839* (Cambridge, MA: Harvard University Press, 1934). The framework of the Eastern Question, however, does not allow for complexity and implications of changes within Ottoman politics, but tends instead to reinforce a polar opposition between reform and conservatism within Ottoman politics and to place most of the dynamism and potential to enact change in the hands of the Great Powers.

8. Even as far back as March 1823, Foreign Minister George Canning recognized the

Greeks as belligerents, mainly to protect British commercial interests in the Aegean, which were prey to both Greek and Ottoman piracy. The 1824 Congress of Verona touched on the issue of the Greek rebellions but focused much more on the situation in Spain (Harold Temperley, *The Foreign Policy of Canning, 1822–1827: England, the Neo-Holy Alliance and the New World* [London: G. Bell and Sons, 1925], 324). In September 1825 a Greek delegation had traveled to London to demand the protection of Great Britain "and offered to accept a supreme chief [i.e., ruler or king] from her." The demands were refused by Canning, who maintained the policy of neutrality (ibid., 341).

9. The Duke of Wellington went on a special mission to St. Petersburg in February 1826, and two months later an Anglo-Russian protocol was issued. See M. S. Anderson, *The Great Powers and the Near East, 1774–1923* (London: Edward Arnold, 1970), 31–33. The terms of this protocol would form the basis for the first Treaty of London, signed on July 6, 1827, by British, French, and Russian governments.

10. Regarding the Ottoman refusal of offers: "Repeated representations had already been made to the Porte by the ambassadors, but had elicited no other answer than that the Greek rebellion was a purely internal matter of no legitimate interest whatever to the European powers. On August 16 [1827] the three dragomans [of the foreign embassies] carried to the *Reis Efendi*—the Foreign Minister—a note which he refused to receive. On the 29th they repeated their visit, and were assured that the Sultan would never accept any proposals regarding the Greeks and that he would persist in his resolve until the day of judgment. On the 31st they were sent again with a further declaration, which the minister, after a childish pretence of not understanding, again refused to accept" (Dodwell, *The Founder of Modern Egypt*, 81–82). While fascinating new studies have come out in recent years regarding the life, projects, and modern legacies of Mehmet Ali, none has addressed this first phase of the "Eastern Crisis" in much detail. Therefore, I rely on Dodwell's study for this information, though it's somewhat dated in other respects.

11. Regarding the Battle of Navarino, see Dodwell, *The Founder of Modern Egypt,* 91. Multilateral military intervention was not premeditated in that battle. Rather, British foreign minister Canning noticed Russian troop movements toward the Danubian Principalities and, anticipating Russian military presence along the Danube, sent British naval forces to the Morea in late 1825. (In the meantime Tsar Alexander died in December 1825, which was followed by Decembrist revolts and a struggle between two brothers for succession to the throne. Nicholas emerged victorious as the new tsar, and the revolts in Petersburg were put down.) (Temperley, *The Foreign Policy of Canning,* 352)

12. Many Greek historians would argue that the Greek Revolution ceased to be an intra-Ottoman conflict when rebels drafted a constitution and began to form a government, a process that can be traced to late 1821 and early 1822 (in Epidauros, December 1821 and January 27, 1822; see Anderson, *The Great Powers and the Near East,* 30). First, this seems to be a retrospective view, since other groups could have attempted the same initiatives but still lost the military conflict and failed to secure legitimacy from other states in the end. Second, from the Ottoman point of view this began as and continued to be an internal conflict (note the reference to the "intrigues" *[fesad]* still underway in the Morea in 1825–26, which prevented the customary collection of funds to pay the imperial dragoman, in BOA, Name-i Hümayun defteri: no. 989: 326). It was only with the formal acknowledgment and "tute-

lage" of foreign states such as Britain, Russia, and France that Greece became an independent state, and for this reason I refer to the Greek Revolution as an intra-Ottoman conflict until foreign powers got involved in 1827.

13. This had been going on before, because Britain had gained possession of the Ionian Islands at the turn of the nineteenth century, and Russia had long been striving to gain control of the Danubian Principalities.

14. "Castlereagh . . . spoke of the Greeks as the counterparts of the Carbonari of Italy, of the Constitutionalists in Spain, and of the Radicals in England" (Temperley, *The Foreign Policy of Canning*, 324). Metternich was solidly in this camp as well, one of several reasons for which Austria did not play the major role in the Greek and Mehmet Ali negotiations that Russia, Britain, and France did (Schroeder, *The Transformation of European Politics*, 637).

15. C. W. Crawley, *The Question of Greek Independence: A Study of British Policy in the Near East, 1821–1833* (New York: H. Fertig, 1973), 30.

16. Mavroyeni, the Ottoman chargé d'affaires in Vienna and the only member of the diplomatic corps remaining in Europe through the 1820s, and Namık Bey were sent to London in 1832 to observe the conference, but by the time they arrived it was already being concluded (PRO: FO, 78/212: 33). A marginal note in Greek on one of Mavroyeni's presentations to the conference in August 1832 causes us to wonder whether he was speaking for the new Greek state, the Ottoman Empire, or the Rum population of the Ottoman Empire: "May the English or the French be our masters but not the Russians. They [the Russians] left us in the mud three times, and they want to remove the snake with our hands. No. Better than the Russians are not only the Turks but the devil" (PRO: FO, 78/218).

17. See Crawley, *The Question of Greek Independence;* and William W. McGrew, *Land and Revolution in Modern Greece, 1800–1881: The Transition in the Tenure and Exploitation of Land from Ottoman Rule to Independence* (Kent, OH: Kent State University Press, 1985), 41–52, for succinct summaries of the diplomacy of Greek independence.

18. See Anderson, *The Great Powers and the Near East*, 33–35.

19. "On 3 February 1830, the London Conference issued *the* protocol which established an independent Greek state under the guarantee of the three powers." Petropulos goes on to comment, "The fact that the London Conference made both decisions, without consulting the Greeks, shows how real Allied domination had become" (Petropulos, *Politics and Statecraft in the Kingdom of Greece*, 47–48).

20. The convention was concluded on May 7, 1832, and the exchange of ratifications took place, again in London, on June 30 of that year (PRO: FO, 78/212). Stratford Canning had returned to İstanbul on January 28, 1832.

21. A panoply of issues were dealt with in connection to the establishment of a new Greek state out of Ottoman territory. See BOA, D.BŞM.9720 (A.H. 1246), for information about aid given to refugees from the Morea *(mora muhacirleri)* who had settled in the neighborhood of Eyüp and rented houses at the expense of the government. See also George Gavrilis, *Dynamics of Interstate Boundaries* (Cambridge: Cambridge University Press, 2008).

22. PRO: FO, 78/212, November 27, 1832; PRO: FO, 78/210, May 17 and April 29, 1832.

23. See Crawley, *The Question of Greek Independence,* appendix 6, for the names and dates of service of ambassadors from all relevant states in İstanbul and European capitals at this time.

24. Akif (1787–1845) served as *reis efendi* until 1836.

25. The receiver was known as the *amedçi;* see Gibb and Bowen, *Islamic Society and the West,* 122–23, for an extensive definition. The director of the Office of the Imperial Divan was known as the *beylikçi;* see ibid., 121–22, for an extensive definition. Regarding Akif's rise, see A. H. Tanpınar, "Akif Pasha," in *İA,* 1: 242.

26. Ahmed Fevzi was an Ottoman admiral as of 1833; see Findley, *Bureaucratic Reform in the Ottoman Empire,* 72–73.

27. The chief physician was known as the *hekimbaşı* or the *reis-ül-etıbba.* Avigdor Levy lists the chief physician as a "key position" in the central government in the 1820s, along with, for example, the *şeyh-ül-İslam,* the army judges *(kaziasker),* and the *kadı* of İstanbul. In May 1826, chief physician Mustafa Behcet Efendi was in attendance at the secret meeting to draft a new military law in preparation for the abolition of the Janissary Corps (Levy, "The Officer Corps in Mahmud II's New Ottoman Army," 15, 17). Heyd discusses the role of *ulema,* such as the *şeyh-ül-İslam,* chief physician, and astrologer, not only in court politics but also in diplomatic negotiations. In the late eighteenth century, for instance, the *şeyh-ül-İslam* "took a leading part in official talks and negotiations with foreign diplomats" in the Ottoman capital. Furthermore, while *ulema* "were apparently not willing to serve as visiting or—after the late 18th century—resident diplomatic representatives in Christian countries," they did serve as ambassadors to Persia, and they were "conspicuous among the Ottoman plenipotentiaries at armistice and peace negotiations with European Powers," such as at the Treaties of Bucharest (1812), Akkerman (1826), and Edirne (1829), all of which were attended by a *molla* (Heyd, "The Ottoman Ulema and Westernization," 84–85).

Abdülhak Efendi was the brother of Mustafa Behcet Efendi, and he had assumed the position of chief physician when the latter died in 1828. Abdülhak Efendi served as chief physician, then, from 1828 until 1848, with three interruptions (1837/38–40, when the surgery director *[cerrahhane müdürü]* Ahmed Necib Efendi occupied the post; 1845–48, when İzmirli İsmael Efendi took over from Abdülhak; and in later 1848, when the office passed for the last time from Abdülhak to Salih Efendi). Interestingly, since 1861/62, Rum and Armenian subjects served in this office, such as Marko Paşa (1861/62), Kabalyon Efendi (1876), and Mavroyani (Mavroyeni) Efendi (1876). See Mehmed Süreyya Bey, *Sicill-i Osmani* [Register/index of Ottoman officials], 6 vols. (İstanbul: Kültür Bakanlığı ile Türkiye Ekonomik ve Toplumsal Tarih Vakfı'nın ortak yayınıdır, 1996), 6: 1728–29.

Mustafa Reşit Bey (1800–1858) was later to become Mustafa Reşit Paşa. He was appointed receiver in late 1831 and assumed the post in June 1832. Shortly after, in 1834, he went on to reopen the Ottoman Embassy in Paris, and upon his return to İstanbul he took a leading part in politics, particularly in the Tanzimat, until his death almost twenty-five years later. See Reşat Kaynar, *Mustafa Reşit Paşa ve Tanzimat* (1954; Ankara: Türk Tarih Kurumu Basımevi, 1991); and E. Kuran, "Reşid Paşa," in *İA,* 9: 701–5.

Nuri Efendi was the son of Mustafa Reşit's sister. He would go on to serve as Ottoman ambassador in Paris (December 1839—November 1841). See Sinan Kuneralp, *Son dönem Osmanlı erkan ve ricali (1839-1922): Prosopografik rehber* [Late Ottoman officials: A prosopographic guide] (İstanbul: Isis Press, 1999), 99; and Kaynar, *Mustafa Reşit Paşa ve Tanzimat,* 63.

28. This relationship among *reis efendi,* receiver, and director of the Office of the Imperial Divan can also be deduced from the order of advancement of men such as Akif and

Pertev paşas, who were promoted from director of Divan Office to receiver and finally to *reis efendi*.

29. Heyd, "The Ottoman Ulema and Westernization," 85.

30. The grand vezir, for his part, was occupied with the battle against İbrahim Paşa's forces in Anatolia; by the end of 1832, Grand Vezir Reşit Mehmet Paşa went against İbrahim Paşa at Konya and lost (Dodwell, *The Founder of Modern Egypt*, 115).

31. Ibid., June 7, 1832.

32. Ibid., July 1832.

33. Ibid., July 22, 1832.

34. This they had tried to do before, but in the 1830s they simultaneously engaged in official meetings and used personal direct lines to the sultan.

35. PRO: FO, 78/212, November 27, 1832.

36. See Katerina Gardika, *Prostasia kai eggiyseis: Stadia kai mythoi tes hellenikes ethnikes olokleroses (1821-1920)* [Protection and guarantees: Phases and myths of Greek national integration] (Thessaloniki, 1999), for discussion and documentation of the role of foreign powers and treaties in the establishment and consolidation of the Greek state.

37. Regarding the turbulent relations, in September 1823, for instance, "the island of Samos declare[d] itself independent of the Greek central government—refuses to furnish its quote of money—or to admit the Eparch who has been named its governor—and proclaims equal hostility against the Turks and the Greeks of the continent and of Hydra, Spezzia, and Ipsara. In fact Samos is now blockaded by a squadron from the latter place" (PRO: FO, 78/110, September 25, 1823).

38. BOA, Sisam İradeleri; AMAE, Consular correspondence from the cities of the Ottoman Empire: Constantinople, file D and Samos 1830-35 subfile.

39. PRO: FO, 78/199, June 11, 1831.

40. PRO: FO, 78/210: 55.

41. PRO: FO, 78/212: 101, 252, 331.

42. PRO: FO, 78/221: 51, 175.

43. PRO: FO, 78/223: 138, 141. Ponsouby was British Ambassador from November 27, 1832, until 1841, when Stratford Canning resumed the post.

44. Ibid., 141.

45. David Urquhart, *The Sultan Mahmoud and Mehemet Ali Pasha* (London: J. Ridgway, 1835), 64, my emphasis.

46. Toledano, "Muhammad Ali Pasha," 426.

47. Mehmet Ali also had direct contact with European powers (Austria and Britain) in 1827 as they weighed the possibility of military intervention on the side of the Greeks. See Dodwell, *The Founder of Modern Egypt*, 89.

48. See Avigdor Levy, "The Officer Corps in Mahmud II's New Ottoman Army, 1826-1839" 21-39, for abundant evidence of the nonfunctioning imperial military in the 1820s and 1830s. R

49. See Toledano, "Muhammad Ali Pasha," 426. See also Levy, "The Officer Corps in Mahmud II's New Ottoman Army," 17: "The projected military reorganization could thus be presented not as an imitation of Western-Christian patterns but as the adoption of a modern Islamic method."

50. PRO: FO 78/221, February 23, 1833.

51. Muraviev arrived in Alexandria on January 12, 1833 (Dodwell, *The Founder of Modern Egypt*, 114).

52. Halil Rıfat arrived on January 21, 1833 (ibid.). He was accompanied by then Amedçi Reşit Bey, later to become Reşit Paşa.

53. PRO: FO, 78/222, March 11, 1833.

54. In fact, Russian statesmen exploited fears of Mehmet Ali as a Muslim by spreading rumors that he and his son were planning to depopulate the Morea of Christians and repopulate it with Africans. See Schroeder, *The Transformation of European Politics*, 642.

55. AMAE, Correspondance diplomatique, MD Turquie: tome 21, docs. 43, 56, Boislecomte report to Broglie on his conversation with Vogorides, dated November 25, 1833.

56. Urquhart, *The Sultan Mahmoud and Mehemet Ali Pasha*, 6–7, my emphasis. Dodwell made the same point one century later when he wrote, "The pasha might claim to be regarded with the same sympathy as Europe had accorded to the Belgians and the Greeks, but even his persuasive tongue could not disguise the fact that he was fighting for his own hand. He did not represent any nation struggling to be free. *His military superiority over the Turks could give no moral claim to special consideration. His only moral claim—if so it can be called—lay in the superior order, justice, and regularity which it might be expected he would introduce into his new conquests as he had introduced them into Egypt. But even then, since his methods would certainly be those of oriental administration, western statesmen would still find opportunities for criticism and doubt. Political expediency was therefore the only standpoint from which the matter could reasonably be discussed at Paris and London*" (Dodwell, *The Founder of Modern Egypt*, 120–21, my emphasis).

57. See Georges Drouin, *La mission du Baron de Boislecomte: L'Égypte et la Syrie en 1833* (Cairo: Imprimerie de l'Institut français d'archéologie orientale du Caire, 1927), introduction, for a discussion of French ties with and sympathy for Mehmet Ali.

58. BOA, C., Hariciye: 2500: "Beyoğlunda Asmalı Mescit civarında yeni yapılan . . . dükkanında yunani muteber tüccardan Cani Hrisodilonunun nakli—cem'i duvvelde bir karışıklık var. Ve cümlesi tedarikte oluyor. Ve Mehmet Ali Paşa dahi tedarikte oluyor. Bakalım kabak kimin başına patlayacak."

59. See AMAE, Correspondance diplomatique, MD Turquie: tome 21, docs. 43, 56.

60. Dodwell, *The Founder of Modern Egypt*, 122–23.

61. Drouin, *La mission du Baron de Boislecomte*, lvii.

62. Ibid., iv.

63. PRO: FO, 78/212, Mandeville to Palmerston, December 19, 1832.

64. Ibid.

65. BOA, HAT: 20168. Unfortunately, only the year, in *hicri*, not the day or month, is given on the document: 1248, which corresponds to 1832–33 on the Christian calendar. Because of the topics discussed, it seems likely that the memo is from 1832, before the offer and acceptance of Russian military aid to the Ottomans. Other conversations, with Canning, with the French chargé d'affaires (presumably de Varenne), and with the French consul in Alexandria (Mimaut) are mentioned indirectly in the report as well.

66. Ibid.

67. See also BOA, C., Dahiliye: 12037, for scenarios being discussed in İstanbul coffeehouses.

68. BOA, HAT: 20168.

69. See BOA, C., Dahiliye: 12037; and BOA, C., Hariciye: 2500.

70. A story of Husrev Paşa's intrigues against his own protégé, Halil Rıfat, was told to the sultan and then reported by an informant, who had been told the story by Mehmet Efendi, the clerk working at the Seraskerate.

71. AMAE, Correspondance diplomatique, tome 21: docs. 43, 56.

72. Ibid.

73. Ibid., "Rapports avec le drogman de la Porte, Vogoridi, prince de Samos," November 25, 1833.

74. Ibid.

75. Ibid.

76. Ibid.

77. The term *diplomatic corps* is in quotation marks, first, because this is the term Boislecomte used in his dispatch (ibid.) and, second, because, as far as we know, the diplomatic corps did not yet exist as a formal entity (see Findley, *Bureaucratic Reform in the Ottoman Empire*, 132). I argue, for one thing, that this official social gathering was an indication of a new culture of formal diplomacy and, for another, that such official gatherings could also be (and were) used to conduct unofficial politics, as shown by Vogorides' actions. Contrast this fête held by the sultan to one referred to by Rev. R. Walsh on his sojourn in İstanbul in 1821. He refers to having met Constantine Muruzi, grand dragoman, days before the outbreak of Greek insurrections, at a "Frank party, a circumstance of social intercourse not usual with the Greeks" (Walsh, *A Residence at Constantinople*, 1: 308).

78. It is unclear at what point after the 1820s these fêtes began, but from Boislecomte's passing mention of the gathering, this particular event does not seem to have been the first of its kind. It would perhaps be misguided to look for a smooth development of social gatherings such as these, for the politics of diplomacy under discussion here, like the new civil-bureaucratic elite, which are the subject of Carter Findley's studies, "emerged with relative abruptness and acquired a broad-ranging influence" (Findley, *Bureaucratic Reform in the Ottoman Empire*, 155). Levy notes that Sultan Mahmud II began holding receptions and concerts after the 1829 Treaty of Edirne but does not specify a date for the first of these (Levy, "The Officer Corps in Mahmud II's New Ottoman Army," 30).

79. AMAE, Correspondance diplomatique, tome 21: doc. 4: "Je n'avais pas un occasion de reconnaître l'effet que mon langage porte au Divan par différens canaux y produisait, quand arriva la fête donnée par le Sultan au corps diplomatique à *Kiat-ana [sic]*."

80. Ibid. While Boislecomte does not specify, we presume either that the gathering included a receiving line, where he was formally introduced to Ottoman ministers and diplomats, or that it was the kind of party where guests mingled freely.

81. Ibid., my emphasis.

82. Ibid.

83. See Christine Philliou, "The Community of Izmir/Smyrna in 1821: Social Reality and National Ideologies," MA thesis, Princeton University, 1998, for a more in-depth discussion of Blaque's time in İzmir and his newspaper there, *Spectateur Oriental*. See also PRO: FO, 78/200, October 11, 1831.

84. PRO: FO, 78/212, Mandeville to Palmerston, December 19, 1832.

85. AMAE, Correspondance diplomatique, tome 21: docs. 43, 56.

86. Ibid.

87. PRO: FO, 78/222, March 11, 1833: "The Russian Admiral accompanied by some of the principal officers of the squadron which is still at Büyükdere went to the Imperial Mint and were received there in a distinguished manner by the Director [Düzoglu] and Monsieur [Vogorides], who accompanied the Russian officers in their visit to this establishment. Several medals in gold were struck upon this occasion and distributed to the Admiral and to the officers of his suite."

88. In reference to the second Mehmet Ali crisis, in 1838–39, Philip Mosely noted, "England, alarmed at the danger that the straits might pass into Russia's direct possession, was directly injured by the growing power of Mohamed Ali, whose new state straddled the two chief trade routes between Great Britain and India. *It was certain in 1838 that England would not be, as in 1833, an idle spectator of what might occur in the Levant*" (Mosely, *Russian Diplomacy and the Opening of the Eastern Question*, 6).

89. Here I make the correlation between discussions and promises of "territorial integrity" for the Ottoman Empire, on the one hand, and the decision to uphold the "political integrity"— that is, the formal structure of politics—on the other.

90. Levy, "The Officer Corps in Mahmud II's New Ottoman Army," 29.

91. Findley, *Ottoman Civil Officialdom*, 73.

92. See Levy, "The Ottoman Ulema and Westernization," 13–39, especially 29; and I. Sungu, "Mahmud II'nin, İzzet Molla, ve Asakir-e Mansure hakkında bir hattı," *Tarih Vesikaları* 1 (1941): 162–83 (a document about Mahmud II, İzzet Molla, and the post-janissary army [Triumphant Soldiers of Muhammad]).

93. Findley, *Ottoman Civil Officialdom*, 73.

94. See ibid., 74.

95. The Bagno was run by Admiral Ahmed Fevzi Paşa, an ally of Akif's (ibid.).

96. Ibid., 70–80.

97. Ibid., 135.

98. Ibid.

99. Regarding the translation service personnel, see Findley, *Bureaucratic Reform in the Ottoman Empire*; and Findley, *Ottoman Civil Officialdom*. Keçecizade Fuat was the son of Keçecizade İzzet Molla, who had served as *kadı* of Galata, been an ally of Halet Efendi, and then a supporter of janissary reforms. See Bayat, *Keçecizade Mehmed Fuat*; and Mardin, *The Genesis of Young Ottoman Thought*. Regarding Ahmet Vefik, see Ahmed Hamdi Tanpınar, "Ahmet Pasha," in *İA*, 1: 207–10; see also Sir A. Henry Layard, *Sir A. Henry Layard: Autobiography and Letters from His Childhood until His Appointment as H.M. Ambassador at Madrid*, 2 vols. Edited by William N. Bruce (New York: J. Murray, 1903), 2: 47, for biographical information and reminiscences of evenings spent with Ahmet Vefik and his father in their İstanbul *konak* in the late 1830s.

100. Ibid.

101. Findley, *Bureaucratic Reform in the Ottoman Empire*, 139.

102. Findley, "The Foundation of the Ottoman Foreign Ministry: The Beginnings of Bureaucratic Reform under Selim III and Mahmud II," in *IJMES* 3, no. 4 (1972): 409.

103. Ibid., 410.

104. Ibid., 409–10; Levy, "The Ottoman Ulema and the Military Reforms of Sultan Mahmud II," 31.

105. PRO: FO, 78/209, March 17, 1832.

106. Walsh, *A Residence at Constantinople,* 1: 345.

107. Findley, *Ottoman Civil Officialdom,* 135–36. This was Yanko Mavroyeni, the nephew of the legendary dragoman of the fleet and *voyvoda* Nicholas Mavroyeni, who died in 1791.

108. Findley, *Bureaucratic Reform in the Ottoman Empire,* 136. Mustafa Reşit Paşa had reportedly learned French during his tenure as ambassador in France in 1834 and not before, when he had served as receiver and met regularly with foreign statesmen. See Kaynar, *Mustafa Reşit Paşa,* 64.

## BIOGRAPHY OF AN EMPIRE V

1. Circa 1828 (A.H. 1244), Grand Vezir Mehmed Selim (Benderli Mehmed Selim Sirri Paşa, grand vezir, September 1824—October 26, 1828) requested (and was granted) pardon for "sabık Divan-ı Hümayun tercümanı Yakovaki ve Boğdan Kaymakamı sabık Istefanaki" (former grand dragoman Yakovaki [Argypropoulo] and former Moldavian Kaymakam Stefanaki) because of their experience, loyalty, and moral rectitude (TKSA, Evrak: 9241).

2. Dimitrios Stamatopoulos, "Othomanikes metarrythmyseis kai Oikoumeniko Patriarcheio: Ho politikos antagonismos gia ten epharmoge ton genikon kanonismon" [Ottoman reforms and the ecumenical patriarchate: The political contest over the promulgation of the general regulations], PhD diss., Aristotle University, 1998, 29 n. 82. Sturdza says that Vogorides was sent to St. Petersburg with Halil Paşa for preliminary negotiations for "a peace," and upon his return Vogorides was given a *nişan* (honor, decoration) and was involved again for preliminary negotiations for the Treaty of Edirne (1829) (Sturdza, *Dictionnaire historique et généalogique,* 448). The earlier peace Sturdza refers to could be the Treaty of Akkerman, but Sturdza does not mention Vogorides' involvement in the 1833 negotiations.

3. If Vogorides did go to Petersburg in 1833, it was presumably in the spring or summer of that year, for he was certainly in İstanbul in March, when he received the Russian admiral at the imperial mint, and through the autumn, when he was meeting with French envoy Boislecomte (PRO: FO, 78/222; AMAE, Correspondance diplomatique, tome 21: docs. 43, 56).

4. Stamatopoulos, "Othomanikes metarrythmyseis kai Oikoumeniko Patriarcheio," 29 n. 82; Sturdza, *Dictionnaire historique et généalogique,* 448.

5. AMAE, Consular correspondence from the cities of the Ottoman Empire: Constantinople, file D: Samos 1830–35 subfile, 123.

6. In an Ottoman communiqué he wrote in the 1840s regarding the history and politics of Moldavia and Wallachia, Vogorides explained the establishment of the autonomous principality of Samos and the rationale of fixing the tribute in proportion to the population, which would be four hundred thousand *guruş* for Samos according to the same formula that had fixed the tribute at four million *guruş* for the Danubian Principalities (MP, Ottoman file II: 2: 18).

7. See PRO: FO, 192/102, February 22, 1833, Spathi (British consul at Samos) to Mandeville.

8. Yanko served for a time in the translation sections of the Ottoman embassies in Paris and London before being declared disturbed (the Ottoman *muhtal-al-demağ* and Greek

*phrenovlaves*) and sent to Samos in the late 1840s with a cleric named Gavril, for a "change of air" (BOA, İrade: Hariciye, 2078). Yanko was eventually sent to Vienna, treated there by doctors, and died in that city in 1867 (Sturdza, *Dictionnaire historique et généalogique*, 449). Constantine's full name and title were Constantine (Kostaki) Musurus Paşa (1807–91). His father, Pavlos, was a merchant from Crete who had migrated to İstanbul in the late eighteenth century and entered the service of Wallachian *voyvodas*. Constantine had accompanied the Austrian diplomat Prokesch-Osten on a reconnaissance tour through the Balkans and in 1832 entered the retinue of Vogorides. After his term as governor in Samos, Musurus became the Ottoman representative in Athens (1840–47), Vienna (1848), and London (1851–85). See Sinan Kuneralp, "Bir Osmanlı diplomatı: Kostaki Musurus Paşa, 1807–1891" [An Ottoman diplomat: Kostaki Musurus Paşa], *Belleten* 3 (1970): 421–35; and Philliou, "The Paradox of Perceptions."

9. Alexandros Photiades had long been the first secretary at the İstanbul patriarchate and had collaborated with Vogorides in Church politics in İstanbul. Later (in a ceremony attended by Sultan Abdülmecit in 1851) he would marry off his son Yanko to Vogorides' daughter Maria. Yanko, in turn, would go on to serve as Ottoman minister in Athens (1860–70) and in Rome (1886) and as governor of Autonomous Crete in the early 1890s. See Sturdza, *Dictionnaire historique et généalogique*, 466. Gabriel Krestides (1817–98), a.k.a. Krustevich and Krestovich, was a fellow hellenized Bulgarian, also from the village of Kotel. He had attended the Patriarchate Academy in the Kuruçeşme quarter of İstanbul, presumably in the 1830s, and had continued on to study in Paris, funded by Vogorides himself (Gedeon, *Mneia ton pro emou*, 293–95). Demetrios Ioannides was the uncle of Constantine and Pavlos Musurus and possibly of the same Ioannides clan as the cleric Anthimos VI Koutalianos. Ioannis Adamantides was reportedly Musurus's right-hand man, following the latter as the first secretary of his Athens Embassy in the late 1830s and charged with special missions (MP, Musurus-Vogorides correspondence: file IV: 18, 21, 29).

10. On bringing the monasteries under the direct authority of the patriarchate, see EPI: codex IH': 144–46, 1836. On changing the archiepiscopate to a metropolitanate, see ibid., codex K': 245 (2), June 1841.

11. Ibid., codex KΔ': 75–76, October 1844.

12. MP, Musurus-Vogorides correspondence: XIX: 156. The term *phanariot* was also pejorative in the modern Greek state, as antagonisms between *autochthones* and *heterochthones* in the Greek civil service and government raged. See Helle Skopetea, *To protypo basileio kai he megale idea: Opseis tou ethnikou provlematos sten Hellada, 1830–1880* [The model kingdom and the great idea] (Athens: Ekdoseis Polytypo, 1988); and Petropulos, *Politics and Statecraft in the Kingdom of Greece.*

13. See Alexis Sevastakis, *Hoi Karmanioloi sten epanastase tes Samou—Ioannes Lekates* [The Karmanioloi in the revolution of Samos] (Athens, 1980).

14. MP, Musurus-Vogorides correspondence: microfilm no. 26. Buyukli had been imprisoned in 1835 in Anatolia and then moved to Samos, where lived until his death in 1846. See Mercia Macdermott, *A History of Bulgaria, 1393–1885* (London: Allen and Unwin, 1962), 112–15.

15. After Vogorides (1833–50) the following men, many of familiar family names, served as prince of Samos, all of whom save Kallimaki resided on the island during their tenure:

Alexander Kallimaki (1850–54), Ioannes Ghika (1854–59), Miltiades Aristarchi (1859–66), Pavlos Musurus (1866–73), Georgios Georgiades (1873 and 1907–8), Constantine Adosides (1873–74 and 1879–85), Constantine Photiades (1874–79), Alexander Karatheodori (1885–93), Georgios Verovitch (1894–96), Stephanos Musurus (1896–99), Constantine Vagiannes (1899–1900), Michael Gregoriades (1900–1902), Alexander Mavroyeni (1902–4), Ioannis Bithynos (1904–6), Constantine Karatheodori (1906–7), Andreas Kopases (1908–12), and Gregorios Begleres (1912–13) (Alexis Alexandris, "Hoi Hellenes sten Hyperesia tes Othomanikes Autokratorias: 1850–1922" [Greeks in the service of the Ottoman Empire], *Deltio tes Historikes kai Ethnologikes Hetaireias tes Hellados* 23 [1980]: 365–404; Blancard, *Les Mavroyènis*, 2: 559). In 2001, one İstanbul Greek even recalled with pride having attended the girls' school attached to Robert College with the daughter of the last bey of Samos (Gregorios Begleres), implying that the position carried near-royal status.

16. See Rangavi, *Livre d'Or,* v ff.

17. Ibid., "Aristarchis" entry.

18. Ibid.

19. BOA, C., Hariciye: 2500.

20. BOA, HAT: 21659 (A.H. 1248; M. 1833).

21. Layard, *Sir A. Henry Layard,* 2: 65–66.

22. See Findley, *Ottoman Civil Officialdom,* 74, especially n. 112, wherein Findley cites a private note from Ponsonby to Palmerston in July 1837 requesting a "very handsome present in money" for "Voghorhedes, Prince of Samos," who "has immense influence just now with Pertev Pasha . . . and is extremely well with the Sultan also."

23. On the appointment as special counselor to Ahmet Fevzi Paşa, see Rangavi, *Livre d'Or,* "Aristarchis" entry. See Findley, *Ottoman Civil Officialdom,* 78, especially nn. 136 and 137, for Aristarchi's role in court factions.

24. Findley, *Ottoman Civil Officialdom,* 78.

25. Ibid. Findley cites an Austrian memo from Baron Stürmer to Metternich in August 1839, which reported that Aristarchi had been receiving three thousand *guruş* per month from Russia.

26. On Prince Milosh and Serbian developments, which were going on in parallel with Greek, Moldavian-Wallachian, Egyptian, and Samos negotiations, see, for example, Leopold Ranke, *The History of Servia and the Servian Revolution, with a Sketch of the Insurrection in Bosnia,* trans. Alexander Kerr (London: H. G. Bohn, 1853), chapters 18–23.

27. Lay notables were known as, for instance, *prokritoi, archontes, prouchontes;* upper clergy were known as *gerontes;* and leaders of the guilds *(esnaf* and *syntechnies)* were known as *oustades,* from the Turkish *usta.*

28. Gedeon, *Mneia ton pro emou,* 426–27. See p. 427 for a picture of the Sublime Porte, with a procession marching toward it, in 1802.

29. Gedeon's own father had arrived in İstanbul from Leros (where he had been a ship-builder) in 1828 at the age of sixteen and entered the service of Nikitaides, a palace architect—yet another example of how the networks from the provinces to the Ottoman metropolis continued to function in the 1820s and 1830s (ibid., 62). This also seems to have been the same Hatzi (Hacı) Nikoli who built an Aristarchi relative's house in Arnavutköy in the 1830s.

30. Ibid.

31. See Macfarlane, *Constantinople in 1828,* 281–93, for a list of clerics and lay phanariots encountered by Macfarlane in 1828.

32. Gedeon, *Mneia ton pro emou,* 190–91.

33. Later, and in a very different political and historical context, the "Mixed National Council" was formed out of the Community Council, in 1862 (ibid., 189).

34. Stamatopoulos, "Othomanikes metarrythmyseis kai Oikoumeniko Patriarcheio," 29; Rangavi, *Livre d'Or,* "Aristarchis" entry.

35. See PRO: FO, 78/109, July 1822.

36. PRO: FO, 78/114. Regarding Aristarchi's meeting with Patriarch Anthimos III for the Episcopal establishment of the Ionian Islands, the British envoy wrote, "The Patriarch is a very excellent, but in truth, a very troublesome person. He is exceedingly jealous of his spiritual jurisdiction within the Ionian states [under British rule at this time], which it must be confessed will be circumscribed within very narrow limits by the arrangement I am charged to carry through" (ibid.).

37. PRO: FO, 78/356. The quotation continues, "The same man who accompanied Achmed *[sic]* (now Capitan Pasha) on his Embassy to St. Petersburg and who aided more than anybody to carry through the convention signed there in 1834. He continues to direct Achmed Pasha in that subserviency to Russia which is evident in his conduct. The Patriarch owing his place to the intrigues and money of Mr. Aristarcki is used by him to extort money from the Greek Community, Ecclesiastical and lay, and to serve all Russian political objects."

38. See EPI: codex IZ´: 40 (4), document to Metropolitan Gregorios of Chios ordering the income from the exarch of Volissos (village in the north of Chios) to be paid to M. Logotheti . . . , October 13, 1830; and from 1836, another patriarchate document: to Gregorios, Metropolitan of Drostra, regarding the request from M. Logothetis Nich. Aristarchis, exarch of Kavarna (ibid., codex IH´: 278–79).

39. Sturdza defines the office of exarch as follows: "ecclesiastical dignitary, most often a Metropolitan, whose jurisdiction covers a province" (Sturdza, *Dictionnaire historique et généalogique,* 638). He offers the modern-day example of Archbishop Makarios of Cyprus, who was referred to as the exarch of that island. Another well-known example is that of the Bulgarian exarchate (1870–), which broke off from the Orthodox patriarchate and whose leader was referred to as exarch so as not to challenge the supremacy of the patriarch. Regarding the association of the offices of exarch and grand *logothete,* a patriarchal letter in 1811, for instance, announced the grand *logothete* Alexander Manos to be the exarch of the area around Lake Pourous, next to Xanthi (EPI: codex IB´, 104–6). In 1819, an order was issued specifying the rights of a grand *logothete* with respect to the proceeds he would receive from his exarchate and its clergy (ibid., codex IΓ´: 175).

40. See Ioannis Psychares, *Epistolai I. Psychare (ephorou ton Chion eis Constantinoupole) pros Demogerontian Chiou* [Letters of I. Psychares (agent for Chiotes in İstanbul) to the Demogerontia of Chios] (Chios, Greece, 1962).

41. EPI: codex K´: 152.

42. Stamatopoulos, "Othomanikes Metarrythmyseis kai Oikoumeniko Patriarcheio," 29; Manouel Io Gedeon, "Kanonismon Apopeira," *Ecclesiastike Aletheia* 43 (1919): 215–16.

43. Ibid.; "Community Treasury" is the translation of "Tameio tou Koinou."

44. Manouel Io Gedeon, *Engrapha patriarchika kai synodika peri tou boulgarikou zetem-atos (1852–1873)* (İstanbul: Ek tou Patriarchik. Typ., 1908), introduction.

45. See EPI: codex IΘ': 136 (2): "Receipt of payment to Hatzi Nikoli Kalfa for Elengo (Eleni) Aristarchou, spouse of Grand Postelnik Soterios Kalliades, for building her house in Arnavutköy" (1839–40). While the word *gambros* in Greek, like the Turkish *damat*, can mean both "brother-in-law" and "son-in-law," Kalliades must have been Aristarchi's brother-in-law, given Aristarchi's age and recent marriage in 1833–34.

46. Stamatopoulos, "Othomanikes Metarrythmyseis kai Oikoumeniko Patriarcheio," 29–30.

47. Anthimos VI Koutalianos was a member of the Ioannides family and hailed from the small island of Koutali (T. Kaşık ada), in the Sea of Marmara. He was a close associate of Vogorides and Kostaki Musurus and was an important figure, on the side of Vogorides, to co-opt the movement for a church in İstanbul in which Bulgarian would be spoken in the late 1840s.

48. See ibid., 31, especially n. 93, wherein Stamatopoulos cites Gedeon's speculation that the removal of Gregorios in 1840 was the result of upper clergy's objections to their exploitation at the hands of Aristarchi and Kalliades.

49. Gedeon, *Patriarchikoi pinakes*, 293.

50. BOA, İrade Series: Mesail-i Mühimme: 916. This was at the end of the patriarchate of Anthimos VI, a known Vogorides collaborator and notorious for his intrigues. See Gedeon, *Mneia ton pro emou*, 687–88, where he calls Anthimos *"poneiros,"* or "sneaky."

51. Soutzos, *Mémoires du prince Nicolas Soutzo*, 62.

52. Ibid., 64.

53. See R. Florescu, *Essays on Romanian History* (İaşi, Romania; Portland, OR: Center for Romanian Studies, 1999), chapter 19, on the Règlement Organique.

54. Soutzos, *Mémoires du prince Nicolas Soutzo*, 64.

55. Ibid., 95.

56. Nicholas Soutso, son of Michael Soutso, the last phanariot *voyvoda* of Wallachia, proudly stated, "In fixing my domicile in Moldavia, I enjoyed the rights of a native, which, according to the anterior customs consecrated by the Règlement, were given to those who had married natives; I found myself, consequently, eligible for all public employment" (ibid., 98). See also Zallony, *Essai sur les fanariotes*, 25, for the importance of İstanbul and Greek-identified phanariots marrying the daughters of native boyars before 1821.

57. Even when Ghika, the new Moldavian *voyvoda*, took power in 1849, he would "in his political perplexities . . . consult ordinarily with the Greeks who had his confidence and on whose discretion he could depend: these were Mavrocordatos the father, his son-in-law, my [Nicholas Soutso's] brother, myself, and sometimes Alexander Muruzi" (Soutzos, *Mémoires du prince Nicolas Soutzo*, 170).

58. One of the first acts of Prince Ghika, before leaving İstanbul for his post in 1822, was "to procure a divorce from his wife, the daughter of the late [phanariot] Prince Hantzerli [Hançerli], who fell a victim, some years ago, to the vengeance of the celebrated Hüseyin Pasha. The Caimacam *[kaymakam]* just sent to Wallachia, is the bearer of this Intelligence to the Princess, and he is also charged with orders to remove her immediately from Bucharest" (PRO: FO, 78/109).

59. PRO: FO 78/109, July 18, 1822.

60. Soutzos, *Mémoires du prince Nicolas Soutzo*, 122–23.

61. In the 1826 Treaty of Akkerman, *hospodar*s or *voyvoda*s were to be elected from "among the old and most capable native boiars *[sic]*," by the Moldavian and Wallachian Divans, or councils, and were to be approved by the Porte on the basis of seven-year terms. In the 1829 Treaty of Edirne, life terms for *voyvoda*s were established, and any removal of a *voyvoda* had to meet with Russian approval. At this time, the Ottoman grain monopoly in the principalities was ended. Finally, at the 1834 Convention of St. Petersburg, Russian troops were to be evacuated within two months, the tribute to the Porte was fixed at three million piastres, and Russia became the spokesman for Moldavia and Wallachia. Seton-Watson, *A History of the Roumanians*, 203, 206, 212.

62. Soutzos, *Mémoires du prince Nicolas Soutzo*, 103.

63. See Sturdza, *Dictionnaire historique et généalogique*, 466; and appendix A for the Vogorides family tree.

64. Rangavi, *Livre d'Or*, "Aristarchis" entry.

65. Alexander Ghika was the brother of Gregory Ghika, who had been *voyvoda* of Wallachia in the turbulent 1820s (1822–28). Alexander Ghika continued as *voyvoda* of Wallachia from 1834 until 1842, when he was replaced by George Bibescu. See Seton-Watson, *A History of the Roumanians*, 214.

66. Soutzos, *Mémoires du prince Nicolas Soutzo*, 108.

67. Ibid., 147; MP, Musurus-Vogorides correspondence: microfilm no. 25.

68. Despite Vogorides' efforts to gain access to Moldavian politics with "local" boyar status, he harbored resentment and hatred for the local boyars as a group, for the role they apparently played in the Hypsilanti-Soutso "apostasy" in 1821 (MP, Musurus-Vogorides correspondence: microfilm no. 29).

69. See, for instance, Nicolae Iorga, *Byzantium after Byzantium*, trans. Laura Treptow (Iaşi, Romania; Portland, OR: Center for Romanian Studies, 2000).

70. On the mediation by *voyvoda*s, see Georg Cioran, *Scheseis ton roumanikon Choron meta Tou Atho kai de ton monon Koutloumousiou, Lauras, Docheiariou kai Haghiou Panteleimonon he ton roson* [Relations of the Romanian lands with Mt. Athos and its Koutloumous, Laura, Docheiariou, and Haghiou Panteleimon of the Russian monasteries], in *Texte und Forschungen zur byzantinisch-neugriechischen Philologie*, no. 25 (Athens: Verlag der byzantinisch-neugriechischen Jahrbuecher, 1938), 88–89. On the mediation by the İstanbul patriarchate, see EPI: codex KH': passim: various documents. On the adjudication of disputes between boyars and abbots, see EPI: codex KH': 124.

71. Cioran, *Scheseis ton roumanikon Choron meta Tou Atho*, 89. Cioran demonstrates the significance of the Moldavian and Wallachian monastic holdings for Mt. Athos just before 1821, for instance; the *voyvoda*s would oversee the collection of proceeds from the monastic holdings and distribute them to Mt. Athos, out of which the Mt. Athos monasteries would pay their yearly taxes to the Ottoman state, the salaries of their İstanbul and Salonica agents, the travel expenses of their monastic personnel, the salary of their Ottoman administrator, sums of money to the *"epistates"* of each of the twenty monasteries, their yearly taxes to the collector for Mt. Athos, and the monthly salaries of the four *serdar*s who composed the "Albanian guard."

72. EPI: codex KZ': 22. Vogorides, too, used this passage in the apologia he wrote in the early 1850s. In Vogorides' text, the passage becomes, "Enlightened by the theory of the evangelical Logos, which commands us to render unto Caesar what is Caesar's (idol-worshipers though they were then)" (MP, Musurus-Vogorides correspondence: IX: 69).

73. EPI: codex KΓ': 289.

74. Ibid.

75. Sturdza, *Dictionnaire historique et généalogique*, 448; EPI: codex KH': 154.

76. EPI: codex KE': 3.

77. Sturdza, *Dictionnaire historique et généalogique*, 448.

78. In 1848, for example, when Vogorides' son-in-law Michael Sturdza had lost the *voyvodaship* of Moldavia, the new *voyvoda* (Ghika) and his cronies apparently tried to wrest the position of *kapıkahya* from Vogorides. Vogorides writes, "Thank God and the beneficent insistence of our Reşit Paşa Efendi, things have calmed down" (MP, Musurus-Vogorides correspondence: microfilm no. 29). Under the new *voyvodaship* of Gregorios Ghika, Vogorides' son Aleko was appointed *kapıkahya*, with Reşit Paşa's sanction. Ottoman authorities still held on to the customs of the old investiture ceremony, because Vogorides noted who had been appointed *davetçi*, or inviter for the new *voyvoda* initiates: for Wallachia, the *davetçi* was the *teşrifatçı* Kamil Bey, and for Moldavia it was Nürettin Bey, the *tercüman vekili*, or dragoman.

79. Ibid., microfilm no. 25.

80. The *mabeyn*, meaning "in between," was the room between the inner and outer areas *(haremlik* and *selamlık)* of the palace. Since that was the space where visitors were received and matters of foreign politics conducted, Vogorides and others referred to the palace itself as the *mabeyn*.

81. MP, Musurus-Vogorides correspondence: microfilm no. 26.

82. Ibid., microfilm no. 32.

83. On Vogorides' requests for promotions, see, for instance, ibid., microfilm no. 26: "Regarding your *nişan* [honor/medal of honor], I beg you to send me the second *'resmi'* ["official," as in official request], as I wrote to you before. I never cease, however, to constantly send requests to the Darphane [imperial mint] asking for the striking of your medal to be done faster. . . . I did hear that it should be struck in the next few days and will be sent to the Sublime Porte." Regarding his connections at the imperial mint, Vogorides was a close ally of the Düzoğlu family of Armenian jewelers and bankers, members of which ran the imperial mint in the 1830s. The Düzoğlu home was in fact on the same (Musurus-owned) estate as the Vogorides home in Arnavutköy, on the Bosphorus.

84. On the establishment of the system of ranks, see Levy, "Ottoman ulema and the Military Reforms of Sultan Mahmud II," 31.

85. A Greek under Austrian protection, Baltazzi was described by Vogorides in 1844 as "today the first friend and counselor of the Maliye Nazırı." See MP, Musurus-Vogorides correspondence: microfilm no. 25, October 1844. "Vogorides raised Musurus's salary, as Ottoman ambassador in Athens, from his other son-in-law, the 'Boğdan bey,' or Michael Sturdza" (ibid., microfilm no. 26).

86. Ibid., microfilm no. 32.

87. The Supreme Council of Judicial Ordinances, this "collegial body with legislative pow-

ers" was founded in 1838 and "functioned as a supreme court of appeal and as the excheq-uer and audit department" and as an advisory body for Mahmud II. At its inception it in-cluded five members and met "at the ancient Kubbealtı section of Top Kapı Palace" (Selçuk Akşin Sömel, *Historical Dictionary of the Ottoman Empire* [Lanham, MD: Scarecrow Press, 2003], 275). For mention of Vogorides' appointment to the council in 1856, see Davison, *Reform in the Ottoman Empire*, 93.

88. *"kai na pragmatopoiesei to anexarteton tes Krataias emon Vasileias"* (MP, Musurus-Vogorides correspondence: microfilm no. 29).

89. Ibid.

90. BOA, İrade: Dahiliye, 7225. While the document does not specify which home of Vogorides, presumably the banquet was at his home in Arnavutköy, on the grounds of the Musurus estate. Members of the diplomatic corps at the banquet included Mumtaz Efendi, Muhtar Bey, and Sarım Paşa, for instance.

91. These events were known as "Ta Mousourika," or "the Musurus events."

92. Quoted phrase is from MP, Musurus-Vogorides correspondence: microfilm no. 27.

6. IN THE EYE OF THE STORM

Epigraph source: MP, Musurus-Vogorides correspondence: file IX: 69, November 1852.

1. See Goldfrank, *The Origins of the Crimean War*, 103, for a reference to Wellington's funeral in late November 1852.

2. MP, Musurus-Vogorides correspondence: microfilm 29, November 23, 1851.

3. See Mardin, *The Genesis of Young Ottoman Thought*, 133, for a discussion of Young Ottoman notions about history. He points to an article written by Namık Kemal in *Hürriyet* in 1868, titled "Hubb ul-Watan min el-iman." See also Albert Hourani, *Arabic Thought in the Liberal Age 1798–1939* (Cambridge, U.K.: Cambridge U. Press, 1983), p. 101, and Ussama Makdisi, *Artillery of Heaven: American Missionaries and the Failed Conversion of the Middle East* (Ithaca and London: Cornell Univ. Press), p. 207, for Butrus al-Bustani's use of this hadith post-1860.

4. MP, Musurus-Vogorides correspondence: microfilm 29, November 3, 1851.

5. In the 1840s, controversies had also arisen—and been contained to the Ottoman arena—regarding Armenian claims to the same Holy Sites. In that case, the Ottoman central state had consulted prominent Ottoman Christians associated with the Orthodox patriarchate to resolve the issue. In 1846, Nicholas Aristarchi and Vogorides were both asked by the Ottoman foreign minister (Ali Efendi)—in a request sent through the İstanbul patriarchate—to give their opinion regarding the matter of the keys to the outer door of Bethlehem, which was going to be given to the Armenians, and the matter of appointing an Ottoman guard for the church "like the one at the Holy Sepulchre." EPI: codex KE': 3.

6. R. W. Seton-Watson, "The Origins of the Crimean War," in *The Origins of the Crimean War*, ed. Bryson D. Gooch (Lexington, MA: Heath and Co., 1969), 25.

7. While there was a Roman Catholic population in the Ottoman Empire, its constituents did not have the institutional, and therefore the political, presence in the sphere of Ottoman governance that the Orthodox Christian population had. The Orthodox Christian popula-

tion was by far larger, more dispersed throughout Ottoman territories, and more politically significant, even if the calculus of multistate diplomacy was coming to rival that of domestic Ottoman governance, giving more weight to Catholic claims.

8. A. J. P. Taylor, for instance, argues that the Crimean War followed from the events of 1848, writing, "British opinion would never have turned so harshly against Russia had it not been for Austria's victory in Italy, and, still more, Russia's intervention in Hungary. The Crimean War was fought for the sake of Europe rather than for the Eastern Question; it was fought against Russia, not in favor of Turkey." Through this prism, Christian subjects of the Ottoman Empire do not even deserve mention. A. J. P. Taylor, *The Struggle for Mastery in Europe 1848–1918* (Oxford: Clarendon Press of Oxford University Press, 1971), 61.

9. See, for instance, ibid.; Bryson D. Gooch, "A Century of Historiography on the Origins of the Crimean War," *American Historical Review* 62 (1956): 33–58; Goldfrank, *The Origins of the Crimean War;* and Ann Pottinger Saab, *The Origins of the Crimean Alliance* (Charlottesville: University Press of Virginia, 1977).

10. On the military aspect of the Crimean War from the Ottoman perspective, see Virginia Aksan, *Ottoman Wars,* chapter 10.

11. See, for instance, *The Siege of Kars 1855: Defence and Capitulations,* reported by General Williams (London: Stationery Office, 2000), for a series of documents and journal entries from a British general fighting alongside French and Ottoman troops in Kars. In these entries, Williams reports on-the-ground realities of Ottoman military life as he tries to manage a military campaign in cooperation with Ottoman military leadership.

12. See, for instance, Kemal Karpat, *Ottoman Population, 1830–1914: Demographic and Social Characteristics* (Madison: University of Wisconsin Press, 1985).

13. Sturdza, *Dictionnaire historique et généalogique,* 448.

14. See Saab, *The Origins of the Crimean Alliance,* 12–13; and Goldfrank, *The Origins of the Crimean War,* 98–99.

15. See Goldfrank, *The Origins of the Crimean War.* On Aali and Fuat, see, among others, Mardin, *The Genesis of Young Ottoman Thought.* While Aali and Fuat would be roundly criticized by Vogorides on the "conservative" end of the political spectrum, they would also be criticized in the 1860s by the emerging group known as the Young Ottomans. Mardin writes, "These two men had . . . held in their grip the formulation of the policies of the Porte. . . . They were accused of personal rule, of brewing wrong policies in an ivory tower, and of building an oligarchy of sycophants" (11).

16. Since the Treaty of Küçük Kaynarca, in 1774, it had been debated whether the Russian Empire was claiming or could claim such a right. See Goldfrank, *The Origins of the Crimean War,* 42–44.

17. See ibid., chapter 7.

18. He frequently uses the verb *Rossizo,* meaning literally "to Russify."

19. MP, Musurus-Vogorides correspondence: file IX: 69.

20. Kostaki Musurus would later play up the importance of this factor in his 1853 dispatches to Reşit Paşa, claiming that the British would without question support the Ottomans against Russia. See Saab, *The Origins of the Crimean Alliance,* 70–75. Interestingly, while Saab cites dispatches from Musurus to Reşit Paşa that she found in the Ottoman state archives, she mentions that she can only assume Musurus is responding to memos sent him by Reşit.

Given the ongoing correspondence between Vogorides and Musurus and Vogorides' sustained contact with Reşit Paşa in İstanbul, Musurus was also likely responding to Vogorides' reports of Reşit's directions.

21. MP, Musurus-Vogorides correspondence: file IX: 69. Regarding the extension of privileges to the Greeks by "Omer Hatab," Vogorides is referring to the Pact of 'Umar, the authenticity of which from the early years of Islam has been called into doubt. It was said to have been made between the Caliph 'Umar and the Christians of Syria, although Vogorides seems to be conflating them here with the Byzantine State and Orthodox Church in toto. See Jonathan Berkey, *The Formation of Islam: Religion and Society in the Near East* (Cambridge: Cambridge University Press, 2002), 92.

22. MP, Musurus-Vogorides correspondence: file XVI: 65a.

23. MP, Musurus-Vogorides correspondence: file IX: 75; ibid., file XVI: 65a (July 5/17, 1853). Regarding the empirewide Muslim uprising against possible Russian (Orthodox) success, there were reports of tensions among Muslims in İstanbul in response to Russian moves and riots in 1853. See Saab, *The Origins of the Crimean Alliance*, 82–83.

24. On the Menshikov visit, see Taylor, *The Struggle for Mastery in Europe 1848–1918*, 49–54; Saab, *The Origins of the Crimean Alliance*, chapter 2; and Goldfrank, *The Origins of the Crimean War*, chapter 9.

25. MP, Musurus-Vogorides correspondence: file XVI: 65a.

26. MP, Musurus-Vogorides correspondence: file IX: 69.

27. In general the *usul-ü meşveret*, or the practice of consulting with eminent men, would be hailed by Young Ottomans of the next generation as the Turkish forerunner of European parliamentary democracy. See Mardin, *The Genesis of Young Ottoman Thought*, 133–34.

28. MP, Musurus-Vogorides correspondence: file IX: 69.

29. Even though, later in the same letter, Vogorides emphasized the importance of the British overseeing reforms to ensure the survival of the Ottoman state, thereby effacing the boundary between domestic and international governance.

30. MP, Musurus-Vogorides correspondence: file IX: 69, my emphasis. The following quotes of Vogorides' can also be found in this source.

31. Ibid.

32. This is a fascinating suggestion that fundamentally contradicts modern nationalist notions, which project a clear distinction between Byzantine/Christian and Ottoman/Muslim onto the fourteenth and fifteenth centuries, and one that supports the arguments of historians such as Cemal Kafadar about the eclectic culture of the early Ottomans. See Kafadar, *Between Two Worlds*.

33. See Stoianovich, "The Conquering Balkan Orthodox Merchant."

AFTERLIVES

1. Δάντου ὁ Ἅδης. Μετάφρασις Κωνσταντίνου Μουσούρου [Dante's *Inferno*, translated into Greek verse by Constantine Mousouros *(sic)*], 2nd ed., p. ιβ′ (1882; London and Edinburgh: Williams and Norgate, 1890).

2. See Davison, *Reform in the Ottoman Empire*, 327.

3. Ibid., 347.

4. Ibid.

5. Selim Deringil provides a vivid depiction of this in his *Well-Protected Domains*.

6. T. W. Riker, "The Concert of Europe and Moldavia," *English Historical Review* 42, no. 166 (1927): 227–44. See also Seton-Watson, *A History of the Roumanians*.

7. His wife, Catherine Conaki, was later remarried to Prince Ruspoli de Poggio-Suassa, mayor of Rome. See Sturdza, *Dictionnaire historique et généalogique*, 466.

8. Ibid.

9. Ibid., 465.

10. See E. Engelhardt, *La Turquie et le Tanzimat; ou, histoire des réformes dans l'empire Ottoman depuis 1826 jusqu' à nos jours* (Paris: A. Cotillon, 1882–84); and Davison, *Reform in the Ottoman Empire*.

11. For background on the September 6–7 events, see, for instance, Fahri Çoker, *6–7 eylül olayları fotoğraflar-belgeler Fahri Çoker arşivi* (İstanbul: Tarih Vakfı, 2005); and Speros Vryonis, *Mechanism of Catastrophe* (New York: Greekworks, 2006).

12. "According to court records, 4,214 houses, 1,004 workplaces/business establishments, 73 churches, 1 synagogue, 2 monasteries, 26 schools along with factories, hotels, bars, and other places were among the 5,317 places attacked" that night. Damages totaled about "150 million Turkish lira, or 54 million U.S. dollars" (Çoker, *6–7 eylül olayları*, ix).

# BIBLIOGRAPHY

## I. UNPUBLISHED ARCHIVAL SOURCES

AMAE: Archives du Ministère des affaires étrangers (Archive of the Ministry of Foreign Affairs), Quai d'Orsay, Paris; Nantes

a. Consular correspondence from the cities of the Ottoman Empire: Smyrna, Bucharest, Istanbul, Samos, Constantinople (file B: 243; file D: Samos 1830–35 subfile)

b. Correspondance diplomatique: MD Turquie: tome 21, docs. 43, 56

c. Mémoires et correspondances diverses: tome 30, doc. 29

ASB: Archivele Statului București (National Archive of Romania), Bucharest

a. Soutso (R. Suçu) family archive

b. Ottoman Turkish collection

BOA: Başbakanlık Osmanlı Arşivleri (Prime Ministry Archives), İstanbul

a. A.DVN 863–70; A.DVN.KLS.930; A.DVN.Kanunname-i Askeri 1 (A.H. 1241; M. 1826)

b. Ahkam defterleri: Boğdan: 80/4: 282; Eflak; Sisam; İstanbul

c. Bulgaristan İradeleri

d. Cevdet Series (C.)

    i. MTZ: 528, 818, 927, 1000,

    ii. Dahiliye: 3650, 7225, 9295, 10747, 12037

    iii. Hariciye: 148, 1039, 2078, 2500, 6632

    iv. Evkaf: 24427

    v. Askeriye: 159, 236, 657

e. D.BŞM.9720

f. Hatt-i Hümayun Tasnifi (HAT): 2134, 2443, 5476, 5530, 7153, 7560, 7562, 7872, 8839, 9799, 10925, 11170, 11363, 11418, 11633, 11674, 12550-A, 12565, 13081, 13375, 13645, 13662, 13745-A, 13754-A, 14731, 16066, 20168, 20896, 21659, 23768, 24611, 43189-A, 43200, 45405

g. İrade Series: Dahiliye; Hariciye; Mesail-i mühimme: 916, 930

h. Name-i Hümayun defteri: no. 989

i. Sisam İradeleri: 1

CML: Cyril and Methodius Library, Orientalia Collections, Sofia

a. Bulgarian newspapers collection

b. Ottoman documents: Istanbul dossier, Eflak/Bögdan dossier (uncataloged)

EPI: Archive of the Ecumenical Patriarchate of İstanbul

Outgoing correspondence to metropolitan sees, 1800–60: codices IB': 104–6; IΓ': 175; IE': 116; IZ': 40 (4); IH': 144–6, 278–9; IΘ': 136 (2); K': 152; K': 245 (2); KΔ': 75–6; KE': 3; KH': 124, 154; KΓ': 289; KZ': 22

MP: Constantine Musurus Papers, Gennadius Library, Athens

a. Musurus-Vogorides correspondence: box IV: files 18, 21, 29; IX: 69, 75; X: 15; XVI: 65a; XIX: 156; microfilm nos. 25, 26, 27, 29, 32

b. Ottoman file (uncataloged), file II, unit 2, doc. 18

c. "Samiaka" files

PRO: FO: Public Records Office: Foreign Office, Kew Gardens, London

PRO: FO 78/18, 78/19, 78/21, 78/100, 78/101, 78/109, 78/111, 78/114, 78/115, 78/116, 78/199, 78/200, 78/201, 78/202, 78/203, 78/204, 78/205, 78/206, 78/207, 78/208, 78/209, 78/210, 78/211, 78/212, 78/213, 78/214, 78/216, 78/217, 78/218, 78/220, 78/221, 78/222, 78/223, 78/356, 78/668, 78/719, 78/764, 78/1496, 192/102, 195/3, 195/38, 195/102, 352/40, 881/280A

TKSA: Topkapı Sarayı Arşivi, İstanbul

a. Evrak: 1144, 1874, 2358, 3600/1–2, 3676, 3732, 4268, 4286, 5163, 5535, 8140, 8234, 9241, 9291, 11746/1–8

b. Defter: 4864

## II. PUBLISHED MANUSCRIPTS, DOCUMENTS, AND SECONDARY SOURCES

Abou-El-Haj, Rifa'at 'Ali. "An Agenda for Research in History: The History of Libya between the Sixteenth and Nineteenth Centuries." *International Journal of Middle East Studies* 15, no. 3 (1983): 305–19.

———. "The Formal Closure of the Ottoman Frontier, 1699–1703." *Journal of the American Oriental Societies* 89 (1969): 467–75.

———. *Formation of the Modern State: The Ottoman Empire, Sixteenth to Eighteenth Centuries.* 2nd ed. Syracuse, NY: Syracuse University Press, 2005.

———. "The Ottoman Vezir and Pasha Households, 1683–1703: A Preliminary Report." *Journal of the American Oriental Society* 94 (1974): 438–47.

Abramea, Anna. "Toponymia Blachias ston charte tou Rega" [Wallachian place-names in Rigas's map]. *Ho Eranistes* 17 (1981): 100–119.

Abu-Manneh, Butrus. "The Naqshbandiyya-Mujaddidiyya in the Ottoman Lands in the Early 19th Century." *Die Welt des Islams* 22, no. 1 (1982): 1–36.

———. *Studies on Islam and the Ottoman Empire in the 19th Century (1826–1876).* Istanbul: Isis Press, 2001.

Adanir, Fikret, and Suraiya Faroqhi, eds. *The Ottomans and the Balkans: A Discussion of Historiography.* Leiden, Boston, Köln: Brill Academic Publishers, 2002.

Akarli, Engin. "Gediks: Implements, Mastership, Shop Usufruct, and Monopoly among Istanbul Artisans, 1750–1850." *Wissenschaftskolleg Berlin Jahrbuch* (1986): 223–31.

Aksan, Virginia. "Ottoman Political Writing, 1768–1808." *International Journal of Middle East Studies* 25, no. 1 (1993): 53–69.

———. *Ottoman Statesman in War and Peace: Ahmed Resmi Efendi, 1700–1783.* Leiden: Brill Academic Publishers, 1995.

———. *Ottoman Wars, 1700–1870: An Empire Besieged.* London: Pearson-Longman, 2007.

———. "Whatever Happened to the Janissaries? Mobilization for the 1768–1774 Russo-Ottoman War." *War in History* 5, no. 1 (1998): 23–36.

Akyıldız, Ali, and M. Şükrü Hanioğlu. "Negotiating the Power of the Sultan: The Ottoman Sened-i ittifak (Deed of Agreement)." In *The Modern Middle East: A Sourcebook for History,* ed. Camron Michael Amin, Benjamin Fortna, and Elizabeth Frierson, 22–30. Oxford, New York: Oxford University Press, 2006.

Alexandrescu-Dersca-Bulgaru, M. M. "Les rapports économiques de l'Empire Ottoman avec les principautés Roumaines et leur réglementation par les Khatt-i Sérif de privilèges (1774–1829)." In *Économie et sociétés dans l'Empire Ottoman (fin du XVIIIe—debut du XIXe siècle),* ed. Jean-Louis Bacque-Grammont and Paul Dumont, 317–26. Paris: Éditions du Centre national de la recherche scientifique, 1983.

Alexandris, Alexis. "Hoi Hellenes sten hyperesia tes Othomanikes Autokratorias: 1850–1922" [Greeks in the service of the Ottoman Empire]. *Deltio tes Historikes kai Ethnologikes Hetaireias tes Hellados* 23 (1980): 365–404.

Altundağ, Şinasi. *Kavalalı Mehmet Ali Paşa isyanı, Mısır meselesi 1831–1841* [Kavalali Mehmet Ali Paşa's insurrection]. Ankara: Türk Tarih Kurumu basımevi, 1988.

Anagnostopoulou, Anastasia. *Mikra Asia, 19os aionas—1919: Hoi hellenorthodoxes koinotetes, apo to Millet ton Romion sto helleniko ethnos* [Asia Minor, 19th century—1919: Greek Orthodox communities, from the Rum Millet to the Hellenic nation]. Athens, 1997.

Anderson, Benedict. *Imagined Communities: Reflections on the Origins and Spread of Nationalism.* London: Verso, 1983.

Anderson, M. S. *The Eastern Question 1774–1923: A Study in International Relations.* New York: St. Martin's Press, 1966.

———. *The Great Powers and the Near East, 1774–1923.* London: Edward Arnold, 1970.

Angelopoulos, G. G., and G. P. Angelopoulos "Anecdotos ekthesis episemou kai autoptou omogenous" [Unpublished essay of an official and eyewitness fellow Greek]. In *Ta kata ton aiodimon protathleten tou hierou ton hellenon agonos ton Patriarchen Konstantinopoleos Gregorios ton V* [The events of the patriarchate of Gregorios V, champion of the holy struggle of the Hellenes]. Athenai: Ethnikon typographeion, 1865–66.

Anscombe, Frederick F., ed. *The Ottoman Balkans, 1750–1830.* Princeton, NJ: Markus Wiener Publishers, 2006.

Arnakis, G. Georgiades. "The Greek Church of Constantinople and the Ottoman Empire." *Journal of Modern History* 24, no. 3 (1952): 235–50.

Artan, Tülay. "Architecture as a Theatre of Life: Profile of the Eighteenth-Century Bosphorus." PhD diss., Massachusetts Institute of Technology, 1989.

———. "Eyüp." *Türkiye Diyanet Vakfı İslam Ansiklopedisi* 12 (1995).

Asdrachas, Speros. *Hellenike oikonomike historia, 150s-190s aionas* [Greek economic history, 15th–19th century]. Athena: Politistiko Hidryma Homilou Peiraios, 2003.

Assad Éfendi, Mehmed. *Précis historique de la destruction du corps des janissaires par le sultan Mahmoud, en 1826*. Paris: Firmin Didots Frères, 1833. [Translation of *Üss-i Zafer* (Base of victory).]

Auldjo, John. *Journal of a Visit to Constantinople and Some of the Greek Islands in the Spring and Summer of 1833*. London: Longman, Rees, Orme, Brown, Green and Longman, 1835.

Aynural, Salih. *İstanbul değirmenleri ve fırınları, zahire ticareti (1740–1840)*. İstanbul: Türkiye Ekonomik ve Toplumsal Tarih Vakfı, 2002.

Ayverdi, Ekrem Hakkı. *19. Asırda Istanbul haritası* [Map of nineteenth-century Istanbul]. İstanbul, 1958.

Bacque-Grammont, Jean-Louis, and Paul Dumont, eds., *Économie et sociétiés dans l'Empire Ottoman (fin du XVIIIe—debut du XIXe siècle)*. Paris: Éditions du Centre national de la recherche scientifique, 1983.

Baghdiantz-McCabe, Ina. *Shah's Silk for Europe's Silver: The Eurasian Trade of Julfa Armenians in Safavid Iran and India, 1530–1750*. Atlanta, GA: Scholar's Press, 1999.

Baghdiantz-McCabe, Ina, Gelina Harlaftis, and Ioanna Pepelasis Minoglou, eds. *Diaspora Entrepreneurial Networks: Four Centuries of History*. Oxford: Berg Publishers, 2005.

Bakirtzes, I. D. "Vogorides, Stephanos." *He megale hellenike encyclopedia* [Great Greek encyclopedia], vol. 7. Athens, 1931.

Balta, Evangelia. *Karamanlidika: Nouvelles additions et compléments*. Athens: Centre d'études d'Asie mineure, 1997.

Barkey, Karen. *Bandits and Bureaucrats: The Ottoman Route to State Centralization*. Ithaca, NY: Cornell University Press, 1994.

———. *Empire of Difference: The Ottomans in Comparative Perspective*. Cambridge: Cambridge University Press, 2008.

Bartle, G. F. "Bowring and the Near Eastern Crisis of 1838–1840." *English Historical Review* 79, no. 313 (1964): 761–74.

Batur, Afife. "Selimiye Kışlası." *Dünden bugüne İstanbul Ansiklopedisi* 6 (1993–94): 515–16.

Bayat, Ali Haydar. *Keçecizade Mehmed Fuat Paşa'nın nesirleri şiirleri nükteleri hakkında şiirler* [Poems by and about Mehmed Fuat Paşa]. İstanbul: Türk Dünyası Araştırmaları Vakfı Yayınları, 1988.

Berindei, Dan. "The Nineteenth Century." In *Romania: A Historic Perspective*, ed. D. Giurescu and S. Fischer-Galati. New York: Columbia University Press, 1998.

Berkes, Niyazi. *The Development of Secularism in Modern Turkey*. Montreal: McGill University Press, 1964.

Berkey, Jonathan. *The Formation of Islam: Religion and Society in the Near East*. Cambridge: Cambridge University Press, 2002.

Beydilli, Kemal. "Sekbanbaşı risalesinin müellifi hakkında" [Regarding the author of the Sekbanbaşı *risale*]. *Türk kültürü incelemeleri dergisi* 12 (2005): 221–24.

Birge, J. K. *The Bektashi Order of Dervishes*. London: Luzac and Co., 1937.

Blancard, Théodore. *Les Mavroyènis: L'histoire d'Orient*. 2 vols. Paris: E. Leroux, 1909.

Blanqui, M. *Voyage en Bulgarie pendant l'année 1844*. Paris, 1845.

Bouchard, Jacques. "Nicolas Mavrocordatos et l'Époque des Tulipes." *Ho Eranistes* 17 (1981): 120–29.

Bouquet, Olivier. *Les pachas du sultan: Essai sur les agents supérieurs de l'État ottoman (1839–1909).* Dudley, MA: Peeters, 2007.

Bourdieu, Pierre. *The Logic of Practice.* Palo Alto, CA: Stanford University Press, 1990.

Bratianu, G. I. "Études sur la approvisionnement de Constantinople et le monopolie de blé à l'époque Byzantine et Ottomane." In *Études Byzantines d'histoire économique et sociale.* Paris, 1938.

Braude, Benjamin. "Foundation Myths of the Millet System." In *Christians and Jews in the Ottoman Empire: The Functioning of a Plural Society,* 2 vols., ed. Bernard Lewis and Benjamin Braude. New York: Holmes and Meier Publishers, 1982.

Bulliet, Richard W. *Islam: The View from the Edge.* New York: Columbia University Press, 1994.

Byzantiou, Scarlatos D. *He Konstantinoupolis he perigraphe topographike, archaiologike kai historike tes perionymou tautes megalopoleos* [Constantinople, or topographical, archaeological, and historical description of this famous megalopolis], vol. 2. Athens, 1862.

Cahen, Claude. "Dhimma." In *Encyclopedia of Islam,* 2nd ed., ed. P. Bearman, Th. Bianquis, C. E. Bosworth, E. van Donzel, and W. P. Heinrichs. Brill Online, 2008.

Camariano, Nestor. *Alexandre Mavrocordato, le grand drogman: Son activité diplomatique, 1673–1709.* Thessaloniki: Institute for Balkan Studies, 1970.

Camariano-Cioran, Ariadna. "Écoles grecques dans les principautés danubiennes au temps des phanariotes." *Symposium l'Époque Phanariote* (1974): 49–57.

———. *Les Académies princières de Bucharest et de Jassy et leurs professeurs.* Thessaloniki: Institute of Balkan Studies, 1974.

Campbell, John K. *Honour, Family, and Patronage: A Study of Institutions and Moral Values in a Greek Mountain Community.* Oxford: Oxford University Press, 1970.

Cantemir, Dimitrie. *Dimitrie Cantemir, Historian of South East European and Oriental Civilizations: Extracts from "The History of the Ottoman Empire."* Edited by Alexandru Duţu and Paul Cernovodeanu, translated from the Latin by N. Tindal. Bucharest: Association internationale d'études du sud-est européen, 1973.

Certeau, Michel de. *The Practice of Everyday Life.* Berkeley: University of California Press, 1988.

Cevad Pasha. *Tarih-i askeri-i osmani* [Ottoman military history]. İstanbul, 1879–80.

Cevdet, Ahmet. *Tarih-i Cevdet.* Vols. 5, 11–13. Dersaadet (İstanbul): Matbaa-yi Osmaniye, A.H. 1309; M. 1893.

Cezar, Yavuz. "Osmanlı devletinin mali kurumlarından zahire hazinesi ve 1795/1210 tarihli nizamnamesi." *Toplum ve Bilim* 6–7 (1978).

Cioran, Georg. *Scheseis ton roumanikon Choron meta Tou Atho kai de ton monon Koutloumousiou, Lauras, Docheiariou kai Haghiou Panteleimonon he ton roson* [Relations of the Romanian lands with Mt. Athos and its Koutloumous, Laura, Docheiariou, and Haghiou Panteleimon of the Russian monasteries]. In *Texte und Forschungen zur byzantinisch-neugriechischen Philologie,* no. 25, 1–308 (Athens: Verlag der byzantinisch-neugriechischen Jahrbuecher, 1938).

Ciurea, Al. "Quelques aspects essentiels de l'époque phanariote dans l'histoire de l'Église Or-
thodoxe de Roumanie." In *Symposium l'époque phanariote 21–25 octobre 1970*, 17–29.
Thessaloniki: Institute for Balkan Studies, 1974.

Cobham, C. D. *The Patriarchs of Constantinople.* Cambridge: Cambridge University Press,
1911.

Cohen, David. "Des relations commerciales entre les principautés roumaines et les terres bul-
gares au cours des années 40–70 du XIXe siècle." *Bulgarian Historical Review* 3 (1974):
70–98.

Çoker, Fahri. *6–7 eylül olayları fotoğraflar-belgeler Fahri Çoker arşivi.* İstanbul: Tarih Vakfı,
2005.

Columbeanu, Sergiu. *Grandes exploitations domaniales en Valachie au XVIII-e siècle.* Bucharest: Editura Academiei Republicii Socialiste Romania, 1974.

Craig, Gordon. *The Politics of the Prussian Army, 1640–1945.* New York: Oxford University
Press, 1955.

Crampton, R. J. *A Concise History of Bulgaria.* Cambridge: Cambridge University Press, 1997.

Crawley, C. W. *The Question of Greek Independence: A Study of British Policy in the Near East,
1821–1833.* New York: H. Fertig, 1973.

Crews, Robert D. *For Prophet and Tsar: Islam and Empire in Russia and Central Asia.* Cambridge, MA: Harvard University Press, 2006.

Cunningham, Alan. *Collected Essays.* 2 vols. Edited by Edward Ingram. Portland, OR: F. Cass,
1993.

Dagron, Gilbert. *Empereur et Prêtre: Étude sur le "Césaropapisme" Byzantin.* Paris: Gallimard,
1996.

Dante. *The Inferno.* Translated into Greek verse by Constantine Mousouros [sic]. 2nd ed. 1882;
London and Edinburgh: Williams and Norgate, 1890.

Daskalakis, Ap. "Les phanariotes et la revolution grecque de 1821." *Symposium l'Époque Phanariote* (1974): 71–77.

Davison, Roderic. *Reform in the Ottoman Empire, 1856–1876.* Princeton, NJ: Princeton University Press, 1963.

Deringil, Selim. "The Invention of Tradition as Public Image in the Late Ottoman Empire,
1808–1908." *Comparative Studies in Society and History* 35, no. 1 (1993): 3–29.

———. *The Well-Protected Domains: Ideology and Legitimation of Power in the Late Ottoman
Empire, 1876–1909.* London: I. B. Tauris, 1998.

Diamandouros, Nikiforos, ed. *Hellenism and the First Greek War of Liberation (1821–1830):
Continuity and Change.* Thessaloniki: Institute for Balkan Studies, 1976.

Dodwell, Henry. *The Founder of Modern Egypt: A Study of Muhammad Ali.* Cambridge: Cambridge University Press, 1967.

Dojnov, Stefan. "Le mouvement de libération nationale bulgare au début du XIXe siècle." *Bulgarian Historical Review* 1 (1975): 60–77.

Dragut, Vasile. "Le monastere de Vacaresti: Expression des relations artistiques roumanogrecques." In *Symposium l'époque phanariote 21–25 octobre 1970*, 265–94. Thessaloniki: Institute for Balkan Studies, 1974.

Drouin, Georges. *La mission du Baron de Boislecomte: L'Égypte et la Syrie en 1833.* Cairo: Imprimerie de l'Institut français d'archéologie orientale du Caire, 1927.

*Dünden bugüne İstanbul ansiklopedisi.* İstanbul: Kultur Bakanlığı Yayınları, 1995.

Duţu, Alexandru. *Political Models and National Identities in "Orthodox Europe."* Bucharest: Babel, 1998.

Duţu, Alexandru, and Paul Cernovodeanu, eds. *Dimitrie Cantemir, Historian of South East European and Oriental Civilizations: Extracts from "The History of the Ottoman Empire."* Bucharest: Association internationale d'études du sud-est européen, 1973.

East, W. Gordon. *The Union of Moldavia and Wallachia, 1859: An Episode in Diplomatic History.* Cambridge: Cambridge University Press, 1929.

Eldem, Edhem. "Istanbul: From Imperial to Peripheralized Capital." In *The Ottoman City between East and West: Aleppo, İzmir, and İstanbul,* ed. Edhem Eldem, Daniel Goffman, and Bruce Masters, 135–206. New York: Cambridge University Press, 1999.

Eliade, Pompiliu. *De l'influence française sur l'esprit public en Roumanie: Les origines, étude sur l'état de la société roumaine à l'époque du règne phanariote.* Paris: E. Leroux, 1898.

*Encyclopaedia of Islam.* 2nd ed. Ed. P. J. Bearman, Th. Bianquis, C. E. Bosworth, E. van Donzel and W. P. Heinrichs, et al. 12 vols. Leiden: Brill Academic Publishers, 1960–2005.

Engelhardt, Ed. *La Turquie et le tanzimât; ou, histoire des réformes dans l'empire Ottoman depuis 1826 jusqu'à nos jours.* Paris: A. Cotillon, 1882–84.

Fahmy, Khaled. *All the Pasha's Men: Mehmet Ali, His Army, and the Making of Modern Egypt.* Cambridge: Cambridge University Press, 1997.

———. *Mehmet Ali.* Makers of the Muslim World series. New York: OneWorld Press, 2008.

Faroqhi, Suraiya. *Making a Living in the Ottoman Lands, 1480–1820.* Istanbul: Isis Press, 1995.

———. *Subjects of the Sultan: Culture and Everyday Life in the Ottoman Empire from the Middle Ages until the Beginning of the Twentieth century.* London: I. B. Tauris, 2000.

Fincanci, May N. *The Story of Robert College, Old and New.* Istanbul, 2001.

Findley, Carter. *Bureaucratic Reform in the Ottoman Empire: The Sublime Porte, 1789–1922.* Princeton, NJ: Princeton University Press, 1980.

———. "The Foundation of the Ottoman Foreign Ministry: The Beginnings of Bureaucratic Reform under Selim III and Mahmud II." *International Journal of Middle East Studies* 3, no. 4 (1972): 388–416.

———. "The Legacy of Tradition to Reform: Origins of the Ottoman Foreign Ministry." *International Journal of Middle East Studies* 1, no. 4 (1970): 334–57.

———. *Ottoman Civil Officialdom: A Social History.* Princeton, NJ: Princeton University Press, 1989.

Fleischer, Cornell. *Bureaucrat and Intellectual in the Ottoman Empire: The Historian Mustafa Ali (1541–1600).* Princeton, NJ: Princeton University Press, 1986.

Fleming, Katherine E. *The Muslim Bonaparte: Diplomacy and Orientalism in Ali Pasha's Greece.* Princeton, NJ: Princeton University Press, 1999.

Florescu, Radu R. *Essays on Romanian History.* Iaşi, Romania; Portland, OR: Center for Romanian Studies, 1999.

Foucault, Michel. *Discipline and Punish: The Birth of the Prison.* New York: Vintage Books, 1979.

———. "Governmentality." In *The Foucault Effect: Studies in Governmentality.* Edited by Graham Burchell, Colin Gordon, and Peter Miller. Chicago: University of Chicago Press, 1991.

————. "On Governmentality." In *The Foucault Reader*, 87–104. Edited by Paul Rabinow. New York: Pantheon Books, 1984.

————. *The Order of Things: An Archaeology of the Human Sciences*. New York: Vintage Books, 1994.

Gardika, Katerina. *Prostasia kai eggiyseis: Stadia kai mythoi tes hellenikes ethnikes olokleroses (1821–1920)* [Protection and guarantees: Phases and myths of Greek national integration]. Thessaloniki, 1999.

Gavrilis, George. *Dynamics of Interstate Boundaries*. Cambridge: Cambridge University Press, 2008.

Gedeon, Manouel Io. *Aposemeiomata Chronographou (1800–1913)* [Historian's notes]. Athens, 1932.

————. *Engrapha patriarchika kai synodika peri tou boulgarikou zetematos (1852–1873)* [Documents from the patriarch and synod on the Bulgarian Question]. İstanbul: Ek tou Patriarchik. Typ., 1908.

————. "Kanonismon Apopeira." *Ecclesiastike Aletheia* 43 (1919): 215–16.

————. *Mneia ton pro emou: 1800–1863–1913* [References of my forefathers]. Athens, 1934.

————. "On phanariot society until the beginnings of our century." (in Greek). *Journal of the Constantinople Philological Society* 21 (1887–88; 1891).

————. *Patriarchikoi pinakes: Eideseis historikai biographikai peri ton patriarchon Konstantinopoleos, apo Andreou tou Protoletou mechris Ioakeim III tou apo Thessalonikes, 36–1884* [Patriarchal portraits: Historical and biographical information on the patriarchs of Constantinople]. Constantinople: Lorenz and Keil, 1890.

Gennadios, Metropolitan of Heliopoulis. *Historia tou Megalou Reumatos (Arnaoutkiogi)* [History of Mega Reuma (Arnavutköy)]. İstanbul, 1949.

Gibb, H. A. R., and Harold Bowen. *Islamic Society and the West: A Study of the Impact of Western Civilization on Moslem Culture in the Near East*. 2 vols. London: Oxford University Press, 1957.

Göçek, Fatma Müge. *Rise of the Bourgeoisie, Demise of Empire: Ottoman Westernization and Social Change*. Oxford: Oxford University Press, 1996.

Goldfrank, David M. *The Origins of the Crimean War*. London: Longman, 1994.

Gölpınarlı, Abdülbaki. "Şeyh Galib." In *İslam ansiklopedisi: İslam alemi tarih, coğrafya, etnografya ne biyografya lugatı*, vol. 11, 462–67. İstanbul: Milli Eğitim basımevi, 1970.

Gondicas, Dimitri, and Charles Issawi, eds. *Ottoman Greeks in the Age of Nationalism: Politics, Economy, and Society in the Nineteenth Century*. Princeton, NJ: Darwin Press, 1999.

Gooch, Bryson D. "A Century of Historiography on the Origins of the Crimean War." *American Historical Review* 62 (1956): 33–58.

Gradeva, Rossitsa. "Osman Pazvantoğlu of Vidin: Between Old and New." In *The Ottoman Balkans, 1750–1830*, ed. Frederick F. Anscombe. Princeton, NJ: Markus Wiener Publishers, 2006.

————. "Secession and Revolution in the Ottoman Empire at the End of the Eighteenth Century: Osman Pazvantoğlu and Righas Velestinlis." In *Ottoman Rule and the Balkans, 1760–1850: Conflict, Transformation, Adaptation*, ed. Antonis Anastasopoulos and Elias Kolovos, 73–94. Rethymno, Crete: University of Crete, Department of History and Archaeology, 2007.

Greene, Molly. *A Shared World: Muslims and Christians in the Early Modern Mediterranean.* Princeton, NJ: Princeton University Press, 2000.

Guboglu, Mihail. *Catalogul documentelor turcesti.* Vols. 1 and 2. Bucharest: Academy of Sciences, 1960.

Güçer, Lütfi. *XV–XVII Asırlarda Osmanlı İmparatorluğunda hububat meselesi ve hububattan alınan vergiler* [Grains and grain taxes in the Ottoman Empire from the 15th to the 17th centuries]. İstanbul: İstanbul Üniversitesi, İktisat Fakültesi, 1964.

Güran, Tevfik. "The State Role in the Grain Supply of Istanbul, the Grain Administration, 1793–1839." *International Journal of Turkish Studies* 3, no. 1 (1984–85): 27–41.

Hammer-Purgstall, Joseph. *Histoire de l'Empire ottoman, depuis son origine jusqu'à nos jours.* 18 vols. Paris: Bethune et Plon, 1835–43.

Harlaftis, Gelina. *History of Greek-Owned Shipping: The Making of an International Tramp Fleet, 1830 to the Present* (London, New York: Routledge, 1996).

———. "Mapping the Greek Maritime Diaspora from the Early Eighteenth to the Late Twentieth Centuries." In *Diaspora Entrepreneurial Networks: Five Centuries of History,* ed. Ina Baghdiantz-McCabe, Gelina Harlaftis, and Ioanna Papelasis-Minoglou, 147–72. Oxford: Oxford University Press, 2005.

Hasluck, F. W. *Christianity and Islam under the Sultans.* 2 vols., ed. Margaret M. Hasluck. New York: Octagon Books, 1973.

Hathaway, Jane. *The Politics of Households in Ottoman Egypt: The Rise of the Qazdaglis.* Cambridge: Cambridge University Press, 1993.

Hattox, Ralph. *Coffee and Coffeehouses: The Origins of a Social Beverage in the Medieval Near East.* Seattle: University of Washington Press, 1985.

Hatziioannou, Maria-Christina. "Crossing Empires: Greek Merchant Networks before the Imperialistic Expansion." *Diaspora Entrepreneurial Networks: Five Centuries of History,* ed. Ina Baghdiantz-McCabe, Gelina Harlaftis, and Ioanna Papelasis-Minoglou, 371–82. Oxford: Oxford University Press, 2005.

Hedin, Astrid. *The Politics of Social Networks: Interpersonal Trust and Institutional Change in Post-Communist East Germany.* Lund, Sweden: Lund University, 2001.

*He megale hellenike encyclopedia* [The great Greek encyclopedia]. Athens, 1931.

*He Pandora.* Athens: Ch. A. Doukas, 1850–72.

Herzfeld, Michael. *The Poetics of Manhood: Contest and Identity in a Cretan Mountain Village.* Princeton, NJ: Princeton University Press, 1985.

Heyd, Uriel. "The Ottoman Ulema and Westernization in the Time of Selim III and Mahmud II." *Scripta Hierosolymitana* 9 (1961): 63–96.

Hitchins, Keith. *The Romanians, 1774–1866.* Oxford: Clarendon Press, 1996.

Hobsbawm, Eric. *Nations and Nationalism since 1780: Programme, Myth, Reality.* New York: Cambridge University Press, 1990.

Hobsbawm, Eric, and Terence Ranger, eds. *The Invention of Tradition.* New York: Cambridge University Press, 1983.

Hope, Thomas. *Anastasius, or Memoirs of a Greek Written at the Close of the Eighteenth Century.* 2 vols. 1819; London: John Murray, 1836.

Hopwood, Derek. *The Russian Presence in Syria and Palestine, 1843–1914: Church and Politics in the Near East.* Oxford: Clarendon Press, 1969.

Hourani, Albert. *Arabic Thought in the Liberal Age 1798–1939*. Cambridge: Cambridge University Press, 1983.

———. "Ottoman Reform and the Politics of Notables." In *The Beginnings of Modernization in the Middle East: The Nineteenth Century*, ed. William R. Polk and Richard L. Chambers, 41–68. Chicago: University of Chicago Press, 1968.

Hurewitz, J. C. "The Europeanization of Ottoman Diplomacy: The Conversion from Unilateralism to Reciprocity in the Nineteenth Century." *Belleten* 25 (1961): 455–66.

Inalcik, Halil. "Application of the Tanzimat and its Social Effects." *Archivum Ottomanicum* 5 (1973): 97–128.

———. "Centralization and Decentralization in Ottoman Administration." In *Studies in Eighteenth Century Islamic History*, ed. Thomas Naff and Roger Owen, 27–52. Carbondale: Southern Illinois University Press, 1977.

———. *Essays in Ottoman History*. Istanbul: Eren, 1998.

———. "Husrev Pasha." In *İslam ansiklopedisi: İslam alemi tarih, coğrafya, etnografya ne biyografya lugatı*, vol. 5, 609–16. İstanbul: Milli Eğitim basımevi, 1967.

———. *The Middle East and the Balkans under the Ottoman Empire: Essays on Economy and Society*. Bloomington: Indiana University, Turkish Studies, 1993.

———. "Sened-i İttifak ve Gülhane Hatt-ı Hümayunu." *Belleten* 28 (1964): 603–22.

———. "Timariotes chrétiens en Albanie au XVe siècle d'après un register de timars Ottoman." *Mitteilungen des Osterreichischen Staatsarchivs* 4 (1951): 118–38.

Ingle, Harold. *Nesselrode and the Russian Rapprochement with Britain, 1836–1844*. Berkeley: University of California Press, 1976.

Institute for Balkan Studies. *Symposium l'époque phanariote, 21–25 Octobre 1970*. Thessaloniki: Institute for Balkan Studies, 1974.

Ionaşcu, Ion. "Le degré de l'influence des Grecs des principautés roumaines dans la vie politique de ces pays." *Symposium l'Époque Phanariote* (1974): 217–29.

Iorga, Nicolae. *Byzantium after Byzantium*. Translated by Laura Treptow. Iaşi, Romania; Portland, OR: Center for Romanian Studies, 2000.

———. *A History of Roumania: Land, People, Civilization*. Translated by Joseph McCabe. London: T. F. Unwin, 1925.

———. *Osmanlı İmparatorluğun Tarihi/Geschichte des osmanischen reiches*. Turkish translation, İstanbul: Yeditepe Yayınevi, 2005.

*İslam ansiklopedisi: İslam alemi tarih, coğrafya, etnografya ve biyografya lugatı* [Encyclopedia of Islam]. 13 vols. İstanbul: Milli Eğitim basımevi, 1940–88.

İslamoglu-İnan, Huri, ed. *The Ottoman Empire and the World Economy*. New York: Cambridge University Press, 1987.

Ismail, F. "The Making of the Treaty of Bucharest, 1811–1812." *Middle Eastern Studies* 15, no. 2 (1979): 163–92.

Itzkowitz, Norman, and Max Mote. "Eighteenth-Century Ottoman Realities." *Studia Islamica*, no. 16 (1962): 73–94.

———, eds. and trans. *Mübadele: An Ottoman-Russian Exchange of Ambassadors*. Chicago: University of Chicago Press, 1970.

Janos, Damien. "Panaiotis Nicousios and Alexander Mavrocordatos: The Rise of the Phanariots and the Office of Grand Dragoman in the Ottoman Administration in the Second Half of the Seventeenth Century." *Archivum Ottomanicum*, 23 (2005): 177–96.

Jelavich, Charles, and Barbara Jelavich. *The Establishment of the Balkan National States, 1804–1920*. Vol. 8: *A History of East Central Europe*. Seattle: University of Washington Press, 1987.

Jonkov, Hristo. "Alexandre Exarque: Contribution à sa biographie." *Bulgarian Historical Review* 3 (1990): 69–82.

Juchereau de St. Denys, A. de. *Les révolutions de Constantinople en 1807 et 1808, précédés d'observations générales sur l'état actuel de l'Empire Ottoman*. 2 vols. Paris: Brissot-Thivars, 1819.

Kafadar, Cemal. *Between Two Worlds: The Construction of the Ottoman State*. Berkeley: University of California Press, 1995.

———. "Janissary and Other Riffraff of Ottoman Istanbul: Rebels without a Cause?" In Baki Tezcan and Karl K. Barbir, *Identity and Identity Formation in the Ottoman Empire: A Volume of Essays in Honor of Norman Itzkowitz*. Madison: University of Wisconsin Press, 2008.

———. "Yeniçeri-Esnaf Relations: Solidarity and Conflict." MA thesis, McGill University, 1981.

Karal, Enver Ziya. *Halet Efendi'nin Paris Büyük Elçiliği (1802–1806)* [Halet Efendi's Paris Embassy]. İstanbul: Kenan Basımevi, 1940.

———. *Selim III'ün Hatt-ı Humayünları—Nizam-ı cedit—1789-1808* [The imperial rescripts of Sultan Selim III]. 7 vols. Ankara: Türk Tarih Kurumu basımevi, 1946.

Karateke, Hakan, ed. *An Ottoman Protocol Register Containing Ceremonies from 1736 to 1808: BEO Sadaret Defterleri 350 in Prime Ministry Ottoman State Archives, Istanbul*. Ibrahim Pasha of Egypt Fund Series. Istanbul: Royal Asiatic Society/Ottoman Bank Archive and Research Centre, 2007.

———. *Padişahım çok yaşa! Osmanlı devletinin son yüz yılında merasimler* [Long live the sultan!]. İstanbul: Kitap yayınevi, 2004.

Karathanassis, Athanassios E. *L'Hellénisme en Transylvanie: L'activité culturelle, nationale, et religieuse des companies commerciales helléniques de Sibiu et de Braşov aux XVIII–XIX siècles*. Thessaloniki, 1989.

Karpat, Kemal. *Ottoman Population, 1830–1914: Demographic and Social Characteristics*. Madison: University of Wisconsin Press, 1985.

Kasaba, Reşat. *The Ottoman Empire and the World Economy: The Nineteenth Century*. Albany: State University of New York Press, 1988.

Katsiardi-Herring, Olga. "He hellenike diaspora: He geographia kai he typologia tes" [The Greek diaspora: Its geography and typology]. In *Hellenike oikonomike historia 15os-19os aionas* [Greek economic history, fifteenth to nineteenth centuries], ed. Spyros I. Asdrachas, 237–47. Athens: Politistiko Hidryma Homilou Peiraios, 2003.

Kaynar, Reşat. *Mustafa Reşit Paşa ve Tanzimat*. 1954; Ankara: Türk Tarih Kurumu Basımevı, 1991.

Kenanoğlu, Macit. *Osmanlı millet sistemi: Mit ve gerçek* [The Ottoman millet system: Myth and reality]. Aksaray, İstanbul: Klasik, 2004.

Kerr, Paul. *The Crimean War.* London: Channel Four Books, 2000.

Khoury, Dina Rizk. *State and Provincial Society in the Ottoman Empire: Mosul, 1540–1834.* Cambridge: Cambridge University Press, 1997.

Kioutouskas, Georgios. "He voulgarike paroikia sten Konstantinoupole os ta 1878" [The Bulgarian colony in Constantinople until 1878]. In *He parousia ton ethnikon meionoteton sten Konsantinoupole ton 190 aiona* [The presence of ethnic minorities in Istanbul in the 19th century], ed. Penelope Stathe. Athens: Syndesmos ton en Athenais Megaloscholiton, 1997.

Kırlı, Cengiz. "The Struggle over Space: Coffeehouses of Ottoman Istanbul, 1780–1845." PhD diss., State University of New York, Binghamton, 2001.

Kitromilides, Paschales. *The Enlightenment as Social Criticism: Iosipos Moisiodax and Greek Culture in the Eighteenth Century.* Princeton, NJ: Princeton University, 1992.

———. *Neoellenikos Diaphotismos: Hoi politikes kai koinonikes idees.* Athens: Morphotiko Hidryma Ethnikes Trapezes, 2000.

Koliopoulos, John. *Brigands with a Cause: Brigandage and Irredentism in Modern Greece, 1821–1912.* Oxford: Clarendon Press, 1987.

Komnenou-Hypsilantou, Athanasiou. *Ekklesiastikon kai politikon ton eis dodeka biblion H', Th' kai I' etoi ta meta ten Alosin (1453–1789), ek cheirographou anekdotou tes hieras mones tou Sina.* Ekdidontas Archim Germanou Afthonidou Sinaitou [Ecclesiastical and political events from after the fall (1453–1789) in twelve books from an unpublished manuscript in the Monastery of (St. Catherine's of) Sinai. Published by Archimandrite Germanos Afthonides of Sinai]. Athens: Bibl. Note Karavia, 1972.

Konortas, Paraskevas. *Othomanikes theoreseis gia to Oikoumeniko Patriarcheio: Beratia gia tous prokathemenous tes Megales Ekklesias (170s—arches 200u aiona)* [Ottoman views of the Ecumenical Patriarchate: Berats for the ordinations of the Great Church, 17th—early 20th century]. Athens: Ekdoseis Alexandreia, 1998.

Koromelas, G. D. "Kallimaches." *He megale hellenike encyclopedia* [The great Greek encyclopedia], vol. 13. Athens, 1931.

Kritovoulos. *The History of Mehmed the Conqueror.* Translated from the Greek by Charles T. Riggs. Princeton, NJ: Princeton University Press, 1954.

Kubilay, Ayşe Yetişkin. "Davutpaşa Kışlası." *Dünden bugüne İstanbul Ansiklopedisi* 3 (1993–94): 11–12.

———. "Rami Kışlası." *Dünden bugüne İstanbul Ansiklopedisi* 6 (1993–94): 306.

Kuneralp, Sinan. "Bir Osmanlı diplomatı: Kostaki Musurus Paşa, 1807–1891" [An Ottoman diplomat: Kostaki Musurus Paşa]. *Belleten* 3 (1970): 421–35.

———. *Son dönem Osmanlı erkan ve ricali (1839–1922): Prosopografik rehber* [Late Ottoman officials: A prosopographic guide]. İstanbul: İsis Press, 1999.

Kunt, Metin. "Ethnic-Regional *(cins)* Solidarity in the Seventeenth-Century Ottoman Establishment." *International Journal of Middle East Studies* 5 (1974): 233–39.

———. *The Sultan's Servants: The Transformation of Ottoman Provincial Government, 1550–1650.* New York: Columbia University Press, 1983.

Kuran, E. "Reşid Paşa." In *İslam ansiklopedisi: İslam alemi tarih, coğrafya, etnografya ne biyografya lugatı,* vol. 9, 701–5. İstanbul: Milli Eğitim basımevi, 1964.

Landros, Christos, ed. "Historiko archeio Samou—to archeio ton Genikon Syneleuseon" [The historical archive of Samos—the archive of General Assemblies]. *Topike Historia kai Archeia* (1992): 129–41.

Langer, William L. *Political and Social Upheaval, 1832–1852.* New York: Harper and Row, 1969.

Layard, Sir A. Henry. *Sir A. Henry Layard: Autobiography and Letters from His Childhood until His Appointment as H.M. Ambassador at Madrid.* 2 vols. Edited by William N. Bruce. New York: J. Murray, 1903.

Leger, L. "Le Boulgare sous Pasvan oglou" (Memoires de Sophroni). In *Mélanges orientaux: Textes et traductions pub. par les professeurs de l'École spéciale des langues orientales vivantes à l'occasion du sixième Congres international des orientalistes réuni à Leyde (septembre 1883)*, vol. 9, 383–429. Paris: E. Leroux, 1883.

Levon Barsoumian, Hagop. "Armenian Amira Class of Istanbul." PhD diss., Columbia University, 1980.

Levy, Avigdor. "Mahmud II." In *Encyclopedia of Islam,* 2nd ed., vol. 6, 58–61. Leiden: Brill Academic Publishers, 1960–2005.

———. "Military Policy of Sultan Mahmud II, 1808–1839." PhD diss., Harvard University, 1968.

———. "The Officer Corps in Mahmud II's New Ottoman Army, 1826–1839." *International Journal of Middle East Studies* 2, no. 1 (1971): 21–39.

———. "Ottoman Attitudes to the Rise of Balkan Nationalism." In *War and Society in East Central Europe during the 18th and 19th Centuries,* ed. B. K. Kiraly and G. E. Ruthenberg, vol. 1, 325–45. New York: Columbia University Press, 1979.

———. "The Ottoman Ulema and the Military Reforms of Sultan Mahmud II." *Asian and African Studies* 7 (1971): 13–39.

Lewis, Bernard. *The Emergence of Modern Turkey.* London: Oxford University Press, 1968.

———. *The Muslim Discovery of Europe.* New York: W. W. Norton, 1982.

Lewis, Bernard, and Benjamin Braude, eds. *Christians and Jews in the Ottoman Empire: The Functioning of a Plural Society.* New York: Holmes and Maier Publishing, 1982.

Lieven, Dominic. *Empire: The Russian Empire and Its Rivals.* New Haven, CT: Yale University Press, 2001.

Lignos, Antonios, ed. *Archeion tes koinotetos Hydras, 1778–1832* [Archive of the community of Hydra]. 2 vols. Piraeus, Greece, 1921.

Lycurgos, I. *He Samos kai ho Vogorides* [Samos and Vogorides]. Athens, 1849.

Macdermott, Mercia. *A History of Bulgaria, 1393–1885.* London: Allen and Unwin, 1962.

Macfarlane, Charles. *Constantinople in 1828: A Residence of Sixteen Months in the Turkish Capital and Provinces; With an Account of the Present State of the Naval and Military Power, and of the Resources of the Ottoman Empire.* 2 vols. London: Saunders and Otley, 1829.

Makdisi, Ussama. *Artillery of Heaven: American Missionaries and the Failed Conversion of the Middle East.* Ithaca and London: Cornell University Press, 2008.

———. *The Culture of Sectarianism: Community, History, and Violence in Nineteenth-Century Lebanon.* Berkeley: University of California Press, 2000.

Mango, Cyril. "The Phanariots and the Byzantine Tradition." In *The Struggle for Greek Independence,* ed. Richard Clogg, 41–66. Hamden, CT: Archon Books, 1973.

Mantran, Robert. *Istanbul dans la seconde moitié du XVIIe siècle: Essai d'histoire institutionelle, économique, et sociale.* Paris: A. Maisonneuve, 1962.

Marasoiu, Gabriela, ed. *Relaţiile Romano-Otomane: Documente turcesti 1711–1821* [Romanian-Ottoman relations: Turkish documents]. Bucharest, 1984.

Marchiş, Ierom. Iustin. *Stavropoleos.* Bucharest: Stavropoleos, PriceWaterhouseCooper, 2005.

Mardin, Şerif. *The Genesis of Young Ottoman Thought: A Study in the Modernization of Turkish Political Ideas.* Princeton, NJ: Princeton University Press, 1962.

Marinescu, Florin. *Étude généalogique sur la famille Mourouzi.* Athens: Kentron Neoellenikon Ereunon, Ethnikou Hidrymatos Ereunon, 1987.

Marinescu, Florin, Georgeta Penelea-Filitti, and Anna Tabaki, eds. *Documents gréco-roumains: Le fonds Mourouzi d'Athènes.* Athens, 1991.

———. *Roumanika engrapha tou Haghiou Orous: Archeio Hieras Mones Xeropotamou* [Romanian documents of Mt. Athos: The archive of the Xeropotamou Monastery]. Athens, 1997.

———. *Roumanika engrapha tou Haghiou Orou: Archeio Protatou* [Romanian documents of Mt. Athos: The Protatou archive]. Athens, 2001.

Markova, Zina. *Le mouvement ecclésiastique national Bulgare jusqu'à la guerre de Crimée* (in Bulgarian with summary in French). Sophia: BAN, 1976.

Markovits, Claude. *Global World of Indian Merchants, 1750–1947: Traders of Sind from Bukhara to Panama.* Cambridge: Cambridge University Press, 2000.

Marsot, Afaf Lutfi al-Sayyid. *Egypt in the Reign of Muhammad Ali.* Cambridge: Cambridge University Press, 1984.

Matalas, Paraskevas. *Ethnos kai orthodoxia: Hoi peripeteies mias scheses, apo to "Helladiko" sto Boulgariko schisma* [Ethnos and orthodoxy: The adventures of a relationship, from the "Helladiko" to the Bulgarian schism]. Heracleion: Panapistimiake Ekdoseis Kretes, 2002.

Matthee, Rudi. *The Politics of Trade in Safavid Iran: Silk for Silver, 1600–1730.* Cambridge: Cambridge University Press, 1999.

Mayer, Arno. *Persistence of the Old Regime: Europe to The Great War.* New York: Pantheon Books, 1981.

McGowan, Bruce. "The Age of the Ayans." In *An Economic and Social History of the Ottoman Empire,* vol. 2, ed. Suraiya Faroqhi, Bruce McGowan, Donald Quataert, and Şevket Pamuk, 637–758. Cambridge: Cambridge University Press, 1994.

McGrew, William W. *Land and Revolution in Modern Greece, 1800–1881: The Transition in the Tenure and Exploitation of Land from Ottoman Rule to Independence.* Kent, OH: Kent State University Press, 1985.

Mengous, Petros. *Memoirs of a Greek Soldier: Containing Anecdotes and Occurrences Illustrating the Character and Manners of the Greeks and Turks in Asia Minor and Detailing the Events of the Late War in Greece.* New York, 1830.

Meriage, Lawrence P. "The First Serbian Uprising (1804–1813) and the Nineteenth-Century Origins of the Eastern Question." *Slavic Review* 37, no. 3 (September 1978): 421–39.

Meriwether, Margaret L. *The Kin Who Count: Family and Society in Ottoman Aleppo, 1770–1840.* Austin: University of Texas Press, 1999.

Messick, Brinkley. *Calligraphic State: Textual Domination and History in a Muslim Society.* Berkeley: University of California Press, 1993.

Miller, William. "Europe and the Ottoman Power before the Nineteenth Century." *English Historical Review* 16, no. 63 (1901): 452–71.

———. *The Ottoman Empire and Its Successors, 1801-1922.* Cambridge: Cambridge University Press, 1923.

Mitchell, Timothy. *Colonising Egypt.* New York: Cambridge University Press, 1988.

———. "Society, Economy, and the State Effect." In *State/Culture: State Formation after the Cultural Turn,* ed. George Steinmetz, 76-97. Ithaca, NY: Cornell University Press, 1999.

Mosely, Philip E. *Russian Diplomacy and the Opening of the Eastern Question in 1838 and 1839.* Cambridge, MA: Harvard University Press, 1934.

Mosse, W. E. "The Return of Reschid Pasha: An Incident in the Career of Lord Stratford de Redcliffe." *English Historical Review* 68, no. 269 (1953): 546-73.

Mouradjea d'Ohsson, Ignatius. *Tableau général de l'Empire Othoman, divisé en deux parties, dont l'une comprend la législation mahométane: L'autre, l'histoire de l'Empire Othoman.* 6 vols. Paris: Imp. de Monsieur Firmin Didot, 1824.

Murphey, Rhoads. *Ottoman Warfare, 1500-1700.* New Brunswick, NJ: Rutgers University Press, 1999.

———. "Provisioning Istanbul: The State and Subsistence in the Early Modern Middle East." *Food and Foodways* 2 (1988): 217-63.

———. "Yeni Çeri." In *Encyclopedia of Islam,* 2nd ed. Leiden: Brill Academic Publishers, 1960-2005.

Mutafcieva, Vera. *Le temps de Kirdjalis* (in Bulgarian). Sofia: Izd-vo na Bŭlgarskata akademiia na naukite, 1993.

Naff, Thomas. "Reform and the Conduct of Ottoman Diplomacy in the Reign of Selim III, 1789-1807." *Journal of the American Oriental Society* 83, no. 3 (1963): 295-315.

Nagata, Yuzo. *Muhsin-zade Mehmed Paşa ve Ayanlık Müessesesi* [Muhsinzade Mehmed Paşa and the *ayan* institution]. Tokyo: Institute for the Study of Languages and Cultures of Asia and Africa, 1976.

———. *Studies on the Social and Economic History of the Ottoman Empire.* İzmir, Turkey: Akademi Kitabevi, 1995.

———. *Tarihte ayanlar: Karaosmanoğulları üzerinde bir inceleme* [Ayans in history: A study on the Karaosmanoğlus]. Ankara: Türk Tarih Kurumu Basımevi, 1997.

Necipoğlu, Gülru. *Architecture, Ceremonial, and Power: Topkapi Palace in the Fifteenth and Sixteenth Centuries.* Cambridge, MA: MIT Press, 1991.

Neumann, Christoph. *Araç tarih, amaç Tanzimat: Tarih-i Cevdet'in siyasi anlamı.* [History as vehicle, Tanzimat as goal: The political significance of Cevdet's *History*]. İstanbul: Tarih Vakfı, 1999.

Nieuwenhuis, Thomas. *Politics and Society in Early Modern Iraq: Mamluk Pashas, Tribal Shayks and Local Rule between 1802 and 1831.* The Hague: Martinus Nijhoffs, 1982.

Olson, Robert. "Jews, Janissaries, Esnaf and the Revolt of 1740 in Istanbul." *Journal of Economic and Social History of the Orient* 20 (1978): 185-207.

Ömer Efendi, Cabi. *Cabi Tarihi.* Vol. 1. Ankara: Türk Tarih Kurumu Basımevi, 2003.

Ortaylı, İlber. *İmparatorluğun en uzun yüzyılı* [The empire's longest century]. İstanbul: Alkım, 1983.

———. *Tanzimatdan cumhüriyete yerel yönetim geleneği.* İstanbul: Hil Yayın, 1985.

Oţetea, A. "La désagrégation du régime phanariote." In *Symposium l'époque phanariote 21-25 octobre 1970,* 439-47. Thessaloniki: Institute for Balkan Studies, 1974.

Pakalin, Mehmet Zeki. *Osmanlı tarih deyimleri ve terimleri sözlüğü* [Dictionary of Ottoman historical terms and expressions]. İstanbul: Milli eğitim basımevi, 1946–56.

Paliouras, Athanasios D. *The Monastery of St. Catherine's on Mount Sinai.* Glyka Nera Attikis, Greece: E. Tzaferi, 1985.

Pamuk, Şevket. "Evolution of the Ottoman Monetary System," part 5 of *An Economic and Social History of the Ottoman Empire,* vol. 2, *1600–1914,* ed. Halil İnalcık with Donald Quataert, 945–80. Cambridge: Cambridge University Press, 1999.

Paparrigopoulos, Konstantinos. *Historia tou hellenikou ethnous apo ton archaiotaton chronon mechri ton neoteron* [History of the Greek nation from ancient to modern times]. 5 vols. En Athenai: Ek tou typographeio N. Passare, 1865–74.

Papelasis-Minoglou, Ioanna. "The Greek Merchant House of the Russian Black Sea: A 19th-Century Example of a Traders' Coalition." *International Journal of Maritime History* 10 (1998): 61–104.

———. "Toward a Typology of Greek Diaspora Entrepreneurship." In *Diaspora Entrepreneurial Networks: Five Centuries of History,* ed. Ina Baghdiantz-McCabe, Gelina Harlaftis, and Ioanna Papelasis-Minoglou, 173–90. Oxford: Oxford University Press, 2005.

Paun, Radu G. "Sur l'investiture des derniers princes phanariotes: Autour d'un document ignoré." *Revue des Études Sud-Est Europeennes* 35 (1997): 63–75.

Peirce, Leslie. *The Imperial Harem: Women and Sovereignty in the Ottoman Empire.* New York: Oxford University Press, 1993.

Peneva, Irena. "Neizvestia biographia na Stephan Bogoridi ot Neofit Hilendarski (Bozveli)" [Biography of Stephan Vogorides by Neophytos Hilendarski]. In *Studia in honorem Professoris Verae Mutafcieva,* ed. E. Radushev et al., 293–300. Sofia: Amicita, 2001.

Pertusier, Charles. *La Valachie, la Moldavie, et de l'influence des Grecs du Fanal.* Paris: Painparré, 1822.

Petmezas, Socrates. "L'organisation ecclésiastique sous la domination Ottomane." In *Conseils et mémoires de Synadinos, prêtre de Serrès en Macédoine,* ed. P. Odorico. Paris: Éditions de l'Association "Pierre Belon," 1996.

Petropulos, John A. "Forms of Collaboration with the Enemy during the First Greek War of Liberation." In *Hellenism and the First Greek War of Liberation (1821–1830): Continuity and Change,* ed. Nikiforos P. Diamandouros. Thessaloniki: Institute for Balkan Studies, 1976.

———. *Politics and Statecraft in the Kingdom of Greece: 1833–1843.* Princeton, NJ: Princeton University Press, 1968.

Philliou, Christine. "Communities on the Verge: Unraveling the Phanariot Ascendancy in Ottoman Governance." *Comparative Studies in Society and History* 51, no. 1 (January 2009): 151—81.

———. "The Community of Izmir/Smyrna in 1821: Social Reality and National Ideologies." MA thesis, Princeton University, 1998.

———. "The Paradox of Perceptions: Interpreting the Ottoman Past through the National Present." *Middle Eastern Studies* 44, no. 5 (September 2008): 661–75.

———. "Worlds Old and New: Phanariot Networks and the Remaking of Ottoman Governance, 1800–1850." PhD diss., Princeton University, 2004.

Photeinos, Dionysios. *Historia tes palai Dakias ta nyn Transylvanias, Wallachias, kai Molda-*

*vias ek diaphoron palaion kai neon syngrapheon syneranistheisa para Dionysiou Photeinou* [History of the former Dacia, the current Transylvania, Wallachia, and Moldavia compiled from various old and new sources by Dionysios Photeinos]. 3 vols. Vienna: Typ. Io. Varthol. Svekiou, 1818–19.

Phrantze, Anteia. *Mismagia: Anthologio phanariotikes poieses kata tes ekdose Zese Daoute (1818)* [Mismagia: Anthology of phanariot poetry, from the Zese Daoute edition (1818)]. Athens: Vivliopōleion tēs "Hestias," 1993.

Pippidi, Andrei. *Hommes et idées du sud-est européen à l'aube de l'âge moderne.* Bucharest: Editura Academiei Republicii Socialiste Romania, 1980.

———. "Jean Caradja et ses amis de Génève." In *Symposium l'époque phanariote 21–25 octobre 1970,* 145. Thessaloniki: Hidrema Meleton Chersonesou tou Haimou, 1974.

———. "Notules phanariotes II: Encore l'exil de Jean Caradja à Genève." *Ho Eranistes* 17 (1981): 74–85.

———. "Phanar, phanariotes, phanariotisme." *Revue des Études Sud-Est Europeennes* 13, no. 2 (1975): 231–39.

Psychares, Ioannis. *Epistolai I. Psychare (ephorou ton Chion eis Constantinoupole) pros demogerontian Chiou* [Letters of I. Psychares (agent for Chiotes in Istanbul) to the Demogerontia of Chios]. Chios, Greece, 1962.

Quataert, Donald. "Clothing Laws, State, and Society in the Ottoman Empire, 1720–1829." *International Journal of Middle East Studies* 29 (1997): 403–25.

Rangavi, E. R. *Livre d'Or de la noblesse phanariote et des familles princières de Valachie et de Moldavie.* Athens, 1892.

Ranke, Leopold. *The History of Servia and the Servian Revolution, with a Sketch of the Insurrection in Bosnia,* trans. Alexander Kerr. London: H. G. Bohn, 1853.

Raymond, André. *Artisans et commerçants au Caire au XVIII siècle.* Damascus: Institut français de Damas, 1973.

———. *Le Caire des janissaires: L'apogée de la ville ottomane sous 'Abd al'-Rahman Katkhuda.* Paris: CNRS Éditions, 1995.

Redhouse, James W. *Redhouse Yeni Türkçe-İngilizce sözlük / New Redhouse Turkish-English Dictionary.* İstanbul: Redhouse Yayınevi, 1968.

Reed, Howard. "The Destruction of the Janissaries by Mahmud II in June 1826." PhD diss., Princeton University, 1951.

Riker, T. W. "The Concert of Europe and Moldavia." *English Historical Review* 42, no. 166 (1927): 227–44.

Runciman, Steven. *The Great Church in Captivity: A Study of the Patriarchate of Constantinople from the Eve of the Turkish Conquest to the Greek War of Independence.* New York: Cambridge University Press, 1968.

Saab, Ann Pottinger. *The Origins of the Crimean Alliance.* Charlottesville: University Press of Virginia, 1977.

Sadat, Deena. "Rumeli Ayanlari: The Eighteenth Century." *Journal of Modern History* 44, no. 3 (1972): 346–63.

———. "Urban Notables in the Ottoman Empire: The Ayan." PhD diss., Rutgers University, 1969.

Said, Edward. *Orientalism*. New York: Pantheon Books, 1978.

Sakaoğlu, Necdet. "Etmeydanı." *Dünden bugüne İstanbul ansiklopedisi*, vol. 3. İstanbul: Kültür Bakanlığı ve Tarih Vakfı'nın ortak yayınıdır, 1993–.

Salzmann, Ariel. "An Ancien Régime Revisited: 'Privatization' and Political Economy in the Eighteenth-Century Ottoman Empire." *Politics and Society* 21, no. 4 (December 1993): 393–423.

———. "Measures of Empire: Tax Farmers and the Ottoman Ancien Regime, 1695–1807." PhD diss., Columbia University, 1993.

———. *Tocqueville in the Ottoman Empire: Rival Paths to the Modern State*. Leiden, Boston: Brill Academic Publishers, 2004.

Şanizade, Mehmet Ataullah efendi. *Tarih-i Şanizade* [Sanizade's history]. 4 vols. İstanbul: Ceride-i Havadis Matbaasi, 1290 (M. 1873).

Şaşmazer, Lynne Marie Thompson. "Provisioning Istanbul: Bread Production, Power, and Political Ideology in the Ottoman Empire, 1789–1807." PhD diss., Indiana University, 2000.

Schroeder, Paul W. "Bruck versus Buol: The Dispute over Austrian Eastern Policy, 1853–1855." *Journal of Modern History* 40, no. 2 (1968): 193–217.

———. "Did the Vienna Settlement Rest on a Balance of Power?" *American Historical Review* 97, no. 3 (1992): 683–706.

———. "Old Wine in Old Bottles: Recent Contributions to British Foreign Policy and European International Politics, 1789–1848." *Journal of British Studies* 26, no. 1 (January 1987): 1–25.

———. *The Transformation of European Politics, 1763–1848*. Oxford: Clarendon Press, 1994.

Scott, James C. *Seeing Like a State: How Certain Schemes to Improve the Human Condition Have Failed*. New Haven, CT: Yale University Press, 1998.

Seton-Watson, R. W. *A History of the Roumanians: From Roman Times to the Completion of Unity*. Cambridge: Archon Books, 1963.

———. "The Origins of the Crimean War." In *The Origins of the Crimean War*, ed. Bryson D. Gooch. Lexington, MA: Heath and Co., 1969.

Sevastakis, Alexis. *Hoi Karmanioloi sten epanastase tes Samou—Ioannes Lekates* [The Karmanioloi in the revolution of Samos]. Athens, 1980.

———. *To Kenema ton Karmaniolon ste Samo, 1805–1812* [The movement of the Karmanioloi in Samos]. Athens, 1996.

Shaham, Ron. "Christian and Jewish 'waqf' in Palestine during the Late Ottoman Period." *Bulletin of Oriental and African Studies, University of London* 54, no. 3 (1991): 460–72.

Shaw, Stanford. *Between Old and New: The Ottoman Empire under Sultan Selim III, 1789–1807*. Cambridge, MA: Harvard University Press, 1971.

———. "The Nizam-ı Cedid Army under Sultan Selim III 1789–1807." *Oriens* 18 (1965–66): 168–84.

———. "The Origins of Ottoman Military Reform: The Nizam-ı Cedid Army of Sultan Selim III." *Journal of Modern History* 37 (1965): 291–306.

*The Siege of Kars 1855: Defence and Capitulations*. Reported by General Williams. London: Stationery Office, 2000.

Skiotis, Dennis. "From Bandit to Pasha: First Steps in the Rise to Power of Ali of Tepelen, 1750–1784." *International Journal of Middle Eastern Studies* 2 (1971): 219–44.

————. "The Greek Revolution: Ali Pasha's Last Gamble." In *Hellenism and the First Greek War of Liberation (1821–1830): Continuity and Change*, ed. Nikiforos P. Diamandouros. Thessaloniki: Institute for Balkan Studies, 1976.

Skopetea, Helle. *To protypo basileio kai he Megale Idea: Opseis tou ethnikou provlematos sten Hellada, 1830–1880* [The model kingdom and the Great Idea]. Athens: Ekdoseis Poly-typo, 1988.

Sofuoğlu, Adnan. *Fener Rum Patrikhanesi ve siyasi faaliyetleri* [The Greek Orthodox Patri-archate of Phanar and its political activities]. İstanbul: Turan yayıncılık, 1996.

Sömel, Selçuk Akşin. *Historical Dictionary of the Ottoman Empire*. Lanham, MD: Scarecrow Press, 2003.

Soutzo, Démètre Skarl. "Les familles princières grecques de Valachie et de Moldavie." *Symposium l'Époque Phanariote* (1974): 229–55.

Soutzos, N. *Mémoires du prince Nicolas Soutzo, grand logothete de Moldavia (1798–1871)*. Vienna: Gerald and Cie, 1899.

Sözen, Zeynep. *Fenerli Beyler: 110 yılın öyküsü (1711–1821)* [Phanariot princes: 110-year story]. İstanbul: Aybay Yayıncılık, 2000.

Sphyroeras, Vasileos. *Hoi dragomanoi tou stolou: Ho thesmos kai hoi foreis* [The dragomans of the fleet: The institution and its occupants]. Athens, 1965.

————. "O Kanounnames tou 1819 gia ten ekloge phanarioton stis hegemonies kai sten dragomania" [The Kanunname of 1819 for the election of phanariots to the principali-ties and the dragomanate]. *Ho Heranistes* 11 (1974): 568–79.

Stamatiades, Epameinondas. *Viographiai ton hellenon megalon diermeneon tou Othomanikou kratous* [Biographies of the Greek grand dragomans of the Ottoman state]. Thessaloniki, 1973; originally published 1865.

Stamatiades, Nicholaos. *Ta Samiaka, hetoi analexeis tes neoteras historias tes Samou di'epis-temon engraphon, on protassontai ai biographiai ton Logoethetou Lycourgou kai Konstan-tinou Lachana* [Samos events, or selections from the modern history of Samos through scientific documents, which are preceded by the biographies of Logothetis Lycourgos and Constantine Lachanas]. Samos, 1899.

Stamatopoulos, Dimitrios. "Constantinople in the Peloponnese: The Case of the Dragoman of the Morea Georgios Wallerianos and Some Aspects of the Revolutionary Process." In *Ottoman Rule and the Balkans, 1760–1850: Conflict, Transformation, Adaptation*, ed. An-tonios Anastasopoulos, 148–68. Rethymno, Greece: University of Crete Press, 2007.

————. *Metarythmise kai ekkosmikeuse: Pros mia anasynthese tes historias tou Oikoumenikou Patriarcheiou ton 190 aiona* [Reform and secularization: Toward a resynthesis of the his-tory of the Ecumenical Patriarchate in the 19th century]. Athens, 2003.

————. "Othomanikes metarrythmyseis kai Oikoumeniko Patriarcheio: Ho politikos an-tagonismos gia ten epharmoge ton genikon kanonismon" [Ottoman reforms and the Ecumenical Patriarchate: The political contest over the promulgation of the general reg-ulations]. PhD diss., Aristotle University, 1998.

Stavrianos, Leften. *Balkans since 1453*. New York: New York University Press, 2000.

Steingass, Francis Joseph. *A Comprehensive Persian-English Dictionary including the Arabic Words and Phrases to Be Met with in Persian Literature*. 1892; London: K. Paul, Trench, Trubner and Co., 1930.

Steinmetz, George. *Regulating the Social: The Welfare State and Local Politics in Imperial Germany*. Princeton, NJ: Princeton University Press, 1993.
——, ed. *State/Culture: State Formation after the Cultural Turn*. Ithaca, NY: Cornell University Press, 1999.
Stoianovich, Traian. "The Conquering Balkan Orthodox Merchant." In *Economies and Societies: Traders, Towns, and Households*. Vol. 2 of *Between East and West: The Balkan and Mediterranean Worlds*. New Rochelle, NY: A. D. Caratzas, 1992.
——. "Model and Mirror of the Premodern Balkan City." In *Economies and Societies: Traders, Towns, and Households*. Vol. 2 of *Between East and West: The Balkan and Mediterranean Worlds*. New Rochelle, NY: A. D. Caratzas, 1992.
Strauss, Johann. "The Millets and the Ottoman Language: The Contribution of Ottoman Greeks to Ottoman Letters (19th–20th Centuries)." *Die Welt des Islams* 35, no. 2 (November 1995): 189–249.
Sturdza, Mihail-Dimitri. *Dictionnaire historique et généalogique des grandes familles de Grèce, d'Albanie, et de Constantinople*. Paris: M.-D. Sturdza, 1983.
Subrahmanyam, Sanjay. *Explorations in Connected History: From the Tagus to the Ganges*. New York: Oxford University Press, 2005.
——. *Penumbral Visions: The Making of Polities in Early Modern South India*. New York: Oxford University Press, 2001.
Subrahmanyam, Sanjay, and C. A. Bayly. "Portfolio Capitalists and the Political Economy of Early Modern India." *Indian Economic and Social History Review* 25, no. 4 (1988): 401–24.
Sugar, Peter F., and Donald W. Treadgold, eds. *Southeastern Europe under Ottoman Rule, 1354–1804*. Vol. 5 of *A History of East Central Europe*. Seattle: University of Washington Press, 1996.
Sunar, Mert. "Cauldron of Dissent." PhD diss., State University of New York, Binghamton, 2004.
Sungu. "Mahmud II'nin, İzzet Molla, ve Asakir-e Mansure hakkında bir hattı." *Tarih Vesikaları* 1 (1941): 162–83.
Süreyya Bey, Mehmed. *Sicill-i Osmani* [Register/index of Ottoman officials]. 6 vols. İstanbul: Kültür Bakanlığı ile Türkiye Ekonomik ve Toplumsal Tarih Vakfı'nın ortak yayınıdır, 1996.
Svoronos, Nicholas. *Episkopese tes neoellenikes historias* [Survey of modern Greek history]. 2nd ed. Athens: Themelio, 1976.
Syndesmos ton en Athenais Megaloscholiton [Association of Great School Alumni in Athens]. *He parousia ton ethnikon meionoteton sten Konstantinoupole ton 190 aiona* [The presence of ethnic minorities in Istanbul in the 19th century]. Athens, 1997.
——. *Romioi sten Hyperesia tes hypseles Pyles* [Orthodox Christians in the service of the Sublime Porte]. Athens, 2002.
Tanpınar, Ahmed Hamdi, "Ahmet Pasha." In *İslam ansiklopedisi: İslam alemi tarih, coğrafya, etnografya ne biyografya lugatı*, vol. 1, 207–10. İstanbul: Milli Eğitim basımevi, 1950.
——. "Akif Pasha." In *İslam ansiklopedisi*, vol. 1, 242. İstanbul: Milli Eğitim basımevi, 1950.
Tanyeli, Uğur. "Bâbiâli Mimari." *Dünden bugüne İstanbul ansiklopedisi* 1 (1995).
*Tanzimat*. Vol. 1. İstanbul, 1940.
Taylor, A. J. P. *The Struggle for Mastery in Europe, 1848–1918*. Oxford: Clarendon Press of Oxford University Press, 1971.

Tekindağ, Ş. "Halet Efendi." In *İslam ansiklopedisi*, vol. 5, 123. İstanbul: Milli Eğitim basımevi, 1967.

Temperley, Harold. *England and the Near East: The Crimea*. Hamden, CT: Archon Books, 1964.

———. *The Foreign Policy of Canning, 1822–1827: England, the Neo-Holy Alliance and the New World*. London: G. Bell and Sons, 1925.

Țipau, Mihai. *Domnii fanariotii in Țarile Romane (1711–1821): Mica enciclopedie*. Bucharest: Editure Omonia, 2008.

Tocqueville, Alexis de. *The Old Regime and the French Revolution*. Translated by Stuart Gilbert. Garden City, NY: Doubleday, 1955.

Todorova, Maria. *Imagining the Balkans*. New York: Oxford University Press, 1997.

———. "Stefan Bogoridi: A Bulgarian Phanariote in the Ottoman Empire" (in Dutch). In *Oost-Europa in het verleden: Liber amicorum Z. R. Dittrich*, ed. A. P. van Gouoever, 177–87. Groningen: Wolters-Noordhoff/Forsten, 1987).

Toledano, Ehud. "The Emergence of Ottoman-Local Elites, a Framework for Research." In *Middle East Politics and Ideas*, ed. Ilan Pappe and Moshe Maoz, 145–62. London and New York: I. B. Tauris, 1997.

———. "Muhammad Ali Pasha." In *The Encyclopaedia of Islam*, 2nd ed., vol. 7, 423–31. Leiden: Brill Academic Publishers, 1960–2005.

Toprak, Zafer. "Bâbiâli." *Dünden bugüne İstanbul ansiklopedisi* 1 (1995).

Treptow, Kurt W., ed. *A History of Romania*. Iaşi: Center for Romanian Studies, 1997.

Trikoupes, Spyridon. *Historia tes Hellenikes Epanastases* [History of the Greek Revolution]. 4 vols. Athens: Ek tou typographeiou tes "Horas," 1888.

Tschudi, R. "Bektashiyya." In *Encyclopedia of Islam*, 2nd ed., vol. 1. Leiden: Brill Academic Publishers, 1960–2005.

Tuğlacı, Pars. *Bulgaristan ve Türk-Bulgar ilişkileri* [Bulgaria and Turkish-Bulgarian relations]. İstanbul: Cem Yayınevi, 1984.

———. *Osmanlı mimarlığında batılılaşma dönemi ve Balyan ailesi* [Westernization and the Balyan family in Ottoman architecture]. İstanbul: Yeni Çığır Bookstore, 1990.

Turan, Ş. "Pertev Pasha." In *İslam ansiklopedisi: İslam alemi tarih, coğrafya, etnografya ne biyografya lugatı*, vol. 9, 554–56. İstanbul: Milli Eğitim basımevi, 1964.

Türker, Orhan. *Fanari'den Fenere: Bir Haliç hikayesi* [From Phanari to Fener: A bay of the Golden Horn story]. İstanbul: Sel Yayıncılık, 2001.

———. *Halki'den Heybeli'ye: Bir ada hikayesi* [From Chalki to Heybeli: An island story]. İstanbul: Sel Yayıncılık, 2003.

———. *Mega Revma'dan Arnavutköy'e: Bir Boğaziçi hikayesi* [From Mega Reuma to Arnavutköy: A Bosphorus story]. İstanbul: Sel Yayıncılık, 1999.

*Türkiye Diyanet Vakfı İslam ansiklopedisi*. 13 vols. İstanbul, 1995.

Unat, Faik Reşit. "Başhoca İshak efendi." *Belleten* 28 (1964): 89–116.

Urquhart, David. *The Sultan Mahmoud and Mehemet Ali Pasha*. London: J. Ridgway, 1835.

Uzunçarşılı, İsmail Hakki. *Osmanlı devleti teşkilatından kapukulu ocakları* [Kapukulu ocaks as Ottoman institutions]. 2 vols. Ankara: Türk Tarih Kurumu Basımevi, 1944.

Vellianites, Th. "Mourouzes." *He megale hellenike encyclopedia* [The great Greek encyclopedia], vol. 17. Athens, 1931.

Vracanski, Sofroni. *Vie et tribulations du pecheur Sofroni: Introduction traduction et notes établies par Jack Feuillet.* Sofia: Sofia-Presse, 1981.

Vryonis, Speros. *Mechanism of Catastrophe.* New York: Greekworks, 2006.

Wallerstein, Immanuel. *The Modern World System.* New York: Academic Press, 1974.

Walsh, Rev. Robert. *A Residence at Constantinople, During a Period Including the Commencement, Progress, and Termination of the Greek and Turkish Revolutions.* 2 vols. London: Richard Bentley, 1838.

Wilkinson, William. *An Account of the Principalities of Wallachia and Moldavia: With Various Political Observations Relating to Them.* London: Longman, Hurst, Rees, Orne, and Brown, 1820.

Wortman, Richard S. *Scenarios of Power: Myth and Ceremony in Russian Monarchy.* Vol. 1: *From Peter the Great to the Death of Nicholas I.* Princeton, NJ: Princeton University Press, 1995.

Yi, Eunjeong. *Guild Dynamics in Seventeenth-Century Istanbul: Fluidity and Leverage.* Leiden: Brill Academic Publishers, 2004.

Yıldırım, Onur. "Transformation of the Craft Guilds in Istanbul during the Seventeenth and Eighteenth Centuries (1650–1826)." *Revue des Études Sud-Est Europeennes* 37 (1999): 91–109.

Zallony, Marc-Philippe. *Essai sur les fanariotes, où l'on voit les causes primitives de leur élévation aux hospodariats de la Valachie et de la Moldovie, leur mode d'administration, et les causes principales de leur chute; suivi de quelques réflexions sur l'état actuel de la Grèce.* Marseille: A. Ricard, 1824.

Zens, Robert W. "The Ayanlik and Pasvanoglu Osman Paşa of Vidin in the Age of Ottoman Social Change, 1791–1815." PhD diss., University of Wisconsin, 2004.

———. "Pasvanoglu Osman Pasha and the Pashalik of Belgrade, 1791–1807." *International Journal of Turkish Studies* 8 (Spring 2002): 88–114.

Zervos, Socrate. "Recherches sur les phanariotes: Àpropos de leur sentiment d'appartenance au meme groupe social." *Revue des Études Sud-Est Europeennes* 27 (1989): 305–11.

———. "Recherches sur les phanariotes et leur idéologie politique (1666–1821)." PhD diss., L'École des Hautes Études en Sciences Sociales, 1990.

Zilfi, Madeleine. *The Politics of Piety: The Ottoman Ulema in the Postclassical Age (1600–1800).* Minneapolis: Bibliotheca Islamica, 1988.

ACKNOWLEDGMENTS

In June of 2000 I set off for İstanbul to begin research for the doctoral dissertation that would, after more than one incarnation, develop into this book. Since that time I have witnessed crises and transformations of virtually every order, from that of international politics to the constellation of my own family. These experiences, more than any single class, book, or individual, have shaped my ability to capture the predicament of Ottoman subjects and rulers roughly two centuries ago.

This is not to underestimate the value of the generous assistance of a large number of institutions and individuals, without whom it would quite literally not have been possible to conceive of, research, or write this book. I take this opportunity to thank them.

I acknowledge the U.S. government for FLAS Title VI funding for the study of Turkish and Arabic through the Department of Near Eastern Studies at Princeton and for the Fulbright-Hays International Dissertation Research Fellowship; Princeton University's Council on Regional Studies and the Center for International Studies, the Program in Near Eastern Studies, for the J. F. Costopoulos Foundation graduate fellowship and the Stanley J. Seeger summer and academic year fellowships through the Hellenic Studies Program at Princeton; the Social Science Research Council (Middle East and North Africa section), the American Research Institute in Turkey, especially ARIT Director Tony Greenwood, and the National Endowment for the Humanities; the American Council of Learned Societies (Southeast European Studies section), Yale University's Center for International and Area Studies and Program in Hellenic Studies; Columbia University's Department of History, the Faculty of Arts and Sciences, and the University Seminars Program; and Ms. Güler Sabancı, Mr. Tosun Terzioğlu of Sabancı University, Mr. Üstün Ergüder, and the members of the jury for the 2007 Sakıp Sabancı International Research Award for Turkish Studies for their generous support. The Institute of Turkish Studies provided the final round of financial support in the form of a generous subvention grant, and for that I am very grateful.

Much appreciation goes to the archivists and librarians who facilitated my research in Greece, Turkey, Bulgaria, Romania, France, and Britain: Andreas Sideris and Maria Volterra at the Gennadeion Library of the American School of Classical Studies in Athens; the staff at the Prime Ministry Archives in İstanbul; Patriarch Bartholomew and the Holy Synod for permission to work at the Ecumenical Patriarchate Library and Archive in İstanbul and at the Library of the Theological School of Chalki (Heybeliada), with its archivists Father Nicholas Petropellis and Father Dorotheos and with the Patriarchate librarian Yorgo Benlisoy; Margarita Dobreva, at the Cyril and Methodius National Library Oriental Collection and Professor Nadia Danova in Sofia; the staff at the Romanian State Archives in Bucharest and at the Archives of the French Foreign Ministry in Paris and Nantes; the Public Record Office in Kew Gardens and the British Library for their willingness to help. Special thanks go to Head Archivist Christos Landros at the Samos branch of the General State Archives of Greece, who shared so much local knowledge and the photograph of Stephanos Vogorides that is on the cover of this book.

Professors to whom I owe much gratitude for shepherding me through the fundamentals of Ottoman history and challenging me to think outside the boxes of area studies include Rifa'at Abou-El-Haj, Peter Brown, Khaled Fahmy, Erika Gilson, my advisor Molly Greene (who deserves a special thanks for her perseverance), Şükrü Hanioğlu (whose four years of training me in Ottoman Turkish were, I hope, not wasted), Norman Itzkowitz, Steve Kotkin—who dared me to write a history of the Ottoman nineteenth century without using the word "Tanzimat" (and I almost managed it)—Heath Lowry, and the late Şinasi Tekin. Dimitri Gondicas of the Program in Hellenic Studies at Princeton warmly facilitated the practical as much as the intellectual side of graduate studies. I also appreciate that Karen Van Dyck, Nikiforos Diamandouros, and Nick and Anne Germanacos encouraged me to set out on this long odyssey (without ever losing sight of Ithaka) and thank Cemal Kafadar for several helpful conversations along the way; colleagues such as Stathis Kalyvas and Laura Engelstein at Yale; Rashid Khalidi, Mark Mazower, William Harris, Karen Barkey, Sam Moyn, Susan Pedersen, Valentina Izmirlieva, Adam Kosto, Dave Cuthell, Greg Mann, and Carol Gluck at Columbia for their time and advice; and Astrid Benedek of the Middle East Institute at Columbia for the support.

Grateful acknowledgment goes to Sinan Kuneralp, Edhem Eldem, and Mihai Maxim, who all helped with the general and the specifics of archival work at Başbakanlık, and to Ayhan Aktar and Alexis Alexandris for their scholarship and enthusiasm. Anthi Karra, Vangelis Kechriotis and Ceyda Arslan, Alexandros Petsas,

Eri Renieri, Bahman Panahi and Afroditi Kamara, Kosta Eftimyadi, and Strato Leana were generous with their company in both Greek and Turkish. In Romania, Andrei Pippidi and Bogdan Murgescu were nice enough to meet with me and discuss the phanariots in their regional context, and Gabriel Leanca showed me and my family around modern-day Iaşi. In Greece, Antonis Liakos was a reliable source of interesting ideas and Elizabeth Zachariadou a source of encouragement. Haris Exertzoglou and the late Popi Stathi provided me with the opportunity to present the case of Stephanos Vogorides for the first time and to the people who in many ways are the most important audience—the İstanbullu Rum of Athens.

Fond thanks go to Persis Berlekamp, Amy Mills, Stefanie Tcharos, Caterina Pizzigoni, Chuck Wooldridge, Amanda Wunder, Janet Klein, İpek Yosmaoğlu, Jamie Cohen-Cole and Eugenia Lao, Tarik Amar, Yossi Rapaport, Baki Tezcan, Nenad Filipovic and Esma Pasic-Filipovic, George Gavrilis, Eileen Kane, Jack Fairey, George Syrimis, Sada Aksartava, Gerasimus Katsan and Meral Kaya, Francesca Trivellato, Youval Rotman, and Sooyung Kim for their company and ideas. Warm gratitude to Vassiliki Giakoumaki, Magda Dimaki, and the Apostolakis, Hainoglou, Stogiannes, Papadopoulos, Sourmelis, Drakoulis and Artuğ families for their hospitality. And to Caitlin Dixon, Ann Walsh, and their families for years of friendship.

Special thanks to Niels Hooper at the University of California Press for his enthusiasm and prescience and to his colleagues, especially editors Laura Harger and Robin Whitaker, for their careful and much-needed attention. Many thanks to Marie Tracy, Merve Tezcanlı and Abhishek Kaicker for their comments on a near-final version of the manuscript, and to Dan Taeyoung Lee for his priceless technological assistance.

Gratitude to my brother Jim and sister Thea, to my parents, Peter and Helen, for encouraging studies of any kind, and to my late grandparents, Constantine and Dorothy Spiridon and May and James Philliou, for their mysterious recollections that lured me into the Ottoman past. Reza, Daphne, and Erfan always waited patiently and gave me the fortitude to see this project through to completion.

. . .

Some of the material in this work is drawn from articles and book chapters I have published elsewhere and is used here by permission: "Communities on the Verge: Unraveling the Phanariot Ascendancy in Ottoman Governance," *Comparative Studies in Society and History* 51, no. 1 (January 2009): 151–81, copyright © 2009 Society for the Comparative Study of Society and History, reprinted with the permission of Cambridge University Press; "The Paradox of Perceptions: Interpreting the Ottoman Past through the National Present," *Middle Eastern Studies* 44, no. 5 (September 2008): 661–75; and "A Tale of Two Cities and an Archive," *International Journal of Turkish Studies* 14, no. 1 (Fall 2008): 11–24.

# INDEX

Italicized page numbers refer to figures.

TEXT
10/12.5 Minion Pro

DISPLAY
Minion Pro

CARTOGRAPHER
Bill Nelson

INDEXER
Sharon Sweeney

COMPOSITOR
Integrated Composition Systems

Milton Keynes UK
Ingram Content Group UK Ltd.
UKHW012002131123
432501UK00005B/165